CW01108678

POLITICAL LANGUAGES OF RACE AND THE POLITICS OF EXCLUSION

For my children and for Liz

Political Languages of Race and the Politics of Exclusion

ANDY R. BROWN
Bath Spa University College

Ashgate
Aldershot • Brookfield USA • Singapore • Sydney

© Andy R. Brown 1999

All rights reserved. No part of this publication may be reproduced, stored in a retrieval system, or transmitted in any form or by any means, electronic, mechanical, photocopying, recording or otherwise without the prior permission of the publisher.

Published by
Ashgate Publishing Ltd
Gower House
Croft Road
Aldershot
Hants GU11 3HR
England

Ashgate Publishing Company
Old Post Road
Brookfield
Vermont 05036
USA

British Library Cataloguing in Publication Data
Brown, Andy R.
    Political languages of race and the politics of exclusion.
    - (Research in ethnic relations series)
    1. Racism - Great Britain 2. Great Britain - Politics and
    government 3. Great Britain - Race relations
    I. Title
    305.8'00941

Library of Congress Catalog Card Number: 98-73857

ISBN 1 84014 516 1

Printed in Great Britain

Contents

List of Figures vi
Preface vii
Acknowledgements xxx

1 The Erasure of Race in Public Space   1

2 Back to the Future: The New Racism Revisited   38

3 Racism and Parliamentary Discourse (I): 1957-68   75

4 Racism and Parliamentary Discourse (II): 1968-88   106

5 Smethwick and the Rise of a 'Political Racism'   140

6 Enoch's Island: Race, Nation and Authoritarianism in the
   Language and Politics of Powellism   189

Conclusion 264
Notes 270
Bibliography 309
Subject Index 337
Name Index 340

List of Figures

Figure 1.1: *The Racialisation of Migrant Labour*   9

Figure 5.1: *Political Racism*   152

Preface

This book is concerned with what I take to be the *problem* of the theory of the New Racism[1] (Barker 1981): the account of the discursive formation of a political language of exclusion of black migrants in postwar Britain. It is based on research conducted over a period of 9 years,[2] which focused on the impact of Smethwick and Powellism on the formation of a political racism in Parliamentary and public debates in the period 1957-1988. It is a discourse based study, since the focus of the book is that history that can be collected, organised and interrogated within the texts and talk produced by politicians and political and public institutions during this period. The most importance sources here are Parliamentary Debates (Hansard) on Immigration, Race Relations and Nationality; political speeches and writing, journals, commentaries and newspapers.

Although I am a sociologist by inclination, the book addresses the question of the political analysis of racism in terms of the theories of neo-marxism, post-marxism, post-structuralism and discourse analysis. However, the book's chief virtue is that it engages such ideas at the level of detailed analysis of Parliamentary and public debates and their social and political frameworks. The focus of the book is necessarily historical since the moment of Smethwick and Powellism has long gone, but the question of their relationship to, and impact upon, the formation of what some have claimed as a New Racism is very much a contemporary question, as the book will seek to reveal.[3]

The purpose of this opening section will be to map out some of the key issues, concepts and debates that the book will address and how these issues correspond to the chapter layout and overall structure of the book. The content of the book is organised into three broadly thematic sections. Part one looks at the problem of racist political language, as exemplified in the language and politics of Peter Griffiths and Powellism, and how this problem has been addressed by (I) neo-marxist accounts of racialisation and (ii) in the exposition of the New Racism thesis. The argument pursued in the these opening chapters is that the theoretical problem the New Racism opens up is a challenging one for racialisation approaches, and for sociology in particular, but that the New Racism argument itself does not engage sufficiently with sociological arguments that precede it or the structural account of political racialisation developed by the neo-marxists. What is needed, I argue, is an approach that can combine insights from both within an approach that recognises the specific features of the postwar political conjuncture and the role of political language analysis within it.

Part two of the book examines the substantive evidence from Parliamentary Debates concerning the discursive formation of what I define as Parliamentary *Commons' sense*, and the extent to which this evidence is consistent with the claim for the emergence of a new racist discourse that marks the transition from Smethwick to Powellism. This section, drawing on extensive textual evidence from Parliamentary Debates from 1957-1968, and from 1968-81, argues that the significance of Powellism cannot be contained within the framework the New Racism theorists offer and that the evidence does not support their argument for a break in the formation of a discourse of exclusionism centred around the emergence of Powellism. On the contrary, there is much evidence to show that Powellism reveals a textual affinity with the development of a anecdotally based, backbench racism and that the discursive relationship it forms with this discourse is both parasitic and transformative.

These arguments prepare the way for the detailed analysis of the discursive significance of Smethwick and Powellism, in terms of their relationship to and impact upon the formation, within Parliamentary and political debates, of a racist language of exclusion, which is achieved within Parliamentary Debates from the mid 1950s onwards. The success of this language is the way in which it manages to re-articulate the absent signifier of 'race' within an emergent discourse of the beleaguered Englishman, awoken to a community transformed by the impact of postwar black migration. It is a discursive formation that is centred by the anecdotal language of local experience and political neglect, and it is this discourse that is refined within the local campaign conducted by Peter Griffiths, at Smethwick, which finally achieves national impact within the politics and language of Powellism in 1968. However, Powell is the elite beneficiary of this language strategy not its author. Part three of the book presents the evidence that can support such an interpretation: chapter 5 offers a detailed analysis of the impact and interpretation of the Smethwick campaign in British party politics, particularly its impact on Labour. While chapter 6 presents the most detailed account of the language and politics of Powellism, yet attempted.

Preface ix

This final chapter shows how Powellism articulates the anecdotal discourse of the local politics of immigration with a revived authoritarian patriotism and political populism. While the resultant mixture is peculiarly Powellist, the chapter argues, such a political articulation is only possible because of the prior development of the backbench racism of the absent signifier, which Powell is able to connect with a receptive political audience, outside of Parliament. The wider explanation for this event are the special political context obtaining, involving the institutional prohibition on 'race' talk, and the inability of Labour to contest the articulation of this racism at the grass roots level. The remainder of this opening section will address the issues and ideas that underpin the development of the argument we have just outlined.

The Problem of the New Racism

I define the theoretical problem of new or modern racism as the problem of the decipherment and designation of public-political languages of group separation and exclusion as racist, when such language forms are encoded by a cultural logic of difference and accompanied by elite disclaimers of racism, in a debate context which is understood by critical-linguistic, sociological and other approaches as informed by discriminatory motives, and which results in the production of legislation that confirms such fears (cf. Reeves 1983; van Dijk 1993b). It is clear from this summary definition that the *new racism thesis* does not address all aspects of the problem it has come to define but it does provide the most consistent theoretical account of key aspects of the phenomenon.[4]

Previous theorists had noted the tremendous significance of a transformation in the public language of 'race', pointing to the speeches of both Griffiths and Powell as exemplars of this new tendency (Banton 1969; Rex 1970). Addressing this debate and seeking to resolve it, Reeves offered the influential concepts of *discursive deracialisation* and *sanitary coding* (1983). The analytical error in the formulation of the former conception is that it depends upon the idea that discourse was previously racialised. But Reeves provides not a single example of such discourse in British politics. The latter concept depends upon this distinction but offers a view that in the context of racial conflict and inequality a politician can publicly communicate racism without acknowledging that this has taken place. The fact that Reeves assumes this context as given, rather than showing how racialised discourse either achieved or contributed to its formation, does not lessen the importance of this distinction. I will argue that it is essential to the understanding of the success of Powellism.

The New Racism thesis rests upon a claim for theoretical novelty which I will challenge in chapter 2. The early contributors to the development of the concept (Barker 1981; CCCS 1982; Gilroy 1987) acknowledge no precursors in either sociology, political science or Marxist political economy. The novelty of what is claimed, in these seminal accounts, centres on the claim of a break or interruption in the form and content of radicalised discourses and, in particular, their public political form. Central to this break is the overwhelming role and significance of Powellism. With the notable exception of Miles (1987; 1989) the *new racism thesis* has met with little critical scrutiny. This book attempts to redress that imbalance. In particular, it highlights the claim that Powellism invents or articulates a new commonsense racism that becomes hegemonic within the political field thereafter.[5]

The reason for this approach are because I want to offer a modification to the New Racism argument and its treatment of Powellism. Drawing on my own research findings I argue that public-political racism in Britain, since at least the mid 1950s (and most certainly before),[6] has taken a predominantly anecdotal form. If we can define an anecdote as a 'detached narrative' of an event, it is the particular ideological quality of such narratives of the local politics of 'race', detached from any specific referent, that has allowed the development of a powerful populist-political *commonsense*[7](Gramsci 1971; Hall et al 1978). I propose that we define this form of commonsense discourse as *Commons' sense* in order to distinguish its location and significance: Parliamentary Debates. I argue that it has been the anecdotal form of expression of such racism that is the key to understanding its success and the source of its tremendous political and ideological power. My modification of the New Racism thesis therefore depends upon the analytical primacy afforded the relationship between commonsense *on the ground* and commonsense in Parliament and political discourse. This significance is crucial to a deeper understanding of the role and success of Powellism.

The New Racism Thesis

While racial political discourse, particularly in the form of Parliamentary Debates, has been little studied (cf. Reeves 1983; van Dijk 1993b: 66), major claims about the significance of public political racism in Britain have been advanced on the basis of surprisingly little empirical evidence (cf. Barker 1981; CCCS: Race and Politics Group 1982; Gilroy 1987; Brown 1997).[8]

The novelty of the New Racism thesis, as it was developed in Britain, was that it appeared to offer a comprehensive theoretical account, in the form of a 'bite-size' concept, of the emergence and rise to political hegemony of a new form of public political discourse. The theory claimed that it was the self conscious development of this discourse that secured the ascendancy of the populist politics of the New Right on the British political scene for over two decades (cf. Barker 1981; CCCS Race and Politics Group 1982; Gilroy 1987; Mercer 1994; Smith 1994). The central element in this emergent discourse was a transformation in the discourse of 'race' into a new form of political commonsense that had become normalised across the political field by the mid to late 1970s (cf. Barker 1981: ch.2 CCCS Race and Politics Group 1982: ch.1, 2). The prime mover and the point of emergence or rupture in the political field was that associated with the dramatic appearance of Powell and Powellism in April and November 1968, with his Birmingham and Eastbourne speeches.

This idea of a point of rupture, and the figure and impact of Powell, are central to the claims of the New Racism thesis and, in particular, the distinction integral to an idea of a discursive shift in the imagery and signifying properties of racist language, that between the 'old' and the 'new racism'. Paul Gilroy, for example, argues that Powellism marks a transition point between the older and more modern discursive forms of racist reasoning. He also offers the idea that what is involved in the outcome of the moment or period of discursive transition represented by Powellism, is what amounts to an epistemological break (Gilroy 1987: 85). Presumably he means here that racist discourse, post Powell, refers to a different range of social objects (that there has been a change in the entire filed of reference of the discourse).[9]

However, it is in the work of Barker (1979; 1981; 1983) that the argument for a *point of transition* is most clearly stated. Barker's argument is that after this *point of transition* a new semi-biological or pseudo-biological discourse, advocating racial separation, is able to arise and become the official orthodoxy (Barker 1983: 2).[10]

More recent contributions to this debate, such as the arguments of Mercer (1994:305-7) and those of Smith (1994: 54-7) uncritically adopt the New Racism distinction, and the centrality of Powellism it proposes, although they do go on to develop an account of Powellism as a *nodal point* or point of re-articulation of the concept of 'race'.[11] These latter approaches unquestionably owe a considerable debt to the work of Hall (1978: 154; Hall et al 1978). For Hall, Powellism is a precursor of the discourse of *authoritarian populism* which is central to the success of Thatcherism and the New Right (1979; 1988). I will argue in chapter 2 that the theory of the New Racism and the account of Authoritarian Populism are not consistent with each other. The significance of this distinction concerns the development of a neo-Gramscian theory of commonsense and the role it plays in accounts of the New Racism (cf. Barker 1981: 22-5; Lawrence 1982: 48-9).

The significance of these distinctions to my argument centre on the broad claim the New Racism thesis advances: that a profound discursive shift accompanies the rise of popular Powellism, sustaining or making possible the development of a populist-political relationship, secured through a novel re-articulation of the conceptual language of racism. For Barker, the mechanism that secures this relationship is a new theory of 'race' which is concealed within, and which informs the formulation of political arguments, statements and policy itself. This new political commonsense provides the political audience with a new language which racializes the experience, or rather *perceived* experience, of immigration and 'black' settlement (1981: 22-5). For the CCCS writers, popular racism is achieved because such political racism connects with existing commonsense (Lawrence 1981: 4; 1982: 89).[12]

This important distinction is never made clear in the dialogue between, for example, Barker and Lawrence. What is clear is that while the CCCS are arguing that the working class are already racist, the impact of Powellism is to re-articulate such racism. Whereas Barker is arguing that it is only after and because of the intervention of Powell that a new commonsense racism can be successful. Prior to this, racist arguments would be rejected as extremist.[13]

My position, in relation to these arguments, is that all advocates of the New Racism argument privilege the moment of Powellism and 1968, whether they see this moment of transition as a break or point of re-articulation. However I concur with the CCCS writers, particularly Lawrence, in arguing that the New Racism reorganises existing commonsense racism, but at *both* the political and non-political levels. It is clear that commonsense racism exists in the postwar period in elite and popular locations, however Barker is correct to argue that racism, as a political phenomenon, has to be reconstructed because there is a political prohibition on its expression. This prohibition is consciously experienced in both the public and political spheres.[14] For Barker, Powell is the first politician to break through this barrier.

Preface xiii

My argument is that this new language is longer in the making and that Powellism is the beneficiary of it rather than the inventor. Central to such a modification is the argument that the New Racism is, first and foremost, a political racism and it is how this political racism is able to articulate an ideological account of the local politics of 'race' in a public language of Englishness that allows it to be normalised across the political field. However this process is a protracted not a dramatic one. It is a process of discursive formation or re-articulation and central to it is the significance of the racialised anecdote.

A Modified Version of the Thesis

In the light of these remarks I propose the following modification to the New Racism thesis: that (i) Powellism cannot be explained entirely in terms of the novelty of its discursive content since, (ii) the content of Powellism has a great deal of continuity with other accounts that are historically prior to it and, upon which, it is both parasitic and transformative. Therefore, (iii) if we are to sustain an argument for a discursive shift or transition in postwar racial discourse then we must establish it through a greater attention to the content and dynamics of Parliamentary and Public Debates, taking place from at least the 1950s onwards.

These sources indicate that if we are to claim any sort of validity to the distinction of a New Racism emerging in postwar political discourse then we must abandon any strong sense of the conceptual transformation achieved *through* Powellism. Here we are confusing different sorts of claims about the 'success' of Powellism. Namely, that the political impact of Powellism is uniquely due to the impact of the conceptual transformation inherent in his novel discourse of 'race'. But this distinction, of the old and the new racism, is also a distinction about the relative lack of success of the old racists. This is misleading on two counts. Firstly, both the (so called) old racists and Powell share a similar kind of political exclusion. The distinction between Powell and Powellism is one that allows, in the New Racism thesis, the idea that Powell's ideas pass into the political mainstream while Powell does not. In this sense Powell's political career has been a spectacular failure (Schoen 1977).

Secondly, it could be argued that the political benefactors of the New Racism are it real authors: the backbench old racists[15] who remain within the Parliamentary process, *post* Powellism. Thus it is my argument that the *external* success of Powellism is an indicator of the *internal* achievement in the political discursive realm the Powellism exemplifies. Central to this distinction is the claim for 1968, and Powell's Birmingham and Eastbourne speeches. If we examine the evidence of public political discourse, constituting Parliamentary Debates and speeches prior to and post 1968, the paucity of evidence supporting the distinction is clearly revealed, as I will show.

A detailed examination of the discursive record of postwar political debates clearly supports the argument that the significance of Powellism is in highlighting, in admittedly dramatic fashion, discursive shifts and changes that had already taken place and were well established within, what I would term, Parliamentary *Commons' sense* by 1968. If this is not the case then we have, for example, precious little explanation for the passing of the 1962, 1965 and 1968 Immigration and Race Relations' Bills. Very obvious sources of public political racism which the New Racism writers are entirely silent about.[16]

This modified argument will be substantiated through a discussion of discursive materials that form the 'archive' of enunciative statements of Parliamentary Commons' sense and public discourse on Immigration and Race Relations over the period 1957 to 1988;[17] although our method will be a selection from this extensive body of material (cf. Foucault 1972). Such a slicing across a period of discursive history allows both a synchronic and diachronic analysis of a political discourse formation. This procedure will illuminate the emergent patterns of continuity in the form and content of postwar racist discourse in British public-political life, the purpose of which will be to modify arguments for a 'break' or 'interruption' in their trajectory by 1968.

Central to this continuity will be the form and figure of the anecdote and its mediation of the discursive ideology of 'race'. We will argue that the element that secures this is the development and use by Powell of 'anecdotal' or 'hearsay' accounts of 'ordinary English people' and their views i.e., Powell's political impact is secured through the development of an anecdotally based, detached racial narrative which Powell delivers to the press and media. The persuasiveness of the public-political racism of Powellism lies in the interior development of these anecdotal themes within Powell's elite speeches and the selectivity of media exposure of them (cf. Seymour-Ure 1974).

My modified argument for a more theoretically and historically consistent account of Powellism rests on the (controversial) view that the idea of 'race', imbricated within the black country vignettes that form the centre of *those* speeches, is a discourse of the *old* racism not the new.[18] This assertion involves a theoretical claim that racism, as a text, is co-produced by its writers and readers, since the meanings of its language depend upon, or rest upon, an appeal to a shared knowledge of the world to which that discourse assigns meanings or achieves 'truth' effects (cf. Kress and Hodge 1981; Fowler 1991). Thus the meanings of New Racism are negotiated through the framework of old racism's old meanings. Old racism, in this sense, refers to the deep structure of the modalities of the ideology of 'race'. Anecdotal discourse allows a conduit into this reservoir, the flow of which is operated by the audience, who are able to complete the meanings referred in the play of the discourse of politicians.

Powellism is thus illustrative of the central feature of the success of racialised commonsense in public life in postwar Britain, in offering an account of social and political reality, through the development of a discourse of anecdotal racism, that appeals to an idiom of hearsay and is qualified in terms of personal experience. This central reference to personal experience, that produces personal knowledge, allows a conceptual division to inhere in such discursive accounts between those who accept racialised discourse as authentic and those that are deemed to be excluded from the experience and are, therefore, not qualified to pass judgement or condemn those that do.

The discourse of the local and familiar allows racist ideas to be appealed to and invoked within a detached narrative that deploys disembedded empirical features as constitutive of the racialised urban location of black settlement. Here the power of racist discourse depends upon acknowledging the power of the idea of 'race' as a profoundly conceptual power of metaphor, allegory, etc. It is incumbent on me to provide a theoretical account of racism consistent with this assertion. I will do this through a brief discussion of racism as a social and political fiction and as a type of discourse.

Racist Fictions

I define the concept of racism as a 'biological fiction' (Fuss 1989: 91). Although in asserting this I am well aware that scholars have expended a considerable effort in attempting to clearly trace and periodize the varieties of types of racial classification over historical time, and the concomitant differences in social meaning that the term 'race' has signified (cf. Banton 1983: ch.3; Guillaumin 1995: *passim*). Like Miles (1989) I do not believe that such evidence should be interpreted to mean that the term racism can never achieve analytical clarity. On the contrary, the term racism should quite clearly refer to types of discourse which employ, refer or otherwise metonymically invoke, the historical fiction of 'race' by seeking to ground social and political forms of domination and inequality within 'a concept which signifies and symbolises socio-political conflicts and interests in reference to different types of human bodies' (Winant 1994: 270).

This discourse, as Seidel (1988a) (drawing on Guillaumin) has argued, since the nineteenth century, has been a biological one; one grounded in a conception of 'man's nature'. It is this 'biological discourse (the discourse of nature) which perpetuates both racism and sexism, the class system and male supremacy' (1988a: 12) in defining the social order as underpinned by the natural and thereby justifying (through forms of argumentative reduction) socio-cultural inequalities. Thus '[t]he biological rationalises the political' (Seidel 1988a: 11). To this formulation we must add the caveat that '[a]lthough the concept of 'race' appeals to biologically based human characteristics (so-called phenotypes), selection of these particular human features for purposes of racial signification is always and necessarily a social and historical process' (Winant 1994: 270).

Racism is an ideology and therefore an untruth (Miles 1982; 1989; 1993). However its historical existence depends upon its articulation within specific discourses. All discourses are claims to truth or rather carry truth claims within them (Foucault 1980). A discourse of truth must persuade us through the mobilisation of evidence, concepts, etc. Racism is the most enduring of historical discourses because it appeals for truth-effects to the most fundamental, non-rational, non-cognitive site of human truth: the body/ nature: the bio-physical sub-structure of existence. Various claims for profound difference at this level are signified by recourse to a range of physical, cultural and political symbols or markers of social difference.

Racist discourse works through a conceptual articulation of social symbolism ultimately reducible to a discourse of the non-social. The political persuasiveness of racism lies in its social referentiality, i.e. connecting profoundly determined difference to social effects or consequences. This is the articulatory power of racist discourse. In this important sense racism empowers its articulators by providing a powerfully simple explanation of social complexity. But the pattern of this explanation is reductionist: it explains the constitution of the social through the prior constitution of the non-social. Therefore, it is the articulation of types of social problem discourse, directed at empirical referents in the immediate environment, and their successful articulation to the determinism of racialised discourse, that explains the public purchase of such narratives in Powellism and other political discourses. My discussion of textual examples of Parliamentary racism and public speech will seek to illuminate this process.

A Referential or Constitutive Theory ?

We cannot simply oppose referential and constitutive accounts of language (cf. Voloshinov 1973). Those theorists that take a discursive approach are theoretically pre-disposed to a constitutive theory. But this in itself does not preclude the scope of claims for the role of discourse in constituting social phenomenon such as racism. When we examine the role of public political discourses of 'race' then we are testing out the limits of the constitutive power of languages without assuming *a priori* that such languages determine their object. Paradoxically it is the referential success of modes of discursive practice that realise the power of racism. The power of racism, as a public political discourse, depends upon its transformative power via its referents. It is the particular way, in particular circumstances, that discursive strategies assign meaning to already existing phenomenon that provides the necessary basis for mapping fields of racist discourse.

To say that racist discourse constitutes its object may over simplify the discursive interplay already at work in particular urban contexts of economic and social conflict. This conflict is at once both real and imagined, involving action, reactions and reflections. When we say that such fields have been subject to a process of racialisation we should, at the same time, acknowledge that economic and social forces raise and highlight the significance of salient features of the urban scene. In other words, certain features are more likely to be racialised than others. It follows that accounts of racialisation must be both empirical and textual, and they must pay attention to the dynamics of a process that is complexly achieved (cf. Miles 1989; 1993; Brown 1997: ch.1).

Political Language

The idea of political language allows a concentration of the concerns of linguistics and sociology in the intersection of language and power in the constitution of relations of signification and those of social structure. This is not to suggest that societies can be collapsed into the structures of language. But rather that within the context of persisting 'structural asymmetries' in unequal societies, discourse - in the form of texts - 'is a site of struggle[...]a terrain, a dynamic linguistic, and, above all, semantic space in which social meanings are produced or challenged' (Seidel 1985: 44). It is the fully social study of semantics, syntactics and other properties of elite text and talk which is required (cf. van Dijk 1993a).

The aim or objective of such analysis is to show the interactional strategies of individuals and groups, in the practice of language usage, that can most illuminate the constitutive role of language in the construction of symbolic power and the political ends to which such power can be directed. Quite how political language constitutes or accompanies political interventions is not clear. As Edelman has argued, to study the detail of political text and speech enunciation is to study the reality constituting role of public language (cf. Edelman 1977; 1988: 103-5). To analyse political language is to be concerned with both the public performance of language and its meaning as text.

While 'political speech' making or enunciation may conform to the idea of 'genre' (Voloshinov 1973) in that, '[e]ach period and each social group has its own repertoire of speech forms for ideological communication' (Voloshinov, cited in Seidel 1985: 45) the political is, as Seidel reminds us, 'ubiquitous' and 'cannot be prematurely foreclosed within the rule of a unit designated as genre, domain or field' (p.45). However, political speech making, particularly in the context of Parliamentary Debates, is most certainly a social practice in the sense that it has a recognisable *language-etiquette* or *speech-tact* that defines appropriateness of expression and reception and that, ultimately, such symbolic forms are expressive and constitutive of the wider society, and the hierarchical organisation of such societies.

What is striking about the political language of 'race' in postwar Britain, is that, while Parliamentary Discourse does conform to a genre of etiquette, in the case of 'race', such an etiquette is simply absent in the early postwar period.[19] The period from the mid 1950s to the early or mid 1960s is the process of its Parliamentary formation. In this sense the notion put forward, in a much criticised study, of a period of language instability leading to a period of definition is appropriate (Katznelson 1976).

What we clearly need to emphasise is that the formation of the political language of racism was not governed by an etiquette of expression but of suppression. The nearest equivalent to such a view is the conception of the control of language by Foucault (1979: 17-18). Such control strategies and positions are a major feature of the impact and idea of 'race' upon the political scene and change irrevocably the idea that 'race' enters politics or becomes the empirical subject of it. 'Race' is suppressed, dismissed, denied, revealed, disputed and condemned in speeches and articles and debates; it is suggested, referred to and alluded within debate; it is euphemised and deracialised. Despite all of this, 'race' is the deep structure of the politics of containment and of the politics of advancement of racist exclusions. It is the referent against which all signification's work and its public erasure is the basis upon which its social referentiality is transformed.

The 'Erasure' of Race

In this section, through a brief dialogue with post-structuralist positions which claim a de-centring of the concept of 'race', post-Powellism, I claim that any adequate account of forms of post-'race' signification practice, particularly ones constitutive of political discourse, must be able to negotiate the distinction between old and new racisms as relating to distinguishable periods that are consistent with empirical evidence of Parliamentary Debates and political speeches in postwar Britain. My argument is that if we are to meaningfully employ a conception of the 'old racism' then we must situate this type of racist expression as hegemonic up to the period of the Second World War in Western Europe. I claim empirical support for such a view in the accounts of historical scholars of racist discourse (cf. Rex 1970; 1973; 1983; Banton 1977; 1983; 1987; Guillaumin 1995; Miles 1989; Goldberg 1993) and as the necessary basis for any adequate account of the emergence of a New Racism as a postwar political phenomenon.

My argument, simply stated, is as follows: The growth and development of public racism in Great Britain in the postwar period has been made possible by, and inexplicably has been guaranteed its political impact upon the electorate, because of a profound and deliberate official political erasure of the signifier of 'race' from public political discourse, i.e. a political racism has been achieved without explicit use of its dominant signifier. Since the liberation of the Nazi death camps and the UNESCO statements of the 1950s and 60s (cf. Montagu (ed) 1972), the 'race' signifier has been, in the sense advanced by Derrida, erased in public space (cf. Derrida (Spivak (ed) 1976: xv-xviii).[20] The effect of this erasure has had a de-centring effect on explicit biologizing racisms, (i.e. discourses that refer to 'race' and 'races'), but the most notable development has been the proliferation of discourses that erase 'race', while in their place has arisen discourses of post-'race' signification, which form a flux around the signifying space, and which work through the articulation of it absent presence.

We cannot argue the finer points and evident complexities involved in the neo-Foucaultian and post-structuralist debate about racist discourse and 'race' signification here (cf. Goldberg 1993). But a few points of inevitable engagement arise: thus Omi and Winant have argued that 'race' is 'an unstable and de-centred complex of social meanings constantly being transformed by political struggle' (1986: 68). Such a process of flux seems to deny that there was/is any certitude to what 'race' means, prior to re-articulation, but crucially they argue that the meanings of 'race' are reinterpreted by articulating 'similar elements differently' (p.64). Thus it is the principle of articulation not what is articulated that has changed: 'race' is still the signifier but what it means, *post rearticulation*, is open to political contestation. The parallels with neo-Gramscian accounts are striking but the authors do not offer a theory of commonsense. Rather, political struggles over the signifier of 'race' take place in the context of the activities of postwar new social movements, and through policy politics aimed at the state. This appears to be a bottom-up, rather than top-down theory of political struggle, (as advocated by the British Gramscians), but it depends upon a claim for 'racial formation' as identity *giving*. It is not clear how such identities can be both determined and re-negotiated.

These accounts are more consistent than those that claim that the concept of 'race' is 'virtually vacuous, reflective of dominant social discourses' and thus 'inherently political[...] assuming significance as it orders membership and exclusions from the body politic' (Goldberg 1992: 543). This position seems to confuse a methodological principle (we should seek to discover what 'race' means in a given context) with a theoretical claim: that it has no distinctive content of its own. This ought to be an argument about the stability of the relationship between the 'race' signifier and its signifieds. In this sense the New Racism thesis claims a radical or permanent interruption in such a relationship. Thus Mercer argues that, post Powellism, 'race' is a 'signifier without a signified' (Mercer 1994), meaning that what 'race' might mean after the break is open to contestation. It is probably more accurate to argue that what has occurred in the postwar period is a breakdown in the relationship between signifier and signified, and the way that relationship works at the level of communication. Laclau's (1994) notion of an 'empty signifier' is suggestive here.

The question Laclau poses is how is signification possible without a stable signifier, or more pertinently, when the signifier appears to be absent? His answer, although he does not apply it to the question of racism, is that racist signifieds are able to act themselves as signifiers of that which they are not. Smith (1994), while supporting Laclau's approach, claims that 'race has been re-coded as crime, immigration, civil disorder, etc. But I would argue that this function needs to be located historically, in terms of the 'erasure' of 'race' as a public-political signifier, in the context of the preservation of its socially located 'conceptual primitives',[21] which are not eradicated, neither are they replaced, by the *moment* of decolonisation or the post-holocaust pronouncements that accompanied the public-political critique of scientific racism (Benedict 1983, orig. 1942; Barzun 1965, orig, 1937; Montagu (ed) 1964; cf. Miles 1989: 42-50).[22] Consequently, the space of 'race' is available to be reconstituted, since racism is a social ideology not a voluntarist politics derived from 'bad science'.

The essential 'articulatory' elements of this resurrection of racism in the postwar world is the persistence of the signifieds of old racism in private elite, official and public/popular spaces. Thus, paradoxically, the effect of political erasure has been a subterranean proliferation of racisms' many social signifieds in these very sites. It follows that the story of the development of postwar 'race' politics (or the racialisation of British politics) is the story of the infiltration or permeation of these ideologies to the centre of public political debates about 'black' immigration. The often claimed metonymy of immigrant=black is symptomatic of the success of such a semiotic reconfiguration. What follows is a tentative account of the rise of the New Racism as an account of the rise of a politically loaded anecdotalism whose chief virtue was its ability to get around the public prohibition on the explicit discourse of the 'old' racism.

Postwar British Racism as an Ideology of Englishness

The unique problem facing ideological racists in postwar British politics was the political prohibition on the explicit reference or employment of the idea of 'race' in respectable debate. The political achievement of exclusion legislation is the result of the successful construction of a Parliamentary discourse that was able to communicate the ideology of racism without the give away signifier of 'race' itself. This process of discursive re-formation was gradual and fraught with difficulties; restricted for the most part, to Question Time and Supply Days, where frequently their centre-liberal and left colleagues would deride and ridicule their dedication to this topic (cf. Layton-Henry 1984: ch.3). The elite response was often high minded and disdainful. However, through perseverance, which is the preserve of the ideological driven, and encouraged by their local successes and support, this group fashioned a particularly distinctive political narrative that allowed the translation of the local politics of 'race' into a narrative of neighbourhood nationalism and white identity politics. This is not to suggest that this group of driven Backbenchers knew what they were about. They practically understood that it was necessary to submerge or redefine 'race' within other social topics or concerns that would act as conduits for it; that would operate as public symbols of the dangers it posed for British society.

Early versions of this emergent formation included the discourse of disease and contamination: health scares, TB outbreaks, tropical diseases, etc. (Barker 1979: 1). Secondly, there was the discourse of vice (linked to the incidence of sexually transmitted disease), moral turpitude and degradation; the delineation of 'red-light' areas and thinly disguised miscegenation discourse directed at the imputed sexual liaisons between black men and white women (*Hansard vol. 634* 17 February 1961: 1963-70; Pannell and Brockway 1965). Thirdly, there was the discourse of crime. This often involved combining prostitution, pimping, etc., with the idea of violence and drug trafficking, and the creation of 'no-go areas' (cf. Gilroy 1987: 79-85).

These emergent local evils, attendant upon the development of black immigration, were often imbricated within a discourse of protection of the working class neighbourhood and local area from moral and social decline As Foot (1965: 36-7) records, the early Immigration Control Associations were welcomed by the locals because, *at last here were people who were going to clean up the town*. As Miles and Phizacklea (1979: 94) have convincingly argued, this perception of decline was closely associated with the arrival and settlement of black migrants. Contained within the development of this discourse was a local nationalism that involved an idea of the decline of Britain as a dominant world power and the arrival and mixing of inferiors, viewed as a direct result of this fact.

The acceptance of the idea of decline often involved a perception of a threat to the character and English*ness* of the areas. Here nation was fused into class; the working and lower middle-class, white locals become the nation and the repository of the virtues and values by which the Empire, and world leadership, had been achieved; a white-order that was realised as it was at the same moment threatened by decolonisation (cf. Schwarz 1996).

At the emergent centre of this discursive formation was the figure of Coates and Silburn's *Forgotten Englishman*[23] (cf. Carter and Joshi 1984: 67-8). A figure discovered to exist in poverty when poverty had been officially eradicated. He lived in the inner city, unable to move away, while the blacks moved in next door. It is no surprise that the key site of struggle over racism at the local level has been that of housing (cf. Rex and Moore 1967; Smith 1989). It is the forgotten Englishman, living in the 'areas most affected', who is spoken up for and on behalf of by the Backbenchers involved in supporting Cyril Osborne's campaign for exclusionary legislation of 'coloured immigration' (*Hansard* 5 December 1958: 1552-1597; *Hansard* 17 November, 1959: 1121-1130; *Hansard vol. 634* 17 February, 1961: 1929-2024; *Hansard, vol.645* 1 August, 1961: 1319-1331; *Hansard* 16 November, 1961: 687-823).

As this discursive formation develops, the Forgotten Englishman becomes the Ordinary English person. A person who is tolerant, well disposed to be civic in his community, but finds himself unable to tolerate the extent of changes that have recently occurred and, in particular, the introduction of foreign elements into his neighbourhood. It is widely believed that Powell exposed or invented this figure in his Birmingham 'rivers of blood' speech. But the quite ordinary Englishman is the central figure in the campaign for controls. It is on behalf of this tolerant and exasperated person that legislation must be achieved. It is this mythical community Cyril Osborne articulates: 'Speaking as an Englishman for the English people about conditions in England, I feel deeply that the problem of immigration must be tackled, and tackled soon' (*Hansard vol. 634* 17 February 1961: c.1930).[24]

The political success of racism in postwar British politics and society is the achievement of dedicated campaign by a group of inter-party Backbenchers and the work of Immigration Control Associations and the assistance, declared and undeclared, of organised fascist and racist groups and individuals (cf. Foot 1965; Walker 1977; Layton-Henry 1984: ch.3; 1992). This dedicated campaign does not achieve success until 1961 when the Conservative government agrees to support a modified version of Cyril Osborne's Private Member's Bill, presented in February of the same year (*Hansard vol. 634* 17 February: 1929-2024; *Hansard vol. 649* 16 November: 687-823). This earlier debate was itself the culmination of a series of Private members Bills and attempted interventions by Osborne and his supporters from 1955 onwards (Layton-Henry 1984: 31-2).

As we have observed such Supply Day Debates and Question Time comments were met with indifference and with elite support for the principles of the Open Door and Commonwealth ideal. Scholarly work now reveals that the State had a Janus face during this period, since publicly it expressed the unity of the Commonwealth; in private and official memos and minutes, it deplored and feared the arrival and settlement of 'inferior' blacks. There can be little doubt that the state elite's response to black migration is a profoundly racialised one, despite the fact that this process is uneven and does not produce restriction legislation until 1961 (cf. Harris 1987: 72; Miles 1988). We must conclude that the success of public-political racism in postwar Britain is the result of the conjunctural alliance of the State elite and racist Backbenchers, which takes place within a more generalised shift in the whole ideological field of racism in this period (cf. Guillaumin 1995: 37-40).[25]

If the claim for the New Racism is to be at all consistent with such accounts then it must address this discursive processes as part of wider transformation of the ideological field of racism in the period 1945 to the early 1960s. Powellism is a privileged confidant of this elite and backbench racism and Powell fashions his own elite/populist version of it in 1968. Prior to this political intervention he is unmoved by the theme (Foot 1969: ch.2).

Researching Smethwick

The original research sources for this project were the seminal accounts of the 'Smethwick phenomenon' and the politics of 'Powellism' recorded by Paul Foot in: *Immigration and Race in British Politics* (1965) and *The Rise of Enoch Powell* (1969). These two slim volumes, as Solomos has suggested, have been virtually ignored by scholars (CCCS: Race & Politics Group 1982: ch.1; Layton-Henry 1984; Solomos 1986a). Written for a popular audience, published in paperback by an investigative 'political' journalist, their significance were as politically defensive interventions into a period that was to have damaging effects upon the popular-alliance that Foot and his colleagues had sought to create.[26]

My re-examination of the framing terms of Smethwick, as it emerged out of the writings of Foot and other sources, focuses upon the interplay between the national political impact of the Smethwick incident in party politics and Parliamentary Debates and the constitution of the local event and its impact. Thus I was led to frame the question of the significance of Smethwick as one expressive of a double-bind: as both a scandalous local event occurring within local election campaigns, and then infamously in the 1964 General Election, and how this local campaign is subsequently expressed within the public language of the national political arena. In other words what sort of interplay took place between the shaping of the picture of Smethwick at the local level and the construction of the political myth of Smethwick? A key neglected source discovered here is the 1964 Expiring Laws Debate and the 1965 Race Relations Bill Debate, both of which are peculiarly disturbed by the impact and reverberations of the stone of Smethwick plummeting into the political pond.

The Local Politics of Race

What the story of Smethwick tells us is that the politics of 'race' arises out of the politics of the local constituency. The Smethwick campaign, in its context, allows us to begin to define and periodise the elements that construct the local politics of 'race' as a potential lever or catalyst of national concerns. First, there is an active fascist element: such far right groups as the British Union of Fascists and the dissident League of Empire Loyalist had recognised the potentiality of the anti-immigration issue and set about securing support by leg-work and campaigning in the areas with a higher concentration of immigrant workers (cf. Walker, 1977: ch.3). The primary, and most necessary element, is the formation of local anti-immigration ginger groups, in this case The Immigration Control Association (cf. Foot, 1965; Rex identifies this development as crucial, cf. 1973: 107; Rex & Tomlinson, 1979: 52).

The second element is probably the precipitator of the first: the structurally mediated antagonism between black, former colonial, 'settlers' and the indigenous white working class and petty-bourgeoisie, created in the context of 'urban blight' of decaying, once traditional and hierarchically ordered suburbs; now open to 'newcomers' and to unsettling urban change (Rex and Moore, 1967). Given this context the situation is ripe for the ideological collision of the global politics of post-colonialism, labour migration, poverty and urban industrial decline, in the context of global capitalist restructuring.

However, for this situation to become 'political' such elements have to be articulated by public language expression. Such articulation takes place through the rise of a local discourse of 'race'; and it is this discourse and how it operates in relation to the local political economy which begins to construct the recognisable features of the postwar politics of 'race' (cf. Drake, 1955; Solomos, 1988: 54-5). This conception of the discursive formation of a political racism must encompass the admittedly complex process of firstly, the practico-ideological construction, through the combination of commonsense notions and elements of more theorised ideologies, of an idea of the problems inherent in the 'influx' of black workers into the national and local economy and, secondly, the processes, which are exclusively discursive, by which the signifieds of 'race' and 'colour' construct a negative or positive account of 'race relations' at the local level; and how such constructions, oral and written, are called forth and centred by: (i) politicians, councillors and public spokesmen and often, decisively, in constructing a local political agenda: (ii) local press coverage (cf.Butterworth, 1967; Foot, 1965; Critcher, et al, 1975).

The third, and significant link in this process, is the way in which politics at the national level can choose to articulate these elements. Such a process may take place in the context of, or in response to, national press coverage or 'exposure'. At each stage there is no necessary momentum for the issue or construction to be articulated or taken any further. The fact that, in the structural and ideological context of postwar Britain, such processes do advance and become political in the full sense of the word is a specific event requiring an analysis that addresses this process as *sui generis*.

Researching Powellism

The approach to Powellism, although broadly framed in this way, had specific differences. Powellism, unlike the event of Smethwick, was not a localised historical political event. If Smethwick can be characterised as a bottom-up political racialisation, then Powellism was the opposite, i.e. a top-down political project. Despite the fact that the term is employed to identify a sense of grass roots extremism, crucially the success of Powellism, I will argue, is how the political discourse of Powellism articulates itself to the materials of the local politics of 'race'. This ideological articulation involves a complex and conjunctural alignment of heterogeneous factors, some very peculiar to Powell, but made possible by an existing reservoir of 'discursive' signifieds of 'old' racism. Thus I will argue that Enoch Powell's racism is almost entirely borrowed; what is significant is the elite attempt at articulation, and the political direction in which Powell attempts to direct these newly combined elements. The persuasiveness of my argument therefore depends upon being able to establish (a) the evidence for the formation and content of the social signifieds of 'old' racism in public and Parliamentary debates: a formation I define as Parliamentary Commons' sense; chapters 3, 4 and 5 all make a specific contribution to this task. (b) The heterogeneous content, discontinuous intellectual and political formation of Powellism, (defined originally as an economic doctrine), and the disinterestedness of Powell as regards the signifying properties of racism, prior to his attempt to harness electoral support for a new populist Toryism. (c) Powell's political and ideological success in constructing a novel discourse of post-'race' signification that echoes and refines that of his Backbench precursors, (who he of course joins once sacked from Shadow cabinet responsibilities) and how that success depends upon the rearticulation of old racism through the space of the absent 'race' signifier. The empirical basis for such claims are (i) Powell's published speeches and statements and (ii) Parliamentary Debates taking place from 1958 to 1962 and from 1968 onwards, also including Powell.[27]

Discourse, Documents and Sociological Research

The principal sources for the research behind the book have been, as indicated earlier, secondary source texts: public documents, recorded speeches and reports. I have principally been concerned with the constitutive properties of the various kinds of texts that I have investigated. However, as a sociologist, I have also been concerned to analyse such texts within their political and historical context of emergence. It is therefore the case that I view the formation of various acts of enunciation to both reflect broadly the context of their production and to play a role in modifying and changing that context. The question of Powellism begs this sort of analysis. To claim that Powellism signifies a shift in political discourse is to make a very radical claim about the role of Powellism as a discourse in shaping new relations of political signification and social regulation. My work shows that this claim is consistently overblown and the reasons for this are contained in the tendency to over-generalise the significance of discursive shifts or transformations on the basis of selective empirical sources. When such errors are made then inappropriate generalisations are often the result.[28]

Methodology

At a general level of analysis I have pursued a quasi-Foucaultian approach, by attempting an 'archaeology' of discourses occurring within the 'enunciative field' of my enquiry (cf. Foucault 1972: 100). But such a task, in establishing the archive and ordering of discursive statements historically, is too general: at best descriptive accounts can be established of the field of enquiry or focus. Such an approach produces a research position that is over-theoreticist and lacks empirical validation (p.27). Thus, for example, I have established, through exhaustive research, using the *IRR Newsletter* (1960-9) as principal source, and cuttings on Powellism for the period 1960 - 1988, that there is, within the discourse of 'race' reporting and speech making, (i.e. the enunciative acts that compose the field of 'race' discourse), a use of common metaphors and symbols; and that such symbols appear to operate at the level of a 'metalanguage'. Such a metalanguage allows journalists, politicians and others to speak of 'race' as an empirically real social phenomenon with inherent characteristics and social effects. The cumulative effect of this field of enunciation is to constitute 'race' as an idea in the language of politics and press commentary as a *sub-political phenomenon*. It is this entity, which is only visible in the field of such discourse, that I have defined as 'political racism'.[29] However, such an account cannot hope to sustain validity unless it can be substantiated by means of comparative examples and illustrations of the detail of debate and exchanges within the political field of public language construction. I have attempted such an analysis at two levels: I have analysed various debates about 'race' in terms of a claim about Powellism and the idea that there has been a shift in the constitutive role of 'race' discourse in the period commencing with Powell's intervention into the 'race' debate. By analysing Powell's discourse in great and exhaustive detail, within a comparative analysis of Parliamentary Debates before and after 1968, I am able to establish if this is a plausible thesis. The evidence suggests it is not and this is consistent with my judgement of the lack of fit of such a thesis within the wider political context. Thus my analysis is able to place such discursive texts within a wider social and political context in a manner able to illustrate the presence or absence of contiguous and contingent elements and factors; since claims for a key text rest on being able to establish, as well as merely claim, such correspondence.

Secondly, I have attempted to analyse the discourse of Smethwick within the field of the enunciation of the idea of 'political racism'. On this methodological basis I am able to assert that the unifying feature of 'race' discourse within public and Parliamentary discourse in this period is *discursive repression*. The source of such repression is to be located within the Labour cabinet elite social democrats, like Richard Crossman and Harold Wilson; and the Liberal Tory centre. It is this discursive context that has allowed the play and closure of 'race' positive and 'race' negative narratives of expression and control which have pushed at, and challenged, the boundaries of official discourse. Only one of these discourses is Powellism and it arises in opposition and alliance to the existing fields of 'race' narration.

Research Claims

The strengths of the study are that it offers a detailed analysis of documentary sources which can clearly reveal the impact, via the conceptual transformation and penetration of racial political language, upon political *Commons'sense* and debate during this period. These detailed sources are discursive ones; consisting of speeches, at the local and national political level; within Parliamentary Debates; as well as detailed press commentary and reportage. Such sources are used as forms of documentary evidence for the presentation of a plausible explanation for the impact of the phenomenon of Smethwick and Powellism upon political debates. Such explanations, employing conceptions of social ideologies and discourses of 'race', are built up carefully through the accretion of extensive detail, quotation and analysis of debates, political statements and commentaries. Such argument quite properly must involve a reconceptualization of the debate concerning the concept of racism and political language and how such terms may be more fruitfully employed.

Acknowledgements

Many people have contributed so much more than they could ever have realised to the formation of the personal and intellectual strategies that have resulted in the production of this book. Some of them have guided and chided me as a thinker; others have aided and abetted me in the research that I undertook over a period of eight or nine years, resulting in the production of the vast amount of material from which this much more compact book is drawn.

In the first category I would like to thank Vernon Philpot, Mr. Love, Tracy Farmer, Andy Damms, Dave Lee, Pat Towning, Martin Fennel and Richard Hinchcliffe. And my parents. In the second category: Martin Barker for his excellent influence and example; Madge Dresser and Peter Jowers; John Solomos for supervising my research and much else besides; Bob Miles, Michael Keith and Simon Cottle for encouraging me at times when I most needed it; Colin Burgess, Derek Williams, Marc Picthal, Andy D. Brown and Ian Barker and former colleagues and friends at Filton college; Peter Kent and the library staff for obscure loan materials form all over the British library circuit; Heather Lynn and the Resource Library at the Centre for Research in Ethnic Relations at Warwick; the office staff at 10 Gower Street, Birkbeck college and the library at Gresse street; my colleagues and friends at Bath Spa. ESRC for funding the fieldwork that provided the material.

Last, but not least, John Wrench for commissioning the title for the Research in Ethnic Relations series; Kate Trew (nee Hargreave) and the editorial staff at Ashgate; and Rachel Hedges for picking up on so much that I missed. Of course, the final responsibility for what remains is mine.

1 The Erasure of Race in Public Space

Why not say 'race'? Why not come out with it?
Mr. Ivor Richards (Barons Court) *Commonwealth Immigrants Bill*,
28th February 1968: col.1475.

The Racialisation of Postwar Immigration Control Debates

This chapter offers a critical engagement with neo-marxist approaches to the postwar racialisation of official debates concerned with the politics of immigration control (cf. Solomos 1986d)[1] i.e., approaches that define the research problematic as one concerned with the analysis of 'racism' and the politics of migration rather than the ideological notion of 'race relations' (cf. Miles 1982; 1984; 1993).[2] It does so from the point of view that claims for the racialisation of British politics and the *Commons' sense* (in the Gramscian sense) of public and Parliamentary Debates do not afford the rhetorical and discursive properties of political language greater explanatory significance in achieving such ideological effects. Such an argument is based upon the view that an epistemologically guaranteed theory of ideology is unable to specify how ideological interests/ forms of mystification are achieved within the production of official language without recourse to a view of racism as a discursive phenomenon which achieves rather than guarantees dominant meanings (cf. Hall 1988).[3] Herein lies the question of the power of ideological language and the power such language has over the definition and interpretation of social meanings (cf. Hodge and Kress 1979; 1993; Kress and Hodge 1988; Fowler et al 1979; Fowler 1991).[4]

This chapter will seek to place the problem of political language at the centre of the debate about the racialisation of black migration in postwar Britain. It will argue that the concepts of commonsense and racialisation, developed by neo-marxist sociologists to explain the emergence of political racism in postwar British politics, assume or impute, rather than demonstrate, the relationship between ideology, racism and language involved in achieving this process.

This obviously raises the question of the relationship between generalised ideologies and particular languages; between discursive signification and political representation and, most specifically, the extent to which the forms of discourse of politics are determined by their official context of production? Here it is clear that along with the lack of attention paid to what we might call, political textuality, not enough consideration has been given to the influence of the institutional context of production upon official discourse and debate, and how this allows an understanding of the sense in which the signifier of 'race' is under official political 'erasure' in the post 1945 period.[5]

It will be claimed that this order of discursive repression is a key determinant of the unique 'mode of thematisation' of 'race politics' as it has emerged in this period (cf. Brier and Axford 1975).[6] The evidence of such repression, despite intending the public control of racism, is more likely to have provided a more effective means of its subterranean encoding within mainstream Parliamentary Debates.

In parliament, at least, there is no language of 'race' but rather a discourse of racial signification within which the term 'race' is most often absent. The distinction is a crucial one. The term 'race' is erased in public space. It cannot be spoken of. Yet, like the Derridean signifier, its 'trace' or immanence remains and more importantly we have no agreed language beyond it; no language which is free of its signifying chains, its linguistic dispersions. A key element of the argument with which we will engage is that racialisation is a ideological process that produces discursive effects within the production of political language, party politics and state policy. Ideological effects must be achieved and any ideological process requires consideration of the material and significatory properties of public language construction.

The institutional process of public language exchange and debate that has resulted in the racialisation of black migrants as a problematic and divisive minority within postwar Britain has been viewed, to a large extent, as a determined 'site' of societal reproduction rather than a process in it itself. Of course, once such a site is afforded significant autonomy then its relationship to wider structures and relations becomes contingent. This however is a necessary price to pay in illuminating the role and significance of political discourse in constructing political realities (cf. Edelman 1977).

Such a micrological focus upon language, text and debate does not impute the autonomy of discourse nor does it abandon a wider macrological focus, since such an analysis of the process of language construction is not intrinsically incompatible with a wider structural account of the political economy of migrant labour and the politics of racialisation and exclusion (cf. Miles 1989) simply because the language, syntactic rules or grammar expressive of these 'relations of signification' are shaped and given meaning within this wider context.

What such a focus can more clearly indicate is the role of political languages in imagining and seeking to achieve the ideological transformation of the meaning and explanation of those inequalities and conflicts of the social realm as they are drawn into its semantic structure. Here we are speaking of the dominant language of the social and how that language must draw ideologies of the social into itself as it is publicly made. Such a language is a language of determinism. The forces of determination of the social world are not seen to be social and economic but natural and biological. The social ideology of 'race' is rooted in this determinism. Political language holds itself aloof from such talk, attempting to persuade of its neutrality and technical reason (Habermas 1973; 1976). The legitimacy of political language depends upon the maintenance of the illusion of it separation from the social domain. However, in the face of the experience and the representation of social relations and processes within the context of social class inequality; gendered and racialised divisions; in seeking to ideologically include those excluded by existing structural inequality; in seeking collective sentiments and popular support in the midst of actual and potential divisions and conflicts of the social, the language of the political re-traces a pattern of determinism familiar to its audiences; re-traces the ghost of 'race', biology and destiny.[7]

This chapter will develop this argument, analytically and inductively, around the following points:

1   The NR theorists make the absence of 'race' a critical point of focus in their account; by contrast, racialisation approaches do not privilege this element. This creates a problem for racialisation theory in that it challenges what it is that is being achieved via the process of discursive racialisation ? If 'race' is absent from political discourse, most of the time, then how can we sustain an argument for the racialisation of British politics?[8]

2   In point of fact, the racialisation approach can offer two types of response to this. It can point to the analytical distinction between the process of racialisation, which involves the construction of deterministically constituted categories, without necessarily the explicit notion of 'race', and the concept of racism which involves the attribution of additional negative characteristics. This allows the approach a good deal of variability in treatment and in approach. It means, most specifically, that the idea of 'race' does not need to be present in racialisation, and racism can be expressed without the explicit use of the idea of 'race'. However there are discrepancies and wide variations in adherence to the full implications of this distinction.

3   These reservations notwithstanding, the racialisation perspective, grounded in a political economy of migration and state regulation, provides a very

sophisticated approach to the 'politicisation' of black migration to postwar Britain. In this respect the framework of such a racialisation approach is more likely, than say a 'new racism' approach, to sustain an account of the historical and structural features necessary to generate the raw material referents of symbolic and ideological discourse, to which political language refers and upon which it attempts to work.[9]

4   A closer examination of successful instances of the approach reveal problems with the analysis of the content of racial language and the extent to which such a language should be examined as a discursive-ideology. In particular, many racialisation approaches, while well grounded in a political economy of labour migration and the regulatory state, fail to define or acknowledge the ideological character of racial political discourse and the extent to which it must take a discursive form of expression. This reveals a putative theory of language as 'epiphenomenon' or effect of class forces/modes of incorporation. This is traceable to a downgrading of the importance of the public sphere and need for ideological legitimation (cf. Habermas 1973; 1976); especially of the process of debate construction where political ideologies are made.[10]

5   An examination of the reality constructing role of political language (cf. Edelman 1977) is central to the issue of the absence or suppression of the racial signifier. Some accounts of racialisation do focus particularly upon public language as the ideological face of state legitimation of exclusion. By the same token the theoretical space of the absence of 'race' is also addressed. Two influential accounts, that of Reeves (1983) and Miles (1989; 1990; 1993), address this problem through the deployment of the concepts of *deracialisation* and *ideological articulation*.

6   However there are problems with these approaches also. Reeves, for example, does not offer a coherent theory of racial discourse as a discursive-ideology but rather as a practically adequate means of concealment of political pragmatism or extremism. Miles' analytical interrogation reveals the deterministic logic of non-'race' specific discourse, that both racialises and is an expression of racism, but does not fully explore racisms' cultural proliferation or social articulation.[11] Racism borrows the language of society.

7   This means that the process of signification is richer but more elusive than supposed; it is affected by the political as well as the repression of structure; it is also, in the last instance, determined by wider economic and social dynamics, although it cannot be 'read off' from them. Political racism is written through public language and such language is bound up with the representation and legitimation of the social imaginary as an unequal and conflictually experienced

social totality. The political language of the racial imaginary is less official and more an address to the social constitution of popular experience; it seeks the language of society in its articulations within the semantic space evacuated by the ghostly traces of biological science and physical anthropology.

8   This, in turn suggests, that what is required is an account of racialisation which opens up the signifying power of discourse to achieve racial meanings in a context which takes full account of the dynamics of political process and the influence and reference to external social and economic frameworks. It is the relative balance of forces that will inevitably determine their decisive effect or otherwise in a political context in which erased traces await activation. Although such a contingent process has no guaranteed outcomes.

Racialisation Theory

Racialisation theory has provided the most adequate framework for thinking the relationship between racism, ideology and state control of populations within the context of global migration within late capitalism and the significance of these elements to the political formation and cultural homogenization of the European and Western nation state system (cf.Miles 1989; 1993). However the politicisation of racism and its articulation with nationalism have produced ideological configurations which appear to possess a great deal of autonomy in the current conjuncture. The salience of this aspect has grown as research into interior state processes and procedures, involved in the development of racial politics and racial political language in the postwar conjuncture, has advanced.

What has not been fully examined is the extent to which this involves a complex relationship between racial politics and racial political language. While theorists working within a racialisation problematic have clearly identified this dimension they have not given it analytical priority, and often the examination of the conceptual content of political language, and its relationship to policy outcomes of official and public debates, has not been pursued with any great theoretical or empirical rigour (cf. Solomos 1988). It is not an exaggeration to argue that political language achieves the legitimacy necessary to allow the state to impose entry controls upon former state members by stigmatising them as an undesirable and problematic source of labour.

Despite the fact that such theorists define the process of racialisation (Miles 1989; and in Cashmore (ed) 1994: 274-7) as an ideological process of signification, they do not recognise the extent to which social policy outcomes, such as the control of 'black' migration, are achieved through a complex ideological struggle *within* political language and political debates. This is because such theorists do not conceive of the process of political racialisation as taking place, in and through public language, despite the fact that there is agreement that the term racialisation is to refer to the 'use of the idea of "race" in discourse' (Miles 1989: 76; Reeves 1983: 173-6). In this respect such theorists conceive of the process of racialisation in too structurally determined a manner, in not allowing the processes of language production and mediation more autonomy in achieving the outcome of racialisation situations.

The Racism Problematic

Our discussion of the racialisation approach must be placed within a wider examination of the so called Neo-Marxist racism problematic which has, arguably, defined the theoretical terms of debate over the past decade in Britain (cf. Miles 1993; Solomos and Back 1993). Neo-Marxist approaches minimally agree that a racist form of political commonsense has accompanied or allowed the development of state racism in postwar Britain. Such racism has developed in the context of the use of 'black' labour which has been racialised or stigmatised and subject to forms of exclusionary legislation, state surveillance and internal regulation. Here racialisation occurs when the 'idea of race' enters into a process resulting in the construction of racial categories which connotate additional negative attributes and/or determined characteristics. When this process is focused upon the state and political institutions then we can say that 'race' has been politicised (i.e. political racialisation has been *achieved*), in that the idea of 'race' has entered into the political process and began to inform and influence decisions taken towards migrant groups (Reeves 1983; Miles and Phizacklea 1984; Solomos 1988).

These developments have taken place within the context of the reconstruction of 'British society in the face of a series of political and ideological conflicts which have occurred in a conjuncture characterised by the declining profitability of British capitalism' (Miles 1989: 39) and, for many writers, the concomitant social and political crisis of the dominant class fraction or bloc. For some this amounts to a 'crisis of hegemony', i.e., a crisis of moral and cultural leadership which has been articulated through the social ideology of 'race' (Hall et al, 1978; CCCS: Race and Politics Group 1982).

This signals the principal area of disagreement *within* the neo-marxist approach: the role and significance of postwar racism as an ideological phenomenon. At its theoretical core this disagreement is one grounded in a view that ideology is either determined at the political/superstructural level or at the economic/production relations level. Broadly speaking this means that theorists will either tend to support an argument about its function within an economic processes, whereby the racialisation of migrants attempts to conceal the role of migrant labour usage, and the extent of the state's involvement in this sphere; as opposed to a more politically autonomous argument, where racism is articulated to achieve more broadly hegemonic objectives. This is also, as I shall show, an argument about the conceptual inflation of the concept of racism as an ideology (cf. Miles 1989: ch.2) and the extent to which racism has began to proliferate as a transformed cultural discourse; or the extent to which 'race' signifies the semiotic site of contested and changing political meanings (cf. Donald and Rattansi (eds) 1992).

It is the distinctive argument of the New Racism theorists that a new racist commonsense has been fashioned within the discourse of right wing strands of British conservatism, as those strands have become more dominant in contemporary British politics. It is this process which clearly reveals the development of a new kind of racist language, one which is free of the negative political censure of the old language of 'race' but which is fully racist in its conceptual structure and in its political effects (Barker 1981; CCCS Race and Politics Group 1982).

Earlier debates over such issues (cf. Miles 1984a) have established that the differing approaches are agreed that the problem of postwar racism is the problem of accounting for how racism is articulated within public and political debates and the degree to which this involves the entrenchment of state power and dominant interests, as well as the evident increase in popular forms of racism. This has lead both sorts of approaches to argue that a political articulation of forms of popular racism have allowed the growth of a greater state authoritarianism, through the construction of 'folk devils' and 'enemies within', and the emergence of exceptional forms of state power, including covert repatriation policies, internal surveillance, policing and forms of quasi-fascism (Barker 1979; 1981; CCCS: Race and Politics Group 1982; Miles and Phizacklea 1984; Carter, Harris and Joshi 1987; Gilroy 1987; cf. Solomos 1986a).

These approaches can be said to constitute the major claims of the 'racism problematic' developed within neo-marxist sociology in the 1980s (Miles 1993; Solomos and Back 1993). It is important to stress that the CCCS: Race and Politics work, in developing a more broadly cultural studies focus to this area, is greatly indebted to the work of Stuart Hall and colleagues, both at CCCS: Birmingham and via the collective involved in Marxism Today (cf. Hall 1978; 1988; Hall et al 1978; Hall and Jacques 1983; 1989). Hall's coining of the terms

'Thatcherism' and 'authoritarian populism' involve claims about Powellism and popular racism which are taken up by CCCS: Race and Politics Group (1982) and Gilroy (1987). However, while both Barker and the CCCS collective share the use of the term 'new racism', the relationship between Barker's analysis of Thatcherism and 'new racism' and Hall's is clearly divergent (see chapter 2).

What all these theorists shared in the 1980s, Miles and Phizacklea and Harris et al included, was a concern to develop a non-reductionist, neo-marxist analysis that could highlight the perceived crisis of the British state in the postwar period, and the extent to which racism and increasing forms of cultural nationalism and authoritarianism were a feature of it. This approach drew, variously, upon the ideas and revisions of Gramsci, Althusser, Poulantzas and Laclau. A common feature of all these analyses was a concern with the deployment of a Gramscian idea of racism as a form of popular and political commonsense. Although it was Hall and CCCS: Race and Politics Group who viewed the securement of popular commonsense ideologies of racism as the basis for winning political hegemony, Barker and Miles less so.[12]

For our purposes here, the key aspect of divergence of the 'racism' approaches is how they differ in their claims and treatment of the role and impact of Smethwick and Powellism in the racialisation of British politics. While the New Racism theorists (and Hall) privilege Powellism (and Smethwick); by contrast, theorists of racialisation do not. This distinction coincides with a divergence of focus upon the language of Powellism and the British Conservative New Right. For the New Racism (and Thatcherism) writers the construction of popular racist commonsense depends upon the hegemonic activities of this group or alliance. The racialisation approaches either explicitly or implicitly contest this view (Miles 1987; 1989). For them, racialisation and racial ideologies arise because of the migrant labour system and the way in which such ideologies are a 'type of distorted thought which remains trapped in the appearances of reality and which, therefore, masks and conceals the real relations and social contradictions' (Larrain 1994: 292) that exist interior to capitalism as a global system of economic domination.[13]

It is the racialisation approach I want to examine here. Our interrogation of the 'new racism' approach will be delayed until chapter 2. The focus of our examination here will be the extent to which theorists, within the racialisation approach, acknowledge the problem of racial political language and the role of such language in the construction and securement of racial ideologies within the politics of migration control. Such remarks reflect the empirical observation that while racialisation theory has been applied in a number of historical and empirical instances, including postwar Canada, France and Britain, it has not been the object of any sustained critical examination. Such an engagement is long overdue particularly given that the term has become an established concept that can be found across a range of theoretical and empirical work on racism (e.g. Smith, S. 1989; Solomos 1989; Miles in Cashmore 1994: 274-6).

The Racialisation Approach on Britain

The empirical/historical object of the British analysis has been the post 1945 racialisation of West Indian and South Asian migration, resulting in the stigmatisation of such groups as unwanted and socially divisive. Miles (1982) has most clearly articulated a model of this process as the result of the articulation of existing commonsense ideologies of racism within a political process, resulting in the ideological signification of the incoming migrant groups as 'races'.

Figure 1.1   The Racialisation of Migrant Labour

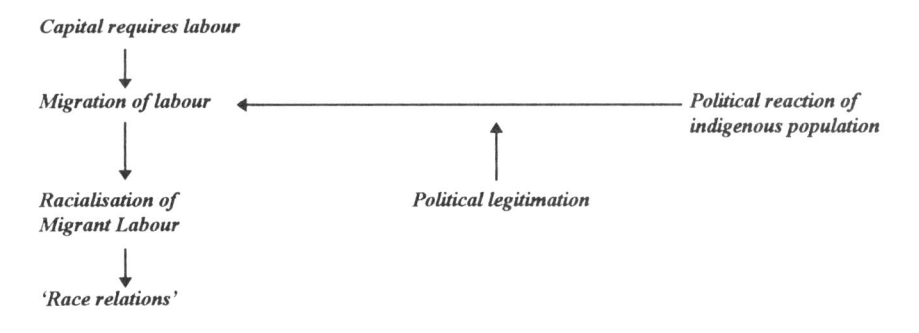

Capital requires labour
↓
Migration of labour ←—————————————— *Political reaction of indigenous population*
↓   ↑
Racialisation of   *Political legitimation*
Migrant Labour
↓
'Race relations'

Source: R. Miles *Racism and Migrant Labour* (1982: 169).

Racialisation theorists would argue that the determined process of utilisation of migrant labour is subject to the distortion and mystification of an ideology of 'race' (which is viewed as epistemologically false), an ideology which conceals the fact that the incoming group are units of labour, members of a global working class, under the sway of international capitalism.

Thus ideological racialisation is an outcome of a process of social construction whereby economic migrants are represented as black immigrants, which is an inversion and concealment of their real relations within the process of capital accumulation. This ideological process of signification is not, necessarily, an outcome of the political functioning of the state but a result of different forms of racialised reaction, at all levels of British society, to a particular group of migrants 'marked' by 'colour' signifiers. Thus, racism often appears as a contradictory effect of the economic and political demands of capitalist state formations, where the demand for migrant labour is racialised by social and political forces within and outside of the state (cf. Miles and Solomos 1987). Thus Miles argues that:

> The development of the capitalist world economic system has been accompanied historically by large scale migrations of people, not least because of the need to constitute a labour force for commodity production, and by the formation of the nation-state. Herein lies a contradiction between, on the one hand, the need for the international mobility of human beings and, on the other, the drawing of territorial boundaries via the construction of citizenship as a legal category which sets legal barriers to human mobility. In this context, the state is central to the reproduction of the capitalist mode of production by virtue of both having the responsibility for organising the conditions under which potential labourers might enter the territory that it administers but also for organising the political and ideological conditions under which the nation state itself might be reproduced (Miles 1988: 438).

This structural framework means that the process of racialisation may arise for different reasons and meet different functions. In some instances it may accompany and make possible the use of migrant labour, or it may act to exclude that labour when the political significance of the racialisation of a group is more important than its racialised incorporation as 'cheap' labour.

Therefore it is not entirely correct to state that a political economy of migration approach confines the analysis of racism to its functional role in migrant labour regulation (Solomos and Back 1993); however it *is* the case that the approach in general wants to confine the autonomy of racism, as a discursive phenomenon, to its role in categorising and regulating or excluding racial Others. Thus, Satzewich argues that 'the process of racialisation, which may or may not involve elements of racism, can be thought of as a mechanism which the state can use to exclude people from entry to a social formation, include people and allocate people to sites in production relations' (Satzewich 1991: 51). Here the signifying power of racism is subordinate to the role it might perform within the securement of the accumulation cycle. In this way racialisation is a complimentary moment within the primarily economic reproduction of structures.

A Case Study: The Postwar Conjuncture and Black Migration

An appropriate 'case study' of racialisation theory would be the small series of path breaking studies variously undertaken by the researchers, Carter, Harris and Joshi, focusing on the 'postwar conjuncture', which clearly reveal the ideological stigmatisation of postwar black migrants by the British political and administrative elite (cf. Carter and Joshi 1984; Carter, Harris and Joshi 1987; Harris 1987).[14] These studies are significant precisely because they highlight the centrality of racial ideologies, in revealing their role in structuring the perceptions of the personnel of the secret state in pre-determining subsequent policies. Yet at the same time they do not confer analytical attention upon the concepts by which such an ideologically mediated process can be understood or the production its textual existence presupposes.

After sifting through elite memos, committee minutes and internal communiqués of the Labour government and civil service in the period 1945-51 and the Conservative administration of 1951-5, and thereby revealing the racist and culturally determinist rationale informing the proliferation of statements, the authors claim evidence of a 'deep racism and extreme racialisation of black migrants' (Harris 1987: 72). They also claim that this process centrally involved the state 'development of a racialised construction of 'Britishness' which excluded and included people on the grounds of 'race' defined as colour' (Carter et al, 1987: 16). Yet the authors do not, at any time, seek to define the concept of racialisation or that of racism and its connection to the evidence of the discursive forms of internal state communication documented. This is important, given that the subject of these studies is the internal discourse of the 'secret state' (a state kept secret because of the Thirty Year rule), manifestly revealed in the official memos and documents of elite political and administrative personnel. It is these revealed sources that provides the prima facie evidence of the political motives and institutional reasoning lying behind the 'contradictory' official face of the state.[15]

Despite the fact that the authors refer to the 'discourse of the state' there is no attempt to situate this conceptual language within a broader theoretical framework. This is not the case for the political economy framework, within which the discussion of postwar black migration is conceptually engaged within the study: a framework which utilises, and critically engages with, marxist debates about *relative surplus population* (RSP), global labour supply dynamics and *industrial reserve army* theory (IRA). Indeed, at one point in Harris' argument, he asserts that 'racialisation was to form part of the mode through which the industrial reserve army was to be ideologically reproduced consistent both with notions of "citizenship" and the "subjective right to work" embodied in the Keynesian ethos of "full employment'" (Harris 1987: 72). It is unmistakable, therefore, that the authors intend a subordinate relationship for ideology: it is the smoke from the train, not the train itself.

It is obviously important, within a systemic theory, to assign due weight of importance to the determining and contributory elements within the social totality of relations examined. Here the researchers ranking of importance is clearly signalled. Given the centrality afforded the evidence of official racism to the analysis of the postwar conjuncture and the racialisation of the secret state, the maintenance of such a subordinate status seems wholly untenable. On this point the contrary evidence appears overwhelming. At this particular historical conjuncture, with less than 500 Jamaicans the subject of an internal state 'moral panic' over black migrants, there can be no convincing economic rationale to the generation of this stigmatisation discourse; especially since it was not a publicly expressed one. Therefore, the separation between the economic and the political becomes critically apparent here. Certainly the writers are right to stress the importance of this racialisation as, in many senses, a rehearsal for future labour restriction legislation. But this in itself does not endorse a political logic; it rather provides us with the motive force for the momentum which does get under way to achieve that restriction act some years later. Its immediate expression, as the authors state, was 'a number of covert, and sometimes illegal, administrative measures designed to discourage Black immigration' (Carter, Harris and Joshi 1987: 3). However the motive for resorting to covert practices, as Carter et al argue, 'coalesced around the fear that the "gathering momentum" of Black immigration would bring about "a significant change in the racial character of the English people" '(1987: 6). In other words, a persuasive, consistent and powerful ideology of racism formed the inferential framework or 'deep structure' of the various expressive statements and minutes of state personnel documented. This the authors quite clearly reveal, and yet they seem unwilling to acknowledge that the implicit acceptance of this racist ideology informed the messy and uneven progress towards a public restriction Bill, consistent with these views. And that this ideological element was, therefore, very largely, *determinant*.

The problem for the state was, as Harris puts it, that 'the movement from administrative to legislative measures was [...] fraught with contradictions' (1987: 72): the central one being that the states' public face contradicted its private one. The resolution of this dilemma, the researchers argue, required the active persuasion and recruitment of the 'public' in the interests of preserving the homogeneity of its unrecognised 'racial character'. This is why the internal state busied itself, at this time, with the collection of information which it was hoped would clearly reveal the 'problem' of the racial incompatibility of black labour; a negative interpretation to which ministers and civil servants already subscribed (Carter and Joshi 1984; Carter et al 1987). Here the authors collectively tilt towards a state-racism theory, albeit short of a conspiracy claim. They suggest a unity of intent to persuade the public, or rather to prepare the public for the necessity of exclusion legislation, at a later date. Here, clearly, is an argument for a unity of state political action.

To summarise then, we have seen that the researchers explicitly foreground an idea of racialisation and deracialisation as the central dynamic informing the, of necessity, covert collective attitude and action of senior state personnel. The result is the official interpretation of the incoming migrants as a racial group with particular characteristics which mark them out as another 'race'. This process of racial categorisation is contrasted with the deracialisation or de-categorisation of the Irish, at this time the largest statistical category of migrant entering the economy (Solomos 1989: 42). The researchers trace out a process of discursive construction, revealed by the evidence of a problem oriented state language, which achieves racism through the attribution of a range of negative characteristics, which are considered innate to the group so stigmatised, and which form the commonsense justification for initially discouraging, and eventually seeking to permanently exclude, black labour units. The authors do not specify a theory of racialisation explicitly but they provide the evidence for, and the salient features of such a process; and they specifically attribute the initiation and authorship of such a process to the state which, they claim, 'undertook nothing less than a political project in which notions of "belonging" and "community" were reconstructed in terms of "racial" attachments and national identity organised around skin colour. This reconstruction simultaneously involved the deracialisation of the Irish' (Carter et al 1987: 16-17).

In the various studies, therefore, it is clear that the motive force for the restriction of black migration is racism. The groups are racialised; this involves a process that is clearly documented in Cabinet records. It also involves the claim for the deracialisation of the Irish, i.e. the revoking of 'race' category status and the absence of additional characteristics of attribution to a previously racially signified group. It is not simply that the researchers do not acknowledge the theoretical concepts that underpin their analysis, but that they do not recognise or fail to acknowledge the extent to which the explicit deployment of these concepts must significantly alter the theoretical determination of the historical reality which they are attempting to account for. This raises the problem of the conceptualisation of racism as an ideology and the extent to which the construction of racial ideologies has a determinate effect upon the constitution of social relations and political processes.

The Autonomy of Ideology

As Solomos (1986d) has clearly indicated, what internally divides the racism problematic is the degree of autonomy which is afforded the ideological and political constitution of racism as an autonomous element with its own internal laws of determination (see also Solomos in Cashmore 1994: 210-6). What we need to add to this discussion is the recognition of the form of production of racist discourse i.e., elite and official language, within both private echelons and within public arenas. It is important to be clear that there are two dimensions to be addressed here. Firstly, that the production of political language is a material practice which is institutionally mediated. Therefore, any account of the role and impact of political language must be able to account for this dimension. Secondly, we are examining the relationship between the form and content of political discourse and the wider framework of group relations of domination and social subordination which lie outside of it.

The difficulty, of course, with the analysis of language forms is that they are a material practice which produces a form of consciousness; a type of representation.[16] In addressing this dilemma we need to be clear that we are speaking of racism as an ideology and that the form of appearance and the means of construction of ideologies depend upon the social production of language. In considering the social production of language, as a means of ideological representation, we need to consider the importance of the concept of discourse. As Kress points out:

> The relation between language and ideology depends on the category of discourse. Any linguistic form considered in isolation has no specifically determinate meaning as such, nor does it possess any ideological significance or function. It is because linguistic forms always appear in a text and therefore in a systematic form as the sign of the system of meaning embodied in specific discourse that we can attribute ideological significance to them (Kress 1985: 30).

What does this mean for the study of the ideological functioning of language? It suggests that the ideological meanings contained within forms of written expression and public speech are understandable, to the extent that they refer to and draw upon an ideological system of terms and meanings absent at the level of specific language content, i.e. the recognition of the discursive formation of types of language. This relationship is a determinate one in that '[t]he defined and delimited set of statements that constitute a discourse are themselves expressive of and organised by a specific ideology'. Thus '[t]he systematic organization of content in discourse, drawing on and deriving from the prior classification of this material in an ideological system, leads to the systematic selection of linguistic categories and features in a text' (Kress 1985: 30). Here Kress is arguing that the construction of public or private texts will conform, in some broadly determined way, to the ideological system of signification which establishes the life of the ideology within the dominant relationships of that social formation or structure.

These theoretical insights should dispel the anxiety of political economists that language as ideology is somehow an autonomous domain with its own independent effects. Language cannot be theorised outside of the system of relationships which it expresses and which it attempts to represent. Since language is, in the words of Halliday and others,[17] a *social semiotic*, i.e., 'forms of language encode a socially constructed representation of the world' (Fowler 1991: 37). Thus the mode of address, its representational strategies and syntactics, will work to naturalise the discourse by concealing its constructedness and thereby aiding its reception. But the ideological structuring of a text or speech comes from the way in which language is always already value-laden, i.e. '[i]deology is already imprinted in the available discourse' (Fowler 1991: 42). Or to put it more provocatively, 'the writer is constituted by the discourse' since '[d]iscourse [...] is socially and institutionally originating ideology, encoded in language' (p.42). In this respect discourse is 'systematically organised modes of talking' (Kress in Fowler 1991: 42). Thus, the discursive conventions that cohere public speech and parliamentary debate, for example, answer, ideologically the economic and institutional requirements of the speaker and her positioning within wider systems of power and control.

Therefore, ideology is not an autonomous determinant of politics. Rather the construction of racism, at various historical points, and at particular conjunctures, is a material practice whose conditions of existence and means of production affect both its form and content. This is because the production of meaning in language is determined by the constitution of the social to which it refers. This is so at the level of (i) the positioning of the speaker, revealed by topic selection and ordering of themes, which provide an 'index of ideological activity' (Kress in Fowler 1991: 42) and (ii) the expression of ideological content, where the pattern of dispersion of elements, within a text, achieves the articulation of ideological meanings. Kress spells out the implications of this argument, when he argues that, '[i]f discourses are the organizations of ideological materials in discursive forms, and if these discourses exist in an already established repertoire of discourses in a social group, then the individual speaker will not in fact be creating the discourse but rather will simply reproduce the discourse' (Kress 1985: 31).

However, as we argued in the Introduction, we must also recognise the significance of the distinction between discourse and text. The production of texts, political texts included, are realised within specific genres, therefore it is possible for the speaker to employ existing discursive rules but to give them a relatively novel inflection or treatment. In the case of the discourse of post-'race' public talk this practice is the necessary basis for the emergence and proliferation of post-'race' signifying discourses that allow the covert racialisation of minorities and outsiders. The structural determination which provides the impetus for its appearance is the linguistic suppression of the language of 'race' in public speech. The development of the discursive strategies of the black country 'race' populists and the eventual emergence of the political discourse of Powellism are reflective of this dimension.

It is important to note that the critical linguist model of ideological language has perhaps an overly-deterministic emphasis, suggesting that ideological meanings can be 'read-off' from underlying social relationship. Its importance lies in how it offers a structural relation between ideologies, understood as epistemic systems or discourses, and patterns of language expression and construction. We may want to question the extent to which such meaning construction is a function of the influence of the deep structure of syntax and grammar structures, which reflects the structural location and power of particular groups, rather than reflecting the ideologically contested, but dominating system of language communities, around which ideological meanings cluster. Here dominant relationships and their contestation are played out within competing language forms, although such forms tend to be structured in dominance. In other words, the clustering of words and concepts within systems of ideology may occur, in the Voloshinovian (1973) sense, via the establishment of language communities, that have formed through the struggle and contestation of social meanings central to the relationship between dominant and subaltern groups. This system of domination may not lie within the 'deep structure' of grammar or syntax but in the interrelationship of language usage to social inequality and the struggles to articulate oppositional interpretations of its meanings. These positions are not necessarily antithetical, as long as language is not conceived as a closed system, internally referential, to which the social has no access (cf. Jameson 1972).

With these arguments in mind, it will be our 'strong case' argument that the retention of the political economy/racialisation framework is a necessary, but not completely sufficient basis, for the analysis of racial political language and claims for a transformation in the conceptual structure of racist discourse, consistent with the rise of Powellism. Such an advocacy is made, with the proviso that existing work into processes of racialisation have tended to either be concerned with the analysis of periods when conjunctures were racialised, or how the process resulted in the reproduction of racial ideologies. Very rarely does such analysis concentrate on the detail of the textual content of such ideological processes. When theorists have done so, the concept of racialisation has become problematic. Part of the problem here is the way in which such a process must involve an ideological mediation, in and through political language, and the way in which this contributes to the reproduction of capitalist relations in the context of migrant labour flows. A critical point here is that processes of racialisation do not necessarily secure capitalist interests in any guaranteed way. Miles clearly recognises the complex and contingent interrelations involved when he argues,

> [T]o define racism as functional to capitalism is to presuppose the nature and outcome of its articulation with economic and political relations, and with other ideologies. Such a definition mistakenly assumes that a homogenous ruling class inevitably and necessarily derives economic and/or political advantages from its expression. The use of racism to limit the size of the labour market is not necessarily in the interests of those employers experiencing a labour shortage, while racism and exclusionary practices that result in civil disturbance will not necessarily be welcomed by capitalists whose business activity has been disrupted as a result, or by the state that has to increase expenditure to maintain social order [...] Racism is therefore a contradictory phenomenon because what is 'functional' for one set of class interests can be 'dysfunctional' for another set of such interests, and because the conditions that sustain its[...]advantageous expression are rarely permanent (Miles 1989: 100).

However, I would contend that the contingency of racist articulation is not simply because interests are likely to be conflictual within particular sectors of the economy, but because the reproduction of ideologies of racism is a function of discursive production, and the interrelation of these discourses, within a framework of political racialisation. While it is absolutely important to theorise the production of discourses, within the wider context of labour migration and state policy developments, we must not assume a casually determinate relationship between these elements, but rather their interplay and contingent articulation (cf. Miles and Solomos 1987).

This argument allows us to suggest the following response to the work of Carter, Harris and Joshi, concerning the significance of the racism of the 'secret state' in the period leading up to the 1961 Bill and legislation. Firstly, this work is

18 *Political Languages of Race and the Politics of Exclusion*

important in demolishing the widely accepted notion of a period of political laissez-faire, before the introduction of controls upon the free movement of 'black' migrant labour into Britain (cf. Solomos 1989: 66). It is now clear that the period obtaining between 1948 and 1961 was one when 'black' migration, from the Caribbean and South-Asia, was officially racialised; a process whose end result was the generation of Official support for a *(black) Commonwealth* restriction Bill. As Carter et al state:

> The period between the 1948 Nationality Act and the 1962 Commonwealth Immigration Act is frequently characterised as one in which the principle of free entry of British subjects to the UK was only relinquished with great reluctance and after considerable official debate. This was not the case. On the contrary, the debate was never about principle. Labour and Conservative Governments had by 1952 instituted a number of covert, and sometimes illegal, administrative measures designed to discourage Black immigration (Carter et al, 1987: 3).

While this summative statement should be celebrated for the research space it opens up, what is entirely absent from this notion of the years of silence over 'race', is any sense of how the public language that accompanied its ideological control, in 1961, was shaped and formed. The very fact that evidence of racism has been revealed in the private echelons and chambers of government should define our research agenda in very definite ways. It is simply not adequate to accept the implications of this that such a secret racism then emerged, a decade and a half later, cloaked in the official rhetoric of a Government restriction Bill. Rather such an official language, accompanying the 1961 Debate over the Bill, had to be developed.[18]

As chapter 3 will show, previous Private Member's 'restriction' Bills reveal a clear thematic development which culminates in the first Government sponsored Bill.[19] But the background to this is the unmistakable, official denial of the importance of the issue of 'race' and the effects or consequences of 'black immigration', which obviously contradicted private 'official' thinking. This is the double edged silence we must decipher and explain. It seems evident that for all Carter et als' talk of the 'discourse of the state', they do not intend, by this phrase, the various voices of the state. But rather the idea that the state, as defined by its unitary purpose and underlying intention, consistent with its functioning, was *revealed* in Cabinet memos.

This also extends to their conception of the degree of autonomy of state discourses. They clearly show that the dilemma of black migration is consistently racialised in state personnel language. And on this basis they argue that the reason for the proliferation of such discourses is because of the difficulty of achieving the racial exclusion, agreed by all such voices, given the political and diplomatic climate. It seems to me that this is not correct empirically or theoretically. Firstly, because there simply are more voices than these researchers allow and therefore, the evidence, if it were examined, for a contestation and diversity of 'race' discourses.[20] Secondly, theoretically speaking, the role of ideology is central to the argument advance by Carter et al, therefore it cannot be confined to a functional epiphenomenon of an economistically derived purpose, despite the fact that this is suggested rather then explicitly stated. It simply is the case that ideological relations do have a great deal of autonomy in constructing the meaning of the political situation in this period, and in the political realisation of restriction. It is surely a triumph of ideology that such restriction occurs and that its benefit is not necessarily economic, but a more complexly political one, a good deal of which is simply unintended.

I will develop this argument shortly. Firstly, though, I want to examine the methodological success of racialisation approaches that *do* take racial political discourse more seriously and do afford it both empirical and theoretical autonomy.

Racialisation Theory and the Non-'Race' Signifier

As we have already indicated, the absence of the racial signifier in much of the record of political discourse, concerned with the control or exclusion of migrant 'black' labour, does present something of a conceptual dilemma for racialisation theory. We have suggested that a more adequate approach to the racialisation of the policies and politics of black migration requires a greater attention to the (i) content of discourse and (ii) theories of language as an ideological system. These criticisms not withstanding, we can point to the approaches adopted by Reeves (1983) and Miles (1989; 1990; 1993), which *do* offer an analysis of racialisation that is focused upon the role and significance of political language in achieving a racialisation of political meanings within Parliamentary Debate. In the following two sections I will consider the value of these approaches in terms of (a) the extent to which they offer a solution to the problem of post-'race' political language and (b) the theoretical development of a critical theory of political language as racism.

Firstly, these approaches can be said to have significantly developed the concept of racialisation, as a means of operationalisation of the conception of racism as an ideology. This could not be more clearly indicated than in the assertion that discursive racialisation refers to 'any circumstance where the idea of "race" is employed in discourse' (Reeves cited in Miles 1989: 74). Miles, in a recent summary, offers this definition: 'there is minimal agreement that the concept be used to refer to a representational process whereby social significance is attached to certain biological (usually phenotypical) human features, on the basis of which those people possessing those characteristics are designated as a distinct collectivity' (1989: 74)

Miles has stated that he prefers to refer to the theory of racialisation when examining the ideological construction of 'race'; thus in effect departing from the rigidly defined conception of it as a doctrine particular to Victorian science, in particular by rejecting the idea that racism can only be present in discourse if a claim is made for a hierarchy of 'races' (cf. Banton 1977; Phizacklea and Miles 1980; Miles 1989). Thus he is, in practice, prepared to accept, *as racist*, claims which do not explicitly assert a hierarchical justification or evaluation. The theoretical justification for this is that involved in claiming that racism is best understood as an ideology that has allowed, through various articulations with other ideologies, for example nationalism, the signification of in-group/out-group relations based on a claim for inherence and population group permanence.

For Reeves (1983) the claim for hierarchy is absolutely definitive of racism as a doctrine and presents the intractable problem of rendering the existing definition of racism inadequate to designate contemporary racial usage as racist. Let us examine this view first in order to see how Reeves arrives at this judgement and what responses he offers theoretically and methodologically to it.

British Racial Discourse: Racism without 'Race'?

Reeves defines British racial discourse as: 'spoken and written material (e.g. speeches, books, articles, debates, conversation) that makes use of a racial category' (1983: 10). However, such a definition is rendered problematic by the claim Reeves wishes to advance: 'I wish to argue that there is a strong tendency in British political ideology to "deracialise" situations which would appear racial to the social observer, and which may be judged by him *(sic)* to be racially discriminatory in their consequences' (1983: 11). This claim provides the central analytical thread in Reeves' often detailed and closely argued thesis.[21] We can best represent the main strands of this argument as follows: (a) current sociological definitions of racism tend to refer to 'bio-scientific' arguments common to 19th century thought; this leaves them ill-prepared to identify current political racial uses of apparently non-racial arguments (eg. Powell) (1983: 21-

24); (b) the designation 'racial discourse' must, if it is to have any validity, be identified by the use of racial categories; unfortunately, much current discussion of 'race' operates without recourse to such categories; (c) if we are to advance from this impasse we must extend the term 'racism' to encompass cultural explanations and other forms of deterministic categorisation (p.22); (d) at the same time we must develop conceptual tools of analysis able to identify 'racial discourse' by other criteria than the presence of racial categories.

Reeves' attempt to resolve the contradictions thrown up by his analytical aims provides the central value of the study: the development of a number of techniques, and examples, for identifying 'racial discourse' that is either free of racial categories of any kind; or explicitly disavows any connection to 'racialism' but is nevertheless racist in either intention, or effect (Reeves 1983: 17-20).

The inherent contradictions between the aim of the study, and the nature of the phenomenon studied, leads Reeves to abandon the attempt to employ a content analysis of political discourse, because he does not believe that (i) it is possible to establish the presence of racial categories in such discourse and (ii) that the debate about what should qualify as racism cannot be resolved satisfactorily. The consequence of this is that (as he acknowledges) he is unable to identify *racial discourse* i.e., as specifically discourse that employs 'racial categories' (p.14). The project that Reeves *does* attempt is one which concentrates on the political dynamics of racial situations and the development of functional language forms for the communication of various forms of 'hidden' or disguised racism by politicians.

The question Reeves' study tries to answer is how a political discourse can be designated racist when its explicit content evades current or effective identification? His answer is to look in detail at the institutional and discursive context in which such discourse operates and to construct from the imputed intentionality and/or imputed effects and/or reception of such discourse a number of analytical designations of how such discourse is racist (cf. Reeves 1983: ch. 6, 7).To this end, Reeves develops a number of concepts by which racist intent, prescription, evaluation or attribution can be identified. The most important of these are 'discursive (surely discursive?) deracialisation' (1983: 176-89), and 'sanitary coding' (1983: 189-97). The process of 'discursive deracialisation' is defined in contradistinction to that of *racialisation* i.e. 'the introduction into discourse of racial categorisation, racial explanation, racial evaluation, or racial prescription' (p.175).

Deracialisation is the elimination, cleaning up or simple concealment of 'race' categories which were formally present in a given discourse. Ideological deracialisation consists in the 'attenuation of, elimination of, or substitution for racial categories in discourse, the omission or de-emphasis of racial explanation, and the avoidance of racial evaluation or prescription' (Reeves 1983: 176-7). For Reeves, evaluation of the character of the 'discursive situation' is determined by the direction in which the process operates. The clarity of this conception does not resolve the problem of how it is possible to recognise a racist discourse that no longer employs recognisably racial categories? Reeves' answer is to place the process of deracialisation within a particular social and historical context in which the process can be observed, negatively or positively, to be occurring. The measure of such occurrence rests upon an appeal to the objectivity of social scientific judgement: 'If the social observer notes a wide discrepancy between his *(sic)* informed assessment of a situation as "racial", and the account offered by the social actors, in which no mention is made of racial processes, then he might legitimately assume a state of asynchronism where some form of systemic ideological deracialisation is taking place ' (Reeves 1983: 178).

The confirmation of this judgement would follow if it were ascertained that the situation subsequently resulted in a 'racial' effect of some kind. Such normative criteria provides a good fit with a situation where 'racial' legislation is passed, while the discourse that allows its passage is studiously non-racial. The claimed objectivity of such an approach to the discursive situation crucially relies upon the criteria that the social observer or social scientist brings to the observed situation. It follows that such criteria cannot be deduced from the deracialised discourse itself. Consequently, this element now becomes critical to the validity of this method. More specifically, the features of the context that the observer employs to establish its racial nature become, in effect, the proof of the assertion. Reeves identifies this context in the following way:

> [T]he tendency for immigration controls to operate in a racially selective manner is most marked, while the justification offered for the Bills rarely makes use of specifically racial description, evaluation, and prescription. The observer is entitled to remark on the discrepancy between the actual racial context and the politicians' account of it [...] While the real intentions of the legislators cannot be unquestionably established, there is ample evidence that their purpose was the placation of a racially hostile electorate (Reeves 1983: 204).

Here, stated quite plainly, is the basis for the judgement: that a racialised 'climate' existed prior and during the debate. Or even more explicitly:

> [D]eracialised discourse succeeds in its purpose [...] by providing other non-racist criteria for discriminating against a group, e.g. shortages of resources in

Britain, and by obscuring the fact that the largest numbers of people to be affected by the legislation under debate are distinguishable by their colour. In the main, exclusion of blacks will be the unstated intention of politicians who, faced with a knowledge of their constituents' strongly expressed views about black people's presence in Britain, support Bills aimed at controlling and reducing black immigration (Reeves 1983: 239).

For Reeves, then, the defining political context in which such deracialisation takes place is one circumscribed by popular racial pressure. Given the centrality of this political dynamic it is puzzling that Reeves does not examine the discursive formation of such a popular racist pressure. He merely takes it for granted. This must point to a flaw in such analysis. Especially since citation, in the form of opinion polls, forms the commonsense justificatory basis for the activity of the politicians who are themselves involved in the discursive denial of racial motive or intent. It is the hidden dynamics of this process that underpins the more explicit discursive operation of: 'sanitary coding' [or] 'the ability to communicate privately racist ideas with a discourse publicly defensible as non-racist' (1983: 190): 'If, in order to placate an electorate, a politician self-consciously seeks to pursue policies with racialist effect behind an ideological edifice in which racist sentiment plays no part' (Reeves 1983: 189).The success of the exercise therefore relies on the politician being able to communicate racial intentions to the electorate, while presenting the proposed measures in non-racial terms. While it is undoubtedly correct that 'publicly expressed language' (p.28) ought to be the focus of 'racial discourse' and 'ideas expressed in language' (p. 28) are the only legitimate object of such a study, the nature of deracialisation as a process depends upon establishing comparative criteria; the validity of such being dependent upon the critical epistemology of the social scientist or observer.

A Critique of Reeves

The difficulty with Reeves' original reformulation of the term racialisation is that, while it is possible to show how a situation, argument or explanation can be racialised, it is only logically possible to demonstrate deracialisation when it can be established that the usage or example was previously racialised. Reeves does offer a comprehensive schema for the identification of deracialisation by comparing the speakers' intention with the effect of the discourse itself. The problem with this model is that it relies on either actor intention or policy effect to establish the function of racial discourse.[22] Such a procedure appeals to *ex-cathedra* criteria when, more often than not, we simply have the discourse to go on. Reeves' discussion of racial discourse proceeds on the basis of identifying content and strategies as reducible to pragmatic action theory, rather than the explanatory or significatory power of language constructions to mediate the meaning and expression of racism. Context takes precedence over content.

Reeves' work is valuable not only in supplying tools of analysis of official discourse concerned with 'race' but also because it attempts to pose the question, hinted at but never made explicit in the debate about racist political discourse, that such discourse exhibits, as its main feature, a denial or effacement of racial prescription, attribution or intent. It could be argued that what Reeves attempts is to render those denied connections explicit by placing political discourse within its racial context and thereby revealing the relationship between context and political intent. Surprisingly, though, such a process is only carried through to a superficial extent and tends to rely upon the assertion of an apparently objective observer for its validity, rather than substantive analysis of the political context. Such an approach ultimately fails to convince because it is unable to resolve the contradictions of the debate from which it arises: a debate that wants to establish racial intent but is unable to reconcile this with the absence of classical racial ideas (cf. Banton 1969; 1970; 1977).

Such criticisms notwithstanding, Reeves can be read to offer an attempted theoretical alignment with the doctrine of racism and actual racial language usage, by proposing a conceptual solution. This involves a conceptual inflation, or more accurately, deconstruction of, so called, classical doctrine, into a number of sequential claims: (a) that races of human beings exist; (b) that these races differ from one another; (c) that the differences are deeply rooted and enduring; (d) that the differences are significant, possibly because they appear in themselves to be explanatory, or because explanations of other social features may be inferred from them; (e) that the differences have social consequences, for example, for social policy. Such statements constitute *weak racism*; weak racism can be extended into *medium racism* by the addition of: (f) that the differences between races are of a superior to inferior, that they occur in some sort of rank order. *Strong racism* goes a step further: (g) that the superior race(s) ought to be entitled to more favourable treatment and the inferior less (cf. Reeves 1983: 12-13).

Weak racism amounts to the acceptance that racial differences exist and that they help to explain the social world, but it omits any overt suggestion of a moral ranking of those differences (1983: 15). Categorising racism in its weak, medium and strong forms allows analysis to account for the strategic and manipulatory use of parliamentary language:

In justifying various actions directed at members of another race, it is plainly not necessary to use a definitive form of racism in terms of belief in genetic inferiority. Other possibilities exist. There is, of course, no requirement to employ arguments that mention a racial group's characteristics at all, but even when they are mentioned, there are a number of ways of avoiding the accusation of racism (Reeves 1983: 213).

Such an analysis of 'modes of argument' is conducted in order to identify, and quantify, the variety of ways in which the recourse to discriminatory legislation of a 'racially' defined group can be justified as non-racial. Reeves *works back* from the projected discriminatory effects of the legislation to the studiously non-racial terms of its presentation.[23] It is therefore not the *presence* of racism but its *absence* that confirms hidden racial intent; a public conspiracy that is shared by the audience towards whom it is directed.

Robert Miles: Racism as Ideological Articulation

Miles, although agreeing with Rex's (1970) defence of the continuing applicability of the concept of racism, by reference to its function in supporting exclusionary assertions and practices, like Banton (1969), wishes to retain the focus upon the content of statements as definitive of their status as racism (Miles 1989: 49-50, 77). For Banton, this means retaining a specific claim for hierarchy within such statements and therefore restricting the applicability of the term specifically to the historical doctrine of 'racial typology' (1970; 1977; 1983). For Miles, it requires the retention of the term racism to designate those discourses that deterministically construct social collectivities as biologically or naturally circumscribed (1989: 79; 1990: 149). This definitional process involves the generation of ideology in the process of the racialisation of groups. Racialisation is thus a process where ideological meanings are constructed and groups are signified as 'Other' by somatic or phenotypical 'markers' (1989: 74-5). Miles has applied this conceptualisation to groups involved in the global process of labour migration, in the context of European capitalist reconstruction, and the concomitant political legitimation of them as a racialised collectivity. In the case of Britain, Miles has pointed to historical periods where the inclusion of migrants for political or economic reasons has produced a concomitant racialisation of their status; two researched examples being Irish and Jewish migration (cf. 1982; 1989; 1993).

However, the legitimation of social discourses of racialisation is not a necessarily determined effect, but rather the variable result of an interplay of social, economic and political factors. Thus Miles has argued,

The migration of neither the Irish nor the Jews was defined as producing a 'race relations' situation in Britain, although both groups were identified as distinct 'races'. Moreover, the acceptance of a group of Vietnamese people in the mid-1970s was not interpreted in terms of 'race relations' as was the (reluctant) acceptance of Kenyan and Ugandan Asians: this difference is significant given that, formally, all three groups were political refugees, although only the former were politically defined as such (Miles 1984b: 253).

Here, the constitution of the political can practically legitimate or attempt to deny the racialisation of a migrant group. A good, illustrative example of this process is the controversy over the 'Honk Kong nationals', when the former Thatcher Cabinet were obliged to secure entry visas for a privileged minority of entrants, against the sound and fury of a party right-wing rebellion, led by Sir Norman Tebbit, and supported by Labour rebels (cf. Times, Guardian, Independent, Telegraph and Mail, 4, 5th and 20th April 1990). Here the discourses of party and media oscillated between defining such racialised migrants as 'Commonwealth Immigrants', 'affluent migrants' or 'political refugees'.

Current criticisms of Miles' approach (Solomos and Back 1993: 7-9) suggests that it is reductionist in grounding the ideological racialisation of migrants within a framework of labour regulation. However, the model of the racialisation of such migrants suggests that the process of economic regulation and ideological racialisation are contingent, not deterministic, elements of an historical process. Racialisation is a process of ideological signification, which occurs in specific material and historical contexts, as a 'component element of allocative and exclusionary mechanisms'. However, Miles argues that racism 'should be identified by its ideological content rather than by its function' (1989: 79). Thus what distinguishes racism as an ideology is its signification of some biological characteristic as 'the criteria by which a collectivity may be identified' The effects of this is to establish the idea of natural *inherence* and *difference*. In addition, the groups must be attributed with other negative characteristics or consequences following from their presence. Such characteristics may be biological or cultural. It follows that the group occupying the category of natural, biological collectivity, possess such (negatively evaluated) characteristics as a sign of permanent difference in origin and status. Thus,

> [R]acism is a form of ideological signification which constructs a social collectivity as a discrete and distinct, self-reproducing population by reference to certain (real and imagined) biological characteristics which are purported to be inherent, and which additionally attributes the collectivity with other

negatively evaluated (biological and/ or cultural) characteristics. Racism, therefore, attributes meaning to the human body, either somatically or genetically, in order to construct an Other which reproduces itself through historical time and space[...]this definition does not bind the concept of racism to the explicit presence of the idea of 'race'. Neither does it require the notion of hierarchical ranking (Miles 1993: 99).

For our purposes, the value of this conceptualisation is to be judged in its application to actual debate content. The example we will examine is from Miles (1990) and is based on the reported speech of Conservative MP, John Townesend (Bridlington), voicing opposition to the right of entry of former colonial subjects from Hong Kong, despite holding British passports, on the following grounds:

> The fact the Hong Kong Chinese are very hard working and hold British passports does not make them British. If millions of Chinese came to the UK they would not integrate and become yellow Englishmen. They would create another China, another Hong Kong in England, just as former immigrants have created another Pakistan in Bradford[...]This possibility should make us consider what has already happened to this green and pleasant land - first as a result of waves of coloured immigrants and then by the pernicious doctrine of multi-culturalism[...]Every year that goes by the English are battered into submission in their own country and more strident are the demands of ethnic nationalism. The British people were never consulted as to whether they would change from being a homogenous society to a multi-racial society. If they had been I am sure that a resounding majority would have voted to keep Britain an English-speaking, white country (cited in Miles 1990: 148).

For Miles, such sentiments and arguments are repetitions of an already well established discourse against which the concept of racism can be tested. This testing is concerned with the question of the meaning of the term and how it should be applied to this kind of political language. Firstly, Miles dismisses the idea that Mr. Townesend explicitly claims that people from Hong Kong or Pakistan are racially inferior. But he does distinguish three groups: English/British, Pakistanis and Chinese. In addition such groups are identified in terms of skin colour. This identification takes a binary form of distinction between 'white' and 'non-white'. This distinction of 'colour' is further implicated in the context of an imprecise 'war' that is taking place which is transforming Britain from a 'green and pleasant land' to an unpleasant one.

> [Thus]we find in this speech the view that the worlds population is made up of a number of distinct populations, each biologically distinct from all others.

Furthermore, each of the races is attributed with a fixed character which has inevitable consequences: the populations of Chinese and Pakistani origin in Britain are necessarily recreating China and Pakistan within 'our midst', as if neither 'they' nor 'we' can do anything about it (the consequence of this is that) Britain is no longer 'white' and the British population is thought to be losing a struggle for survival (Miles 1990: 149).

Miles acknowledges that such a set of arguments are not racist in terms of a view of racial hierarchy. But 'such a definition fails to comprehend the generality that underlies these specific empirical assertions' (p.149). What does Miles mean here? His argument must be that the general claim contained within the doctrine of racism can also allow the attribution of determination to fix upon other features as 'racial'. Thus, 'We can define racism as any set of claims or arguments which signify some aspect of the physical features of an individual or group as a sign of permanent distinctiveness and which attribute additional, negative characteristics and/or consequences to the individual's or group's presence' (p.149).

At the same time it is noted that the group is recognised as a population, and therefore as a reproducing entity that has an inherent 'nature' and permanence. Thus the distinguishing features of a racist claim, in this sense, are 'inherence' and 'permanence' (p.149). Given these elements it would be reasonable for Miles to claim that such sentiments constitute a variety of racism. However he argues that to do this would be to concede unwarranted validity to the New Racism school of thinkers, who have designated claims for culture and nation, like those of Townesend, as constituting the expression of a 'new racism'. Miles believes that there is nothing conceptually to be gained from redefining nationalism as racism. What should be recognised is that (i) nationalism and racism have distinctive claims but that (ii) what they have in common is a similar conceptual matrix which revolves around inherence and nature. He points, in other words, to the conceptual similarity of the ideologies. 'Nationalism, like racism[...]entails an exclusion. and bemoans the disintegration of cultural homogeneity. It follows that "Chinese" people should stay "in their own country" were they naturally belong' (p.149). Nationalism thus articulates very closely with the doctrine of racism, and historically has been called upon to serve a similar function within the economics and politics of capitalist social formations. However, conceptually, the two ideologies remain sufficiently distinct to require separate analysis concerned with their historical articulation.

A Critique of Miles

Miles' development of the concept of racialisation to encompass the process of production of racial significations, within public and official texts, allows the possibility of the development of a much more specific analytical method of deconstruction of racialised forms of political language. Such an advance is based upon the rejection of the Banton position that the term racism can only strictly apply to the idea of 'race' inscribed in 19th century scientific doctrine and within mistaken methodologies of 'racial typology', peculiar to the period of intellectual consolidation of industrial-capitalism and concomitant justification of imperialism and colonial expansion (cf. Banton 1977: 74, 54).

The development of the conception of racialisation to involve the practice of signification rather than the search for the empirical categories of 'race' science, allows Miles a potentially more useful analytic method for the deconstruction of racialised 'forms' of politics (Miles 1989: 74). Certainly the pre-condition for this is to jettison the idea of 'race' as definable in terms of a doctrine of 'scientific racism' or 'typology' simply because (i) to withdraw the sanction of science from the discourse of 'race' does not eradicate the non-scientific discourse that proceeded its construction and which escapes its subsequent censure, i.e, the cultural and class purity ideas of lineage, type, etc. Or the cultural and commonsense discourses that interacted with that of claims for scientific 'truth'. (ii) But also by allowing the conceptual inflation of those significatory elements employed in the process of the social construction of 'race' categories through the ideological process of racialisation. Here the racist selects an empirical or imaginary feature or category in order to sustain the existence of the 'race' and then attributes negative attributes to this existence. Miles clearly recognises the arbitrary nature of this construction of conceptual categories but insists upon the idea that a racially defined discourse is one rooted in the idea of permanence and inherence of stigmatised bodies. This move also allows him to anticipate and acknowledge the indirect or inferential way in which the racialised categories will be employed as signifiers which are apparently 'empty'. This distinct conceptual advance achieved by Miles' is bought at the cost of retaining a commitment to an account of ideology that is epistemologically defined (1982; 1989: 42). The problem involved here is that the retention of a conceptualisation of ideology, while no longer supported by a notion of science, is itself critiqued from a position of science. It is to this dilemma we now turn.

The Problem of Ideology

In this final section I want to indicate how an approach broadly in accord with a racialisation/political economy framework, as exemplified particularly by the work of Miles, can address the problem for political language analysis of the post-'race' signifier. This involves considering the extent to which the debate about racism is itself locatable within the interstices of the debate about ideology, epistemology and representation.[24] The significance of the changing debate about the continuing validity and usefulness of the concept of ideology is most pertinent to the question of the significance of political language and the power of public representation and ideologies, and the extent to which such an approach rests upon the assumption of the epistemological falsity of 'race' and the ideologically informed process of racialisation.

As we have noted, the practice of ideology critique advocated by Miles assumes an epistemologically privileged position from which the distortion and mystification of social representations can be recognised.[25] To the extent that social reality presents itself as other than it is requires scientific tools that can rupture or penetrate its surfaces. The implications of such a view, as Foucault has argued, is that 'behind the concept of ideology (is) the nostalgia for a quasi-transparent form of knowledge, free from all error and illusion' (Foucault 1984: 59).[26] As postmodernism questions our ability to reach a truth which is not relative to a particular achieved discourse or discursive effect, and doubts the existence of fundamental social relations and contradictions, the epistemological judgement implicit in ideology critique becomes, if not impossible, not easily reconcilable with competing understandings that themselves play a role in the construction of racialised accounts of the social world (cf. Larrain 1994: 297). The persuasiveness of post-structuralist and post-modernists critiques of scientific knowledge are that they consolidate the critique of science at the centre of the definition of racism as an ideology. Surely the historical relationship between science and racism must persuade us that science cannot be immune from ideology, but is itself a discourse of 'power' and 'desire'? (Foucault passim; Deleuze and Guattari 1984); as well as being deeply perspectival (Lyotard 1984).

Why is this question important? Firstly, because a defence of the ideological quality of racialised discourse retains analytic attention upon its historical effects: forms of exclusion/inclusion, through the formation of regimes of signification, but also attention upon the core characteristics of the racial imaginary as a biological or essentialist fiction. I concur with Miles that too great a departure from an agreed criteria of recognition, render the concept redundant or conceptually vacuous (cf. Miles 1989: ch.2). However it is evident that this limited position is currently under assault and, for some reason, is no longer credible because it involves a commitment to a form of reductionism or essentialism (cf. Solomos and Back 1991).

The point of contradiction which forms the empirical and theoretical focus of our argument, as it has been developed through this chapter, is that claims for discursive racialisation involve the entry or permeation of the 'idea of race' into discourse. Yet the validation of this 'presence' cannot simply be an empirical exercise because 'race' is almost invariably absent in postwar official discourse and Parliamentary Debates. As we have argued, 'race' is 'under erasure' so that its trace remains as it continues to motivate and articulate effects, though its location is elusive and the languages which appear to carry it somehow conceal it at the same moment.

As we have established, it is the unique mode of thematisation of 'race' under official erasure to which we must attend. This is a double closure and inversion because, epistemologically speaking, 'race' cannot exist prior to its representation, therefore its representation must itself always already be an ideological construction. From this it is only a small step to suggest that the thematisations of 'race' are many and likely to be an intertextual phenomenon. When we interrogate such thematisations as emergent from the tactics, strategies and constructions of public and private languages, then we can clearly see that the ideologies of 'race' are numerous, drawing on historically diverse configurations, and articulated with social and political ideologies, as they emerge from the circulation and exchange of public narratives within official debates.

One way of usefully resolving this dilemma is to introduce the distinction between core and secondary racialisation:[27] this would allow the focus upon secondary discourses which arise within the field of discursive racialisation and exist in various texts, documents and ideological and symbolic constructions. This is especially pertinent to the political sphere, especially in the context of the prohibition on the use of the signifier of 'race' in public speech (cf. Montagu (ed) 1972). This secondary level of discourses is necessarily complex and will have, in addition, some degree of autonomy from the core criteria. For example, postwar political debate is characterised by a complex of racist discourses, some of which legitimates the term 'race'; and some of which attempt to delegitimate its application to migrant groups and their subsequent exclusion, because of fears about the social impact of the discourse of 'race' itself.[28] Any exploration of such linguistic complexity requires such a distinction to allow the idea of discursive formation and critical deconstruction. We must pay attention to how racist discourses are achieved and this means examining the mechanisms that allow

Discourse and Ideology

My theoretical resolution to the problem of ideology, as I have already indicated, is to argue that, while it is necessary to define racism as an historical ideology (cf. Banton 1983; 1987; Miles 1989), when we are speaking of the production and exchange of racial ideas, in public and institutional contexts, then we are referring to discourse. It is the term discourse that is best able to encapsulate the sense in which racial ideologies are drawn upon in the social construction of public meanings, as well as how such meanings are contested and exchanged in the dynamic process of official debates. Neither the conceptual content, or mode of expression of racial ideology, can be contained within the inherent functionality of the concept of ideology. In this sense, the production of regulatory and exclusionary legislation is the contradictory effect of the racialisation of political language. While it could be argued that the advocacy of migrant labour controls serve to sustain existing capitalist relations, through the reproduction of racial Others, such a political manipulation is only possible because of the prior development of racial ideologies, which cannot be reduced to the interests of a political elite or dominant class fraction. Thus, not only are racial ideologies relatively autonomous, but their reproduction involves a complex processes of production of discourses whose exchange, conflict and combination, produces racialised public languages.

As we shall show, in chapter 6, the 'core' criteria of a theory of racism proposed by Miles does provide the essential basis upon which it is possible to reclaim the analysis of Powellism from the New Racism theorists. However this gain is not as clearly won as it might appear. The problem of modern or 'new' racism in political language is that it does not explicitly reveal itself as racist by obligingly conforming to the criteria of the 'core'. Our argument will be that racist theorising, and the production of racist discourses, proliferate on the basis of implicit inferential reference to such a core.[29] In this way it becomes possible to interpret the way in which racial ideology is communicated and how it legitimates racism between speakers and audiences.

This analytical focus requires the assumption that articulating the ideology of 'race' within a form of situated communication requires the construction of a discourse, or social and political narrative, able to conform to existing generic rules of production and dissemination of texts. Once we look within the category of the constitution of the political then we discover a micro structure of positions, and rules of exchange, which can be shown to have decisive impact on the production of such discourses. However, conceding this does not automatically create a break in the theorisation of racism as others have claimed.[30] Rather it points to a closer attention being given to the process whereby racism is drawn upon and communicated to its political audience.

Secondly, such an approach does not sufficiently recognise that the political discourse of 'race' is also that language of description generated to deal with the idea of 'race' underlying the political management of the social construction of immigration as a racial phenomenon. This amounts to a double edged conception of the idea of racialisation: that it refers to two kinds of discourses; one a discourse of *management* of racism; the other a discourse of *promotion* of racism. Within this duality there will be many voices of contestation, alliance and ambiguity. This leads us into a discussion of the concept of discursive-racialisation.

Discursive-racialisation

Earlier we examined the adequacy of the concept of deracialisation (Reeves 1983) in accounting for the racial effectivity of discourse that has been subject to a process of discursive deracialisation i.e., the 'cleaning-up' or simple concealment of 'race' categories which were formally present in a given discourse. We concluded that such a conception, and that of 'sanitary coding', go some way towards more clearly illuminating the range of discursive and rhetorical strategies developed within British postwar political debates to covertly promote, or seek to communicate, approval of racism to a partisan electorate.

We now suggest the such an account is inherently functionalist in not more clearly allowing for the idea that such strategies might themselves be a complex effect of the promotion of, and contestation of, the racialisation of official language. Empirical instances of debate content suggest that such a process is infinitely more complex and contradictory in effect than has been supposed, to the extent that the language of resistance to racism often provided the means of achievement of its political expression. The broad answer to why this should be so are to do with the political repression of racial language, which has the effect of pathologising racial expression, as indicative of surrender to psychological or irrational disorder. Language itself becomes the bearer and means of infiltration of racism into politics. It is this narrative of political panic we have called 'political racism'.[31] It is against the 'extremism' of this scenario of the racial agitation of the instinctively prejudiced electorate that a language of liberal moderation and local representation of those *most affected* is constructed and defined.[32] It is this discourse that allows racist Commons' sense not simply to 'enter' but to be *produced* through Parliamentary Debate.

Racialisation theory *can* accommodate such analysis; but the term must be extended to encompass the double process by which political language is racialised: how the ideology of 'race' enters political language but also how such language reacts to and negotiates the impact of that idea, in terms of the meaning and significance it acquires in the course of the conduct of official debates, concerned with the exclusion of racialised migrants. In this respect, the forces that would favour, and those that would resist the racialisation of black migration, are played out within the discourse of public and party debates.

Conclusion

The close interpretative analysis of political discourse, central to the focus of our study of this period, requires that we conceive of racial political language as the product of competing and inter-meshing societal discourses and representations, which have produced a symbolic political narrative of 'race' and immigration which employs and refers to empirical and symbolic, ideological and narrational elements in a complex, inter-discursive way. On the basis of this general assertion we will argue that the articulation of 'race' within political discourse and debates takes the form of a series of societal referencing narratives or *ideological narrative of the social*. Such narratives will be seen to take a ubiquitously anecdotal form in constructing a public account of a social world in which 'race' is seen to be an active force that creates situations, informs actions, and explains reactions. In this respect, 'race' is a discursive ideology, in the sense asserted by writers like Sykes, because it 'provide[s] explanations for why things are as they are by defining the participants and processes in the social world and the relationships between them, as well as the criteria by which the latter may be evaluated and the means by which they may be changed' (Sykes 1985: 87). Such narratives of 'race' construct and unfold the public story of 'immigration' (insofar as that story is metonymically identical with the account of the social and political impact of 'black' migration to postwar British society).

Subsequent chapters will illustrate the complex patterning of such public political discourses and the 'race' narratives they construct. Such narratives are related to, and emerge directly out of the processes involved in the politicisation and racialisation of the issue of black migration from the former-colonial territories of Britain. This development is only possible once a public language idiom, able to speak a language of post-'race', has emerged. The process of this becoming is the single most neglected issue in the analysis of the development of postwar racism within Britain.[33]

As we have argued, accounts of the process of the racialisation of the politics of migration in postwar Britain have paid insufficient attention to the political language within which it has been articulated, in terms of the properties and propensities of the language itself as an achiever of public significations, as well as the routines and practices that have allowed it be officially conducted, especially within Parliamentary Debates; and the wider historical and political elements, economic and ideological, that form the context against which such a language has emerged and been shaped. The reasons for this are complex and inter-causal. However, as we have indicated, a central difficulty here are the problems, theoretical and politically attendant upon theorising the autonomy of racial ideology, and the extent to which the political process of racialisation of black migration depends upon the construction and exchange of competing racialised discourses, which are themselves politicised.

As chapters 3 and 5 will clearly show, as soon as we apply any sort of socio-linguistic model to Parliamentary discourses of 'race and immigration' then it is evident that we are looking for the way in which 'race' debate apparently denies the existence of 'available discourse' but, at the same time, demonstrably, develops a neutral or liberal language of 'race' which defines it as an illiberal irrationalism. Such a language is counterpoised to pro-'race' discourse i.e., political discourse that wants to articulate 'race' as a political category, but has not developed the conceptual categories to allow this to be achieved smoothly.[34]

Both approaches claim legitimacy in being best able to manage the explosive properties of 'race' within political debate.[35] This characterisation goes some way to explaining why it is that the language of 'race' within Parliamentary debates is either absent or it is anecdotal. This is because, increasingly, the only publicly authentic discourse of post-'race' is one based on personal feeling and experience. This underlies a mainstream conception of 'race' as a 'problem' of the emotions and prejudices. Thus the double edged conception of 'political racism' we have previously suggested has its resonance. The idea of 'political racism' must invoke both the idea of the expression of racism, made possible by the activity of the post-'race' promoters, who manage to succeed in persuading the political elite to support racist conceptions and demands on the basis of this. At the same time, the idea of 'political racism' also describes the conceptualisation of racism as a property of political language usage itself.

This conceptualisation of the nature of racial discourse, and its role in the reproduction of racism, involves a claim about the role of language in promoting racism. Such a model of 'race promotion' has its basis in a view of the non-rational basis of 'race' thinking and feeling, which is translated into the elements apparently carried in political language forms. It is on the basis of the development of such discourses of post-'race' management that we can begin to theorise the idea of the effect of racism as the effect of the discourse of its management rather than its promotion. It is the necessity of managing the emotionally problematic notion of 'race' which is responsible for its ideological effects in creating a discourse of regulation of those racialised by it. This is not simply to state that reaction creates racism but rather that the discourse of racial protection actually increases the racist effects of politics upon all levels of British society: this is the deeper significance of racialisation. The official political denial of 'race' talk and yet its covert development and ideological articulation within parliamentary debates is the central conceptual problem that political language racialisation approaches must be able to explain.

What are the implications of these arguments to the study? Our analysis of the emergence of post 'race' discourse within official debates will show that such discourse is to be understood as a political means of narration, which is either euphemistic or coded; or it is anecdotal. These two features are not accidental but reflect their historical formation within the twin determinants of the 'secret state' and the 'black country' 'race' populists. What overdetermines these elements is the political ideological influence of the postwar context; that of the period of decolonisation and the idea of the aftermath of the Holocaust.[36] These political phenomenon create a climate of repression of racial narration and require its reformulation within the coded language of liberal-tolerance. The climate of racial suppression, created by the context of decolonisation and the impact of the idea of the Holocaust, define the idea of racism as an irrational prejudice. The impact of this upon political language and the conceptualisation of racism are profound. Such a language, in seeking to avoid extremism through the suppression of racial language, achieves the suppression of the imputed racial groups in the interests of not wishing to further stimulate passions and emotions definitive of the discourse of 'race', as it retreats headlong from the anecdotal populism of the post-'race' promoters. In these ways, the constitution of the political does have a considerable effect upon the production and uses of official treatments of the idea of 'race'. Thus, despite the inevitable outcome of such a contest, it is from within this discourse of prejudice and the irrationality of 'race' that a discourse of exclusion is constructed; as it is resisted by alternative articulations of the same language.

The next chapter considers the conceptual value of the New Racism thesis in the detailed analysis of post-'race' talk, and the extent to which the concept can reveal and account for the emergence of this particular language form, as well as the questions attendant upon its historical and discursive formation and development within the politics of black migrant exclusion legislation; a legislation made possible, as we have argued, through the development of a parliamentary *Commons' sense*.

2 Back to the Future: The New Racism Revisited

> Mr. Wilson rejected *'the reasoning of those who in these past days have marched from Smithfield and the docks on the House of Commons to proclaim the doctrines of a new racialism'* (IRR: Newsletter, June 1968: 219).

> *I wish to ask, are we to condemn such an attitude as a racialist one? I should say no. I should say that it is a commonsense attitude* (Mr. Geoffrey Lloyd (Sutton Coldfield) *Expiring Laws Bill - Committee*, 17 November, 1964: c.302).

This Chapter looks critically at that concept currently at the heart of claims for the emergence within Britain, during the last two decades or so, of a *new cultural politics* of racism: the 'New Racism' (NR).[1] The NR concept is important because it has been employed as the primary concept in claims for the emergence of (i) a new theoretical approach in the analysis of racism, one concerned with racial subjectivity, the cultural dynamics of signification, and the multi-accentuality of 'race' discourses (cf. Hall 1988; Donald and Rattansi (ed) 1992; Mercer 1994); and (ii) the extent to which this new cultural theorisation of racism is a response to the emergence of new forms of politics and social movements, based on cultural identities and projects, that the approaches of the 1980s can no longer adequately comprehend (Solomos and Back 1993: 20).[2]

This Chapter is thus imagined as a sort of return to the seminal concept of NR in order to explicate its foundational logic, and the scope and focus of its claims, within the theoretical and historical context of its emergence. The metaphor of 'return' is one meant to invoke a theoretical journey back from the debate 'present' to the conceptual 'past'. Although, of course, such a journey is really a reconstruction and recombination of 'found' materials. Our purpose in employing such a method is that it will allow us to show that the concept, as it emerged and developed in the 1980s, was an internally contradictory and problematic one, involving different kinds of claims and foundational theories, which render the concept theoretically ambiguous. Such ambiguity has allowed the concept a political purchase, in meaning many things to many theorists, but at the expense of a critical examination of what it is that the concept can actually tell us about, for example, how the politics of racism and the state has became the politics of, for example, the Rushdie affair, Dewsbury and Tebbit's cricket test?[3]

The primary focus of the chapter will be to critically examine the concept in terms of the role it has played in providing a conceptual 'tool box' for understanding the role of Smethwick and Powellism in the construction of the 'new' cultural political language of racism. This critique is important to the development of the main arguments of the book concerning Smethwick and Powellism, and the meaning and significance of postwar racial political language, because the NR thesis provides the most coherent account of the role of Smethwick and Powellism in the formation of a racial political discourse. An account which is organised around the decisive idea of a conceptual transformation in racial political codes of signification, from 'old' Nazi tainted biologistic language, to a 'new' culturalist language of 'absolute' difference, which occurs between the discourse of Griffiths, at Smethwick, and the emergence of Powellism (cf. Barker 1981: 40-2; 1983: 2; Gilroy 1987: 85).

For the NR writers, it is only after this period of transformation in the conceptual content of racist discourse, engineered by Powell and the rise of the New Right, that racism could capture the heart of the state. The political means and subsequent tool of this 'state racism' is the 'new' racist commonsense that becomes *naturalised* (as *commonsense*) in Parliamentary and public debates, from 1968 onwards, culminating in the 1976 Immigration Debate and the 1981 Nationality Debate (cf. Barker 1981: 13; CCCS: Race and Politics Group 1982: 27-35).[4]

The significance of the NR thesis, as an object of critique, cannot be overestimated because it contests key elements of our argument, as advanced in chapter 1. Firstly, its principal focus is upon the discursive 'content' of public/political language, advanced in the course of debates about ('black') Immigration. Secondly, it seeks to ground such analysis within a conceptual distinction about a shift or transformation in the content of such language. Thirdly, it seeks to locate this micro-logical analysis of debate content within a wider macro-logical account of the structural and ideological forces and relations of postwar British politics and society.

Our account will, by implication, suggest a number of doubts about the adequacy of this conceptualisation to support the current claims and developments being made on the basis of it (cf. Hall 1992a ; Mercer 1994: 305-8).[5] Our central argument must be that the NR concept fails to clearly establish the political newness it asserts or the language transformation that it has supposedly brought about. This should not be taken to mean that such a phenomenon has not been brought into existence i.e., *that no language transformation of any kind has occurred,* but rather that both the empirical method and conceptual means of accounting for it are flawed, particularly in the claims for the popular/political success of a non-biologistic racism. More worrying perhaps, we shall conclude, is the tendency among much 'new left' political culturalism to seek, on the basis of such interpretations, to create a cultural language of 'myth' as a response to the apparent success of such politics among the contemporary 'New Right' (cf. Mercer 1992: 436; 1994: 307-8).[6]

The structure and periodization of our argument can be represented schematically as follows: firstly, that the concept of NR, as it was developed by Barker (1981) and CCCS: Race and Politics Group (1982), was not particularly 'new' or particularly novel. Such an argument had been developed in an earlier period and in order to address the same political object: Powellism. Secondly, the meaning of the concept is deeply ambiguous and, what is more, this ambiguity has been reproduced unresolved in the development and re-application of the concept by others. Thirdly, that the account of the NR, seen as seminal (Barker 1981), does not unequivocally advocate the supersession of a biologistic account of racism, but rather its reformulation: *the new biologism.*[7] Fourthly, that the wedding of the notion of the NR to a notion of neo-Gramscian derived political commonsense is contradictorily realised by NR theorists because of a problematic relationship to the interpretation of the conception of commonsense developed by Gramsci (1971). Finally, that the account of popular racism constructed on the back of such accounts, exaggerates the success of the New Right in winning a political audience, as well as the role of 'commonsense racism' within such a process. We begin with a brief sketching-in of the discursive foundations of the conception in order to reveal its implicit connection to, but denial of, earlier sociological debates concerned with explaining the connection between racist political expression and the concept of 'race'.

The 'New Racism' and the Debate about 'Race Politics': A Reconstruction

As we have already suggested, the debate about the NR does not begin with the publication of *The New Racism* (1981) by Barker; rather it begins, if a moment could be selected, with the discussion by Banton (1969: 551-4) of the appropriateness of the designation 'racist' to the speeches of Peter Griffiths and Enoch Powell.[8] This essay then sparks of a long standing debate concerning the extent to which it is correct to designate explicitly non-biological theories of 'race relations' as racist (cf. Phizacklea and Miles 1980; Miles 1982). Thus the debate about the NR is not in fact actually 'new' and, by implication, neither is the concept. The 'lost' history of the concept has had the effect of severing the relationship between the analysis of political language as ideology from the debate about the concept of 'race' and its relationship to racist discourse. Attempts to further ground the concept within an Althusserian and neo-Gramscian theorisation of ideology have further divided scholars (cf. Hall 1978; CCCS: Race and Politics Group 1982; Miles 1984a; 1987; 1989).[9]

As we argued, in both the Introduction and chapter 1, the NR theorists either developed their account in isolation from the terms of sociological debate about racism as a doctrine or ideology; or they developed their approach specifically by characterising the sociology of 'race relations' as itself a racial ideology (Lawrence 1981; 1982). This is because the point of entry into the debate about racial discourse was the overwhelmingly ominous sense in which the contemporary politics of the 1970s exhibited a ubiquitously racial form. Thus the theorists began from the evidence of the profusion of racial discourses and attempted to 'read' an immanence or presence into them. In the case of the CCCS: Race and Politics Group, the theoretical grid they drew upon, in order to interpret the meaning of the emergence of this discursive formation, was much of the fusion developed by Stuart Hall and colleagues in the writing of the monumental *Policing the Crisis* (1978). There the authors combined a political intervention into 'mugging' with labelling theory, New Criminology, Cohen's development of 'moral panic' theory, Althusserian theories of ideology, and Gramscian theories of hegemony and the *cultural autonomy of the ideological political superstructures*. Much of the impact of this approach was a political synthesis of what we might call the 'New Left', latterly associated with the political positioning around the breakaway communist political/theoretical journal *Marxism Today* (cf. Forgacs 1989).

In the *Policing the Crisis* study the authors developed the idea that the 'predatory behaviour' of 'foot pad theft' became swept up within a moral panic about 'law and order', which was a symptom of deeper shifts in the cultural politics of the management of British capitalism, and the role of the state in securing moral and cultural leadership of an unstable alliance between dominant and subordinate classes. The racialisation of mugging, like the politics of Powellism, was a privileged 'moment' in a series of panics over social and cultural change, rebelliousness, 'affluent' youth and sexual and moral permissiveness, that shook the dominant classes and led to the idea of an 'organic crisis of hegemony' (cf. Hall et al 1978; Hall 1978).

The ideological significance of 'race' was that it was able to thematize this crisis of social authority and the need to regain control over civil society through more authoritarian means. The politics of 'race' 'launched a torpedo' straight 'to the boiler room of consensus politics' (Hall et al 1978: 246) by revealing the first clear signs of how a populist rupture could be achieved in the political re-alliance between dominant and dominated. This set of ideas led Hall into analysing Thatcherism as a continuation of Powellism and the briefer attempt by Heath 'to restore 'Selsdon man' - a close cousin of Neanderthal Man - at the centre of British politics' (Hall 1979) i.e., an attempt to construct an authoritarian alliance between the definition of the meaning of the crisis and the support of the subaltern: *authoritarian populism.*

The collection of essays, *The Empire Strikes Back* (ESB) (1982) moved in the same theoretical grooves as the monumental *Policing*: what it privileged above all though, was the role of 'race' in the definition and management of the crisis of authority. 'Race' was the privileged metaphor of British society in crisis and the ideological means whereby the state and the dominant could draw upon a populist racism in order to regain control. The crisis of hegemony and the popular politics of racism were leading, the authors argued, to an authoritarian statism: an exceptional form of the capitalist state (cf. Poulantzas 1978; see Hall's review article 1980d).

It was the intersection of the development of the idea of popular racism that suggested a similarity with the NR argument developed by Barker. Both theorists highlighted the importance of this concept and how it was associated with Powellism and the rise of the New Right populist politics of 'race'. The ESB book enthusiastically took up the idea as consistent with its own approach to deciphering the 'current conjuncture'. However, such a view is misleading in suggesting a similarity; Barker has recently sought to disavow the association of Thatcherism and the NR (Barker 1992: 81-100). We will argue that the conceptions of popular racism/commonsense and the NR are radically incompatible. The relevance of this theoretical contradiction is important to the development of our argument as it relates to the development of a theory and methodology of analysis of political language.

Firstly, the theorists of the NR do not acknowledge the content of the old racism they distinguish. Secondly, they allow too much autonomy to the political, particularly privileged sites of it, to determine the content of racial discourse and its meanings. In this sense they presage the recent arguments that racial discourse is a signifier in search of a signified; that cultural meanings are the site of racial contestation of ethnic projects and political struggles (cf. Omi and Winant 1986; Mercer 1994). In the same way, the conception of commonsense that anchors the theories is defined politically or it is read back historically in ways which are radically incompatible with the account of the postwar development of racial ideology.[10]

As we have argued in chapter 1, an adequate theory of political racial discourse must afford some degree of political autonomy over against the *core ideology* and its *secondary racialisation*. However this kind of analysis must pay attention to the detailed content of political discourse formation, none of which the NR theorists achieve, since they focus upon selective sources, which often amounts to a misinterpretation of debate content and dynamics.[11] In this respect the analysis of the NR theorists is not sufficiently hermeneutical and/or reflexive in interpreting the content of political/public debates and their languages within a wider historical framework, one that can provide the linguistic and non-linguistic dynamics of change in racial political languages concerned with the symbolic and ideological issue of 'Immigration' and 'Race Relations'.

Thus far we have argued that the NR is not actually new; such arguments have characterised prior political discourse and have been anticipated by other writers. This genealogy has been obscured or remained unrecognised by the theorists. Our second major argument is that the claim for a NR is not a unified one since the concept is employed with varying degrees of consistency by the theorists. There are at least three kinds of claims that can be made for the NR: (i) that racist political language has been subject to 'sanitary coding' which conceals or 'codes' a biological claim; (ii) that such language usage is merely the latest variety of biological reductionism, which conforms to a deep-seated reductionist ontology central to the behavioural sciences, (currently expressed in the arguments of sociobiology (cf. Dawkins 1976; Barker 1981: 100-173); (iii) that the impact of Thatcherite political revolution has unleashed a new culturalist nationalist discourse that has taken up ideas of 'race', nation and tradition in a specifically modern discourse of authority and attempted, divisive hegemony.

Broadly speaking the NR school, while susceptible to the arguments of (i) is most decisively split between claims (ii) and (iii). Section two of the chapter will explore these 'fault lines' through an examination of the relationship between the 'content' and claims of the NR writers. It will demonstrate that there is evidence for the use of the theory as a form of 'coding' in both examples. Claims (ii) and (iii) can be identified and explored in the writings of Barker (1981), Lawrence (1982) and Gilroy (1987). The point of division identified occurs in the scope of (ii), concerning the extent to which the theorists endorse a theory of the necessary biological basis of 'race' argumentation and its conceptual relationship to the cultural form of the NR.[12] On one level this concerns the delineation of the 'old'/'new' racism dichotomy and the extent to which the theorists of the NR offer a general account of the 'old racism' upon which to judge 'newness' (cf. Miles, 1987: 35). The approach to the scope of (iii) throws up further differences of conceptualisation. Of specific interest here are the importance given to the role of

Powell in the construction of the NR and the relationship to Thatcherism. It will become clear that claims for (iii) rest upon widely incompatible theories of 'commonsense' racism which further divide the theorists.

Redefining Racism

The attempt to redefine the scope and meaning of 'race' has been central to recent debates over the concept of 'new', 'modern' or 'symbolic' racism: that essentially a new form of racial theorising and thinking has been developed within British Conservative and 'new right' discourse, (and, for some, the wider Western European social order: cf. van Dijk 1990; Sivanandan 1988; 1989, and France in particular cf.Taguieff 1990; Wievorka 1994; 1995), by the development of certain symbols and metaphors able to naturalise a racist response to black immigration, and endorse calls for repatriation as either a threat levelled at the internal 'enemy' or a practicable 'reality' of legislation. The key element to much of this has been the denial, in this 'new' cultural and symbolic language usage, of the ideas of the old racial typology/hierarchy by which racism was previously identified (Barker 1981: 3-4).

An interesting commentary on this debate is that presented by Banton, who has argued that the concept of 'race', once an intellectually respectable concept, had by the interwar years become redundant and discredited (Banton 1980). Rightly the concept should have died out shortly after this time; unfortunately its public career has been indefinitely prolonged because it has been taken up by politicians, in the postwar era, as an explanation for the problems of New Commonwealth Immigration.[13] Such a use for Banton is inappropriate and has had a number of undesirable consequences; one of which is the terminological confusion about the correct designation of 'race' as an explanatory entity and the discourse of racism that historically could be derived from or attributable to it (Banton 1980: 21-42).

This argument can be seen to further develop a position adopted by Banton in the seminal debate among British sociologists concerning the issue of 'race' and sociology (cf. *BSA Conference on Race and Sociology*, (1969) in: Zubaida (ed) 1970). Banton is notable for his contribution to this debate, on racism and political discourse, when he argued that the discourse of both Griffiths and Powell were inappropriately deserving of the label 'racist', since such speeches did not operate with a classical theory of racial classification or typology (Banton 1969: 551-554). For Banton only this historically short-lived discourse should be appropriately labelled 'racist', specifically one exhibiting a scientific appeal to a theory of racial difference and classification. Both Powell and Griffiths, as Banton demonstrates through quotation, do not appeal to such pseudo-scientific validation but rather appeal to a cultural argument. Commenting on Powell's Eastbourne speech Banton argues:

> If indeed it is the case that those who would deny equal treatment to members of ethnic minorities now appeal primarily to cultural instead of biological variation, should we describe their views as racist?[...]Some commentators have spoken of the "changing nature of racism"; but this is justified only if one defines it in terms of its function. I argue that if we label the new culturally based doctrines "racist" we may mislead people[...] In seeking the distinguishing feature of these new doctrines, one possibility to be examined is that they are new varieties of ethnic nationalism (Banton 1969: 553).

Outlined here are all the main conceptual issues that will occupy the discussion about the NR over a decade later: the appeal to cultural arguments as pseudo-biological in character; the proposition that the 'function' of racism has changed; that the 'new' cultural discourse is a doctrine of nationalism that is arrived at through a suppressed or re-defined use of the concept of 'race' (cf. Miles, 1987).

The 1969 BSA conference, where Banton delivered this paper (cf. Zubaida (ed) 1970), can rightly be designated as the first attempt, within sociology, to discuss the discourse of 'race' politics and to centre such a discussion around the designation of Griffiths and Powell as political racists. Banton's main adversary, John Rex, offered a challenge to Banton in the form of the influential idea of a 'functional equivalent' theory of racist discourse: 'What is a theoretical rather than an ethical question[...]is whether the phenomenon of Powellism or any other contemporary political doctrine or movement is a functional equivalent of the racist doctrines and movements of the thirties' (Rex 1969: 610).

Unfortunately this debate has not been resolved or directly rejoined, despite the efforts of Miles to stimulate such an event (cf. Phizacklea and Miles 1980; Miles 1982; see also Banton 1977: 159-62). The debate between Rex and Banton was concerned with precisely the question addressed in the affirmative by the NR theorists: whether deterministic (or pseudo-biological) arguments about cultural difference constitute racism? Whereas much of Banton's definition would exclude most kinds of racism and all varieties of NR arguments, Rex's criteria would be able to accommodate such arguments. But the imputed function of such racism and its context of emergence would be problematic. For although the context has changed, for Rex racism serves essentially the same function. Thus the articulation of the idea of the nation to a racialised notion of culture would be problematic for Rex's general 'functional' model; yet this is the feature that has the most claim to 'newness'.[14]

Banton's solution is to designate mark II theories as new political forms of ethnocentrism (Banton 1969: 554; 1970: 31). But this conception is not elaborated upon so it is difficult to see how this re-definition leads to greater analytical clarity. It is one thing to say that, as a biological doctrine 'racism is dead', yet the function such a discourse serves in achieving meaning for its audience remains active. Settling for ethnocentrism takes away the power of critique that the designation 'racist' had for types of discourse.[15]

In fact, others had come to similar conclusions. For example, Ankie M. Hoogvelt (1969), a sociologist working on prejudice scaling, on examining the infamous 'letters to Enoch' reviewed by Powell sympathiser, Diane Spearman (Spearman 1968), takes exception to the way in which the post-bag is divided into: (i) those whose remarks are designated racist in terms of conformity to the terms of the existing, biologically determinist model and; (ii) those who employ more broadly cultural arguments or assertions. Thus Spearman is led to reject arguments concerned with the 'defence of national culture' and/or 'historical way of life' as racist since they do not depend upon a theory of biological difference.

The idea of racism re-conceptualised or thought-through in terms of 'fears for British culture' raises the question of what should count as a statement of racism and how such statements should be categorised. For Spearman, such 'cultural fears' are ethnocentric but not 'racist' in the accepted understanding of the term. Hoogvelt disagrees and offers an example from the letters which could quite reasonably form the 'core' of Barker's 'new racism': 'No Briton wants to see his traditional way of life, the country he has loved and fought for, lose it identity and particular character through the over-great acceptance of peoples of quite different cultures and ways of life' (cited in Hoogvelt 1969: 1). This is the 'new racism' as well as the core of Powellist arguments. Hoogvelt concludes: 'the supporters of Enoch Powell who express fears for British culture are in fact expressing ethnocentrism. And it is my further contention that ethnocentrism, in the context of Britain today, has racist implications' (1969: 1).

Hoogvelt supports this conclusion by examining the conceptual division made possible by the consistent application of the concept of cultural group or 'cultural nation': 'Ethnocentrism involves distinguishing between an in-group (culture, nation, folk) with which the individual identifies, and an out-group which is seen as threatening' (1969: 2). The value of Hoogvelt's paper is to suggest that, given the current political climate over 'race', such forms of ethnocentrism do invoke and trade-upon an 'idea of race'. Hoogvelt's innovation, then, is in providing a redefinition of the scope of the concept of 'race'; one which can accommodate current political uses. To his credit Banton does suggest this but his error is in wanting to partition of the 'race' concept from association with this sort of usage. While this sort of operation may be important in supporting an account of epistemic shifts in the discourse of biological science (Banton 1983; 1987) such an account is inconsistent with the wider discursive claims of Banton's account of the 'moment' of *racialisation* 'as a social process[...] whereby a mode of categorisation was developed, applied tentatively in European historical writing, and then, more confidently, to the populations of the world' (Banton 1977: 18-19) and the moment of *de-racialisation* 'in which many politicians and educators seek to correct the mistakes of the past' (Banton 1977: 19).

Banton designates the speeches of Griffiths and Powell as 'new' forms of ethnocentrism, rather than racism, because they appeal primarily to cultural arguments, rather than the language of 'racial typology', peculiar to the classificatory 'science' of the late 18th and early 19th century (Banton 1969; 1970; 1977; 1983: ch.3). The problem with the conceptual limitation imposed by Banton's usage is that it renders almost all of the debate and discourse on 'race' and immigration, since the early 1960s: 'race' free. Thus the effect of Banton's intervention is conservative: it attempts to replace racism with the term ethnocentrism. But defining Powellism as ethnocentric cannot explain the role Powell's speeches have played in shaping the issues of the 'race' and immigration debate; in particular the *threat to the national culture, historical community and way of life of the indigenous* 'English'. In other words, the inferential racism of national character and identity, interwoven through Powell's speeches and writings.[16]

These themes and ideas are the ones echoed and articulated in the letters to Powell, along with the 'old' language of moral and physical 'superiority': blood, stock and 'race'. The profusion of these cultural sentiments and phrases attest to the essential basis of Powellism as a popular construction of a politics of cultural exclusionism, whose end-game is the physical exclusion of certain categories of people legitimated, in all but name, by an idea of 'race'. The self-conscious re-definition of 'racism' as cultural hostility is the essential accompaniment to this project.

The 'New Racism' Thesis

Beginning to recover the lost ground between the NR and earlier attempts to pose the question of racism and political language establishes, at the very minimum, that the idea of racism re-conceptualised as cultural-xenophobia or *tribalism* is not a new one. The conceptual discourse of racism has taken many forms. What has changed is the political context of its articulation.

One of the reasons for the lack of continuity between earlier discussion and the development of the NR thesis is due to the contrary stand-point and assumptions of the approaches. Thus, both Barker (1981) and CCCS: Race and Politics (1982) locate the existence and conceptual logic of the NR through a 'reading' or 'decoding' of contemporary political speech and press editorials. They are able to 'read-off' the theory as immanent from this material because of wider set of assumptions about the consistency or homology of such discourse to wider social and political frameworks: the contemporary crisis of British capitalism, as a refraction of global recession, made visible in the 'lurch' to the right in social policy which had heralded the rise of the 'New Right' in British politics (and the concomitant decline of the New Left); whereas, the earlier theorists' response to Powellism was, in many ways, a departure from a wider, social theory of 'race relations' centred upon the settlement and assimilation of post-colonial migrants. The failure of the sociology of 'race relations' was in the inability or reluctance of theorists, such as Banton and Rex, to translate this debate into a specific theory of the racialisation of politics and the state.[17] The failure of the NR theorists may just be the reverse, the failure to translate the political context back into the conceptual debate, such that racism becomes a reflex of political forces; and thus its critique becomes one of reduction to sophisticated description alone.[18]

For Barker (1981), this distance from the sociological debate initiated by Rex and Banton (Zubaida (ed) 1970), is due to his explicitly philosophical approach to (a) the conceptual and ideological structures underlying contemporary political discourse, and their possible relation to: (b) the debate about Darwinism, and the 'sciences' of ethology and sociobiology (Barker 1983a; cf. Rose 1979). For CCCS (1982) the distance from the sociological debate can be accounted for in terms of the broadly based and specifically focused hostility towards the 'sociology of race relations' and the sociological writings of, in particular, John Rex (Gilroy 1980; Lawrence 1981; CCCS: Race and Politics Group 1982; ch.3; cf. Rex 1983: ch.7).[19] One noticeable effect of this conceptual isolation from sociology is the absence of an adequate definition of, or discussion of, the concept of racism in either work (cf. Miles 1987: 35-36), particularly in CCCS: Race and Politics Group (1982).

What is distinctive about the NR theorists is that they are principally concerned with the analysis of contemporary discourse: that of politicians, press and public debate. Unlike previous sociological analysis they do not translate the evidence of 'racist' discourse into the concepts of a larger theory of 'race relations', whether 'immigrant-host' or 'culture-conflict'; or in terms of the debate about 'race' as a doctrine of late18th century Western 'science' and the regulation of colonial and imperial relations in the 19th century, etc. (cf. Banton, 1977: ch.3; Miles, 1982; 1989). Rather, they retain the discourse as the object of the analysis and not a symptom or indicator of more general theoretical issues. In this respect their very style of approach, despite its shortcomings, does begin to address the question of the adequacy of a critical sociology to account for racialised political discourse.[20]

It could be argued that, whereas existing sociological work attempted to conflate the 'new' racist discourse into received theories of racism and thereby simultaneously reduce and distance the actual discourse; the NR theorists attempted to 'read' a coherence and immanence into such discourse, in its own terms. This 'content/discourse' analysis was then linked to a politically informed diagnoses of the role of such discourse within the current conjuncture; the diagnosis being supported by various evidence sources and at varying degrees of historical depth. Thus it was assumed, by the theorists, that there was a political project involving racism and that this occurrence needed to be addressed. The political focus of this analysis, in itself, marks a particular departure from the theoretical analysis of racism in sociology, as well as suggesting an important theoretical revision of political studies, by challenging the un-theorised account of racism that has formed the substance of much of the account of Powellism, and the 'race politics' of the major parties in the postwar world.[21]

The Scope of the Analysis

The next section will seek to identify and explain the contribution the NR has made to the analysis of postwar racial discourse. The argument will identify the key claims of the theory: (i) that there has been a distinctive shift in the focus and content of racial discourse from the biological to the cultural; (ii) the core of this style of argument is one concerned with the naturalness of cultural hostility; (iii) this illicitly racialised notion of culture has allowed the self-conscious political construction of a new 'organic' theory of the nation by the Conservative 'new right'; (iv) the bridge between the idea of 'race' and nation has been achieved through the widespread acceptance of a new 'political commonsense' able to organise popular experience and understanding of immigration and 'race'; (v) that the 'new racism' has become hegemonic, both within the Tory party itself, and within the wider political culture.[22]

It's Simply 'Human Nature': The 'New' Cultural Racism

The NR does not refer to a unified concept or school of thought. The phrase itself is coined by Barker (1979; 1981) but its usage is common to a number of contributors (CCCS: Race and Politics Group 1982; Duffield 1984; Gordon and Klugg 1986; Seidel 1986a; Gilroy 1987). Again, there is some variation in the kinds of claims and treatment made of the concept in these contributions; however a core theme or idea can be identified:

> [T]he core of the new racism[...]is a theory of human nature. Human nature is such that it is natural to form a bonded community, a nation, aware of its differences from other nations. They are not better or worse. But feelings of antagonism will be aroused if outsiders are admitted (Barker 1981: 21)

> The new racism is essentially a theory of 'human nature' and human 'instinct' and most important among such instincts is the supposed desire of human beings for the company of 'their own kind'. The idea that there is such a human instinct is now widespread on the right (Gordon and Klug 1986: 14).

> The starting point of the new racism is difference not hierarchy. It is held to be human nature to form groups based on similarity which then set themselves apart from other groups perceived as different. The cement which binds a group together is its shared way of life: its culture[...]What people feel about their culture is paramount. If people sense that their way of life is being threatened, since it is so central to their social and individual existence, it will arouse fear and hostility. Immigrants, because they have a different way of life, elicit this response (Duffield 1984: 29).

> Martin Barker has argued that the alleged invasion by foreign culture implies a particular theory of nation and of race. For the New Right, the nation is constituted by homogeneity of culture, and the problem of race lies in the fact of cultural difference. Alien cultures (not inferior, merely different) necessarily undermine social cohesion; this necessity derives from human nature. Such cultures must therefore be eliminated either by assimilation or by removal (Seidel 1986a: 111-2).

> [T]he core of new racist theory is the naturalness of in group preference and outgroup hostility: it is human nature to prefer your own. This invocation of 'human nature' is an idea which was already given scientific legitimacy by the 1960s and 1970s ethologists such as Lorenz and Morris[...]It has more recently been given further academic support in the theoretical developments of sociobiology (Husband 1987: 319-20).

The most extended treatment of the concept comes in the work of Barker (1979; 1981). Some of the themes and ideas in Barker are given different treatments in other accounts, broadly in sympathy with Barker's approach (Duffield 1984; Gordon and Klug 1986; Husband 1987). The most important difference in the use of the concept comes in the work of CCCS: Race and Politics Group (1982: passim), and most significantly in the work of Lawrence (1982) and Gilroy (1987). As for example:

> [R]acist ideologies[...]form the cement of that structural configuration we have referred to as the 'new racism'. [They]are an organic component of attempts to make sense of the present crisis. The fear that society is falling apart at the seams has prompted the elaboration of theories about race which turn on particular notions of culture. The 'alien' cultures of the blacks are seen as either the cause or else the most visible symptom of the destruction of the 'British way of life' (Lawrence 1982: 47).

> The distinctive characteristics of the racism which currently runs through life in Britain[...]which Martin Barker (1981) and others have labelled 'the new racism' will be examined[...]with a view to focusing on the nature of its newness - the job it does in rendering our national crisis intelligible[...]its novelty lies in the capacity to link discourses of patriotism, nationalism, xenophobia, Englishness, Britishness, militarism and gender differences into a complex system which gives 'race' its contemporary meaning. These themes combine to provide a definition of 'race' in terms of culture and identity. What new right philosopher John Casey has called 'The whole life of the people'. 'Race' differences are displayed in culture which is reproduced in educational institutions and, above all, in family life (Gilroy 1987: 43).

Both CCCS: Race and Politics Group (1982) and Barker (1981) characterise the NR project in terms of its political novelty. This superficial resemblance hides more fundamental difference, in particular, the conception of the relationship of a popular working class racism to that of the new Tory populism, and the role of 'race' as an ideological component within Thatcherism and the discourse of the 'new right'. These differences will be explored, especially in terms of how they impact upon the debate about commonsense, between that of Lawrence (1982) and Barker (1981). First, though, we must look at how the general argument for the NR is built up.

Barker's Account

Barker's (1979; 1981) account of the NR has a particular structure of exposition. We can identify this as follows: a new kind of political commonsense has emerged in neo-conservative talk concerning 'immigration/race relations'. This commonsense appears reasonable and restrained in comparison to the language employed by the 'crackpot' Hitlerists of the Far right, National Front, etc. It poses the issue in terms of 'different cultures'/'ways of life' and 'defence of traditions' and 'territory'. Such commonsense reasoning has an inner coherence which guides its usage: the assumption that separation, by dint of culture, conforms to a deep instinct in human nature. This underlying theory is what unifies the seemingly disparate and rhetorical uses of this language in public debate, Parliament and in the columns of the popular press.[23]

Barker characterises this theory as a 'pseudo-biological culturalism' (1981: 23) or as the 'new instinctivism' (1983). Such a theory has been popularised and promoted by the speeches of Enoch Powell and has been further developed within the newly ideological 'right' of the Tory party. It is a theory which links 'race' and nation. This linkage is achieved through the mediation of the commonsense language of cultural separation. In this way the idea of the nation is delivered through an illicit idea of 'race', carried in an account of culture. The popular resonance of this theme, as evidenced by the success of Powell, allowed the emergence of a new 'organic' theory of the nation which was systematically applied in the politics of the 'New Right'. At the centre of this politics was the official (racist) logic of state Immigration policy and the 1981 (actually 1983) Nationality laws (cf. CCCS: Race and Politics Group 1982; Barker, 1983).

Barker's account has been endorsed and elaborated on by other theorists, in broad agreement with it (Lawrence, 1982; Duffield, 1984; Seidel, 1986a; Gordon and Klug, 1986; Gilroy, 1987; Husband, 1987). This agreement has centred on endorsement of the arguments that, the NR: (i) had identified a new theory of 'race' operating in contemporary political discourse; (ii) that Powell and the 'new right' had led a right wing 'back-lash' on the strength of it; (iii) the logic of the theory had passed to the centre of the political consensus, and (iv) created a new popular commonsense which threatened a far more authoritarian solution to Britain's political ills (cf. Barker, 1979; 1981: ch.1; 1983).

The account has also run up against some specific criticisms: (i) that the NR discourse is not a new kind of racism but an articulation of the existing ideologies of racism and nationalism (Miles, 1987: 38); (ii) that the selective and restricted concentration upon Powell and the 'new right' cannot establish generalisations about the extent and character of racism in contemporary Britain (Miles 1987: 36); (iii) or that empirical observation would not support the idea that the NR has become hegemonic, even within the Tory party itself (Rich 1986b: 45-72). (iv) Finally, that the 'new' popular commonsense is either (a) actually new (Lawrence 1982); or (b) particularly popular (Brewer 1983; Miles 1987). Much of these criticisms are fully justified and we will indicate how they can form part of a coherent critique of the theory and its account of Powellism and the impact of 'political racism'. In order to do this we must take the key terms of the argument and analyse the substance of each in turn. Firstly, this must involve the claim for a new theorisation of 'race'.

A New Theorisation of 'Race'?

Put another way, the central claim of the NR thesis is that, since the 1960s, and particularly since 1968 and Powell's speeches, a new language of cultural-nationalism and separatism has become dominant in political Debate concerned with 'Immigration'. This language successfully disavows racist intentions and previous association with the organised racist fringe and yet it is fully racist in its underlying assumptions and grounding concepts. What therefore distinguishes the NR is a new way of speaking and referring to 'race', without the necessity of explicit reference to the concepts and ideas of scientific racism or doctrines of the 'blood', etc.

The NR invokes the idea of 'race' but does so through the use of a completely different conceptual discourse. This discourse involves the frequent use of concepts such as: 'alienness', 'way of life', 'tradition', etc. This is not also to argue that the existing idea of 'race' is not explicitly invoked on some occasions also. Here, however, the concept is either ridiculed or undermined; or it is used as a comparison point to demonstrate the non-racist nature of the discourse politicians now employ to deal with issues of 'Immigration' and 'Race Relations'. Thus one of the NR popularisers, Sir Alfred Sherman, was quite able to offer a definition of racism that left the NR untouched: 'Racialism is the belief that intellectual, cultural and moral qualities are genetically transmitted among the main racial groupings of mankind, that racial groups can be graded according to these qualities as inferior, with the racialists' own group at the apex' (cited in Barker 1981: 3).

In this way the concept of 'race' is placed in parenthesis; its meaning and relevance is disputed or undermined or it is redefined as non-pejorative. Thus the theory of racism has 'evolved' politically. This has been achieved through the development of an everyday, commonsense language, able to discuss the political hot-potato of the 'race' and Immigration issue. This populist language has allowed the New Right to redefine racist reaction to 'black immigration' as essentially grounded in cultural traditions and community. Rather than an expression of irrational hostility racism is an inevitable response to an intolerable situation.

The idea of culture here is one grounded in a historically static and nationally bounded community. It is suggested that such arrangements must inevitably form, that communities, once arisen, will band together and defend their territory and shared identity. Such behaviour is an expression of a common human nature which takes different national and cultural forms. This nature circumscribes the limits of tolerance to alien nationals and provides a warning of the inevitably of hostile response invoked by their presence. Here the postwar migration of 'black' former colonial, New Commonwealth citizens, becomes the invasion of 'foreign cultures' and 'ways of life'.

Therefore, the central questions posed by the NR thesis is: what if racism could express itself in a cultural form? What if cultural antagonism and hostility where the inevitable expression of a divided human nature? Nothing here is essentially 'new', as we have seen. What is important is how this series of questions is seen to arise out of the process of 'mass migration' and the 'indigenous' reaction to this process. The newness of the NR is to describe and account for the racial antagonism and hostility involved in anti-immigrant sentiment, not in terms of the undermined *authoritarian personality* identified in 'prejudice' surveys, but as a legitimate, 'natural' response to a perceived 'threat' of a minority group against a majority group. The 'threat' is that posed to the preservation of the existing culture of the indigenous by the 'alien cultures' of the immigrant populations, settling in towns and cities across Britain. Such a response is legitimated by politicians by demarcating such a response from that of the 'race' extremists. This demarcation exercise allows the legitimation of the response of the audience and the commonsense measures of the polity in dealing with these 'cultural fears' (cf. Barker 1981: ch.2).

The Definition of Racism

Even if we accept the import of the thesis its core ambiguity remains: whether these new cultural arguments represent a new theorisation of 'race' or merely ad hoc political expediency? It remains ambiguous whether 'race' is merely disguised or 're-coded' (through the linguistic technique of 'sanitary-coding'?)[24] or actually thought-through in new conceptual terms? In other words, has there been a fundamental shift in the means of conceptualisation of group difference, specifically a new kind of culturally grounded biological theory (or pseudo-biological theory)? Sometimes Barker suggests the one argument; sometimes the other. For example, in the 1979 essay, the central idea is that the NR theory is the political logic of the 'new inheritors' of biological reductionist arguments.[25]

Certainly, for Barker, the recourse to biology is the distinguishing feature of racist doctrines (cf. Barker 1981: 22, 25-9, 39, 83). This is clearly the import of the following statement: 'Why is it that racists, in search of justificatory arguments, have so often turned to biology? What is it in the nature of certain forms of biological argument that makes them so available to racist[...]positions?' (1981: 7). It is at this very point that we can see a significant internal departure in Barker's account, against that of the received view of the NR position. Barker is actually arguing for a new variety of racist biologism, not just a new way of invoking the idea.[26] This can be seen by the way in which Barker uses the idea of culture; he is not arguing for culture as an illicit slide between 'race' and nation but of the biological underpinning of this idea.[27] For a set of ideas to qualify as a racism they must possess an interior logic of determinism. Thus, we can see that, for Barker, the NR is based on essentially the same biologically reductionist premise as the 'old' racism, and arrives at similar kinds of 'solutions' to the problems it poses in terms of these ideas.

We can clearly see this idea of biological reductionism if we look again at his account of the theory:

> It is a theory that I shall call biological, or better, pseudo-biological culturalism. Nations on this view are not built out of politics and economics, but out of human nature. It is in our biology, our instincts, to defend our way of life, traditions and customs against outsiders - not because they are inferior, but because they are part of different cultures (Barker 1981: 23-4).

Barker evidently believes that a biological imperative, or the logic of it, is operating at the base of this sort of theory. It is the deterministic quality of it that qualifies it as a racist theory. Human nature as a biological imperative that is expressed in a deterministic culture. Not to recognise this is to go against the natural logic of culture. This is consistent with Barker's definition of racism:

> Suppose a theory about human nature puts emphasis on how natural it is to feel hostility towards, or even just essentially different to, members of other populations. To my mind that is racist. Referring barriers between peoples to human nature is racist because of the way it suggests that national separatism is natural and inevitable (Barker 1981: 2).

This definition, one of the few Barker offers, is too vague to allow critical evaluation of what Barker identifies as the central characteristics of racism. Here he seems to be suggesting that racism is any sort of a deterministic theory about human nature. As Miles has pointed out, this hardly enables us to distinguish the NR from reductionist ideas about gender (Miles 1987: 36). However, I think the sense Barker has of this is in terms of the idea of the NR as a theory that is rigorous, like a science; but it is 'in the language' (Barker 1981: 3). For an exposition of this we need look no further than Barker's judgement of Powell's Eastbourne speech:

> Looking back over the three speeches, it is clear to me that this third one is by far and away the most racist. True, it does not use the nastiest examples; its language is relatively restrained. But here, almost fatalistically, a theory is propounded. The consequences of human nature are such that whether he, John Enoch Powell, wants it or not, people are going to resist. It is not that blacks are bad; they are simply different. Therefore their sheer presence in numbers has the same effect as an invasion. Their cultural alienness will bring about the rivers of blood he had talked of those months earlier. It is as if, over the year 1968, Powell had gradually assembled the confidence and the ideas to assert a complete racist programme (Barker 1981: 40).

There are echoes here of Barker's earlier judgement that Powell's Birmingham speech was all 'moral panics and rigged statistics' (1979) with no theory at all, in the idea that Powell gradually arrives at a way of theorising 'immigration' in a new (racist) way. However this assertion is as ambiguous as the other statements we have examined. The idea that racism is a deeply deterministic conception of human nature, based on a pseudo biologic-culturalism, that must inevitably work itself out through collectivities of people, is consistent with the idea of 'race' science, as the same kind of levelling, reductionist conception. Here, the status of language and theories is to reveal the imperatives of nature; nothing can be done to alter this state. Powell's job as a politician has been to point this out and to insist that policy must operate in conformity with this logic if tragedy and 'race war' is not to inevitably occur.

This is the best that we can do with the theory in pushing it to consistency. The deep ambiguity of whether the theorisation is a new form of racism or an attempt to conceal the old one cannot be reconciled. There is not enough evidence to suggest that the theory is a biological reductionism simply because the content cannot provide evidence of this; at the same time the scientific characterisation of the theory is not clearly grounded either. Despite the fact that Barker believes that the recourse to, and emergence of the theory, has parallels with the logic of the emergence of sociobiology, the connection of this theory to politics is not sufficiently established.[28]

The Nation

The other deeply problematic move in the theory is the use of the idea of the nation as a culturally defined entity that is able to operate in a deterministic fashion, as if according to biological imperatives. It is this 'buried logic' that, in rejecting the designation racism as not applicable to the characterisation of cultural belonging, proposes the logic of cultural determinism that creates national-cultural groups or communities. Essentially what is taking place here is that the idea of 'race' is submerged into that of culture; this allows cultures to operate in an exclusionary manner, via the demarcation of cultural boundaries. Such boundaries define the cultural parameters of nations. Nations are the consciousness of such divisions and allow the distinctive expression of cultural traditions and symbols. Such icons/symbols operate to express and signify such divisions. Thus cultural separation is collectively 'lived'. It is through the culture, the 'way of life' of a people that the existence of the nation as an expression of culture is understood. Nations then are constructed out of cultures and traditions; and the distinctiveness of each is expressed in the unique 'way of life' expressed through these institutions and practices: 'At the heart of [the]"new racism" is the notion of culture and tradition. A community is its culture, its way of life and its traditions. To break these is to shatter the community' (Barker and Beezer 1983: 125).

The significance of this theory of the 'nation' is that it is asserted in the context of, and in response to, 'mass Commonwealth immigration'. The idea of the nation circumscribed by culture, and understood through a 'way of life' of its people, is realised at the point when it is most under threat. The threat is one posed by the 'cultural invasion' and 'swamping' of too large numbers of people with 'alien cultures' and 'ways of life': 'People are really rather afraid that this country might be rather swamped by people with a different culture and[...]if there is any fear that it might be swamped people are going to react and be rather hostile to those coming in' (Margaret Thatcher, *The Times*, 1.2.1978; cited in Barker 1981: 22). Here the traditional concerns of the nation are linked to the need to assert identity, through collective instinct, against cultural swamping or invasion. Here groups, forming national units, are defined by cultural characteristics that organise and make possible a 'way of life'. It is in reference to this and in protection of this that 'cultural hostility' will occur. The hostility arises because of the sense of the vulnerability of 'cultural identity' to adulteration or 'swamping'.[29] Mass immigration poses the most important test upon the community because it demands the assertion of the nation and 'way of life' against attack. If the nation is not affirmed in opposition to immigration it is likely to be lost. Here the government is given the responsibility to preserve the conditions of the national and cultural community. Liberal-minded acquiescence to mass immigration is seen as an abnegation of this role which threatens the very existence of the nation. As Barker interprets it 'a nation which, through its government, does not defend its way of life, dooms itself to instability, decay and decomposition' (Barker 1981: 74).

It follows from such ideas that the sense of culture, national consciousness and the 'instinct to defend', are the criteria by which a nation is deemed authentic or not: a national community as opposed to a mere geographical location. Defending the culture is also reaffirming allegiance to the nation. The instinct to defend proves the existence of the nation as a homogenous 'we'. This is asserted most chillingly by Powell: 'An instinct to preserve an identity and defend a territory is one of the deepest and strongest implanted in mankind. I happen to believe that the instinct is good, and that its beneficial effects are not exhausted' (Powell, BBC, 9 June 1969; cited in Barker 1981: 22).

Without the cultural values affirmed in anti-immigrant feeling, the nation would not exist as a focus or suppository of group emotions. Thus the politics of the nation require a popular activism: the nation must be actively realised through group patriotism and loyalty. Such emotions, traditions and sentiments are 'natural' and find their expression in the 'nation'; thwarted they can become explosive. Here is Sherman again: 'National consciousness, like any other major human drive - all of which are bound up with instinct for self-preservation - is a major constructive force provided legitimate channels; thwarted and frustrated, it becomes explosive' (cited in Barker 1981: 23).

It is thus human nature to form bonded units and to want to preserve the 'way of life' of such distinct units. Government and legislation should proceed from this fact, not against it. Once again the linking elements in this part of the theory point towards a central dilemma: to what extent is this the exposition of a racist theory and not a variety of political expediency? The point of weakness must surely be the idea that this process of cultural formation should be so weak and vulnerable to dissolution? What is this but the classical racist notion of adulteration of the aristocratic blood by barbarian contamination of lesser breeds? If we set this against the deeply problematic account of 'the nation' as a racist ideology we are at the point of terminal confusion as to what we are referring to.

Racism or Nationalism?

Right-wing fantasies of the homogenous nation and unitary national consciousness are one thing, but the justification of racism in terms of appeals to 'cultural' arguments raises the question of the extent to which the concepts of racism and nationalism have been conflated or confused by the NR theorists? Has the concept of nationalism become re-defined, in terms of contemporary political uses, as racism? Or is it possible that the NR represents an ideological articulation of the one through the other? (cf. Nairn 1970; Miles 1987: 38).

While Barker explicitly identifies the new Conservative political project as one of re-theorising the nation, he does this without any attempt to refer to the debate about nationalism as an ideology (cf. Miles 1987: 25). In this respect the criteria he selects as distinctive of the NR, and the function such discourse serves in political discourse, all point to the designation of the discourse as one of nationalism. With no explicit discussion of the ideology of nationalism Barker does not clearly distinguish what it is about the function or content of the NR which can distinguish it from a doctrine of nationalism. Consider for example the following distinction offered by Smith:

> The supreme goal for a nationalist is 'national identity' or 'nationhood', a visionary state of authentic self-expression and fraternity in which an historic community realises its unique qualities. The search for nationhood is a long and arduous struggle for self-regeneration. It requires both cohesion and autonomy: the growth of deep bonds of emotional solidarity, and the exercise of the citizens rights of sovereign participation in decision- making. Though mankind, for the nationalist, is 'naturally' divided into unique culture-communities or nations, yet human beings must continually strive to preserve, deepen and fully understand their world of nations. They must jealously guard their sovereign independence, strike deep roots in their native soil, and immerse themselves and their personal identities in that of their own historic community (Smith 1979: 87).

Smith's account of nationalism as an ideology provides us with the idea of the cultural community as an inclusionary collective, within which the individual is invited to participate, and immerse her identity with that of the cultural and historical whole. Racism, by contrast, is an exclusionary doctrine of separation and biological destiny:

> [R]acism may be defined as a doctrine that divides the world into racial castes locked in a perpetual struggle for domination, in which the allegedly

physically superior are destined to rule the inferior and form a racial elite. A racial caste, in turn, can be defined as any social group that is held to possess unique hereditary physical traits which allegedly determine all the mental attributes of the group (Smith, 1979: 87-8).

Despite the fact that these ideal-typical accounts of the doctrines of racism and nationalism are clearly differentiated, as Smith points out, 'the fact remains that the two ideologies have been, and still are, frequently confused or associated' (1979: 88). There are broadly two reasons for this, which are pertinent to the discussion of Barker's account of the NR. Firstly, the ideologies of nationalism and racism arose within half a century of each other in western and central Europe, and both referred to the same social grouping: the national community. But the most likely source of the confusion between the ideologies is the way in which they both refer back to the same basic social unit: the ethnic group or 'ethnie' (cf. Smith 1988; 1989).[30] It is this social collectivity, which is defined culturally or through religious sentiments, not primarily biology. Thus, it is the cultural locus of the 'ethnie' which allows the racialisation of the nation and certainly provides the bridging concept for the theories of the NR.

Consequently, the conceptual effect of much of the NR thesis is a terminological confusion surrounding the concepts of 'race' and 'nation' and their respective ideologies (cf. Miles 1987: 24-43). It is the nation that the new 'instinctivism' wants to get back to, not 'race'; so why call the theory the *new racism* rather than the *new nationalism*?

Political Instinctivism?

The third important element in Barker's account that requires examination is the claim that the 'turn to race and immigration' marks a return to an avowal of a basic ideology within British conservatism (cf. 1981: ch 3, passim). Barker claims that the return to ideology marks the demise of a species of postwar Toryism characterised by its pragmatism and a denial of the nation as anything but an expanding 'economic resource cake' (Barker 1981: 35-6) i.e. the period of Macmillan's leadership characterised, by Barker, as Butskellism (p.36).

Quite another problem with this sort of claim, as Barker recognises, is that most commentators characterise the Tories as supremely pragmatic in approach and avowedly non-ideological in politics (cf. Eccleshell 1990). As Eccleshell has argued this distinction should not be confused with the assertion that Conservatism is not an ideology.[31] Methodologically it is more helpful to seek to identify how the elements of political pragmatism and ideology feature and combine at different point and periods of Toryism. Here Gamble's (1974) account of the politics of 'power' and the politics of 'support' is very astute in identifying the aim of politics, for Toryism, of securing and wielding state power. This is the source of Tory pragmatism (Gamble 1974: ch.1); what Butler has dubbed the 'art of the possible' (Butler 1971). The place of ideology in this scenario is in the need to cohere a mass basis of support for the Tory elite upon which to rule. The 'grass roots' is the ideological base that allows the promotion of the elite (Gamble 1974).

Barker does recognise the logic of this dilemma of practical politics and ideology in the case of the 'boat people', where Mrs. Thatcher is forced to deny the very logic that formed her 'culture swamping' arguments (Barker 1981: 26-9). In other words, ideology had to be sacrificed to the practicalities of state management. However Barker's account of the relationship between politics and ideology reveals a view of politics as driven by ideologies, with 'economics' as a decisively interrupting logic:

> In power, any Government faces pressures other than those associated with its own public image, membership retention and vote managing. There are pragmatic decisions to be taken in the face of economic requirements, international pressures and so on. Famous, now, as expressions in Britain of the diverting of ideology by real pressures, are the nationalisation of Rolls-Royce and the apparent volt-face on Rhodesia in 1979 (Barker 1981: 26-7).

Besides being a misunderstanding of the normal operation of state power in the global capitalist economy,[32] such a view suggests that (i) governments are primarily ideology driven, despite the fact that extraneous elements intrude and (ii) the respective ideologies of Toryism and Labourism are thus ideologically incompatible with their insertion within such an external system.[33]

Notwithstanding the point about whether politics is driven by ideology or capitalist rationality, Barker wants to argue that the impact of the New Right project is in how it is able to deliver a basic ideology to lead the Conservative party again. It is a species of political instinctivism which has its roots in the philosophy of David Hume. Hume, Barker claims, developed a philosophical system of instinctivism as the natural basis of human nature. Not surprisingly this intellectual arrival at the idea of non-intellect is central to Tory ideology. The link Barker is able to make here is with the apparently pragmatic, commonsense treatment of 'race' of the new right populists. As we have seen, such a language is said to be informed by a coherent theory that forms the basis of organic Toryism. It is this new instinctivist theorisation of the nation which constituted the 'real'

Thatcherite project. What the 'new right' 'hards' were about was getting back to, or seeking to develop, the 'instincts' of the people. The paradox of the approach is that this politics has been intellectually arrived at: people *ought* to trust their instincts. Thus the job of politics is to re-create the conditions for the re-emergence of the nationalist instinct, and henceforth politics should be fashioned on this basis (Barker 1981: ch.3).

Barker employs the rhetoric of Whitelaw, in the 1976 Immigration Debate, to suggest how the Tories had developed an account of the 'racial fears' of the British electorate as expressive of a genuine instinct for preservation of the national community. Hence, on this theoretical basis, politicians can view ordinary peoples' genuine fears as reflective of a real threat:

> Not only were the people with the fears, ordinary genuine people, but also they were genuinely afraid; and no politician in his right mind would deny it[...]The argument begins with the apparently unchallengeable statement that these people are ordinary normal citizens; before you can take a breath it adds that the feelings they express are real, powerful sentiments, not to be ignored; and then, as though no change has been made in the argument, it is stated that the object of the fears is real (Barker 1981: 14-5).

What Barker is suggesting here is that such an argument is a syllogism; we have arrived at conclusions which do not logically follow. But the momentum to go to this interpretation is within the structure of the argument. The Tory politicians can slide to the idea that black migrants do represent a threat because the sentiments affirming this interpretation are genuine. Another way to say this is to say the truth 'effect' is in the statement. For Barker such sophistry reflects, at a deeper level, an ideological commitment. Genuine feelings express a truth because they reflect a 'frontbench' acceptance of the idea that cultural hostility is an inevitable acceptance of the 'nature of human nature', consistent with Tory principles. The difference is that the 'new right' sought a consistent acknowledgement of a basic Tory ideology of 'instincts' on which the life of the nation is premised. Political intervention ought then to follow from this basis and ultimately the whole political culture should be shaped in conformity with this view (1981: 50-2).

However, in terms of the example Barker employs concerning the political staging of a 'whole racist programme' in terms of the new (re-discovered) language of instincts, the argument is disappointingly circular. It depends upon accepting that the meaning of 'genuine' carries with it the very theory it is supposed to be creating.[34] This further conceptual ambiguity leads us, finally, to a discussion of the carrier or ideological form of the language of the NR: the politically fashioned 'commonsense' that allows Whitelaw, Powell and Bell to share a common view. An extended discussion of this concept is warranted by its centrality to the account presented by both Barker and CCCS: Race and Politics Group (1982).

Commonsense Racism?

> *The original concept of common sense was based on the belief that there exists an understanding of the world which is 'common' in the sense of natural to everybody. It was part of the belief in Universal Reason, the ideology of a class that was contesting the 'irrational' institutions of Church and King. It was also part and parcel of eighteenth-century individualism and of the belief in a 'natural man' who, if left to himself and uncorrupted by existing social forms, would automatically develop the right ideas about the world* (Nowell-Smith 1977).

> *[T]here has been a conscious bid by the Tories, led from their Right, since 1968, for a new theorisation of race. It is powerful in that it avoids the older definitions of race that were so evidently tainted with Hitlerism. We must see the new theory of race, not as an appeal to commonsense, but as a struggle to create a new commonsense* (Barker 1981).

> *[S]tate racism has been sanctioned and legitimated at the political and ideological levels by the growth of new and virulent strains of racist ideologies that are both coherent and popular. Popular, because they intersect with and re-organise the common-sense racism of the white working and other classes* (Lawrence 1981: 4).

The argument that the 'new racism' forms a new form of commonsense is central to both CCCS: Race and Politics Group (1982) and Barker. Barker argues that the NR represents the consciously organised attempt, on the right of the Conservatives, to construct a new 'philosophy and politics of commonsense' (Barker 1981: 23). The relationship between these two elements is critical in understanding how the NR works in practice. Barker claims the articulation of the theory with commonsense in at least three instances: at the level of prejudice; at the level of political discourse; and in the theoretical science of ethology and sociobiology.[35]

The job this commonsense has increasingly been called upon to do is to present popular hostility to (black) immigration as a natural and inevitable response, rooted in our 'essential natures'. This view is exemplified most infamously in the formulation of 'culture swamping' by Mrs Thatcher. As we have seen, for the Tory politicians, 'fears' of being swamped by alien cultures are genuine, not because they are true or false, but because they arise out of a life-situation; they are a felt, an instinctive, gut response to the situation. What the Tories have done, argues Barker, is to provide support for this ordinary-everyday prejudice, at the political level via a 'theory that justifies racism' (1981: 22). This is the politics of the 'gut' response, of common feeling: hence 'common-sense'. And '[t]he politics of it are made possible by the philosophy of it' (p.23).

However, Barker argues, such public, political support for what the Liberals would designate as 'colour prejudice' could not hold water without recourse to a theory to which it refers: 'If it were not for the presence of a theory behind the "racist common-sense", the obvious lacunae and untested assumptions of its approach would not so easily escape scrutiny' (Barker 1979: 3). This is too brief a comment to be clear at a critical point in the argument. Barker suggests that it is the presence of a fuller theory behind the commonsense talk which guards against or prevents criticism. But the point is not made clearly. He is perhaps suggesting that it is the existence of a theory behind the politics of commonsense racism which allows its production, allows speakers to present apparently unconnected fragments, secure in the knowledge that the full theory from which it is derived, is hidden. In other words, without the theory such commonsense racism would be open to the charge of being precisely that. But the question is now begged of how we can ascertain the existence of this underlying theory? Barker's method follows from his remarks about the nature of the way in which the theory of the NR is held by its speakers. His argument is that an emergent 'racist world view' is carried in particular kinds of language use. What is remarkable about this is that the view of 'racism' that the use of language creates is never fully visible. It can only be recognised as a full theorisation of racism when the fragments are brought together:

> [A] theory about race can be concealed inside apparently innocent language. Its concealment enables it to provide form and structure to people's experiences and reactions, without displaying itself as a whole theory with big and dangerous implications. Only under certain conditions does it display itself as a fully theorized view of human nature. It is only by careful investigation, therefore, using many quotations, that the theory in the language can be exposed. Individual statements may otherwise only appear metaphorical (Barker 1981: 3).

As we have already suggested, what remains the enigma of the NR theory is whether we view the 'presence in 'ordinary language' usage 'of a racist world view' (Barker 1979: 4) as the intentional political construct of the 'old' racists, wishing to wash the discourse of 'race' clean of nazism, in order to make it palatable to a British audience; or as a development, within ideology, of a *new racism* particular to the conjuncture in which it arises, and which constitutes a development within the logic and internality of the discourse of 'race' itself ?

Not surprisingly, Barker wants to have his (theoretical) cake and eat it too! Certainly the account provided of Powell (Barker 1979; 1981: 37-41) suggests that a conscious effort was made to get around the problem of 'race' in British politics. This is what Powellism was all about! In the early account, Barker suggests, Powell could not get free of the language of the old racism (Barker 1979: 1). In fact, records Barker, the anti-immigration groups which preceded the advent of Powellism, went out of their way to avoid connections with the 'race' theories of the Hitlerists: 'It was for this reason that there was a return to metaphors. There was obsessive discussion, in semi-moral terms, of disease: leprosy, T.B., syphilis and other more exotic illnesses were predicted, discovered and agitated over. The emphasis on metaphors of pollution is to be found in Powell's early racist speeches' (Barker 1979: 1). In fact, argues Barker, Powell's 'rivers of blood' speech is remarkable because, 'there is a total absence of any theory of race. It is all and only rigged statistic, cries of pollution, and moral panics' (p.2). Citing this quotation is perhaps unfair because Barker significantly revised this opinion in the book, *The New Racism* (1981). I have referred to it, not to be unkind, but to point to the way in which Barker sees commonsense as a calm, dispassionate language that can carry a racist theory. This is the insight derived from the 1976 Immigration Debate where, amidst this calm dispassionate language, a 'whole racist programme was laid out' (Barker 1981: 13).

At one point in the earlier piece, Barker suggests that the language of racism has evolved. There are two pressures for this evolution. The first is the pressure exerted by the anti-immigration racists. The second is the dynamic towards a racist theory that has come out of the politically motivated attempt to use ordinary language to speak about 'race'. Here we have a view of racism as something in the logic and conceptualising structure of language, or rather theories and ideas, themselves. In other words the racism is not in the intentions of racists who use the language to fit their purposes. Racist language is not a post hoc justification for racist current practice or rhetoric that barely conceals intentions; it is the motive force that can set into play consequences that follow from the logic of the ideas. It is the persuasion exerted by the internal coherence of the ideas. This is a view of racism that allows it to exist 'within apparently innocent language'. Such a theory allows the Tories 'a theoretical reason for supporting prejudice' (Barker 1981: 23).

Thus, to summarise, Barker argues that it would not be possible to argue this case without a theory to organise it. In other words, when Tory backbenchers and the tabloid press use this commonsense, they are applying the theory. The logic of the NR does not come from the natural sounding way it is expressed but in terms of its consistency to an underlying theory. This theory is a new form of commonsense, grounded in a new theory of 'race'. Hence the commonsense of Conservative talk is both an expression of this theory and a way of concealing and protecting themselves from accusations of racism. The motive force for the development of the theory is, as we have already argued, the popular appeal of anti-immigration and, in particular, a way of speaking of it that did not immediately involve the 'old' racism of hierarchy and superiority.

As we have seen, the precursor and point of transition is Powellism (Barker 1979: 1; 1981: 37-42). What Powell has achieved is a way of speaking of 'race' which allows it a popular legitimacy. Such talk is able to legitimate popular prejudice and transform it into a means of political support. The problem of the 'old' racism was that it was tainted with Hitlerism and so, within the terms of British political culture, deeply unpopular. The new theory speaks instead of cultures, but also it makes a virtue of the denial of categorisation in terms of old style racism, in presenting such arguments.

The new Toryism has legitimated prejudice by transforming it into the language of commonsense. With this language the New Right are able to talk about popular racism as derived from 'genuine' (i.e., deeply felt) fears. It is the job of a Conservative politics to speak to and to reflect the commonsense of the people. This allows Barker to argue: 'everyday language now embodies a racist "common-sense", this has come from classic Tory assumptions about society, and a whole racist theory is waiting in the wings to give organised form to that "common-sense" '(1979: 3).

What is missing here is the form and character of the everyday language before such processes. What of the 'fears' themselves? Are they already racist?[36] Or are they commonsense? In the 1981 NR book, Barker declares: 'It would be senseless to deny that there are real problems and tensions surrounding immigration; but in themselves these do not add up to a theory, or a conceptualisation of race. People's experience is particular, and close to their lives' (Barker, 1981: 25). Here the argument is clearly indicating that prejudice pre-exists its' enlistment within new Toryism. A theory of 'race' must be introduced into it for it to be theorised. Such a theory cannot replace 'ordinary language' with a language of racism, rather it must systematise that language usage to make it consistent with an undisclosed theory of 'race'. This is where the new Tory commonsense connects up with the traditional role of commonsense in such politics. Thus, '[t]he Right[...]with its roots in everyday thinking, very often is only making better sense of what appears as common-sense truth, held in a disorganised way' (Barker 1979: 3). However, it is specifically the job of politics to do this work:

> [I]t is important to be clear that there was a struggle to create this new theory[....]After Powell's 1968 speeches, which themselves constituted a first major move in this process, there was an increasingly conscious bid to organise people's experiences and prejudices. Without a doubt, the newspapers - and certain ones in particular - played a very large role in this process[...to] organize people's experiences of immigration, to provide a set of focusing concepts around which reactions would be more than individual prejudice (Barker 1981: 25).

Thus, the new Tory racism was a political commonsense which imbued the everyday language of prejudice, directed at 'black immigration', with a racist commonsense. Once such prejudice had been made into a commonsense the Tories could legitimately claim, consistent with their traditional approach, that it was a 'genuine' feeling that they must acknowledge; and in one sense nothing here departs from traditional Tory paternalism. It is a given of Toryism that human nature cannot be changed. However, it is quite another to organise politics in accordance with that nature, such that it cannot go against the *limits* of that nature. The reason why the politics of commonsense can make sense, argues Barker, is because it is supported by a coherent, underlying theory. What that theory was doing increasingly was to provide an organised, a systematic form for that 'racist common sense'; this organised theory is the NR. As we have seen, for Barker to be able to claim this underlying consistency requires him to challenge the dominant conception of Toryism as non-ideological, pragmatic statesmanship.

Despite these arguments, the use of evidence of speeches and debate, as well as a suggestion of the role of the press in its construction, the process of the articulation of the experience and prejudice of people into a politically constructed commonsense racism is unclear. It is not clear because the concept of commonsense employed by Barker remains itself un-theorised. In the preface to the original text Barker quotes Gramsci: 'Common-sense is the practical ideology of the ruling class'. The usage of commonsense in the argument of the NR is consistent with that claim, but not with the Gramscian theory that underpins it. This is because, Barker theorises commonsense as something existing at the level of politics. It is the commonsense discourse of the Tory politicians and hapless Liberals, such as Roy Jenkins, who are carried along into accepting the emergent world view of the NR (Barker 1981: 19).

This treatment is not adequate for what it wants to claim. Since the 'new' commonsense is worked-up politically, the process of its construction requires identifying at least three distinct phases or moments: (i) the existence of prejudice as a form of commonsense; (ii) the organisation of that commonsense by politics; (iii) the existence of an 'emergent theory' that provides a framework for such commonsense. Barker is unable to achieve this synthesis because he concentrates exclusively on the question of (iii); minimally on the process of (ii) and (i) hardly at all. One possible explanation for this lop sided treatment is that Barker is unhappy with acknowledging the idea of racism as an entity outside of its political articulation.[37]

A possible answer to this problem of conceptualisation is provided by Lawrence (1982: 47-94). Lawrence's argument is not that the NR has constructed a new commonsense, but rather that commonsense racist images form the core of the new, cultural racism. This distinction may appear to be a fine one but is in fact grounded in a different approach to the treatment of the concept of commonsense. For Lawrence, the NR describes those arguments that are able to articulate commonsense racist images to the 'crisis'. What Lawrence means by this phrase is the Gramscian idea of a challenge to the moral and cultural leadership of the elite, possible at a moment of crisis.[38] While such ideological-articulation is historically specific and modern, the ideas and images that compose such commonsense racism precede their articulation. Or to put it more bluntly, the more organised ideologies intersect with commonsense so effectively because that commonsense is itself already racist.

This argument can be seen as the logical outcome of Lawrence's discussion of the concept of commonsense and the idea of commonsense racism. Unlike Barker, Lawrence specifically grounds his discussion of commonsense in the theorisation of Gramsci, as developed by Hall et all (1978: 154). As we have seen, Barker does not define commonsense at all. Neither does he recognise the idea of racist commonsense, outside of the political arena. For Lawrence, pace Gramsci, commonsense is a 'composite' knowledge, containing cultural deposits from the past as well as prejudices and, suggestions of a future order. In essence it is a 'contradictory' source of knowledge about social relations: 'The contradictory nature of common-sense means that it should not be thought of as constituting a unified body of knowledge. It does not have a theory underlying or "hidden beneath" it, but is perhaps best seen as a "storehouse of knowledge" which has been gathered together, historically' (Lawrence 1982: 49; citing Hall et al 1978: 154).

This argument is apparently a specific rebuttal of Barker and the assertion that the NR arguments form a political commonsense, because they are supported by a hidden theory or emergent 'world view' (Lawrence 1982: 89). This criticism is misdirected, simply because Barker is not talking about popular commonsense at all. However this distinction does not impede Lawrence's central argument: '[C]ommon sense embodies the practical experience and solutions to the everyday problems encountered by the popular masses throughout their history, "it is also shot through with elements and beliefs derived from earlier or more developed ideologies which have sedimented into it" (Lawrence 1982: 49; citing Hall et al 1978: 154).

This theorisation of commonsense allows Lawrence to argue that the racist commonsense elaborated by the radical right owes its popular resonance, as a set of themes, to earlier developed ideologies of 'blackness' which structures the history of the emergence of capitalism and the 'peculiarities' of English imperial dominance as well as, in particular, the 'subaltern' experience of the working class (1982: 56-80). The racist images and ideas which construct the 'blacks' are images which are drawn upon and re-work themes that go back beyond English imperialism and capitalism itself. In fact, Lawrence argues, an adequate account ought to be able to: 'trace these ideas back to their historical "roots" and then to reconstruct the subsequent histories of their gradual elaboration[...]into the anti-black racist ideologies we are familiar with today' (Lawrence 1982: 58). Such an archaeology is not feasible, however, a 'historical tracing' of 'the gradual sedimentation of these ideas into common-sense thinking' is (p.58).[39]

We are now in a position to appreciate precisely how the apparently fine distinction, in the way in which Barker and Lawrence present the NR, actually turns on a significantly differentiated view of its relationship to commonsense: 'We would argue that it is precisely because racist ideologies have been elaborated from "common-sense" assumptions, which are already "taken for granted", that they gain popular support and acceptance' (Lawrence 1982: 89). And even more explicitly:

> Our concern to note what is specific about racism in the present[...]does not mean that we consider Britain's imperial past to be irrelevant. On the contrary[...]it provides important clues as to how racist ideologies have come to be such a tenacious feature of the commonsense thinking of the white working (and other) class(es) (Lawrence 1982: 48).

However, on top of this basis Lawrence adds in another tier:

> The past is alive, even if transformed, in the present[...]In our view the more developed racist ideologies are popular precisely because they succeed in reorganising the commonsense racist ideologies of the white working class, around the themes of "the British nation", "the British people" and "British

culture" - themes which explicitly exclude black people. Certainly, this has had the effect of strengthening the mechanisms whereby the working class is reproduced as a racially structured and divided working class (Lawrence 1982: 48).

Here it is proposed that it is on the back of an historically accumulated racist-commonsense that the NR is articulated. Commonsense racism is the necessary basis of this process in providing the materials that can be articulated by Powell, Sherman and co. Thus, at the centre of the account of the NR thesis by Barker (1981) and Lawrence and the CCCS: Race and Politics Group (1982) is a fundamental disagreement about how and why the NR is successful. As we have seen, the distinction turns upon the differing ways in which the respective theorists employ the concept of commonsense. For Barker, the success of the NR is demonstrated by the fact that it has, concealed in official, ordinary language, lodged itself at the heart of the official view. For the CCCS collective, the success of the NR is measured by the extent to which it has coincided with, and articulated, existing commonsense racism in the interests of the dominant 'bloc'. We now need to ask whether these differences are carried over into the treatment of Powell?

The Treatment of Powell

As we have seen, Barker argues that it is Powell's original reformulation of 'race', developed in his 1968 speeches, which offers the basis for an entire rethink of the Conservatism developed in the postwar period by the Macmillanites (Barker 1981: 37-8). It is the return to ideology, signalled by Powell's treatment of 'race', which offers the radical right a model of populist politics, able to secure majority support. Thus Powell is the essential, mediating link to the eventual emergence, with the election of Mrs. Thatcher to the leadership of the party, of an organised and ideologically coherent 'new' Right

The CCCS: Race and Politics Group also acknowledge the key significance of Powellism in providing the essential ingredients of a new ideology of 'race'. Similarly they also endorse the idea of Powellism as a key mediation or 'nodal' point that secures the entry of the NR. However, for them, the old style Powellism has been superseded by new cultural arguments that develop the logic of Powell's claims to the changing terrain of the current ideological-political landscape. It is no longer a case of 'repatriation' but of 'managing the underclass' that is here:

For over a decade now, race has been situated primarily through the discourse of Powellism, as a specific social problem which has been imposed from *outside*. As the bastard children of Empire set up 'camps' in the heartland of the mother country, a degree of *internalization* has been forced on the reluctant Briton. The blacks are now a home-grown problem. They are in Britain but not of Britain (CCCS: Race and Politics Group 1982: 30; emphasis in original).

In the context of mass unemployment, deindustrialization, and major outbreaks of social violence, old-style 'Powellism' was not an adequate mode through which the crisis could be rendered intelligible. The late seventies saw a transformation of racist ideology which took account of these new realities, and provided a more adequate though nonetheless racist interpretation of what was happening. Those re-workings have taken place along two main lines[...]First, there has been a consistent attempt to pin down the dangers posed by specific groups of the black population: the illegals, the young, the militants, the unemployed, and even the white traitors who identify with an 'alien culture'[...]Second, a reworking of the concepts of 'nation' and 'citizen' has taken place which aims to deny even the possibility that black people can share the native population's attachment to the national culture - God, Queen and country. This presents the common-sense logic of repatriation or 're-emigration' (CCCS 1982: 29).

The first point has to be that both Powellism and the concept of the NR are not given as much prominence in the Race and Politics Group as they are in Barker. For them, the concept of Powellism is important in so much as it has (i) provided the leading ideology of 'the blacks', as the 'enemy within', and this is important because: (ii) this usage articulates with the dominant social representations of the 'organic crisis of British capitalism', as a social order under threat from 'within'. (iii) The NR of the late seventies, and early eighties, is a product of these elements: a view of the social and political crisis of authority and social order, thematized through the ideologies of 'race'. As we can see, such a theory is not one concerned with Conservative ideology or the Conservative party specifically, but with a more general perspective of how 'race' has become, in both commonsense and in official thinking, the leading theme of the 'crisis' (Lawrence 1982: 27-35).

A point of intersection in both, quite distinct, accounts is how Barker and the Race and Politics Group both view Powell as a transitional figure in the establishment of the discourse of the NR. They both acknowledge the significant contribution he makes to the development of the ideology of the NR. However, while Barker attributes the originality of the theory to Powell, for the Race and

Politics Group, Powell is a populariser of the idea of the blacks as the 'enemy within'. This is simply because the idea of the blacks as a threat, and as 'enemies' within the heartland of Britain, is already potentially present in the historical commonsense of the 'working (and other) classes'. In this respect, what the discourse of the NR achieves is a successful articulation of these cultural deposits of imperialism, re-articulated to the current concerns of the state and social authority in contemporary British capitalism. In this sense, the NR is not 'new': it is re-worked theory. It has provided the means, on the ideological level, for the *Empire to Strike Back*, i.e., the language of empire racism has been ideologically reworked (cf. Hall 1982).

In conclusion, CCCS: Race and Politics Group (1982) are less concerned with analysing the formation of the NR, via Powellism, than identifying how: (i) the current conjuncture i.e., late 70s Britain and the perception of crisis among the higher echelons of the state, and; (ii) an idea of 'alien cultures', has provided the ideological articulation necessary to secure the popular mandate for the latest phase in the state regulation of Britain's black population. Within the book, *The Empire Strikes Back* (1982), various essays explore aspects of the situation of 'black' people as 'subjects' and 'objects' of the 'new racist cultural politics' and how the logic of such culturalist arguments leads to the political solution of 'repatriation' or 're-immigration'. Given this level of acceptance of the culturalist argument; at the level of the state, and in political and academic discourse, and within the organised working class and sections of the left, the authors conclude that autonomous black struggle is the only viable political solution to the politics of popular racism in Britain (CCCS: Race and Politics Group 1982: ch.1, 8).

Conclusion

How does the NR thesis relate to our study ? It is related in three specific ways: (i) it recognises the role of discourse in the formation of a 'race politics' in Britain, and the need to study the formation and detail of such discourses; (ii) it identifies the key role of Powellism in the construction of the NR and as an ever-present factor in the 'race debate'; (iii) finally, in offering the idea of commonsense as mediating link between audience and discourse (and thus providing the essential basis for the articulation of contemporary 'racist ideologies') it is able to go beyond the reductionist models of prejudice central to the received view of Powellism. These positive features must inevitably be balanced by negative features. The recognition of discourse must be tempered by the criticism that the terms of reference of the theorists is quite narrow; centred upon selected rightist press luminaries, commentators and politicians. The evidence gathered from such a narrow methodological source cannot be over-generalised. This criticism must extend, in the case of CCCS: Race and Politics Group (1982), to the assertion that the image of 'race' is the central articulating element in social representations of the 'crisis'. Such a view is derived from limited evidence, almost exclusively concentrated in a narrow range of right wing press articles. There is a tendency, among both writers, to assume a hegemony of the NR based on these narrow sources.

The NR writers are to be commended for raising the vitally important issue of the public language of racism, and the conceptual forms in which it appears, as well as the question of the postwar transformation of racist discourses. However, their dramatic claim that Powellism and the NR arise, disjunctively in 1968, and begin a deep transformation in the language of racial politics and the deeper racialisation of the state, should be treated with a great deal of scepticism. Firstly, because it exaggerates the impact of Powellism, as well as the transition between one sort of racial signifying system and another. As we shall argue in chapter 6, Enoch Powell's racism is almost entirely borrowed. He simply does not introduce new terms of conceptualisation of racism. On the contrary, it can be shown that his language and politics have a good deal of continuity with previous pre-Powell language strategies.

Accordingly, the next chapters, 3 and 4, set about examining the idea of 1968 as a watershed or moment of emergence of cultural racism. chapter 3 looks at the language and politics of the 1961 Immigration Control Debate, and the debates preceding it, from 1957 onwards, in order to argue that this period is more important in defining the ideological significance of postwar black migration to Britain, not least because it results in *real* legislative effects.

Chapter 4, by contrast, looks at the period after 1968, deliberately in order to examine and contest the empirical basis of NR claims concerning the discourse and conceptual content of debates. It does so in order to show that they are often misleading, and quite selective, in their theorisation and methodological analysis of the handful of key debates which are offered as support for their case. Such analysis will reveal the narrow focus and selection of debate content that underpins the argument of the NR thesis. It is not simply that a linguistic and interpretative theory must examine the non-linguistic context of the production of political discourses, but rather that claims for language transformations should pay attention to the institutional and historical framing of discourses, as well as the way in which language transformations reflect and constitute these structures or regularities.

We must conclude that Barker and the Race and Politics Group have sought textual and historical support for the apparent novelty of the *erased political language of 'race'*, apparent in the late 1970s. This has led them *a priori* to a model of language transformation, conceived as *rapid moments of change that are a function of political demands and projects*. While it is important to afford the political due weight, it is important also to seek controls for statements across historical periods, by examining, for example, the alternative hypothesis: *that the postwar periodization of the formation of post-'race' discourse has a high degree of thematic consistency, including that of Powellism*.

Finally, as a postscript, the conceptual distinction identified by the NR thesis, between a new cultural and old biological racism, has found echoes within more recent analysis concerned to explain the emergence and conceptual characteristics of new forms of (so called) Euro-racism. For example, Taguieff (1987) has identified a conceptual distinction between types of racist discourse: a classical *inegalitarian* and a new, *differentialist* kind (cf. Wievorka 1994: 182; Miles 1994: 199). However, I would concur with Wievorka, who agues that both types of racism are to be found *within* historical expressions of racism; in other words *the new differentialist racism is not new*. Wievorka goes on to show how new differentialist claims for absolute cultural difference disguise a reference to biological/genetic logics which link such discourses to the idea of 'race'. I would go further and argue that expressions of the 'new'/neo racism are only able to create an idea in the minds of their interlocutors if they are able to invoke this dimension. I believe that Barker, despite his confusing treatment of the idea of the nation as pseudo biological, also believes something like this to be the case. This claim that, new cultural arguments operate upon the basis of old racist logics, is presented as part of my analysis of Powellism in chapter 6. The next two chapters examine the documentary evidence for the argument that there is a continuity of development to racial political discourse in the postwar period and that Powellism represents a continuation rather than decisive interruption of this logic.

3 Racism and Parliamentary Discourse (I): 1957-68

This chapter examines, in detail, Parliamentary Debates concerned with Immigration and the discourse of 'race' in the period 1957-68.[1] It is an assumption of this approach that a particular racialised discourse of the social informs these debates, and that the 'race' connotative ideas by which it is achieved can be quite clearly identified in the early to mid part of this period. They become less explicit as the Bill moves from the political-right to the Government frontbenches. This movement would conform to Reeves' 'discoursive (discursive?) deracialisation' concept, although Reeves does not apply it to this period or to account for this phenomenon (Reeves 1983). As we have seen, Reeves employs deracialisation to refer to discourse that was previously racialised or ought to be racialised, as judged by an 'objective observer', but appears in its presentation not to be so; despite the fact that he assumes the prior racialisation rather than establishing it empirically.[2] Others, the New Racism theorists, have gone further in claiming that such apparently 'race free' talk misrecognizes the extent to which a new kind of public discourse has allowed racism to be *naturalized* as the official language of the state. Quite how this process has been achieved remains somewhat ambiguous, as we have seen.[3]

As Miles (1990) has recognised, what is central to such analysis is the relationship between political language and the concept of 'race'. Claims for racist political language depend upon being able to establish the clarity of this linkage. This chapter will argue the case for a re-examination of this relationship, empirically, by showing, firstly, that Parliamentary language from the late 1950s to the early 1960s can be shown to be racist, i.e. to express a clear conceptual relationship to ideas of 'race' that can be said to constitute the social discourse of racism in British society.[4]

Secondly, that the 1961 Immigration Bill Debate should be characterised as racist not because of the strength and validity of the arguments presented by Gaitskell, Gordon-Walker and Royle in support of such a claim,[5] as is conventionally recorded (cf. Layton-Henry 1984; Solomos 1989), but because a clear conceptual relationship can be traced in the language and structure of argumentation of that debate, as well as key personnel and ideologies, to link it clearly to the more explicitly eugenicist, and evidently racist, themes and proposals of earlier debates from the late 1950s. Thirdly, contra accepted research assumptions concerning the fact, if not the process, of the expungement of certain explicit 'race' codes from Parliamentary discourse from 1962 onwards, racial language is still very much in evidence, and this is because such language is able to refer to, invoke or denote, well established societal narratives and images of 'race', which add up to the idea of that which the New Racism theorists call: the 'old racism'.[6]

In addition, this chapter proposes that, contra the New Racism theorists, the period from 1957 - 1968 is of greater significance in the development and understanding of the language of 'race' politics than the period commencing in 1968 with the emergence of Powellism. Surprisingly, the evidence lends itself more towards deepening the conventional assumption that the watershed in 'race politics' comes with the mainstream support for controls by the Conservative Government in 1961.[7] Thus the 1962 Act is apparently a remarkable success for a marginal right wing ginger group of 'race' populists in the Conservative and also Labour party.[8]

However, what is more likely to be going on in the period leading up to the framing of legislation, is the negotiation and development of a public discourse of 'race' that could be supported by the Conservative Frontbench. This process can be traced quite clearly in the debates, statements and exchanges taking place in Parliament and in Official communications during this period. It therefore remains to define this process as one taking place both in secret and in the languages of public exchange and debate, as a necessary process of the development and transformation of racial political language; particularly as it is seen to transmute and transform itself in the passage from the Backbench to the Front. so that it increasingly begins to resemble that *Commons'sense* discourse of 'Race Relations' and 'Immigration', that we have come to recognise.

After 1962 this process deepens and becomes more generalised, not least because Labour acknowledge the necessity of the continuance of restriction, in the 1963 and 1964 Expiring Laws Debates, and as the necessary basis of the 1965 Race Relations Debate.

Parliamentary Debates

It is necessary to warn against the danger of over estimating the significance of language use and the role of Debate in the construction of legislation. As Drewry has argued, if the process of 'law' making can be said to comprise of: initiation, formulation, scrutiny, legitimisation, application and feedback, then the effective role of House of Commons debate is concerned with only two of these: 'scrutiny' and 'legitimisation' (Drewry 1981); and, as Norton has argued, 'by the time both stages are reached, legislation has largely, though not fully, been "made"' (Norton 1981: 82).

Surprisingly, such arguments would accord with the lack of attention given to the 'content' of Parliamentary Debates, or their significance, among radical scholars. Such a view has its sanction in the Marxist theory of the state, and the well observed historical dominance of the executive, as well as the celebrated phrase of Lenin, likening Parliaments to 'talking shops'; or as in the following description:

> Take any parliamentary country, from America to Switzerland, from France to Britain, Norway and so forth - in these countries the real business of "state" is performed behind the scenes and is carried on by the departments, chancelleries and General Staffs. Parliament is given up to talk for the special purpose of fooling the "common people" (Lenin 1977: 271).

According to such a view, determined scholars, concerned to locate the 'origins' of official ideologies, would be far better advised to examine 'secret' committee and cabinet debates, prior to the initiation or formulation of a Bill (cf. Deakin 1968; Carter and Joshi 1984; Carter, Harris and Joshi 1987; Harris 1987).[9] But, as we have already argued, the construction of a discourse of 'race politics' cannot be attributed to an official origin alone. The emergence of a distinctive language of 'race' arises out of an interplay of both public and official discourses, national and local constructions; and this relationship is one that must be unravelled.[10]

Despite the fact that the effectiveness of the function of: (i) scrutiny and (ii) legitimisation is seen to be considerably diminished in the contemporary period, the role of Commons Debate in the formation of Immigration, Race Relations and Nationality legislation deserves careful examination because (a) the function of scrutiny is effectively exercised on a number of Bills: the 1968 Race Relations Bill, the 1971 Immigration Bill and the 1981 Nationality Bill.[11] Although the effect, in aggregate, of these interventions and modifications is minus rather than plus; and (b) with immigration restriction legislation the requirement to debate and legitimise the measures is of paramount importance. This is not, as conventionally assumed, because of a departure from a consensus middle-ground approach, but because such legislation arises 'publicly' from the backbenches and lobbies, rather than as an announced government measure. It therefore requires to carry a good deal of support, secured not at division, but in the passage and treatment of the principles of the Bill through the House.[12]

Structure and Content Analysis

What kind of a discursive structure have the various debates about Immigration, Race Relations and Nationality exhibited? Here, we are concerned with the internal relations that construct the Parliamentary scene. Beyond this we must consider its relationship to the public means of communication that mediate it to mass publics. The discursive connection here is the 'content' of Debates and the extent to which the content and discussion is conditioned and determined by a prior agenda established in the 'public sphere' (cf. Habermas 1973; 1976). At the same time, we must consider the formal relations and styles of presentation and reception of the language forms and strategies of Parliamentary Debates, and the extent to which these formal conditions of production of official discourse determine the treatment of content.

In the debates themselves it is important to note the relationship between the frontbench Government 'spokesman', seconder, and backbench ministers of their own party and, in replica, those of the Opposition benches. It is the task of the frontbench, in the case of Immigration, the Home Secretary, to introduce the measures advocated. The Second Reading allows these measures to be debated in the House and for objections and amendments to be raised. If the passage through the house is difficult the government may want to compromise, by allowing alteration of clauses at Committee. However, a Bill cannot enter Committee until it has been accepted. Obviously if the government has a majority in the House, and has the support of that majority, then proposed legislation will pass through the House and become law, eventually. Only two Bills, since 1907, have failed to do so (cf. Drewry 1981). However, a 'rough ride' through the house can increase dissent from both backbenchers or, at the very least, cast doubt on the overall composition of the Bill; if not the Bill itself.

In 'moving' the Bill the government spokesperson, a Cabinet minister, will want to justify and explain the need for the introduction of another set of measures on to the statute books; s/he will want to either explicitly identify or allude to the social problem, phenomenon or emergency, giving rise to the necessity of legislation. S/he will want to stress the necessity and inherent soundness of the proposals that are 'commended to the house'. The discursive strategy is to smooth the passage of the Bill into law, by anticipating and appealing to opposers and waverers, as to the reasonable and practical solutions offered by the Bill, and in terms of ideological and tactical positions that are held by different MPs and factions within her own party and by the Opposition.

The most critical area to the success of the Debate is how frontbench language is negotiated, challenged and accommodated to by backbench hardliners and opposition critics. The success of frontbench language depends upon invoking the authority and legitimacy involved in the framing of the Bill, of how it addressess the problem or objective in the most efficient, expedient and essential manner. Reeves (1983) has argued, that senior frontbench introductions designed to 'move' a Second Reading are encoded in a formulaic 'description'. Thus, by Second Reading, a Bill is virtually impregnable from critique and therefore its negotiation within the verbal exchanges and routines of the House is merely symbolic:

> Descriptive 'arguments' consist in outlining in detail the various clauses of a Bill, and are especially to be found in the speeches of those who move Second Readings and who reply to debates. Such arguments do not justify the Bills in the sense of providing *reasons* for the acceptance of their prescriptions, but they have a strong persuasive effect in that they project, as taken-for-granted, the Bill's values, to such an extent that the casual listener may not even consider the possibility of other lines of action. By the time a Bill receives its Second Reading, it usually exists in such a polished legalistic form that it is a skilled task to penetrate, let alone undermine, its structure. At its Second Reading, a Bill is almost a fait accompli and as such is capable of providing a limiting mental set for those who read it complacently (Reeves 1983: 238).

Such a view does capture an important part of the reality of the Second Reading. The clauses and arguments of the Bill are often well polished. The language of commendation to the House is one of liberal but reserved equanimity. The language appears oblique; the 'problem' and the projected response are tied very tightly together, clause by clause. A language of reasonableness and sobriety, of officiality and ceremony is required.

Of course, one reason for this is that the arguments are often well rehearsed and merely need to be suggested. It is up to the floor to engage in the more messy exercise of debate. Even here the will of the 'movers' is that the hegemony possessed by the Government will mean that the passage of the Bill will be conducted within the dominant framework proposed by the Government. The dominant hegemony here is a thematic motif of reasonableness and liberal-minded caution: that the Bill addresses a necessary evil with a minimum of bureaucracy. The more tightly this thematic control can be exercised the more successful will the government appear to be.

However, the formal hegemony of the recommendation of the Bill to the House does depend upon the extent to which dissent and controversy is anticipated. This is particularly the case in Debates about Immigration where the movers are often only too well aware of the dissent and arguments against the motion. In these circumstances the opening remarks in support of the Bill attempt to set in place a framework that will both anticipate and attempt to encompass and incorporate, or dispose of, any criticism; so that the Bill can be presented as near reasonable and legitimate as possible.

Such argument will contain appeals to justificatory elements and the invoking of arguments in often oblique outline; these arguments will make sense precisely because they have already been established. In this respect all introductions exhibit this feature. The language is restrained and modest, the arguments are muted, seemingly reasonable precisely because they rest and depend upon a prior framework which is available to the audience. In this respect the success of the presentation of a Bill is in anticipating opposition arguments and heading them off; or attempting to neutralise their effect with a variety of disclaimers, or linguistic and technical devices, designed to distance a contentious issue or clause from the main elements of the Bill. Such themes and ideas form the substance of supporting statements, as they anticipate them, and it is the job of the Bill's seconder, while dealing with member's remarks, to reassert such themes and arguments in finally moving the Bill to assent by the House; or to division.

Methodology

The methods used in the analysis of the documentary material are: (i) content analysis and (ii) discourse analysis. The specific analysis of discursive documents arising from this realm will require and involve (a) a hermeneutic technique, employed to identify and establish the overall textural unity of the document, in terms of the ideological context in which it appears, and the themes and symbols it records, which refer and are in return defined by such a context; (b) content analysis is employed in order, classify and rank these ideological themes, identified as significant in structuring the unity of the document. Such themes are also organised according to sub-divisions, relating to whether they assent or dissent from the official and/or dominant presentation, which opens and closes such accounts.

Content Analysis

In terms of the Hansard debates material, a systematic analysis of the content of speeches is conducted. The recording of this material is organised through a procedure of (i) producing a summary of content; noting themes, points of arguments, reference to previous debates, etc., and phrases used and: (ii) ranking of dominant themes, ideas, established through frequency of occurrence or centrality to argument; (iii) sorted into assenting and dissenting patterns. Content analysis techniques are employed in order to classify and rank those ideological themes identified as significant in structuring the debate.[13]

Discourse Analysis

Such analysis is employed to identify the range of meanings offered and the structure and organisation of the debates in terms of how (a) internal thematic content and argument and, (b) external framework and political context, structure the dominant reading and interpretation of the Debate. The methodology employed combines a hermeneutic analysis employed to identify and account for the structure and unity of the ideological context of the debate. This is done through reference to those factors which are absent, but to which the Parliamentary discourse refers, and to the ideological themes and presentations which have their origins and reference outside and prior to the Debate. It is through a tracing of the interplay of these factors that the ideological meaning of the debates can be established. We can extend these points in the following way:

(i) A core or preferred interpretation is locatable within the Debates. This view is usually, but not exclusively, associated with the Government. It is seen to codify or express its aims or intentions in calling for the Bill. The Reading of the Bill is the public presentation of this intention in the form of an extended argument in support of a precisely worded mandate; the mandate proceeds its defence.

This presentation or interpretation is commended to the House. In order for the Bill to pass through it must get majority support. If the Government has a majority it needs merely to gain a majority assent from its own party. Even here the wording and presentation of the intention and measures of the Bill are important. Obviously the passage of the Bill, and any likely resistance to it, is anticipated and organised in advance of its presentation. The presenters, usually the Government, are looking for a consensual reception and would require to see that the Bill commanded majority support.

(ii) The actual Debate itself involves a public negotiation around the interpretation of the content or intent of the Bill. Contributors modify, assent to or flatly contradict its view.

(iii) This 'preferred view' has an ideological structure which can be traced in the pattern of metaphors and the regularity of the use of terms, predicates, etc.

(iv) Each Debate is unique within its own terms; a micro process of public negotiation and statement of alternative interpretations. Such an interplay, however, takes place within a thematic environment circumscribed by party identification and the agenda set up by media commentators and prior public debate. Thus the terms of the Debate almost inevitably proceed it.

(v) Beyond the Debate itself it is possible to locate a framework of ideological themes which trace and hold in place the dominant view. This thematic history structures and informs the way in which issues are handled, codified and even understood. It will be the aim of the analysis to demonstrate the relationship between this thematic structure and the content of Parliamentary discourse.[14]

Analysis

The analysis conducted will be presented over this and the following chapter. This chapter will present a comparative account of Debates up to 1968; while chapter 4 will deal with Debates, post 1968. The detailed analysis that follows will therefore include those Debates taking place in 1958; 1959; 1961; 1964, 1965 and 1968.[15] This division is important as a comparative device which will allow contrasting and comparable themes and treatments, in the pre-Powellite era and afterwards, to be identified. This most basic division will allow us to begin to refute or confirm the question of the impact of Powellism.[16]

Two of the most important findings that will be indicated here are (i) that the period proceeding the rise of Powellism is of key significance in framing and defining the question of 'race' and Immigration; (ii) that there is a good deal of continuity, rather than discontinuity, in the themes and modes of argumentation employed in these earlier Debates. This will allow us to claim that what distinguishes Powellism is not a change in the style of address, for he adopts this more or less in *toto*, but in the transformation of the discourse of eugenicism that pervades the 1958, 1959 and 1961 Debates.[17] This theme will be identified and its ideological relationship to the 1961 Debate will be mapped-out and accounted for.

Firstly, we will examine the 1961 *Commonwealth Immigrants Bill, Second Reading* (16th November, cc. 687-824). After this we will examine the

Debates that precede it. Working back from the 1961 Debate we will argue that there is an important relationship of continuity of themes, ideologies and personnel, between the debates and interventions that precede the 1961 Bill, i.e. those debates taking place in the late 1950s. In addition, we will assert that the content and structure of the debate cannot be fully understood without, at the same time, recognising the implicit framework of ideological themes that the early debates have established.

Example: *Commonwealth Immigrants Bill - Second Reading, 16, November 1961, Parliamentary Debates (Hansard) Fifth series, vol. 649: 687-824*. Although the 1961 Debate is considered significant, the reference to content, even in the best of the available commentaries, is minimal and selective; concentrating on either the actual clauses of the Bill or on the keynote speech of Gaitskell against the Bill (cf. Foot 1965: 171-4; Layton-Henry 1984: 41; Solomos 1988: 35; 1989). While it is important to argue that the Bill, while carried by a Conservative majority, is considerably damaged by the opposition criticism of Gaitskell, Gordon-Walker and others, the more significant aspect of it for what is to follow is the kind of treatment the Bill receives in both presentation and supporting argument. This aspect is important because (i) it allows close examination of the way in which language is employed to support and justify the intentions of the Bill; (ii) how such language compares to the earlier debates and, (iii) how subsequent debate will proceed in reference to this language treatment, once Labour are in government. Let us now commence an analysis of the language structure of the debate:

Assenting Themes

(1) Despite the honoured tradition of the 'open door' the recent dramatic increase in Commonwealth immigrants threatens to swell the population of Britain's already overcrowded island.
(2) Cannot continue to accept this increasing flow of immigrants particularly because the doctrine of the open door means that a quarter of the world's population is legally entitled to come to Britain.
(3) The sheer weight of numbers will make it difficult to absorb the immigrants into the national life, particularly since excessive numbers tend to create internal communities that will be un-assimilable.
(4) It is only prudent to anticipate the kinds of social problems that continued immigration will cause, in particular
   - increase in racial antagonism and social friction
   - rise in unemployment

- chronic housing shortages.
(5) The immigrants by their overwhelming presence are creating serious social problems, particularly they are associated with:
- certain forms of serious crime
- a number of serious diseases
- relying on the state for hand-outs.
(6) Restriction is inevitable in a world context where the standard of living of the migrants is so much lower than that of Britain so that they will continue to come to take advantage of it. The sheer number of economic migrants could threaten that standard if control is not imposed.
(7) Although restriction will upset the Commonwealth relation such a relation must be understood to work in two ways: the children also have a duty to the parents.

Dissenting Themes

(1) No consultation or agreement attempted or reached with head of Commonwealth countries directly affected by restriction.
(2) Absence of corresponding emigration figures is serious omission
- causing imbalance in ability to arrive at rational assessment of extent of problem
- deliberately withheld to create misleading impression of the numbers involved
- reflects on the hurried and ill considered nature of the Bill.
(3) Social problems associated with immigrants created and exacerbated by government neglect:
- housing shortages
- multi-occupation and rent racketeering
- indigenous antagonism
- racial prejudice.
(4) Motivated by 'colour prejudice'.
(5) A 'colour bar' camouflaged, because of:
- colour prejudice
- fear of indigenous prejudice
- hurried response to campaign of prejudiced individuals
- exclusion of the Southern Irish
- inadequate response to 'real' social problems.
(6) Abnegation of Commonwealth obligations and betrayal of the Commonwealth ideal out of narrow self-interest, particularly now that

Commonwealth is no longer an Empire and there is no economic incentive in continuing to support it.
(7) Commonwealth as historic opportunity to achieve inter-racial harmony and new diplomatic role for Britain which Bill jeopardises.
(8) Failure to apply moral, ethical and Christian principles.

Treatment

The first thing to note is that most, though not all, the assenting themes are contained in Butler's recommendation of the Government's Bill to the House. However, the arguments, images and ideas offered by Butler are only fully understandable when related to (i) the previous debates over motions and Bills offered by (Sir) Cyril Osborne as a Private Member; and (ii) the particular themes, arguments and kinds of language employed in the presentation of those debates; (iii) the 'climate of opinion' constructed in the press and public space in anticipation of the Bill's Debate (cf. Layton-Henry 1984; 1992; Solomos 1989).[18]

We can illustrate these points through a closer examination of Butler's introduction. The first point to note is that the Bill is introduced with 'considerable reluctance' in asking for 'control' of immigration of Commonwealth citizens. This is because the 'free movement', to and from the 'Mother Country', of her citizens is a 'cherished ideal'. Butler links this comforting notion of the traditional 'open door' ('an important link binding the Commonwealth together'), as having a number of unforeseen consequences, the magnitude of which make controls against such a tradition 'justifiable':

> The justification for the control[...]is that a sizeable part of the entire population of the earth is at present legally entitled to come and stay in this already densely populated country. It amounts altogether to one-quarter of the population of the globe (Hansard) *Commonwealth Immigrants Bill*, 16 Nov. 1961: col. 687)[19]

This 'fact', when given 'serious consideration', means that no country can allow an 'indefinite continuance of virtually limitless immigration' (c.678); especially 'an influx on the present scale' (c.678). Here Butler has linked together the prospect of the threat of a huge number of immigrants, potentially able to settle in Britain as members of the Commonwealth, with a recent increase in the quantity arriving. The linking of these two themes is fundamental because it invites comprehension of the threat as explicable in terms of the 'fact' of the present 'problem' of 'inflow' of 'numbers'. Now that Butler has hinged his case upon the ideological conjunction of these two elements he must present the figures that will justify his claims of dramatic 'inflow'. Before he deals with the figures though he wants the House to appreciate the context of concerns against which the figures for Immigration should be measured. A very important theme within this context is the 'fact' that:

> [W]e are a thickly populated country[...]There are fewer countries more densely populated than our own. Over the past ten years the population here has increased by 2 1/2 million, to reach more than 51 1/4 million. Immigration is becoming an increasingly important factor in this problem (Hansard *Commonwealth Immigrants Bill*, 16 Nov. 1961: col. 684).

Here the problem of population expansion is linked quite directly to population inflow. Less than two columns later Douglas Jay (Battersea, North) is asking for the figures for population outflow i.e., emigration; yet Butler does not have these to hand. Without such figures such points are speculatory. But of course the point is an inferential one. It is made because it relates to the image of the 'over crowded island', 'densely populated country' (c.687), 'thickly populated' (c.688); or Osborne's 'the most densely populated little island in the world' (c.733); and the framing image of the 'sizeable proportion of the entire population of the earth' (c.687), 'numbers', 'noticeable figure' (c.689), and the need to 'keep the flow within reasonable bounds' (c.692); 'control the flow' (c.693), 'influx' (c.687), 'unlimited numbers' (c.693-4),'large numbers' (c.694), 'sheer weight of numbers' (c.695), etc, *ad infinitum.*

These images of the 'numbers game' and the threat of 'inflowing masses' into the tiny, overcrowded island are perhaps the central and defining commonsense image in postwar Debates about Immigration, Race Relations and Nationality; (and more recently 'refugees' and 'asylum seekers').[20] The 'problem' of the 'threat' of such 'numbers' proceeds the Debate.[21] Butler's thematic intention here is to connect up the theme of the 'open door', and the Commonwealth ideal, and suggest that such a doctrine has allowed, and threatens a population explosion *caused* by massive immigration. What Butler is doing, quite deliberately here, is to invoke and undermine the key element of the Opposition attack against controls: that of the Commonwealth and Commonwealth relations, and to link this to the threat of 'numbers'. So that by the end of his speech he can argue that the greatest threat to Commonwealth relations will come, not from the imposition of legislation, but from antagonism towards Commonwealth citizens 'at home' should it not be imposed.

Of course, when Butler speaks of the Commonwealth he does not mean Canada, Australia and New Zealand; of which 50,000 a year come but, 'many of these are not immigrants' (c.688). Then there is Ireland: many of the 60,000 or 70,000 are 'seasonal workers' who come and go. Rather, the 'new factor' is immigration from 'other parts of the Commonwealth': the West Indies, India, Pakistan and Cyprus. The numbers from these countries is 'rapidly increasing', despite voluntary agreements with the sending countries to restrict outflow. Such efforts have not kept the 'flow within reasonable bounds' (c.692) and therefore now require the Government, with 'considerable reluctance', to consider such restriction from the 'receiving end'.

In the next section Butler presents a number of other factors that make it necessary to 'control the flow'. First, though, Butler wants to praise the contribution to national life the immigrants have made. By this point nobody can be under any illusion as to which categories of immigrant from the Commonwealth Butler is referring to: 'no one can doubt the value of the contribution which the immigrants have made to our national life. In particular, our hospitals and public transport system would be in difficulties were it not for the services of immigrant workers' (c.693).

Set against this Butler offers a set of less consensual themes than those of the 'overcrowded island':

> We must remember that we are working in a period of full employment. It does not take much imagination to realise what might happen if, unfortunately, there should be a recession of trade and immigrants were competing for jobs with other people in this country. In such circumstances, life would be very difficult for the immigrants already here, and the situation would be very much worse if others continued to flock into this country in unlimited numbers in the hope of finding a job (c.693).

Here a recession is invoked to conjure up 'race conflict'. We are asked to imagine a situation in which, because of a rise in unemployment, immigrants and indigenous workers are competing for the same status of job. Now the previous, patronising remarks about the value of immigrant workers, occupied in Health care and Public transport, connects home. In addition, and more darkly still:

> It cannot be denied that the immigrants who have come to this country in such large numbers have presented the country with an intensified social problem. They tend to settle in communities of their own, with their own mode of life, in big cities. The greater the number coming in to this country the larger will

these communities become and the more difficult will it be to integrate them (c. 694).

Or:

if the numbers of new entrants are excessive, their assimilation into our society presents the gravest difficulty (c. 694).

We have now established the other central commonsense theme of the Debates over the last thirty years. The problem of numbers = the problem of the assimilation of 'alien cultural groups'. The discourse of numbers who 'flow', 'flock' or 'influx' is articulated to whole communities who are un-assimilable because they are *too large*. They set up communities on their own, with their 'own way of life'. They present a problem by their 'great' numbers and by their very concentration. Large numbers are not assimilable. So immigrants from the Commonwealth are by their very nature, a 'problem'. It is not hard to see here already assembled, the key elements that Powell will later use.[22] It is, of course, 'a question of numbers and alienness' as he has reiterated on numerous occasions. We also know, of course that, besides voting with the government, Powell sat silently through these debates.[23]

The Bill is seconded by (Sir) Cyril Osborne and this makes the connection to the earlier Debates explicit. Osborne, on rising, is subjected to vilification from the Opposition benches. He cannot commence his Seconding of the Bill beyond stating:

As the House knows, I have been agitating for this type of legislation for ten years. I make no bones about it and I do not apologise for it. I have received thousands of letters from all over the country, mostly from people who live in the areas[...]These people show an acute sense of distress because of this problem (Cyril Osborne (Louth) *Commonwealth Immigrants Bill* (Hansard), 16 Nov. 1961: 716-7).

This opening statement allows Osborne to shoot an electoral warning across Gordon-Walker's bows; a direct response to the latter's eloquent and principled attack upon the Bill: 'The right hon. Member for Smethwick gave not nearly enough attention to the English people in the great cities who are affected by this problem' (c.718). The full effect of this salvo was not felt until the result of the General Election in Smethwick, when some argued, the 'neglected' got their own back on Gordon-Walker.[24] Of course, the 'areas most affected' phrase becomes a famous one in the hands of Powell. But as our analysis will show, this theme is one constructed by Osborne, and by Harold Gurden, Norman Pannell and others, such as Labour MPs., John Hynd and Harry Hyne. Osborne engages further skirmishes and exchanges until he reaches the core of his argument. It is this core which also forms the interior of the government's Bill:

> [W]hy do immigrants come to this country? Why do they come here? For the simple reason that the standard of living in this country[...]is so much higher than that they can enjoy in their own country[...]As long as that is true they will come. This is the honey pot to which they will come, so long as there is any honey in the pot (Cyril Osborne (Louth) *Commonwealth Immigrants Bill* (Hansard), 16 Nov. 1961: c.719).

Or:

> In Pakistan and India they work harder for a week's wage which is less than they can get here on the dole for doing nothing (c.720)

Once Osborne has established his argument he then attempts a rearguard action to deny the discriminatory intention of such legislation. Osborne believes that if the issues can be separated then such a claim is legitimate:

> I claim that control is inevitable because of the attraction of our country to the coloured people because of their immense poverty and their low standard of living[...]this control which I think is inevitable[...]has nothing to do with coloured skin at all. It is due entirely to poverty and to numbers. I want to say this to Hon. Gentlemen of those immigrants from the coloured part of the Commonwealth. In my opinion, had they faces as white as snow, their great numbers and their great poverty would have made control of their coming into this country inevitable (c.720-1).

Having established the distance of these two points to his satisfaction, Osborne feels confident enough to assert them together in defence of the Bill: 'Therefore, I say that the sheer weight of numbers - nothing whatever to do with the colour of the skin - is a factor that controls the event and makes it imperative that we should have some form of control' (c.722).

Here Osborne has supplied us with another of the great enduring themes of the debates on Immigration, Nationality and Race Relations that have occupied the honourable members over the last thirty years: the problem of the economic threat of a potentially massive migration of poor, third-world migrants who seek an escape route from poverty and find in Britain's liberal open door policy and welfare state, their haven. This theme is a central motif, consistent over twenty odd years; as for example the 1981 Nationality Bill:

[T]here are massive pressures[...]in the world today, in a world that has got smaller, in a world of relatively cheap air travel, from the people in the poorer parts, be it the Middle East, the Indian Sub-continent, or North Africa, to come to the bright lights, the hot spots, the relatively wealthy Western European economies.[...]This pressure has been building up and will continue to do so. In the last year alone, 1 million people visited this country from those parts of the world. Having visited, having seen, having relatives and friends here, having realised the advantages of living in our country, and having set all that against their own backgrounds, there will be real pressures from them to come and settle here if they can, or to come illegally and stay if they can (*British Nationality Bill*, 28 January, 1981: col. 1017).[25]

Of course, such comments must be set against a situation of nil primary immigration and are thus inescapably directed towards the issue of 'relatives', real or 'imputed', of black British citizens.[26]

Further in: Powellism before Powell ?

With the contribution of Harold Gurden (Birmingham, Selly Oak) we move into the racialised landscape of the 'inner city' borough and the politics of the alienated 'Englishman'; a narrative articulated by the 'black country' backbench group, to which Powell did not wish to belong, and from which he kept his political distance (cf. Foot 1969; Schoen 1977). Yet, ironically, it is this backbench political 'rump' of Tory populists that has tirelessly worked for the national-political recognition of the issue of 'race' and Immigration. The language and arguments they have developed to bridge the constituency *experience* of 'race' and Immigration to the national-political arena are arguably the single most important influence, Powellism not withstanding, on the formation and development of legislation.[27]

What is most interesting about these contributions is the way in which they operate upon and rehearse themes and anxieties, issues and concerns, that we now recognise as Powellist. For example, is it not an axiom of the claims for a New Racism and for a ground shift in the form and function of contemporary racism, that Powell's language marks a distinctive break and innovation in terms? Let us further trace these configurations to discover where they lead.

Gurden leaves us in no doubt of the seriousness of the issue under debate: 'This Bill may well prevent an ugly situation in this country' (c.736). This is why, with popular feeling running high in the affected areas, it is wrong to criticise such views as racist: 'it is incredibly dirty politics[...]to accuse those who favour restriction[...]of being actuated by colour prejudice' (c.763).The people who write to their MPs in favour of restriction are 'sincere' and 'have searched their hearts and their consciences'. But to appreciate this and the feeling that 'things are getting out of hand' it is necessary to have experience of the 'areas effected'. This is Gurden's central assertion. It is only those resident in the 'areas most affected' who are qualified to pass judgement; to 'really know' whether Immigration Control is needed or not. This distinction is brought out very nicely through a comparison of local press reporting of the 'problems' of immigrants and the accounts carried in the national press: 'We have had criticism from The Times and that is understandable. The Times is not sold in the areas of difficulty[...]The Times is sold in areas where people never see immigrants and do not understand the problem' (c.738).

Here, again, we find a theme that Powell will commandeer and make his own. In fact it is probably his initial theme; it is the neglect and contempt shown those who *experience* the problem first hand who he belatedly speaks up for.[28] The gulf that separates those who know the problem first-hand and the principles of high-minded liberals is the gulf of 'experience'. Gurden too, uses this sense of having the experience to *really know*, when he asserts: 'Members should see some of the things which go on in Birmingham. They would then think that it was getting out of hand. Certainly the police have more than they can deal with' (c.736). This assertion receives a chorus of protest from the opposition benches. Amidst this, Gurden asserts the darker under-belly of his argument: 'Oh, yes. I am not saying that it is all crime, but I know of cases where the police have been so busy at certain times of night that there has been as much as an hour's delay after making of a 999 call before they have been able to get out' (c.736).

Gurden is unable to disguise his direct identification of crime with Immigration, although he attempts to present his assertions in the form of a reasoned statement, befitting the style of the House. This gives such assertions an absurd logic, as for example: 'Crimes are not committed only by coloured immigrants, but those that are are out of all proportion to the numbers of immigrants, and are of the worst kind - murder, rape, bloodshed, theft, dope, peddling, sex crimes, and so on' (c.739). This obsessive returning to unsubstantiated crime and morality scares rises to a crescendo at the close of his speech:

> Opponents of the Bill say that the housing problem was with us before the immigrants arrived, but Birmingham's problem has been aggravated to an extent never known before. Slums now exist in hundreds, or perhaps even thousands, where previously they could be measured in dozens. Never was

92 *Political Languages of Race and the Politics of Exclusion*

there such filth and such obscenity. The humiliation and degradation of these people are dreadful. That is why I say that it is not only socially but morally right to have this Bill (c.742).

The language of Gurden here is the language of moral and social superiority; seeing in the object of its abhorrence the nightmare of a lower class of humanity.[29] It is a discourse of 'race', not in the sense of reference to a doctrine of scientific typology but in the form of a ideological narrative of the social, which works to identify separable, socially and culturally inferior groups whose practices are not compatible with the standards of the host community. Its relationship to the opening speech of Butler is that it makes explicit what that speech infers: the social crisis of housing and unemployment; the sheer weight of numbers and the formation of communities apart. These themes can suggest the metaphors and nightmares of 'race' without having to voice them; but at the core of the debate they are plainly there.[30]

The Ideological Structure of the 1961 Debate

The ideological contestation at the heart of the 1961 Debate is one posed between, on the one hand, a theory of the Commonwealth, of its future potentiality as a unifier of post-Empire relations between Britain and her former colonies, and, a view of the problem of the potential mass emigration of these colonials, made possible by the continuing fact of this relationship. It is a contestation of broadly, the themes of a 'New Commonwealth' of Labour vs. the politics of protection of an 'overcrowded island' from further occupation. These themes structure the debate and the positions adopted, most noticeably on the side of protecting, by Cyril Osborne and Harold Gurden, while the most notable advocates of the Commonwealth of Labour, are Gordon-Walker, Prime Minister Gaitskell and Charles Royle. The dominant framework is of course that offered by Butler and the Home Office, of 'reasonable grounds' for control; while the opposition struggle to contest that the principles and arguments that underpin such a construction, are economically unsound, and aimed at an effective 'colour bar':

[T]his Bill in intention, in fact and now openly, because of what has been done to the Southern Irish, is a Bill based on racial discrimination[...]In its first form, before the Irish where taken out, the Bill was very careful to cover up this racial discrimination, but this only makes its worse, because a colour bar clothed in hypocrisy provokes even deeper resentment than a straight forward colour bar[...]everyone knows that the overwhelming majority of those trying to get in on the open quota will be coloured people. The net effect of the Bill is that a negligible number of white people will be kept out and almost all those kept out by the Bill will be coloured people (Mr. Gordon-Walker, *Commonwealth Immigrants Debate*, 16 November, 1961: cols. 708-9).

The 'race' populists, as we have seen, by appeals to first-hand experience and anecdotal accounts of crime, and newspaper reports of inner city 'social crisis', construct a situation of acute danger where the 'common people', the 'ordinary Englishman', lives in fear of the 'flood' of social and economic migrants; liable, if kept unchecked, to tear apart and destroy settled communities and traditions. While such metaphors and associations of 'race' weave the pattern of anecdotal accounts of crime and moral decline, there direct provenance is with the projected transformation of the English community and the Englishman himself:

'Surely, it is not illiberal[...]for people to be concerned with preserving their own national character and continuity. A question which affects the future of our own race and breed is not one that we should leave merely to chance' (Mr. Martin Lindsay (Solihull) *Immigration (Control)*, 5th December 1958: col. 1563-4).

It is surely well established that it is this theme, above all others, that we have come to identify as most Powellist? Of course Powell does not formulate this issue explicitly in terms of 'race' but in terms of the 'homogeneity' of the English. But in fact the ground-work for this ideological articulation is already very successfully laid before his use of it. As for example:

Speaking as an Englishman for the English people about conditions in England, I feel deeply that the problem of immigration must be tackled, and tackled soon (Mr. C. Osborne (Louth), *Control of Immigration*, 17 February 1961: col.1929).

Or:

[T]he overwhelming proportion of[...]immigrants stay in England[...]and they form on the map a new coloured city as big as Bedford, Chester, Colchester, Scunthorpe or Worcester. This cannot be allowed to go on indefinitely because in another ten, twenty or thirty years' time the face of England would not be recognisable (c.1932).

And:

Why cannot I say just occasionally in this House, "England for the English"[...]I speak as an Englishman for my fellow countrymen (c: 1936).[31]

We will pursue the implications of this evidence in chapters 4 and 6. For the moment we need to consider the significance of the language used by Osborne and the other 'race populists' to the internal/external thematic of the 1961 Debate. The most important distinction here is the question of the distance of Osborne's language from the 'official view'. What is at issue is the question of the degree of acceptance of this racialised 'world view' on the Frontbenches? Is there evidence of a significant measure of language continuity in the content of language usage? Do Ministers with Portfolio also employ ideas of 'race', in the eugenicist sense, or as a narrative of social and moral decline? Here such a discourse would exhibit the defining criteria of 'race' as a biological fiction able to construct narratives of Self and Others; in this case, the Indigenous and the Newcomers.[32]

The essential difference between Butler and the 'race' populists is that Butler never 'slips' into the 'old' language of 'race'; whereas Osborne and Gurden, although they attempt to dispense with it, cannot manage without it; it creeps in at every point. Yet, as the Opposition suggest, the object of both is a racial one. The essential difference is that the explicit idea of 'race', encoded within the (i) inner city nightmare of the beleaguered Englishman and, (ii) the question of numbers and cities going 'coloured', by Osborne and Co., has undergone a linguistic transformation into the 'social problem' metaphors of the Bill's concern to balance the need to be responsible, in seeking to restrict a potential 'social problem' of excessive numbers, and the idea of the impact of growing numbers, the threat of potential numbers, on the ability of the host community to absorb and cope with the formation of distinct cultural communities, forming within major British cities.

Of considerable importance here to this discursive process is that Butler's address is one consonant with the 'climate of opinion' that has brought the question of Commonwealth Immigration to Parliamentary Debate. Thus the rules of the public Debate and the repetition of terms of signification act together to enclose and absorb the idea of 'race' into a political commonsense of the projected social problem of 'race relations'. The 'race' politics of the Bill become, not the metaphors and invocation of historical ideologies, but the terms of engagement of political advantage and disadvantage in demonstrating the ability to handle this issue within the Parliamentary arena.

It is the job of Butler, as Home Secretary, to present his party's Bill, as befits the House rules, as both reasonable and appropriate to: (i) the social ill or problem it wishes to redress and, (ii) the principles that will command the respect of the whole House. Butler knows he cannot, given the previous agitation and Private Member's Bills of Osborne et al, hope to meet the question of principles.

What he must do is to try to deflect this criticism into the justification and framing of the 'problem'. As we have seen he does this with some skill, managing, to a certain extent, to invoke the dimensions of a problem that the existence of the Commonwealth relation has inadvertently caused. However, he is not completely successful, because his economic arguments are speculative; he cannot substantiate them. He is left therefore to infer and suggest themes he dare not fully articulate.

These themes makes sense and are understood so to do by his audience because they have already been established by Osborne and other 'race' populist in previous Debates. If there was any doubt about the kinds of connections Butler might be suggesting, the contributions of Osborne and Gurden, in a self-consciously populist way, spell them out. It is the association of Butler's intentions with the views of these two that defeats the ideological success of the Debate for the Government, despite the fact that the Bill carried majority support. After this Debate the official language of 'race' will distance itself much more from the popular morality discourse of *crime and disease* established in the Debates leading up to the first piece of Commonwealth restriction legislation.[33]

Interestingly, although the Bill is passed, the arguments of Butler, in alliance with his 'race' populists, Gurden and Osborne, do not carry the House. Ideologically the Bill is defeated within the House, though outside it appears both necessary, commonsense and expedient. The argument of Gaitskell and Gordon-Walker are the ones that are noted; arguments that provide an effective economic and moral critique of the premise of the Bill:

> There is a direct relation between labour demand and immigration. Ninety-five per cent. of immigrants get jobs quickly. They do not just move about casually. They are able to take a share in the workings of our economy (Mr.Gordon-Walker, *Commonwealth Immigrants Debate*, 16 November, 1961: c.710).

And:
> Many people talk about millions of people coming here; [the Home Secretary]talked about a quarter of the population of the world coming here. But a limit is set on the numbers coming here by the economy itself, by the need of the economy for labour[...]The truth is that there is a fairly quick adaption of the numbers to the movement of the economy to and fro (c.710).

Gordon-Walker's remarks are reinforced and deepened by Hugh Gaitskell:

> [T]he rate of immigration into this country is closely related and, in my view at any rate, will always be closely related to the rate of economic

absorption[...]There has been, over the years, if the Hon. Gentlemen cares to consult the figures, an almost precise correlation between the movement in the numbers of unfilled vacancies, that is to say, employers wanting labour, and the immigration figures. As the number of unfilled vacancies goes down, the immigration figures go down, and as the number of unfilled vacancies rises, the immigration figures go up (Mr. Hugh Gaitskell (Leeds, South) c.794).

This is an eloquent and persuasive argument, which had an important constraining effect upon those in the labour movement growing faint hearted at the encroachments of the 'race' rebels. Gaitskell follows this with a strong elite condemnation of the Home Secretary's argument: 'It is, in my opinion, an utter and complete myth that there is the slightest danger or prospect of millions and millions of brown and black people coming to this country. Anyone who is trying to put that across is only trying to frighten people into believing that' (c.794). It is by means of this discourse of economic rationality and facticity that Gaitskell seeks to contest and undermine the validity of the arguments suggested by the Home Secretary and his 'race' populist Seconders (c.794-99).This critique is powerful, in bringing reason and economic logic to bear upon the 'scares' of the Opposition. At one point in his speech Gaitskell rounds upon the Government frontbench and addresses them directly:

What then is the reason for the Bill? The immigrants are healthy, law-abiding, and are at work. They are helping us. Why then do the Government wish to keep them out? We all know the answer. It is because they are coloured and because in consequence of this there is a fear of racial disorder and friction. This is the real question. Why do we have so much hypocrisy about it? Why do we not face up to the matter? (Gaitskell, c. 796).

Here, Gaitskell is referring to the political effect of the Notting Hill 'race riot' in speeding up the move to an official Government Bill. However, despite the importance of this 'moment' is confirming a racialisation of the disorders (Miles, 1984b), the ideological foundations of debate language lie deeper in the development of racial-political language and ideological-political strategy, which we will now demonstrate.

The Racial Imaginary: The Construction of the Ideological Framework of the Commonwealth Immigration Control Debate

In fact, as we have already suggested, the 'problem' of Commonwealth immigration is ideologically constructed in the handful of Debates that precede the 1961 Debate. One of the earliest of these is the intervention by H. Hyne (Accrington),[34] a Labour MP, on *Immigration Policy* (Hansard) 3 April, 1958: cols. 1415-26). This intervention is addressed, and responded to, on behalf of the Home Office, by Patricia Hornsby-Smith, Joint Under Secretary of State for the Home Department (cf.1422-26).

Hyne's Motion is a very basic demand for a consideration of restriction of 'British subjects from other parts of the Commonwealth' (c.1415). The Motion, as the core of his speech makes clear, is concerned with the 'problem' the numbers of immigrants is creating and is likely to create: in health care provision, the risk of carrying diseases into the country; the question of employment; the size of school classes. Perhaps the most urgent of all for Hyne is the 'question of National Assistance': 'When these people arrive in this country they immediately become eligible for National Assistance' (c.1417). This assertion allows Hyne into his central metaphor, that of 'hospitality':

> Hospitality is a very worthy virtue, and we are all proud and pleased to welcome guests into our own homes. But would we be justified in inviting into our homes more guests than can reasonably be housed and fed without serious detriment to our own families, even if those guests offered to pay for their accommodation or even if they happened to be relatives? (c.1417).

The 'guests' Hyne has in mind who 'are stretching our hospitality rather far' (c.1416) are immigrants from the Commonwealth as opposed to refugees or aliens. He quotes one of a 'pile' of letters he has had about 'recently landed coloured folk' and he agrees that: 'certainly they are coming, and they seem to be coming in increasing numbers to this country' (c.1416). Hyne assumes, during the course of his speech, that the term 'immigrants' is synonymous with those 'guests' emanating from: Malta, Cyprus, Pakistan, India and from the Caribbean.

The identification of the problem as one concerning 'coloured immigrants' is central to the Motions' seconder, James Lindsay (Devon, North):

> According to the Report of the Overseas Migration Board for last year, a quarter of the immigrants, that is to say, a quarter of the 178, 000 - 45, 000 - were coloured people. This is a great influx of coloured people into this country, and it will make a great difference to the composition of the

population. We are starting on the road to becoming a multi-racial country, a mixed community. We must face the facts (1419).

For Lindsay, it is the social impact of coloured immigration which forms 'the possible threat behind the present situation' (c.1418).[35] It is the risk of the 'colour problem' arising in Britain which concerns Lindsay. Although Britain is a 'tolerant' society the risk is one that will increase if there is no restriction on 'unskilled' Commonwealth labour, particularly at a time when demand is falling. Already we have seen 'signs of difficulty' in the 'employment of coloured labour'. At the same time, coloured people tend to congregate in certain jobs in segregated sectors of the economy. These elements are 'disturbing': 'I am quite convinced that the worst side could not happen, but there always is the possibility of trouble, and it is the risk of trouble, the threat[...]which is so important' (c.1420). As this quotation clearly shows, the similarities in theme and treatment between the 1961 Debate and this one are evident. The problem of numbers is, of course, central. Here also the population size of the Commonwealth and Dominions is used to suggest a potential 'mass immigration': 'Anyone from the Dominions or Colonies is allowed to come here as and when he wishes. There are no fewer than 630 million people in the Dominions and Colonies. We offer them a very warm welcome and very generous hospitality, and it is not surprising that very many come' (c.1418).

The idea that the total population of the New Commonwealth would emigrate to Britain tomorrow is absurd, but effective.[36] The idea that the migrants received 'generous hospitality' was a patent fiction, but it is consonant with the idea of the immigrants as guests of Britain's hospitality; until they take advantage, at which time it is necessary to get firm and restrict access to that provision. Hyne's legislative suggestion is that the Home Office agree to:

> [C]onsider barring people with no visible means of support, people who are obviously invalids who may be a burden on the National Health Service, and people with criminal records[...]absconding husbands and the like. Also, we might consider taking powers to deport those who break the law, just as we do with people from foreign countries (c.1418).

Here we have the inferences that construct the hidden language of eugenicism: the obsession with healthy population stocks, idleness, the carrying of diseases; the potential for violence and crime, and the lowering of standards and morality that will inevitably accompany the influx of large numbers of 'physically and mentally' inferior 'races'. This eugenicist theme is a very prominent element within all the interventions proceeding the 1961 Debate. It also forms the ideological framework of the speeches in that debate by Gurden and Osborne. It is what Barker and Gilroy would want to identify as the 'old racism'. Certainly the 'core' is composed of the 'old racism'; but on this basis a newly emergent secondary discourse of racial narration and argumentation is developed by these early 'race' populists. The structure of these debates is more subtle and complex than the binary opposition of old/ new racism allows in claiming a break or transition in what appears a complex field of change and continuity, within the inter-discursive context of debates and press and media coverage.[37]

A good example of the implicit eugenicist framework that characterises the debates proceeding the 1961 Bill is the motion proposed by Cyril Osborne: (*Immigration Control,* Hansard, 5 December 1958: Cols.1552-1597):

> That, whilst this House deplores all forms of colour bar or race discrimination, it nevertheless feels that some control, similar to that exercised by every other Government in the Commonwealth, is now necessary, and urges Her Majesty's Government to take immediate steps to restrict the immigration of all persons, irrespective of race, colour, or creed, who are unfit, idle, or criminal; and to repatriate all immigrants who are found guilty of a serious criminal offence in the United Kingdom (c.1552).

Although this theme is hedged in and enclosed within a defensive line of disclaimers and qualifiers, its core is qualitatively eugenicist: the *'unfit, idle and criminal'*. Osborne's rhetorical question as to 'whether the United Kingdom can continue to accept indefinitely unrestricted immigration irrespective of its 'quality and quantity' is resolved on the side of the 'qualitative' (c.1553). The meaning of the term 'qualitative' is made abundantly clear in statements such as the following: 'I think that there must be some control of immigration starting with a limitation on the least desirable types' (c.1556). Or even more nakedly: 'I cannot believe that any hon. Member, even one with the most liberal ideas, could defend the use of this country as a dumping ground for criminals from any part of the Commonwealth' (c.1558).

It could be argued that these are isolated statements that do not represent the overall argument. In fact the discourse that Osborne articulates in support of his motion, is one characterised by a struggle to keep the question of the 'quality' of the immigrants separate from the threat of their increasing numbers:

> [T]he more immigrants we allow into our country, irrespective of their colour or race, the greater the problem we shall have to deal with and the more their children will feel that they have a right to be here and to invite their other

relatives to come. By ignoring the issue now and deferring the decision we shall only be increasing the size of the problem (c.1554).

The problem for Osborne is that he wants to raise the question of colour as central without spoiling the non-racial disclaimers of the motion. His solution is to use a rhetorical device of quoting authoritative sources to speak for him. In this Debate he quotes *The Economist's* warnings of the intolerance of the 'British people' to the quantity of coloured immigrants. This device is only partially successful as it, on the one hand, distances the issue of colour to an inverted commas status, but, at the same time, it suggests the connection between the qualitative and the quantitative which had remained implicit. Labour backbench restrictionist, H.Hyne (Accrington) is moved to protest: 'I am not opposing the hon. Gentleman; I am with him, but I am sorry that he should introduce these quotations about colour. He said that he would not do so' (c.1555). Or Mr. Grey (Durham) with undisguised irony: 'The hon. Gentleman is spoiling the case' (c.1555). Pushed onto the defensive Osborne reveals the syllogistic structure of his motion: 'I am asking that there shall be control irrespective of colour or race. But it is useless denying that opinion in the country is most exercised by the coloured immigrant' (c.1555).

The seconder to the motion, Mr. Martin Lindsay (Solihull), does not seem hampered by such caveats, and identifies the core of the demand and to whom it should apply, quite explicitly: 'The motion refers to the idle, the unfit and the criminal, with the request that they should be excluded and that the criminal should be deported to the country of origin' (c.1561). Added to this however, Mr. Lindsay wants to deport not only those who are criminal but also: 'those who have shown that they are unfit in the sense that they are unable to earn a living in this country' (c.1561). As support for this extension of the demand, Mr. Lindsay asserts:

> We know that many thousands of people have come here from overseas because they prefer to live on National Assistance here rather than in poverty in their own country - men who do not speak English, who are unable to read and write, who have no particular craft and who would be quite incapable of holding down a job even in circumstances of brimful employment such as do not exist today (c.1561-2).

Mr. Lindsay is equally forthright when it comes to the issue of the association of colour with this identifiable group of the 'unfit': 'We all know perfectly well that the whole core of the problem of immigration is coloured immigration. We would do much better to face that and to discuss it realistically in that context' (c.1562).

The problem the proposers have in these early debates, over the need for restriction, is that the language or discourse they use is one that invokes an idea of 'race'. They also know that if this idea is summoned it will go against their case. As for example, the discourse of the 'unfit' is a term that cannot be used in a public context to apply to an identifiable group without bringing forth protest.[38] However, the difficulty for the proposers is that they do not want to let go of this language, because it is this very language that constructs the 'racial imaginary' through which they view the situation. The threat of numbers, of the idle and the unfit, is a 'racial' one and the speakers know this. The reasons then for the form the Debate takes can be best accounted for in terms of the conceptual division internal to the 'race' populists as to whether to defend the use of 'race' or to be consistent in concealing it in order to achieve their objective. This dichotomy exists within the discourse itself.[39]

The most consistently aware of this problem is the member who pursued the issue more than any other, Cyril Osborne. However, although he is manifestly aware of the requirement to present his case in a language that does not formally allude to 'race', his order of presentation often invokes it explicitly, with only the formality of quotation as defence. Hence Osborne quotes a letter denigrating the character of the Jamaicans as anti-British believing that if such sentiments are attributable to a third person they cannot be used to accuse him.[40] At the same time he is rebuked by his own supporters for this practice. Or similarly, while attempting to build a case involving apparently, non-'race' categories: unemployment, social strain, and health services, Osborne cannot resist the need to insist that he is speaking on behalf of the 'white man' or the 'Englishman'; categories which are seen to be virtually indistinguishable.[41]

Behind this defence of the 'white man's country' is a view of the emergent world order and its division among 'colour' lines: 'because of what we as white people, the Western world, are trying to do for the Afro-Asian countries in raising their standards of living, we are helping to industrialise them, and by so doing we are setting up new competition against ourselves in world markets' (c.1556). This argument, of the emerging challenge and confrontation of the coloured nations and the economic crisis that will ensue, calls for arguments of reciprocity: 'I am merely asking that there shall be done for Englishmen what other parts of the Commonwealth readily do for their own people' (1557).[42]

This understanding of the difficulties in using the 'race' concept cannot prevent the need to raise the issue of 'changing the nature of a community':

> We must ask ourselves to what extent we want Great Britain to become a multi-racial community[...]Surely, it is not illiberal[...]for people to be concerned with preserving their own national character and continuity. A question which affects the future of our own race and breed is not one that we should leave merely to chance. I do not believe that it is sensible to make this island a magnet of attraction for the whole of the rest of the Commonwealth by virtue of our superior wealth and Welfare State (c.1563-4).

This conceptual dilemma is highly pertinent in understanding the style of presentation of these early debates. This is particularly so in the way in which it creates an intensified problem of framing the issue at the outset of a debate, i.e., as an introduction. The speakers know from the outset that they are concerned with the question of 'coloured immigration' and that, engaging in this question, must involve the question of 'race'. They also know that the question of 'race' is not an issue that can be discussed in the House. It is these constraints and understandings that produces the particular kind of introductory style they share:

> This is a difficult, delicate and not very pleasant subject to discuss. It is difficult, because we are proud of our traditional open door, and we have been especially glad to welcome to these shores people from our own Commonwealth. It is delicate, because anyone who raises it is immediately open to the suspicion of racialism or of arousing passions and prejudices which no one wants to arouse (*Immigration Policy*, Hansard 3 April 1958: col. 1415).

Once the issue of restriction, of closing the door against the Commonwealth is muted, it is necessary to deny any racial motive. Indeed the opening disclaimers must invoke and then dispel the charge of racism. This is accomplished by removing the motive that could impute such a charge and replacing it with a completely opposite element. Here the choice is organised along the continuum of feeling, passion, prejudice and genuine fears; realism and practicality. Harry Hyne (Accrington) attempts something like this caveat when he asserts:

> I would be the first to object to any kind of bar on the grounds of race, colour or creed. Indeed, my object today is the very opposite. It is precisely because I am beginning to be afraid that these prejudices may develop in this country that I want something done about this uncontrolled immigration before the position becomes more serious (*Immigration Policy*, (Hansard) 3 April 1958: c.1415).

Make no mistake that Hyne is asking for a bar directed precisely at 'coloured immigrants' but he insists he is making it because of the threat that such immigration presents. Racism is being denied here a rationality. It is something that drives prejudices and which is exacerbated or diminished; rather than providing the reasons for a view or a course of action. This account of racism, and Hyne's recognition of his position separate from it, makes it difficult to identify the motives behind the call for controls as itself racist. It is an emergent feature of the debates preceding the 1961 Debate that it is possible to call for the restriction of an erstwhile racial group whilst explicitly identifying the motives for this course of action as non-racial. The way in which this is achieved is by defining a way of describing the problem posed by the group as 'objective', principled and fearlessly dispassionate, rather than subject to the distortions and unreason of the common emotions or passions; particularly since these passions are themselves the tool of 'racialism'. Secondly, that the failure to assent to controls will stimulate those very passions identified as the problem. What enables this caveat to take place is the initial bold attempt to seize upon the definition of racism as something opposite to that which motivates your actions.[43]

It is important to recognise that these language strategies develop out of the discursive need to negotiate the difficulty of the absence of an official language of 'race' in Parliament or in public speech. It is also out of these innovations that a more official language, expunged of eugenicist symbolism and the metaphors of social and moral inferiority, will arise and upon which the construction of the widespread acceptance of the need for Immigration and Nationality controls and restriction, as necessary, can be achieved.

A good indicator of the forthcoming official acceptance is tentatively suggested by the reply of the Joint Under Secretary, for the Home Office, as early as 1958:

> I would like to thank the hon. Member for Accrington (Mr. H. Hynd) for the very objective manner in which he has raised this matter. He has very courageously aired what is undoubtedly a controversial topic in a very fair and factual manner (Joint Under Secretary for the Home Office) (Miss Patricia Hornsby-Smith) *Immigration Policy*, 3 April 1958: col.1422).[44]

Of course, we must account for this reception partly out of the need to preserve the consensual form of the 'race' issue. But the following points are given the same realistic caste:

[W]hile we welcome British subjects to this country, I agree with hon. Members on both sides that we cannot ignore the rising potential of this immigration. In view of the size of the populations of the countries from which these people are coming, we have to take stock of the position as it now presents itself, and to realise that it could in the future possibly constitute a very grave burden on this country if the trend were to increase, or if the numbers arriving in this country were to become out of proportion to those that we can reasonably absorb (c.1422).

Surely the significance of this 'official response' is the way in which it demonstrates clear ideological linkages from the speeches and interventions of the Labour populist and racist right to centre support for the first Government Bill? This must be viewed as a process of transformation, of the racist scares and concerns of the ideological right, to the reasonable 'concerns' and 'balance' of the frontbench. It is a function of the use of official language and increasingly becomes, by repetition and transformation, the legitimate object of that language. What informs the internal continuity of this process are the twin themes, so evidently present in the official discourse of Hornsby-Smith; and common to the reasoned compromise of 'liberal' Butler and the extra-Parliamentary fundamentalism of Powell: *numbers and alienness*.

It is the self-evident 'problem' caused by the un-regulated accumulation of numbers of alien cultural groups that poses the political challenge to the liberal consciousness of the establishment. Within the iconographic landscape of this discourse of English reason and generosity is a racial language of exclusion and isolation fashioned from within. As we will demonstrate, Powellism is not a major departure from this formation, but rather an indicator of how far the framework, within which the political language of 'race' could be conducted, had itself shifted. The difference is one of *degree*. Thus, in Butler's speech, amidst a language of reasonableness, all the themes of 'race' and Immigration, are in place. The Bill is framed by a language of 'balance' and 'reason', underpinned by a set of inferences, which state in a more restrained or 'coded' form, those arguments already established by the 'race populists'. Without this existing set of inferential themes, Butler's arguments would appear spurious. Of course, Butler holds back from claims about idleness, disease or criminality. Ironically it is the very presence of these arguments within the debate that spoils the ideological credibility of the Government's case for restriction. Butler, the liberal, is accused in the quality press of the most heinous illiberality. But such liberalism is already increasingly hollow since it informs an ideological position that no longer commands any institutional support. The *'winds of change'*, in the space of a decade, reap the bitter harvest of Powellism. Within this discursive arcade the language of the right has merely mutated: its vision of the numerical assault upon, and cultural disintegration of, a racially homogenous social order remains a constant and enduring theme. What has changed by 1961 is that such a discourse, transformed by debate and elite support, has fashioned itself into an effective political language able to cohere backbench agitation and public pressure to the retention and maintenance of existing state power. The next chapter will further develop this substantive argument by focusing specifically upon the significance of the available evidence in establishing the degree of impact upon the discursive transformation in the political discourse of Immigration and Race Relations, by the rise of Powellism in 1968.

4 Racism and Parliamentary Discourse (II): 1968-88

As we have already established, advocates of the theory of the exceptional nature of Powellism, argue for 1968 as a watershed in British 'race politics'. In this chapter we examine, empirically, the textual evidence from Parliamentary Debates that can confirm or refute this view. Noted indicators of this are to be located within an apparent transformation in the conceptual content of public and Parliamentary language concerned with the *cultural impact* upon the national community, particularly in terms of their sense of identity, of *continued immigration* of 'culturally alien' groups, and the concomitant formation of 'foreign' areas of occupation within traditional working, and lower middle class, communities of English towns. There is, in short, a decisive claim for a qualitative transformation in the political language of 'race' and the popular presentation of the 'cultural' nature and consequences of immigration, which substantially replaces biologistic and inconsistent 'old' style racism of the Tory 'black country' populists and Empire revivalists.[1]

Conceptually central to this shift and transformation in political language is the call for an 'end to immigration', and for the culturally sanctioned pursuit of a policy of repatriation of incompatible groups, whose accumulation and development, as communities with 'special' demands and characteristics, threatens the political stability and homogeneity of the culturally defined nation:

> The nation has been, and is still being, eroded and hollowed out from within by the implantation of large unassimilated populations - what Lord Radcliffe once in a memorable phrase called "alien wedges" - in the heartland of the state[...]The disruption of the homogenous "we", which forms the essential basis of parliamentary democracy and therefore of our liberties, is now approaching the point at which the political mechanics of "divided community"[...]take charge and begin to operate autonomously (Enoch Powell, *Speech given at Public Meeting of the Hampshire Monday Club*, Southampton, April 9 1976; in Powell 1978: 165).

The most incisive and explicit expression of this argument is that of Gilroy (1987) and Barker (1981), made in support of the claim for the emergence of a New Racism (NR) . As for example, Gilroy has argued:

> It is only by looking in detail at the language and imagery of th(e) discourse on 'race' that the extent of changes which followed Enoch Powell's 'river of blood' speech of April 1968[...]can be appreciated. That speech provides something of a bridge between the older forms and linguistic devices of racism represented in the work of writers like Elton, Griffiths and Pannell, and the recognisably modern forms which identify and address a different range of problems[The speech] can be read as a break in the epistemology of contemporary racism (Gilroy 1987: 85).[2]

While Barker has explicitly claimed,

> [In my book][3] I argued that a new kind of racism had emerged in British politics, first articulately shaped by right wing conservative Enoch Powell, whose speeches on the question of immigration in 1968 lurched politics to the right very sharply. This 'new racism' stressed cultural differences as the primary reason for resisting immigration, and argued that each culture differently arises through national traditions from a common human nature. Thus, we aren't superior to black people, just inevitably different[...]That reference to human nature is a symptom of a semi-biological justification of racial separation emerging.[4] Increasingly since 1968, it has been the main organiser of official state racism in Britain (Barker 1983: 2).

For such theorists the language of 'race' is transformed after 1968 so that a qualitatively different discourse is recognisable in political and press debate. Other more modest claims for the impact of Powellism hold that Powell's extremely well publicised speeches, in April and November 1968, created a climate of public expectation of severe 'immigration control' upon non-white migrants which policy makers where forced to comply with, lest they lose popular support and legitimacy. In other words, Powellism, if not Powell himself, passes into the mainstream political agenda; and, for some, racism enters Parliament as a dominant force.

The evidence for these claims is more qualitative than quantitative. Certainly there is broad agreement that the 1968 Kenya Asians restriction Bill was the 'panic' response to a Powellist orchestration of popular revolt against any liberal line (cf. Layton-Henry 1984: ch.6; Rose 1969). At the same time, textual evidence suggests that the language of panic found its way into Parliamentary debate:

> I very much regret that it is not possible for this country to absorb these persons, to whom we have given the most solemn pledges, at a pace. If we did, I fear that it would cause racial disharmony and explosions (James Callaghan, Secretary of State for Home Affairs, *Commonwealth Immigration Bill*, 22 February 1968: c.662).

But what of the larger claim that a fully racist theorisation of black migration to Britain became the dominant language in debates, culminating particularly in the 1976 Debate on Immigration? As Gilroy has argued, in order to assess the claim for a *qualitative shift* in racial language content, we must make a detailed analysis of the textual evidence that can be cited as support for such assertions.[5] Sources here are the 5th July, 1976 *Immigration Debate*, cited by Barker and, for reasons of comparison, the *Race Relations Debates* taking place earlier in that year, and within days of the Debate on Immigration.[6]

Particular attention will be paid to the 1976 Debate since it is a noted indicator of the pro-thesis. However, much of the significance of the content of the 1976 Debate will be derived from a comparison with the themes that traverse the distinction between pre- and post- 1968 'race' language. In addition, we will examine, in some textual detail, the 1981 *Nationality Debate*, cited as evidence of qualitative shifts in the cultural-nationalist discourse of the 'New Right', beyond Powellism (CCCS: Race and Politics Group 1982: ch. 1, 2).[7]

While a close examination of the 1976 and 1981 debates may satisfy the textual evidence required to support the NR thesis, the broader distinction of the period after 1968 must also be examined, in order to establish what sort of impact (if any) Powellism may have had on political debates and political language usage. It may be the case that Powellism has had an impact on political language but not one that amounts to a shift in the conceptual epistemology of terms. Here we might argue that (i) Powell's dramatic presence has helped to heighten and sustain the issue of Immigration some considerable degree beyond its intrinsic weight and magnitude; or that (ii) Powell's speeches and interventions have resulted in specific effects in their own terms. This consideration is dependent, to a certain extent, on an additional variable; and that is the question of the continuity of Powellism to the 'old right' anti-immigrationists, and the extent to which his political language is separable from theirs. In accordance with these aims, this chapter will also examine and discuss the content of those debates taking place after 1968, particularly involving Powell directly.[8] Given the quantity of material involved, the focus of analysis will be less a detailed content analysis of the language of each debate but rather a more general analysis based on evidence and quotation from selected debates, across the whole period.[9]

Since much of the preceding chapter argued against the notion of 1968 as a conceptual watershed in the development of postwar racial discourse, it is important to establish what sort of claims for the nature of Powellism *can* be supported by the evidence; and the question of the relationship of Powellist discourse to the wider official discourses that characterise this period. In this respect, a key argument made will be that the 1981 *Nationality Debate* is much more important indicator of the conceptual and ideological impact of Powellism. However this claim is not necessarily consistent with those accounts that claim it is the culmination of Powellism or indeed a second phase (CCCS: Race and Politics Group 1982: ch.1; Solomos 1986b,c) in its ideological trajectory. It is only when the debate about 'race' restriction and repatriation gives way to a debate about 'racial identity' and nationalism that Powellism is able to more fully dictate the direction and content of Government legislation.

Prior to this Powell had remained a debate contender, sometimes managing to influence legislation through Committee clause changes, as in his notable success in the Committee stage of the 1971 Bill,[10] but unable to stimulate or lead a debate fully consistent with his ideology.[11] Even here Powell votes against the 1981 Bill, but for Committee, despite the fact that such a Bill comes the closest to the Bill of citizenship he had been calling for as a means to 'end immigration' and to provide a *test of allegiance* for those culturally incompatible with the nation (Powell 1972; 1978). At the same time, the 1981 Debate preserves an essential continuity with prior debates. This conceptual continuity draws together the 'old racist' right with the 'New Right' Powellites in a concern with numbers, the defence of racism, and the need to preserve the cultural homogeneity/racial composition of the population, in the interests of the Englishman and the British 'race' and breed. Such conceptual shifts that do occur, in the period from the late 1950s to the early 1980s, are *ones of degree* within an overarching continuity, inside which, Powellism is a dynamic and motivating force that allows the consistent presence of racism within politics and public debate. In some debates this 'presence' is overwhelming, as for example the 1968 *Race Relations Debate*, but his position 'outside' of the Tory cabinet and then as member for South Down confine his effect to an outside stimulator of ideological climates which, although very effective, cannot produce specific legislation.

Powellism and Political Commons' sense

It seems curious that Barker should view the *Immigration Debate* of 5th July 1976 as the triumph of the NR (1981: ch.2). If we accept that it was, and the argument and interpretation of the debate is persuasive, it still leaves a puzzle as to the relationship of Powell to this Debate, particularly since his contribution to it is minimal, to the extent that he does not actually remain in the chamber and is absent from the division over it.[12] It is of course Barker who claims that the 1976 *Immigration Debate* enshrines the NR theory as *political commonsense*. This raises the question of whether the identification between Powellism and the *Commons' sense* of political Debates is as clear cut as it might appear to be from such accounts. We must therefore carefully consider the argument that Powellism has created a 'new commonsense' which, by 1976, is for Barker and others, clearly at the heart of the frontbench 'political establishment'.[13]

Certainly the Commons' sense language of these debates is very like Powellism, at least from the backbenches. However the language of the Frontbench is certainly not Powellist in the same way. As for example, Whitelaw, opening for the opposition in the Race Relations Debate is very clear what that Commons'sense is: good 'race relations' are only possible if the indigenous, tolerant majority, can be assured that strict immigration control will be enforced. In particular, existing measures must be tightened and illegal immigration must be dealt with; at the same time the public must be informed of the precise numbers of dependants who the country has an obligation to, so that 'an end to immigration' is in sight (*Race Relations Bill*, (Hansard) 4th March, 1976: c. 1570). This certainly reflects the Commons' sense racism which informs the understanding and exchange of debates; but it is not Powellist, even though it represents an 'extremism' of sorts. Powellism is certainly in evidence as providing the ideological pressure to seek support for such demands. But they fall far short of what Powell would have wanted, and he is not the force guiding their formulation. If anything, they are a political reaction or concession to his position.

This alone must throw doubt upon the way in which Barker presents the role of Powell. The account of the Immigration Debate is characterised in the following way: (i) the debate is seen as important because no full debate on Immigration has been conducted for some time; (ii) added to this Powell had managed to obtain and leak the Hawley report, a civil servants' account of the 'queues of dependants' wanting to join their relatives in Britain. In this fashion we get an impression of how Powell, playing the 'numbers game' with the complicity of the press, is able to create the pressure for a debate.

While the details of this account are evidently correct, the political and ideological context of the debate is drawn far too narrowly. The first thing we should recall is that 1976 is remembered primarily for the debate on Race Relations, which took place on the 4th March, four months prior to the Debate on Immigration. Secondly, unlike the Immigration Debate, this debate was initiated by the Government and led to legislation: the 1976 Race Relations Act. By contrast, the Immigration Debate was initiated by the Opposition and was therefore unable to produce any legislation. This, of itself, does not mean that it did not have any effect on the behaviour of the Government in power or the setting of the terms of public debate.

But as soon as we include the March debate within our analysis it produces two important insights which cast doubt on the evidence for the passage of the NR into the political mainstream, and the role of Powellism in this process. Firstly, a considerable amount of the debate is concerned with the issue of 'further immigration' and restrictions rather than 'race relations'; in fact, this argument is the main plank of the Conservative approach. In essence the argument, put plainly by Whitelaw, is that without the reassurance of a 'cut in numbers' of dependants and the prospect of 'an end to immigration' Race Relations policy will not be tolerated by the indigenous population. Here we can plainly see that such a debate position is a precursor of the arguments of the Immigration Debate. In this respect the July debate is a result of this approach and the pressure to agree these measures; to establish the minimum Commons'sense that will underpin government policy.

There are two points that follow here. The first is that, despite this negative concentration upon the rights and expectations of the 'tolerant' indigenous majority, virtually the whole of the Conservative party vote with the Bill. Powell and a handful of 'race' populists vote against it. Many of these are the Tory backbench 'hard-core' racists, such as Ronald Bell, who has consistently contested the fundamental validity of any kind of Race Relations legislation.[14] The others are part of this old guard or they are the new Powellist influenced, 'populists' such as Powell's successor at Wolverhampton, South-West, Nick Budgen; or the populist right: Churchill, Stokes and Stanbrook..

The second point is that, politically speaking, the commitment to 'end immigration', even at the expense of dependants, in order to meet the 'genuine fears' of the indigenous, is the political price Labour must pay in order to pass the 1976 Race Relations Bill. It will be our argument, in the course of this chapter, that the discursive transformation that has taken place here is that to which we have already referred: the passage of the language of racism from the 'old' racist backbenchers to the frontbench. Specifically this has involved public support for the imaginary and beleaguered Englishmen who is viewed as the 'victim' of the social and cultural 'problems' that have followed 'black immigration' into major conurbations, particularly Birmingham, the Black Country and London. As our analysis, in chapter 3, of the debates of the late 1950s and early 1960s made clear, the construction of this 'folk archetype' has taken the best part of twenty years and forms the ideological 'bedrock' of the political (racist) Commons' sense of Immigration and Race Relations Debates.

The 4th March, 1976 Race Relations Debate

The March 4th Debate is chiefly remarkable for the attempt by the Shadow Home Secretary to hijack it from Roy Jenkins and to turn it into a Debate about 'immigration fears'. Underpinning this treatment by the Conservatives is the idea that it is only by addressing these fears that the question of a 'race relations' policy could have any chance of success. This framework was signalled early, when Home Secretary Jenkins' opening remarks, concerning the urgent need for anti-discrimination legislation because of the clearly documented evidence of social and economic discrimination against black British people,[15] are interrupted by Winston Churchill MP (Stretford). Sweeping such gloom aside as applicable to 'only a tiny minority' Churchill asks rhetorically: 'Would [the Home Secretary] pay tribute to the wonderful way in which the British people have accepted[...]a very substantial influx of alien culture and alien race into their midst without any open conflict or racial prejudice?'(*Race Relations Bill* (Hansard), 4 March 1976: c.1550).[16]

Despite the 'culture' centred language of this interjection, it rests on the invocation of the 'tolerant' British people and the imaginary Englishman, under siege in his own community.[17] The political importance of this imagery is in how it allows the articulation of the legitimate feelings of 'many genuine people', 'entirely free from any racial prejudice'[18] who attribute their feelings to the idea that the rate of immigration is not being curtailed and thus the source of their anxieties must grow apace. Since the Official source of entry has been severely curtailed, through a series of draconian pieces of legislation, considerably more severe than anything on the European continent, the focus of anxiety must be on 'abuses' and 'infiltration' of the system: 'illegal entry' and 'overstaying' being the favoured examples. The nasty turn involved in the movement to such a position is the obsession with '*covert* immigration'. The degree of movement in the mainstream can be gauged here most incisively. Thus Whitelaw acknowledges the wish of the Home Secretary to 'root out' illegal immigration, 'Nevertheless,

[...]there is real public anxiety and[...]a case to be investigated and answered' (c.1569). In seeking support for this assertion he refers to the *Daily Telegraph*, then proceeds to read out a spuriously documented article alleging that 'immigrants' from the Asian sub-continent 'troop in endlessly through the arrival terminals'(c.1570). Sidney Bidwell (Ealing, Southall) specifically contests this, 'There is tight control over immigration and there has been for a long time. The right hon. Gentlemen has just said that a stream of people come in. That is not the case' (c.1570). This challenge causes Whitelaw to retreat back behind his 'question raising' role:

> I said that this is what an article says is happening. I have not said whether it is true or not. If an article of this sort is published in a reputable newspaper which has a wide circulation, inevitably it raises questions and one would be hiding one's head in the sand if one pretended that it did not and does not present a case to be answered (Mr. William Whitelaw (Penrith and the Border), *Race Relations Bill* (Hansard), 4 March 1976: c.1570).

This logic is central to Barker's analysis of the NR and the discursive gambit known as the argument from 'genuine fears' (cf. Barker, 1981: 14-6). However, this response is absolutely in line with the use of such arguments and sources by the 'old racists', such as Harold Gurden, who both referred to and consistently used newspaper stories and editorials as 'evidence' of the 'genuineness' of the anxieties of their constituents.[19] The key here is the 'depth of feeling' and the extent to which such feeling reflects a genuine i.e., authentic understanding of the situation. Here feeling is equated with empiricism: those that feel it somehow must *know*. However the lack of proof does not call for official caution in the circulation of such remarks but the opposite; the need to search out incidents that can support such feelings:

> [I]t is no use pretending that this is not something felt on a very widespread basis. This may not be happening. I do not know whether it is happening or not[...]But if they have any substance, I hope that very firm counter-action will be taken immediately, and that proper checks will be instituted to prevent overstaying. Surely that makes absolute sense? (Mr. William Whitelaw (Penrith and the Border), *Race Relations Bill* (Hansard), 4 March 1976: c.1571).

This is a fuller statement of Whitelaw's claim in the Immigration Debate to the effect that,

> There are still too many stories of illegal immigration and over-staying which are widely believed. I do not accept all of them, but the old saying 'No smoke without fire' is usually true, and so I conclude that there are some illegal immigrant rackets which need to be uncovered and smashed immediately (Whitelaw c.966; cited in Barker 1981: 14).

It could be argued that this is traditional Tory pragmatism about a non-traditional Tory issue: public opinion must reflect a bedrock of commonsense; people's experience are grounded in their emotions, and such people are therefore likely to be lead astray unless properly assuaged. This requires a leadership in tune with popular fears. Barker claims this political relationship is the basis of a new politics of (racist) commonsense, as we have seen.[20] However, it could be plausibly argued that the model offered for 'genuine fears' is a re-working of the 'moral panic' argument.[21] The press are central to the framing of such 'popular' anxieties which are then taken up by politicians as proof of the validity of the anxiety. Of course the circuit is a 'self-referencing 'spiral, articulating the political project of moral entrepreneurs and the circulation interests of press barons; but here the main actors are politicians involved in what Barker was subsequently to dub 'flexi-panics' (1984 (ed)):[22]

> [T]he question I am raising relates to what is said by many people, and it is no use pretending that this is not something felt on a very widespread basis. I do not know whether it is happening or not[...]I doubt whether the Home Secretary or the Minister of State knows whether or not it is happening. If these claims can be rebutted, so much the better. But if they have any substance, I hope that very firm counter-action will be taken immediately, and that proper checks will be instituted to prevent overstaying (Mr. William Whitelaw (Penrith and the Border), *Race Relations Bill (Hansard)*, 4 March 1976: c.1571).

The key element here, as Barker correctly identifies, is the overwhelming attention to 'feelings' and 'rumours' of the indigenous. In defence of this public speculation, Whitelaw asserts the further point that popular confusion about statistics has led many to conclude that 'there is something fishy about the whole business' (c.1573). This is equivalent to the 'no smoke without fire' argument cited by Barker. It is the worst kind of spacious logic and represents an extreme concession to populism. At the heart of such a position is the view that the 'ordinary Englishman' must be reassured that 'he' is not being swamped - because Government Departments are not *effectively enforcing immigration control*. On this basis the Conservatives will not consider discrimination legislation until they are satisfied that there is evidence of a 'really strict control of immigration' (c.1573): 'It cannot be said to often that if illegal immigration and overstaying were to be taking place on any substantial scale they would destroy any race relations policy' (Whitelaw c.1569).

It is important to be clear that this is the closest the Conservative Frontbench actually get to discussing 'Race Relations' and it is, in fact, a statement about 'immigration' and reveals the skewed ideological climate in which such a discussion has been placed. The 'logic' of a panic about numbers leads to the logic of the numbers game itself: an obsessive search for 'the truth' about -'the immigrants'. What the sound of the incantation of numbers seeks to confirm, by repetition, is that there are already 'too many of them here.' Denied by office, and an elite code of liberalism, to voice this anxiety as 'truth', Whitelaw confirms the validity of such racial constructions by the very seriousness with which they are treated: 'we need a totally independent inquiry into the way in which immigration statistics are collected, compiled and presented' (c.1569).

Whitelaw argues that only a public inquiry will quieten the feelings of people and satisfy the arguments and allow 'a completely fresh start which will rebuild public confidence and give us an opportunity to reassess the working of strict immigration control' (c.1573). At the close of his speech Whitelaw reiterates and confirms this position: '[The Home Secretary]must demonstrate clearly that there is strict and effective control of the numbers entering the country[...]Provided that the Home Secretary can fulfil that part of his clear compact with the British people[...]the Bill has a role to play' (c.1573).

Firstly, it is incontestable that this logic of presentation is a rehearsal for that cited in Barker. Here of course, the Race Relations Bill Debate, is a much more effective political arena since it relates to the contestation of official proposed legislation. What is missing from Barker's assessment of the significance of the Debate is that politically, for the Frontbench, this speech is a strategic juggling act, aimed at forging a workable alliance between Front and Backbench, able to carry the middle ground with Whitelaw and the Shadow Cabinet Frontbench, as against the racial extremism of the Backbench. The point is that it *allows Whitelaw to manage a party vote for the Bill.*

To be fair to Barker what, of course, remains unacknowledged here by the Conservative elite is how (i) public opinion (ii) concern with numbers and (iii) reference to press debate are a specific and worried concession to Powellism and the construction of a 'climate of opinion' orchestrated by Powell and Sandys (cf. Layton-Henry 1984: ch.6). The idea that the 'ordinary Englishman' must be reassured that 'he' is not being swamped; that government departments are liable to error and that the nature of statistics has become a site of intense scrutiny and anxiety. Finally, that the government of the day is not enforcing *strict immigration control*. Thus Whitelaw's presentation, its conceptual structure and terms of reference, are substantially those Powell delivered in contemporaneous speeches of the time.

This does not mean, however, that Barker is correct to assert that the NR has entered Parliament by this time and become the 'political Commons' sense.' The problem is one of conflation. Powellism, the discourse of the NR identified by Barker; and the Commons' sense identified here, are not the same thing. To argue that they are is to misrepresent the role of 'race language', the political clout of Powellism; and the internal politics of the Tories at this time. Firstly, in terms of language, as we have already argued, the central imagery and logic of this construction of the problem of 'race relations' is one that Powell himself adopts and develops from the 'race populists'. The distinctive change is that now the frontbench accommodation to such racist imagery is more publicly evident.[23] Such a movement is a movement of continuity not discontinuity. Secondly, because there are evident differences in the manner of the presentation of these themes and ideologies by the frontbench and backbench, and by Powell himself; and because they are wedded to incompatible political strategies and positions. A central distinction here is in the treatment of 'racism' as a phenomenon belonging to the negative attitudes and ideas of the indigenous. Powell and the backbench cannot bring themselves to acknowledge the existence of such views among their *ordinary English indigenous*. Not so Whitelaw:

> [I]t is our duty openly to voice the genuine anxieties of many people in this country. In doing so we have equally to differentiate between those genuine anxieties and the real prejudices shown in the vicious correspondence which I am sure all hon. Members receive from the real extremists (Mr. William Whitelaw (Penrith and the Borders) *Race Relations Bill (Hansard)*, 4 March 1976: c.1568).

Although this distinction is a strategic one that operates along the axis of the genuine/prejudiced, it does acknowledge the location of racism within the electorate. It therefore provides the basis for a social democratic articulation against the Powell/backbench position. The position adopted by Whitelaw is, if anything, further modified in the social democratic direction in the Immigration Debate, as we shall show. Before this, however, let us examine more closely the specific character and role Powell plays in the Race Relations Debate and its comparative significance.

The Role of Powell

Unlike the Immigration Debate, Powell does speak in the Race Relations Debate, as well as playing a strong role of contestation in its Committee stages.[24] Like Whitelaw, the subject and object of his intervention is not 'race relations' but 'immigration': 'This Bill is even more irrelevant to the real problems and dangers entailed on this country by the inflow from the New Commonwealth during the last quarter of a century' (Powell, J. (Down, South) *Race Relations Bill* (Hansard) March 4th, 1976: c.1580).

The difference in the stance adopted is that Powell's is a position of absolute radical pessimism: unless the country and its politicians are patriotically aroused to defend their culture and institutions against the 'unarmed invasion' of black migrants the very fabric of the nation as a historical community could be destroyed! However, contra the NR claims for a new cultural discourse of difference, via Powell's intervention, the 'real' concern and point of focus of this phenomenon is: 'birth rate', more specifically 'coloured births'. This elision between terms requires Powell to frame his remarks with an explicit caveat or disclaimer of 'racism', specifically because Powell fully knows that the discursive space or field on which he wishes to pitch his ideological tent is that of 'old racism'; an old racism specifically signified by the theme of 'immigrant births':

> I have never myself at any stage in any discussion on this matter assumed any higher birth rate on the part of the immigrant or non-European population than of the rest[...]We are not talking about birth rates. We are not talking about the proportion of numbers of births to relevant population, which is what birth rate means. We are talking about the proportion of births of a particular year which are of a certain kind and a certain origin, and adding one year to another until we reach a whole generation of 25 years. We are talking about the composition of a generation (Powell, J. (Down, South) *Race Relations Bill* (Hansard) 4 March 1976: c.1582).

Powell's use of the 'numbers game' here and the phrases 'a certain kind' and 'certain origin' are 'motivated' signifiers for the spectre of the 'coloured generation' growing in volume within the general population. It is unmistakable that Powell's treatment of numbers is towards the construction of this inferred racial nightmare: a population apart and growing within the 'heart of the nation' but culturally and politically not in *allegiance* with it.[25]

In the course of his speech, Powell refers to the disclosure of figures requested and supplied by OPCS of the monitor of ('what are popularly called') 'coloured births'. It is the production of this figure which allows the all important comparison of the numbers born to mothers, themselves born in the New Commonwealth or Pakistan, and total births. This allows Powell to launch into a Parliamentary version of his 'numbers game' of *immigrant births*. The geo-spatial imagery of this number count is the dead-pan intoning of the percentage of 'black' births within the '*areas of occupation*' i.e., the Midlands and Inner London: 'Birmingham runs at 17 or 18 per cent'; while, 'Leicester who entered late into the race' [what race is this?], 'rose in six years, 1969 -74 from 18, 19, 20, 23, 25 to 26 per cent' (c.1581). Inner London rates are running at: 'Brent, 36 per cent, Ealing 34 per cent, Haringey, 34 per cent, respectively'.

However Powell's 'black math' is not complete unless it is also able to include within the equation: 'immigrant descended births'. 'These percentages, of course, are not the full proportion of what popularly would be called 'coloured births'. In these years children were also being born to mothers who had indeed been born here, but were as much New Commonwealth in all but a technical sense as the mothers of the children to which these figures relate' (c.1581).

This category follows, of course, from Powell's absolutist ethnicity argument: that a West Indian or Asian cannot be deemed English simply by being born in Britain; first they must pass the culture test; however the numbers eligible to enter such a test are strictly limited![26] Here, the metaphors and politics of the new cultural and the old biological politics of racism collide. Powell's emphasis on the proportionate expansion of the population as coloured, while insisting that there is no assumption of differential birth-rate, is a feature of both the 'new' and 'old' racism. However, such a point can make no sense except in reference to the assumption and focus of the 'old racism', and yet the formality of the presentation of this point is a disavowal of those assumptions. This is the most characteristic feature of Powellism and, for some, the NR (Solomos 1989: 123-6).[27] This proportion of the population that Powell goes to the trouble of collecting statistics about, will automatically reproduce itself and expand, even without assuming a differential birth-rate. What else can the practice of drawing attention to the separation of this population be unless the intention is to racialise it? Thus at the heart of the NR discourse of Powellism is a biological metaphor of differential fecundity which threatens the 'white' ethnic majority, whose cities are being occupied by ever growing numbers: 'this element - the one third of our cities coloured - is being increased by an annual influx assessed at a minimum of 50,000' (Powell c.1583).

The NR theorists are silent about the role the numbers game continues to play in 'new racist' discourse.[28] In this sense, Powellism's relationship to the front bench is very much that of the 'old' style racist: since his central theme was/is and continues to be: 'numbers', colour and immigrant birth rate.[29] For Powellism 'numbers are of the essence': they are the empirical basis on which cultural communities form and become 'wedges' and 'implants'.[30] It is on the bedrock of Powell's biological politics of the birth-rate and the political imperative that Powell is able to construct the 'new (cultural) racism' of the ethno-war raging through Britain's inner cities and conurbations. This well worked scenario has merely to be articulated to the sub-theme and concerns of the debate: that proposed legislation is addressed to white ethnic practices directed against the black ethnic minority:

> This massive segregation is not arising because of discrimination - certainly not of any discrimination which it is within the power of the law to influence or remove. It is arising because of the combination between human nature on one hand and the mass and size of the original movement itself and the rate of its continuance on the other (Powell, J, *Race Relations Bill* (Hansard*)*, March 4th, 1976: c.1584).

This could reasonably said to be a statement of the NR. What defines it as racist is the determinant role that human nature must exercise over the mixing of groups.[31] Thus, for Powell, the effect of the Bill will be counter-productive because the creation of new rights creates new grievances. When immigrants enter the country they instantly become the recipients of traditional and fought-for rights and privileges. In addition the Bill seeks to give new rights, 'the purpose of this legislation is to create new rights, new remedies, which the inhabitants of this country have never enjoyed and never sought, for the sake of this new and growing element which is amongst us' (Powell c.1585). Here we have arrived at the heart of Powellism, phase two.'[32] It is during these years that Powell returns to the Immigration Debate, importing into his analysis of numbers and 'black math', the images and projections of violent civil war on mainland Britain.[33] It is the thread of inner logic of this 'race war' scenario that leads back to the argument about numbers.

Given such a scenario, racism and discrimination are predictable reactions to the expanding foreign presence; they are the down-side of the ordinary Englishman, pushed beyond his endurance. The metaphors of social strain and alien encampments is at the heart of the official construction of Immigration politics as our analysis of, especially, the 1962 Debate makes clear. Powell merely takes this politics to its terminus: *repatriation*.[34] Thus the realism of the Conservative frontbench and backbench support is one forged on the anvil of Powellism. Such a realism though is able, through the layers of the numbers game debate and the politics of (minority) racial harmony, to resolve the nightmares of 'race war' within the ideological incantation of: an *end to immigration*. This is the new (racist) realism:

> After serious consideration, I have come to the view that it is essential in the country's interests, in the interests of the ethnic majority of the population, and, just as important, in the interests of the racial minorities, that further immigration into Britain from the New Commonwealth should be ended at the earliest possible date (Mr. Dudley Smith (Warwick and Lemington) *Race Relations Bill* (Hansard*)*, March 4th, 1976: c.1592).

Since 'over three quarters of the population' want an 'end to immigration' and are by no means racists since 'only a tiny minority of people are racists, as we understand the term[...w]e must have more positive action to stem the tide, which is far greater than most of us realise' (c.1593). Smith anchors his argument by reference to the 'problem of the thousands of illegitimate children' in the Caribbean who are 'anxious to come here' which could prolong immigration for a 'hundred years' unless the rules are changed. His solution is Powell's: 'It is perfectly possible for those who want to rejoin their relatives to do so in their country of origin'(c.1595). The potential infinity factor of Asian and Caribbean dependants is a variation on a well established Immigration Debate theme, established since the late 1950s, of the potentially limitless amount of people wishing to exercise their constitutional right to enter Britain and overburden it.[35]

Mr. George Sinclair (Dorking) believes strict control essential to give the host community, particularly those residing in areas of immigrant concentration, the confidence to adjust to stresses and strains. Such people require a promise that no more immigrants will be allowed to add to their worries (c.1603). To this end two assurances are required, (i) that there will be no relaxation of controls while new measure are considered and (ii) assurances must be given that stronger measures will be taken to check the flow of illegal immigrants and people who overstay their permits (c.1603). Is this not the NR? Only if we confine that term to shifts in a body of discourse that has an essential unity (cf. Solomos 1990).[36] Since what has occurred over the thirty years of Immigration Debate is that Powell and Gurden's people 'who really know' are now been given much more explicit rather than complicit frontbench support. It amounts to a case of 'we believe you now'.

The next exchange and contribution confirms this view. Mr. Thomas Torney (Bradford, South) challenges Whitelaw's spurious rumour validation which he sees (surely correctly) as confirming the unfounded prejudice of the racists? Ronald Bell replies acidly that the Hon. Member is *alone* in not being concerned by the illegal entry of immigrants. Here we arrive at the crux of the Debate and the recognition of the remarkable degree of continuity such Debates have exhibited:

> The House will readily concede that I have concerned myself with this subject for longer than any other Hon. member[...]Although I could say much[...]I shall not do so because *I need a little time to adjust to the sentence of orthodoxy which seems to be passed upon me this afternoon* (Bell, *Race Relations Bill* (Hansard), March 14th 1976:c. 1620-1; *italics mine*).

Such disarming modesty does not prevent Bell from presenting his philosophical defence of the idea of discrimination which has remained the central element in a consistent conceptual attack on the very premise of racial discrimination Bills:

> Discrimination is not merely the supreme human quality; it is the very principle of life itself, whether it be vegetable or animal. Discrimination is everything. The perception and evaluation of difference is a basic function of every sentient creature. A heavy responsibility lies upon anyone who proposes to use a law of a country to declare that people must disregard certain things that they believe that they perceive. The error that should be castigated, whether legal or not, is the attachment of unreasonable importance to an observed difference. However, the process of discrimination is always impeccable. It is always right and should never be discouraged, let alone forbidden[...]I regard laws of this sort as was against the very spirit of the human race (Bell c.1621-2).

Here, as in Powell and much of the NR, racial hostility is placed on a philosophical or anthropological plane where its logical or determined character appears to have no connection to social acts of hostility. Racism is trivialised as a cognate error and discrimination becomes a definer of human attributes. It must be concluded that such logic is mischievous, apparently, as in much New Right discourse, deliberately so (cf. Palmer (ed) 1986).[37]

It is on the basis of Bell's philosophical plea for the freedom to discriminate that allows him to settle upon the question of racial language, lobbing a missile into the contradictory heart of anti-racist liberalism: the role of language in the construction of racial accounts of social relations: 'The Home Secretary is saying that people cannot be allowed to express scandalous opinions in moderate language because it is too dangerous, and that if they are put moderately and rationally, they may persuade people that they are right' (Bell c.1625). This argument goes beyond the concerns of this chapter because it challenges the idea that racism involves an obvious prohibition of those intent upon social hatred, rather than an interrogation of the social construction of 'discursive repertoires' or ways of interpreting/constructing *racialised* 'realities'.[38] Ironically, the example Bell draws upon to support his argument, is ill considered *and* absolutely central to the claims of the old racists:

> We know that in the last year certain geneticists have come close to saying that there is in certain races a certain mental inferiority which could be ineradicable. Never mind whether it is true or not, the situation is that they have reached that conclusion. Are they not to be at liberty to state the view? (Bell, c:1626).

Such an appeal ignores the social and ideological context within which the search for a racial IQ factor has proceeded (Simon 1971; Kamin 1974; Rose 1976);[39] again it displays a mixture of philosophical posturing, fundamentalist moralism and hard edged populism; these are mixed in a malicious and mischievous way, by the apparent simplicity of the issue.[40]

Powell's 'Backbench' New Racists?

While we have shown a clear relationship of conceptual language of Powell to the 'old racists', like Bell; does the same hold good for the 'new racists'? For example, Nick Budgen was Powell's Conservative replacement as MP for Wolverhampton South West, but any claim that he is the Powell heir apparent requires careful consideration. For example, a feature of his contribution is to concede that discrimination is a problem. In addition he unequivocally condemns racial prejudice, 'I define racial prejudice as being blind, unreasoning dislike of any race' (c.1631). However, it is evident that his definition of racism is quite circumspect and quite consistent with the Backbench 'populists' he keeps company with. In this respect his argument replicates and extends the themes and concerns of the racial logic of the ordinary Englishman and the magic resolution of an 'end to immigration' i.e., Budgen's right-politics is a function of a bid for a populist stance:

> [T]he ordinary people of this country - not the media or the gentlemen in Whitehall and Westminster - have displayed an extraordinary tolerance. Let us pay tribute to the people of this country who have borne the burden of this immigration. There have been many tensions and difficulties which have been reduced by the kindliness, decency and good humour of the British man in the

street - the same people that we Tories instinctively trust rather than compel (Budgen c.1633).

Once the issue has been consistently defined in terms of the image of the kind and decent English, the idea of introducing penalties against such an icon is itself criminal. Indeed, for Budgen, the very construction of the categories of penalty will make solid something that is fluid and able to form a benign rather than malign form. What aligns Budgen with Powell and Griffiths before him is the defence of the putative working class victims of such legislation, whose behaviour, if it ever does depart from that of reasonableness and friendliness, is to be sympathised with rather than condemned. Such legislation is likely to be socially divisive because,

> it stirs up the whole issue of racial prejudice once again. It will cause further resentment as it grants yet further rights to the immigrant minority. It will be one more affront, not to the middle class who are here but to the ordinary British people who have to bear the brunt of immigration and have done so with decency and dignity (Budgen c.1634).

The defence of the threatened rights of the mythical Englishmen, his tolerance waning, besieged in a multi-racial city, rapidly transforming into something unrecognisable as 'England' reaches it poetic apogee with the contributions of John Stokes (Halesowen and Stourbridge):

> I begin by declaring an interest. I am an Englishman and a member of the Royal Society of St. George[...]I believe that most hon. Members know in their hearts the views of ordinary English people. They wish to keep this country, which they know and love, basically as a place to which they feel they belong. Fundamentally, they do not wish it to change either its character or its cohesion. In other words, they wish to retain their identity - their homeland (Stokes c.1642).

Here the defence of the rights of the indigenous Englishman reveals itself as a defence of identity and the character of a mythical 'homeland'. Such a defence is necessary because immigration of 'alien people' has changed its character: home is no longer home, i.e., 'something that one knows, loves and returns to' (c.1642). Now the 'immensity' of 'coloured immigration' threatens 'the future'. 'Immigration has completely altered the face of certain parts of the country. It has[...]created foreign enclaves in our midst. It has brought into this country alien people who live alongside us, whose religion, customs and habits are quite different from ours' (c.1643). Here, in impeccably Powellist terms, Stokes draws the 'alien cultural' immigrants as against an ontological-portrait of a formally homogenous English, defined and associated by their customs and national belonging; elements now under assault.

It is inescapable that the content of this speech would not be possible without a thorough absorption of the narrative content and style of Powellism. Stokes even offers a vignette of 'a constituent', 'who found himself and his family the last English persons in a road otherwise totally occupied by immigrants' (c.1643).[41] Stokes anchors this narrative firmly within the theme of the survival of the English in their own land: 'I make no apology for the fact that this problem mainly concerns England and the big English cities. There are certain areas where an Englishman may feel that he is a stranger in his own land' (c.1643-4). This directly paraphrases Powell's statements and Osborne's before him.[42] Does this example therefore demonstrate Powellism or the NR have passed into the mainstream of Immigration and Race Relations debate, by this time? The answer must be that, once again, such language and narrative style, while coupled to Powell, is also firmly anchored in the discourse of Osborne and Pannell; particularly the central metaphors of the Englishman and the character of England.[43] What has changed is the lack of reference to 'race or breed'.[44] So there has been, qualitatively, a shift in the symbolism of the drama but not the central depiction of the story. The Powellist narrative style of Stokes is still one firmly anchored in the style and concerns of the old racists, as I have consistently argued, despite its presentation of cultural fears and feelings.

In point of fact, Stoke's apparently Powellist cultural fears, are very evidently racial ones in the 1981 Debate, despite the fact that formally such debate concerned proposed Nationality legislation:

> The Bill seems to suppose that all or a large part of the human race is much the same in thoughts, habits, customs, religious beliefs and ideals as those who lived here for centuries and have shaped their destiny on the world's stage[...]The great English Jew, Disraeli, said that race was everything, and he was right. But race and racial origin are not mentioned in the Bill, and John Bull becomes a very shadowy figure indeed (John Stokes, (Halesowen and Stourbridge), *British Nationality Bill*, 28 January 1981: c.989).

From the idea of fundamental difference Stokes is moved to insist that the distinctive cultural character of the English requires their status as a separate 'race'; and legislation must recognise this national 'race character'. Mr. Stokes goes on, in the course of this particular speech, to refer to the need to, 'convert the heathen immigrant to Christianity' (c.989), and for the need for parliament to 'safeguard the essential identity of the nation and to preserve its future' (c.989). Here such cultural fears are unmistakably fears for the racial future of the English. This very obvious slide to 'race' from culture must question not only the 'new racism' idea but the penetration of such language forms into Frontbench discourse.[45]

In this respect, Powellism still occupies the same kind of relationship to the mainstream as the 'old racism', although overall, the distance between the frontbench and backbench has narrowed with the growing centrality of racial Commons' sense to political legitimacy[46] and its potential as an issue that is able to thematize party politics and address constituency demands. In addition, as the content of Stokes' speech illustrates, a formal separation of language styles obtains in such presentation. Thus the construction of the Commons' sense language of the frontbench relies more on inference than a shared language. Let us now return to the 1976 Debate, claimed by Barker to demonstrate the ascendancy of the discourse of the NR, in the light of our analysis of the Race Relations Debates.

The 5th July Immigration Debate: The 'New Racism' Pollutes the Commons?

The 5th July 1976, Immigration Debate, presented as the example par excellence of the penetration of the NR into the political culture, was in fact an opposition initiated debate conducted on a supply day. Thus the claims for the penetration of the NR into the heart of official political culture rests upon the conduct and content of a debate without any political 'teeth'. In his opening remarks Whitelaw substantially repeats his remarks of the Race Relations Debate which will go into Committee within days of the Immigration Debate.[47] If anything, Whitelaw is more circumspect in his opening remarks, by adding clauses and caveats not present in the previous debate, which was subject, as we have shown, to some degree of contestation. The effect of this strategy is to distance his public accommodation to populism. For example, when referring to the ('cultural') fears and feelings of the electorate, he adds comments such as 'quite wrong in my judgement' (c. 965), or 'as I believe unjustified' (c.966-7). The effect is to make his position, if anything, less hard-nosed in the Immigration Debate than it is in the Race Relations Debate.

Certainly, as we have shown, Barker is right to stress that the debate is staged and seen as necessary because of the prior press and media construction of Hawley and Powellism.[48] However, this 'climate of opinion' or 'moral panic' over dependants, is one that is central to the Conservative contestation of the Race Relations Debate. And in terms of the impact of such upon Government legislation, the prior debate is obviously of crucial importance. This still leaves a residual argument that the Immigration Debate is important in demonstrating the depth of penetration of the logic of the NR. This proof is bound up in Barker's presentation of the language in which the debate is conducted; particularly in how frontbench language is at the very heart of 'new racist' logic, often in sharp contrast to the uncontrolled and inconsistent backbenchers. Sometimes the role of the latter is to say in blunter terms what frontbenchers must control. Our previous discussion and evidence of debates suggest almost completely the opposite interpretation: that backbench racism is articulated in the treatment it is given by the Frontbench, and that the passage of the Osborne Bill from the political periphery to Government sponsored legislation is reflected in a transformation in Frontbench treatment, not a mutation in the conceptual language of racism necessarily.[49]

This passage of 'race language' legitimacy from back to frontbench could be said to be mediated by Powell's intervention. This is obviously integral to the assumptions of the NR. However, Powell's intervention into the debates comes some time after the adoption of the *language of control* by Frontbench Conservative and Labour ministers, as chapter 3 has already established. Thus, the very Commons'sense of this debate is one consistent with the wide gamut of prior debates in 1958, 1959, 1960, 1961, 1962, 1965, 1971; and so on. In addition, the sacking of Powell from the Conservative Shadow Cabinet, and his subsequent political isolation during this period, is simply not addressed by the NR writers; but is, in terms of the logic of their argument, surely vital to explain? Powell's language is always closer to the backbench than the front. Does this mean the arch 'new racist' is not in fact one at all? Powell is sacked from Cabinet because his language takes-on-board too much of the baggage of the old racists. Frontbench language remains at some distance and creates its language statements in conformity with a politics of the public space, involving legitimation and ritual presentation games.[50]

What is 'new' in the New Right is their political treatment of 'race', in that they are prepared to stretch that language to accommodate populists demands that can provide a political 'fillip', one that may benefit them in terms of general support; or in terms of specific political interventions requiring some degree of popular support.[51]

Barker's Analysis of Labour

We now turn to the analysis of the relationship between the two major parties and the language of the NR. Barker's analysis involves a specific formulation of this relationship. This follows from his argument that the NR emerges from within the ranks of the 'New Right' and is introduced into politics by this group of politicians and leader writers in Thatcher's partisan press. The problem this presents Labour is that they have no alternative and are, in point of fact, on the run from this new formulation of 'race' as human nature. Barker sketches Labour's dilemmas very acutely within the micro drama of the July debate:

> [T]he absence of a whole alternative view of race and immigration from Labour[...meant that] they were prone to half-hearted acceptance of Tory theorizations. What was in fact needed, was a theoretical/political account to counterpose to the Tory racist theoretical/political account together with a wholesale attack on the latter. Because nothing like that existed, Labour slid down the slippery slope, avoided the debate, and ended with platitudes saying they all agreed broadly, but asking the Tory Right not to be so nasty (Barker 1981: 20).

Is this accurate? I believe that it is not accurate, on the grounds, firstly, that the NR or the espousing of a racist world view in the debate, did not go uncontested. And secondly, the extent to which Labour shared such a view is the extent to which they shared a Commons' sense view of 'race' and Immigration already established in previous debates, of which the 1976 Debate was substantially an extension. In addition, it is not correct to characterise the debate as absent of Labour. As the confusion over the order of speakers involving Sid Bidwell (*Immigration Debate*, 5th July 1976; c. 987) makes clear, given that the debate is a Conservative initiated one it is not surprising that there is more pressure from the Tory benches to speak (Barker 1981: 12-13). Secondly, it is misleading to assert that Tory assertions and contributions went uncontested, (Barker 1981: 19-20); (see, for example, the contributions of Mr. A.J. Beith (Berwick-upon-Tweed): c.10006-12; or Mr.George Rogers (Chorley): c.1014-5):

> We have all listened to the strange tales which are told and retold to incite racial hatred. Sometimes concoctions which plainly are not foundered on truth are published in the letter columns of newspapers. Newspaper editors should check the authenticity of some of the stories they publish[...]We all know that according to gossip and rumour a coloured person has only to show his face at a Department of Health and Social Security office to be instantly showered

with untold wealth which he invests in several colour television sets and a variety of motor cars[...]we have a duty to expose such nonsense (Mr.Rodgers, (Chorley), c.1015).

The point can only be substantiated if the assumption is accepted that the Tory front and backbench are secure in a full theorisation of 'race'. It is in the face of this consistency that Labour appear fragmentary and piecemeal, according to Barker. Ultimately this is because the NR was 'the very theory that underpinned Labour's half-hearted response' (Barker 1981: 20). In concluding this Barker ignores the elements of traditional contestation within the political wings of Labour (cf.Foot 1965: ch.8). Such a treatment misses the significance of centre-right Jenkins' presentation of colonialism and inequality relations as 'contingent' as opposed to 'causal' (cf. Barker 1981: 19). Also, Labour backbenchers do draw upon the dissolution of the colonies and the Commonwealth, in the context of the 'end of colonial empire', and theorise immigration as a corollary of the latter.[52]

Despite Jenkins careful re-construction of the 'Commons'sense' terms of the Debate, in favour of a view of immigration as a post-colonial problem, the great majority of his reply is taken up with a 'rather close arguments about numbers' of dependants and a review of British government 'obligations'. From cols. 972 - 982, Jenkins is committed to a running defence and explanation of the 'numbers of dependants' and the 'absolute numbers' *allowed to enter* and, subsequently, a protracted wrangle, with various backbenchers, over the fine detail of this. What implications does this have for the claims for the ascendancy of the NR? What this sequence suggests is certainly that Labour are 'on the run' and on the defensive over the question of numbers, and this is certainly a consequence of Powellism as a powerful public force in the press and media. However, in terms of the theme and content of the discourse in question, the *continuity* of treatment remains; what has been replaced is the poplar mythology of criminals, scroungers and the 'unfit' by: dependants, fiancees and, preceded by the 'illegals' and 'overstayers'. Although their point of unity and identity remains the discourse of *numbers and alienness*.

This relationship of 'folk devils', to front and backbench, is central to the treatment and pattern of the debates. Take for example, Robert Taylor (Croydon, North-West):

> [W]hen I hold my regular meetings with constituents the majority who come to see me are immigrant families and they all have one thing in common. They wish to be reunited with members of their families, and the reunions, of course, must always take place over here (Taylor c.994).

Or:

> Recently a father from the Indian subcontinent came to see me on behalf of his three daughters, each of whom was under 20 years of age and for each of whom he had arranged a marriage with a fiancee in India. Those girls have had marriages arranged for them on the briefest of acquaintanceships (Taylor c.994).

Mr. Taylor then refers to the 'practice' of choosing unseen husbands that have not been 'westernised' in preference to men already settled here and comments: 'This is more racialist than any other action one could think of, because it is a rejection of other races and customs and a rejection of our society's customs' (Taylor, c.995). Barker identifies this treatment as an instance of the NR. Such anecdotal evidence once again provides the authenticity by which general pronouncements about the political nature of Race Relations can be judged. Such evidence is specifically used to vindicate, a priori, the details of the Hawley Report, which Mr. Taylor has not read, (Powell reminds him that a copy is in the House library, his only contribution to this debate): 'The report is correct if it concludes that the problem of marriage to Indians from the sub-continent is infinite' (c.995).

Barker's treatment of this excerpt suggests a vindication of the NR; such a family should be returned to its 'natural environment in Sierra Leone'. Again this apparently strong example can be re-contextualised by other elements of the speech, so that its weight and importance shifts. For example: 'When the case first came to my notice in November 1971, the lady had just produced a fourth child and professed herself dissatisfied with the accommodation provided for her by the taxpayer' (c.996). Here we have the anecdotal construction of a 'folk devil', in the fashion beloved of Conservative party conferences.[53] In this respect it is important to also make the point that Barker's NR discourse sits very securely within 'old style' *moral panic* claims of welfare scroungers, the idle and the socially 'unfit' and undesirable. Barker picks up on the claim for repatriation on cultural grounds but it could equally be argued that Taylor's treatment of this case is predominantly obsessed with her illegal status, and role as a welfare scrounger, in receipt of: 'cash supplementary benefits of £1, 600 together with other benefits of kind', such as a 'subsidised council flat' and 'education' for her children. Taylor complains that the widespread examples of such illegals and overstayers, 'fester sores in the community where such people live' (Taylor, c.997). Such pecuniary assessment, as support for entry restriction or enforced return, are explicit in the debates of the late 1950s, culminating in Osborne's Private Members Bill of 1961, as we have shown.[54]

Labour and the 1976 Race Relations Debate

Any assessment of Labour's position and subordination to the NR argument must involve a discussion of the 1976 Race Relations Debate. This is simply because it is within that debate that Labour are in a position to propose legislation and to define the case for a legislative anti-racism. The importance, therefore, of this debate is in the manner and means by which Labour are able to pass their Race Relations Bill, and the extent to which *they extend a political argument against racism*. Labour's position in this Debate rapidly becomes clear: the purpose and rationale for the Bill is as a necessary balancing measure, to be set against Immigration Control. In other words, there is a clear adherence to a centrally constructed (racist) Commons' sense, i.e., that strict control is necessary if 'race relations' are to be harmonious. Thus,

> [T]here is a clear limit to the amount of immigration which this country can absorb, and that it is in the interests of the racial minorities themselves to maintain a strict control over immigration (The Secretary of State for the Home Office, Mr. Roy Jenkins, *Race Relations Bill* (Hansard), 4th March, 1976: c.1548).

This, while evidently already a racist position, is itself buffeted and driven by the winds of a rampant Powellism; which has, by this time, provided the framing terms of press panic over illegal immigrants and bogus applicants for British hospitality.[55] Thus, Labour's presentation of the Bill, is hedged around with a defensive posturing in a *defensive climate of opinion*. This defensiveness surrounds Labour's attempts to put in place anti-discriminatory legislation which they see as an unpleasant necessity to address the overwhelmingly evidence of economic and social abuse.[56] Yet, incredibly, such a presentation is possible only by working against the prevailing Commons'sense that, as we have seen, the victims are seen to be the indigenous not the newcomers (even when evidently much of this group are second generation):

> The first principle upon which the Government's policy is based is the clear recognition that the vast majority of the coloured population will remain permanently in this country, and that a substantial and increasing proportion of that population belongs to our country in the fullest sense of being born and educated here as fellow citizens (Roy Jenkins c.1547).

Such a principle cannot be accepted by the Tory backbench, since to do so would be to disrupt the dominant meaning of the black presence and the character of the

emotion. I can say quite categorically that none of us have ever played on prejudice' (cited in Foot 1965: 52).

Smethwick as a National-Political Phenomenon

It must be absolutely clear, at this point, that the story of Smethwick is an untold one in the vast majority of political commentary. The reasons for this must now be evident; it quite simply disturbed the view of 'race' and politics that had been held in place by the major political parties and reproduced by academics and commentators since. For sure its impact must have been devastating, despite the distorting lens of its reporting and management by much of the media and party elite. There has been precious little analysis of the fractures and shockwaves which must have reverberated through the parties. We have been denied the material that might have enabled an exploration of the manifold dimensions of its political impact. Rather the meaning of Smethwick as a 'freak' event in British politics has been 'cast in stone'. The very fact that it has passed into political folklore so securely, should alert attention. The interpretation of Smethwick as a political object lesson in the way politics can become contaminated by a racist reaction, has closed off any further meaning to be derived from it.

This mythologising was evident at the time, exemplified most pointedly by Wilson's retort, during the opening of the new Parliament, to the effect that Griffiths, the new Member for Smethwick, would spend the rest of his term as a 'parliamentary leper' (Layton-Henry 1984: 59-60). The Wilson 'police-action' is important in number of ways: (i) because it has come to signify, for many, the way 'race' made its appearance in British politics; (ii) how its populist potential could apparently be harnessed by unscrupulous politicians. This issue was signified, above all else, by the issue of language and the idea of how official language treatment would encourage or dispel the spread of 'race'; (iii) closely allied to this issue of public treatment was the idea, embedded in such language-use, of the idea of 'race politics' as some kind of immoral, anti-rational contagion that the 'leper' metaphor resonated.

This chapter will argue that, encapsulated within the contagion metaphor of 'political leprosy', is an implicitly held theory of 'race' that informs and makes sense of the political treatment of 'race' politics by the Labour cabinet and centre Liberals. It is an idea about the nature of 'race' language and the danger of its potential relationship to the political process. The language of reaction to which we have referred, and the theory of 'political racism' which it invokes, is embedded in and arises out of these 'conceptual primitives'. It is an argument about the political treatment of 'race' as an overwhelmingly politically dangerous idea: since it appeals directly to the emotions and feelings and 'arouses', 'whips-up' or 'inflames' deep-seated 'passions' and 'prejudices' in a manner un-amenable to rationality (cf. IRR 'Newsletter' 1960-9).[7] Such a diagnoses must call forth a treatment: as we argued in chapter1, the central concern with the language treatment of 'race' and the various strategies called forth to meet its potential political impact, describe quite accurately the development of the politics of 'race' in the postwar period as a process dependent upon the construction and use of an ideological language of (liberal) anti-racism.[8]

The Political Treatment of Smethwick

If myth is, as Barthes (1972) has argued, 'an evacuation of history': then the case of the treatment of Smethwick is indicative of the process whereby aberrant meanings are enclosed within the very form the myth assumes. The ideological effect is the suppression of the historical record. The Smethwick result, despite Wilson's public display, is seen to confirm Labour's acceptance of the need for controls to safeguard politics from the threat of a 'political racism' that continued support of open-immigration policy would unquestionably stimulate. This chapter will argue that such a view is both superficial and deeply ideological; it works because it allows a view of politics and an interpretation of events consistent with dominant discourses, of both Left and Right. The following sections will explore and develop this theme. In order to develop our conception of the depth of impact of Smethwick upon party politics and the public domain we must first introduce and discuss the key concepts we will develop in order to describe and explain this phenomenon. These are: (i) political racism (ii) 'race' politics and (iii) discourse formation.

Political Racism

There have been few, if any, accounts of postwar British politics that have attempted to employ the concept of *political racism*. To the extent that the concept has been employed within the literature it has been thought to refer to: 'political parties or movements that have engaged in any sort of mass electoral politics and whose programmes contain an explicit anti-black and/or anti-foreign worker appeal as a central element' (Husbands 1985: 13; n.1). In other words, the concept is to refer to parties and political movements that have explicitly adopted a 'racial' politics and stance of the extreme right or fascist fringe. Within the terms of such a definition there has been no incidence of a *political racism* within postwar British politics. This is simply because none of the major political parties involved in British politics have ever explicitly adopted an anti-black or anti-immigrant stance within their political programmes. A partial exception to such an exclusion is the attempted rise of the National Front in the 1970s, on an anti-immigration/repatriation platform, with which it secured some notable by-election results retaining candidate deposits for the first time (cf.Walker 1977; Husbands 1983; Taylor 1982); and more recently the British National Party (cf. The Mirror, Sun, 18th September 1993).

The only other political movements or 'moments' that can be said to have involved some of the elements contained in our formal definition of political racism are (i) the infamous anti-immigration campaign mounted by Peter Griffiths at Smethwick in 1964 and, (ii) the political interventions and events accompanying the rise and fall of the political fortunes of J.Enoch Powell MP, i.e. Powellism, 1968-74.[9] However, such 'events' or 'moments' rather than being considered to have provided British examples of an *attempted* political racism, are rather employed, when they are discussed at all, to mark the boundary or extent to which the 'race issue' has managed to penetrate the perspectives and programmes of the major parties (cf. Brier and Axford 1975; Layton-Henry and Rich 1986: 1-16; Lawrence 1978/9).

According to this view both attempts, however defined, are examples of political *failure*. Smethwick was certainly thought to announce the potential electoral importance of 'race' as a national-political issue should it be taken-up by a major party (Deakin (ed) 1965:; IRR Newsletter, April 1966; Butler and King 1965: 360-8). However, despite such warnings and forebodings, the projected electoral-populism failed to surface in the 1966 general election (Deakin et al 1966; IRR 1966). The reason was simply because the leadership of both parties had contrived a form of bipartisanship in order to keep 'race' of the electoral agenda (IRR, November-December, 1966). This bipartisan 'consensus of stringency' was composed of (a) a stiffening of anti-immigration measures and pronouncements, which were aimed at an assumed prejudiced electorate and, (b) a tacit agreement, reinforced through leadership pronouncement, to keep the issue out of the election campaign (IRR, April, 1966: 4). In this way the *Smethwick factor* was isolated and removed from the legitimate political arena.

Thus, there has never been an example of the mass political employment of the issue of anti-(black) immigration as a central theme of British politics. Despite a number of minor crises over the potential electoral impact of a Griffiths' style campaign, Powellism as a mass popular movement, and the threat of the National Front as a credible third party - 'race' and immigration have, in the long view, failed to penetrate the legitimate political arena or become a significant party-splitting issue. As a consequence, mainstream political analysis of the 'race' issue in British politics, rather than concentrating on the specific phenomenon of, Powellism or the Front has attempted to focus upon what has seemed, from the observed failure of these episodes or 'moments', the central question: why has 'race' failed to become a legitimate political issue? (cf. Layton-Henry and Rich 1986: introduction; Solomos 1986a). Such a question has been consistently interpreted as involving the analysis of how the British political elite has managed to prevent 'race' from becoming a mainstream or centre stage issue (Katznelson 1976; Studlar 1980; Bulpitt 1986).[10]

Race Politics

Our analysis will employ a less restrictive definition of political racism, not in order to deny the general validity of the previous distinction, of a mass electoral politics organised in opposition to 'alien nationals' or 'other races'; but rather to extend its conceptual scope so that it might apply to any attempt to use or employ racial metaphors, associations or societal referencing arguments, involving or referring to 'race'. This conceptual inflation of the concept of 'political racism' will better enable us to describe that perception of the threat of the articulation of prejudice and political leadership that surrounds the political discourse of, specifically Smethwick and the largely neglected political account of Powellism, (particularly the discourse internal to the Labour party); as well as the failure to prevent the general negative effect of 'race politics' on the political system. Such an account will, by implication, want to question the presently restricted use of the concept of 'political racism' to characterise the far-right and thereby marginalise the centrality of this issue to key periods in the postwar conjuncture.

The place to begin to contest the prevailing reading is in terms of the question of how it has been possible to construct an apparently consensual and unified account of Smethwick and Powell as temporarily volatile episodes but ultimately, failures. Such failure being conceived specifically in terms of whether such incidents resulted in the introduction into British party politics of the question of 'race' as a legitimate political issue. Within this view, the incident of Smethwick and the phenomenon of Powell are characterised as scandalous but ultimately futile attempts to introduce into British politics non-traditional, emotive and illegitimate issues. Such incidents (while given more publicity then there significance deserved) do illustrate the boundaries of the acceptable political agenda around which the two party system is seen to revolve. According to this kind of summation, appeals to racial sentiment and hatred have no place in the legitimate political arena and will not therefore have any success.

However, sitting uneasily within this dominant consensual view, is another which does recognise the impact of Smethwick and Powellism; seeing them as potentially dangerous and destabilising political issues which threatened the political system where it not for the elite-consensus of the establishment politicians in recognising and removing such a threat. Thus Wilson is seen to condemn and vilify the Smethwick campaign as illegitimate and unacceptable; while Heath is forced to sack Powell and to close intra-party ranks against such a dangerous view of the connections between ideas of 'race' and immigration controls. Here the importance of these incidents is recognised but their impact is mediated by the reactive-strategies of the political system when called upon to deal with such illegitimate attempts at destabilisation.

Finally, there is the view that the above factors have led, reluctantly but seemingly inevitably to the introduction of migrant restriction legislation which has acted to (a) de-fuse the threat of political agitation around an anti-immigration platform and (b) to appease popular concern over the 'problem' of large scale immigration which the Smethwick result and the Powell campaign have been associated with in the popular mind. However, this accession to demands for control has been taken reluctantly and pragmatically by the major parties and has not, except for minor periods, been an issue of political contestation between the parties.

Each of these scenarios represents well defined positions over the question of the role of 'race' within British politics. Yet it can also be seen that in another respect they are progressive positions of retreat from the general position of absolute refutation of the idea of the penetration of 'race' politics into the political arena. So position (1): no such politics could survive or gain any mainstream legitimacy. Position (2):'race' has entered but it has been headed off. Position (3): 'race' has entered but the damage has been limited. The lynch-pin that holds these accounts together is the idea that 'race' is not a political issue i.e. that it does not constitute a set of ideas that can be employed in party debates or to develop policies. It is rather a malaise or error of thought which some can be susceptible to. It is this idea of the danger of 'race' as a political issue that accounts for the absolute denial of political employment; 'race' is anathema to politics. This idea has a continuity of logic which passes through all three positions adopted. It allows in position (3) to say that although immigration controls have been implemented they have met genuine anxiety over numbers and have been practical in the need to meet such fears rather than allow them to be distorted by racial fantasies and scare mongering. In other words, in order not to lose the ground to the racists it is necessary to restrict the cause of the problem of racism - the number of immigrants.

The Impact of Smethwick: 'Political Racism' as a Theory of Discourse[11]

What is beginning to emerge out of our analysis of the perceived impact of Smethwick within the political sphere is a conception that some have termed 'race politics' (Bulpitt 1986: 26; cf. Miles 1988: 433) while others have preferred the idea of the 'politicization of 'race'' (Miles and Phizacklea 1984), but which I prefer to call 'political racism'. I take this term simply to describe the attempted political employment of some form of racial categorisation, argument or belief. It thus encompasses the empirical materials and instances involving the use or application of ideas, beliefs or descriptions involving 'race' employed within the political sphere proper. The concept can be sub-divided according to the way it is applied: *political racism*^{1} (PR1) and *political racism*^{2} (PR2). Thus,

PR1: attempted description and explanation of features and principles of the social and political world which refer to or have their basis in an idea of 'race' and which seek political confirmation of such, i.e., action or legislation undertaken in conformity with such a view.

PR2: descriptions and explanations provided by political actors and elites for designating the legitimate and/or illegitimate employment of 'race' discourse and which seek to control its content, uses and circulation.

It is a major assumption of our approach that orthodox institutional political analysis operates with an un-examined theory of 'race' (PR1) from which a theory of its uses and applications in politics is assumed (PR2). In order to unpack the hidden meanings implicit in this usage we need to make visible the larger discourse that is absent but which supplies the conceptual system by means of which the discourse is understood. Our concern in this chapter is with PR2. Once we have developed definition PR2 it will be possible to reintegrate the full concept and its uses as follows:

Figure 5.1   **Political Racism**

$$\text{Political racism} = \begin{cases} \text{PR1} \\ \text{PR2} \end{cases} = \text{PR 1, 2.}$$

The full term *political racism* should be employed to define and invoke empirically verifiable entities and processes involved in the recognition of it, in respect of the following: (a) the extent or degree to which a conception of 'race' has been employed within party politics in the late postwar period; (b) descriptive/evaluative accounts made or employed within the political sphere in order to define and account for its illegitimate/legitimate uses; and (c) the political 'ends' to which such definitional accounts are directed.

A Discursive Ensemble?

PR2 can be seen to arise out of a 'reading' of a number of key institutionally located discourse that are characterised by their attempts to define and interpret the idea of politicization of 'race' and the significance of Smethwick and Powell to this process. The institutionally located discourses we can identify as being involved in constructing a conception of political racism PR2 are the following:

(i) the Institute of Race Relations (IRR) particularly in its *Newsletter* (1960-69) and also in the various research projects and reports it commissions, many of which are incorporated within the monumental, *Colour and Citizenship: A Report on British Race Relations* (Rose et al 1969).
(ii) the Labour party leadership in the form of interventions within Parliamentary Debates (Hansard), public announcements and constituency speeches, party conference reports, diaries and political memoirs.
(iii) the Liberal-Tories such as St.John-Stevas, Humphry Berkeley and Nigel Fisher.
(iv) the national 'quality' press, in particular *The Times*, in its political and parliamentary coverage of the period, leader comment and, in particular, its 'Midland Correspondent' column.

We can characterise this group of discourses that are seen to arise in the late post-war conjuncture as a discursive ensemble because, despite their separate institutional locations, they arise in response to and share a similar view of the politics of 'race' in our period. In addition such an ensemble has played a decisive role in furnishing the 'inferential structure' (Hall et al 1978: 58-9). i.e., the mental map or interpretative framework (composed of key assumptions, values and forms of criteria by which 'issues' can be defined as relevant or non relevant, etc.,) through which, and by means of which, the conception of political racism has been publicly 'thought' in our period. The conceptualisation which underpins such an 'inferential structure' is that which we have referred to as political racism: PR2. We can identify its core theme as a composite of two distinct but overlapping schemas:

(1) 'political racism' has been the direct consequence of an illiberal retreat from principles to the appeasement of the 'public'/populist clamour for immigration controls.
(2) despite attempts to preserve a bi-partisan policy on immigration controls and thereby keep 'race' out of politics unscrupulous politicians have scuttled such a consensus from without; first at Smethwick in 1964, then Sandys and Powell over the Kenyan Asians; finally Enoch Powell's "river of blood" challenge to the establishment in April 1968.

Let us briefly note specific features of the content of these schema. It can be seen for example that: (i) indicates that the central element is a retreat from principles which is manifest at the political/authoritative level. Such principles are being sacrificed for the maintenance of the popular vote. It is thus what the IRR and other commentators have called a 'dutch auction' in illiberalism (cf. Kaufman 1965; Patterson 1969). The central feature of (ii) is the view that the attempt to construct a consensus over the exclusion of 'race' from the polity is thrown or led into crisis and disaster by 1968. In one respect this is because Powellism represents the ultimate auction move, one which Labour cannot follow without stepping irrevocably beyond the political sphere within which their legitimacy/ authority is founded.

It is the argument of this chapter that the social and political interpretation of Smethwick and Powellism which composes the substance of the 'received view' is largely determined by the logic and internal rules of combination of this interpretative schema. In other words, the effect of the operation of such a framework, when faced with the 'events' of Smethwick and Powellism, is to generate the kind of interpretation we have called PR2. PR2 is thus a preferred reading which seeks to limit and confine (or more strictly close-down) the range and kinds of meanings/applications of the phenomena of Smethwick and Powellism, and the ways in which they have employed 'race' at the political level. Such a process involves the employment of criteria and values able to codify and 'fix' the meaning of Smethwick and Powellism, and in particular, as we shall see, the nature of the form of political relations it involves and the significance of such relations to the established polity.

Political racism is thus a conception that serves to characterise i.e., define a political relationship, to register that relation, as it at the same time seeks to condemn and deny the social and political validity of such a relation. It is thus a naming as well as an attempt, made possible through such naming, at social and political closure. Such a conception of political racism can be broadly defined, in the British context, as the extent to which the state control of 'commonwealth immigration' became an electorally contested issue between the major political parties. A dominant conception involved here is that of: bi-partisanship:

(i) the major parties agree to uphold or conform to a particular stance over an issue or strike up a de-facto agreement regulating acceptable and unacceptable issues or treatment of issues;

(ii) there are certain taken for granted ideas, beliefs, etc. which lie outside or beyond the pale of political difference or electoral contestation either because they are associated with religious beliefs, or carry a moral or humanitarian value; such values are thought to transcend the party political divide; i.e. they are humanitarian or philosophic universals that will commend universal assent; they are, so say, beyond politics.

Another way of expressing this is to say that all the major parties operate within the parameters of a 'consensus' i.e., basic agreement over core values that provide the political sphere with its internal legitimacy and standards of procedure. To cross this divide is to incur moral and ethical condemnation and thus to risk the legitimacy of the political sphere in terms of its ability to address its audience according to the central or core values of the society (cf. Shils 1975; Woolf 1968).

From the outset of the postwar period up to the early 1960s, neither Parliament or politicians have had an existing or agreed language with which to address the issue of 'race'. The development of such language, therefore PR1, is not unnaturally a slow and protracted one, based on winning majority consent to a particular discourse; a process made all the more difficult by the intense taboo of speaking publicly about 'race' after the war. Thus it is hardly surprising, given this context, that both PR1 and PR2 will arise and contest the very development of a political language form, and the role of such language in the construction of racialised legislation. Another way of understanding this process is that it describes the construction and mobilisation of a postwar racism and anti-racism and that both these broadly contrasted discourses construct the discourse of 'political racism' as it develops through debates in this period.[12]

The next section will trace the *genealogy* (or history of the present uses of the idea) of Smethwick as a shock episode that dramatises the sudden emergence of 'race' as a political factor on the party platform and its implications for the political system. We will find that this conception of a 'race' free postwar politics is a fiction which itself influences the local construction of Smethwick even before the infamous election defeat of Shadow foreign secretary, Patrick Gordon-Walker.

Smethwick and the Rise of 'Race'

> [U]p to 1964 there was not much reporting in national newspapers about 'race' in an English context, and there was a general consensus that this was a matter which was outside politics and ought to remain so (Dummett 1973: 242).

> The national political parties had all tried to avoid the fact that racial antagonism was an issue which seriously concerned the British public. But when Gordon-Walker was defeated once at Smethwick and again at Leyton it seemed desperately important to a number of people in the Labour party that something be done quickly before race became a monster which devoured British politics (Hindell 1965: 395).

The genealogy of the conception of a 'rise of political racism' begins in 1964 with Smethwick specifically because, as E.J.B.Rose, the then director of the *Survey of Race Relations*[13] put it: 'the 1964 General Election, and in particular the result in Smethwick, made colour and race major factors in British politics for the first time' (Deakin (ed) 1965: *foreword*). In other words, it is the factor or issue of 'race' which is held to be the reason for the surprise election victory, in the teeth of a national swing to Labour, of the midland's Conservative candidate Peter Griffiths at Smethwick, ousting the then Shadow Foreign Secretary, Patrick Gordon Walker (Layton-Henry 1984: 43). Gordon-Walker is said to have been 'bundled out on the racial issue' (IRR Newsletter, October 1964: 2). It is Griffiths's overt use of the racial argument - "If you want a nigger neighbour, vote Labour" - which is seen to *introduce* racialism into the public-political arena for the first time (*IRR Newsletter*, April, 1964: 3). Ann Dummett, a participator in much of the discussion of the time and a reliable commentator observes: 'Against the national trend, and from what since 1945 had been a safe seat, Gordon-Walker had been ousted. There was just one factor to be observed in Smethwick that marked it out as different from other constituencies; the Conservative campaign had been openly and violently anti-immigrant' (Dummett 1973: 243).

Concern about the kind of campaign fought by the local Conservatives forms the most frequent focus of comment. This concern is very markedly present in the Labour leadership post-mortem: 'the defeated Labour candidate Mr. Gordon-Walker[...]said that the campaign had been fought.[...]almost wholly on the question of immigration and had been the dirtiest campaign he could remember[...]His view was shared by Mr. Harold Wilson [who] attributed the result to "the campaign being conducted in a way which I can only regard as a disgraceful exception to the general trend of British politics over the past 100 years" (*IRR Newsletter*, October, 1964: 3).

The material produced by *The Times* Midland correspondent confirms and deepens the impression of the campaign as one dominated to an almost obsessive degree by the 'problem' of 'immigration' for the local community. Much of the detail of this 'dirty-politics' is recorded by Foot (1965), as we have shown. The report commissioned by the Institute of Race Relations: *Colour and the British Electorate* (Deakin (ed) 1965) also suggests that the local history leading up to the general election result is one peculiarly concerned with the campaign over 'race' conducted by the local conservatives. Dilip Hiro, writing in the early seventies, provides a more retrospective judgement: 'For the first time in Britain, racism was *openly* injected into politics at the national level and was seen to pay electoral dividends[...]race and immigration were dragged from the fringe of British politics to its centre' (Hiro 1973: 51).

This evidence suggests that both the contemporaneous reporting, at the local and the national level, and the retrospective reaction to the election result, all incline towards the view that such an 'event' marks a definite watershed in the electoral history of 'race'; or, more specifically, its political treatment. It is this feature, the political employment of 'race' within mainstream electoral contestation, which is seen to mark the boundary between a period of the marginality of 'race' to one of fairly sudden and central national-political significance.

Let us look more closely at the elements that compose this type of interpretation. Firstly, the issue has become political for the 'first time' in Britain and contained within this claim is a strong sense of moral condemnation that such a thing should ever have happened. This is essentially Wilson's view. Also like Wilson, there is an implicit warning that something, therefore, has *gone wrong*. The something in question is the very idea that 'race' should have been allowed any kind of platform within national-political debate. Immediately connected to this idea is the suggestion that the placing of 'race' onto the political agenda will leave it open to electoral exploitation. It is not clearly indicated why this is considered such a terrible prospect. But the inference is clear: 'race' does not belong on the *legitimate* political agenda.

The 'why?' is perhaps most clearly suggested by Wilson and Hiro. Because it could lead to general employment of 'dirty politics' of the type employed in the Smethwick campaign. Such a politics of 'race' could pay 'electoral dividends' by (implicitly) 'stirring-up' racial ill-feeling for electoral advantage. Such a politics would, by definition, be incompatible with the procedures and institutions which are seen to provide the framework for legitimate politics. Such a tradition is encapsulated by Wilson's historical arcade 'the general trend of politics over the past 100 years.' 'Race' must, by definition, remain outside of such a legitimacy. Its sudden and dramatic appearance and the kind of populist, agitational politics it might bring forth could threaten that tradition and those institutions.[14]

This type of view, despite the fact that its detail remains largely unexamined, has been conventionally interpreted as one of 'electoral fears'. Layton-Henry has spelled out how such a view is seen to provide an 'explanation' for the significance Smethwick was though to have for the party political system: 'The result was to have a momentous effect. It appeared to confirm the worst suspicions of those who believed that the general public was deeply racially prejudiced and that if the issue were exploited by unscrupulous politicians it could evoke a massive popular response' (Layton-Henry 1984: 43).

The 'those' in question were leading Cabinet politicians like Richard Crossman, Minister of Housing in the Labour government 1964-66, whose often quoted diary comment expresses the mood: 'Ever since the Smethwick election it has been quite clear that immigration can be the greatest potential vote loser for the Labour party if we are seen to be permitting a flood of immigrants to come in and blight the central areas of our cities' (Crossman 1975: 149-50). Dummett echoes this in her observation of the mood of Labour:

> It was easy to draw the conclusion that popular feeling among voters against black immigrants must be so hostile and powerful that it overrode all other considerations[....]It was necessary, the Labour party clearly then believed, to ditch Gordon-Walker and along with him any reputation the party might have for being soft on immigrants, if it was to maintain electoral success. Within a few weeks of the Leyton by-election new and stringent controls on immigration were announced by the Home secretary (Dummett 1973: 243-4).

Thus the significance of Smethwick and the reason for its permanent place within British political analysis and commentary is because: (i) the campaign conducted by Griffiths marks the debut of the 'colour problem' as a contested issue between the major political parties; (ii) at the same time it announces the potentially devastating electoral power it appears to possess. The combination of these two elements culminates in: (iii) calls by both major parties for 'drastic reductions' in the rate of 'immigration' in line with perceived 'popular feeling' on this issue and thereby the neutralization of its potential electoral impact (Miles and Phizacklea 1979: 6-7; Ben-Tovim and Gabriel 1982: 148; Layton-Henry 1984: 43, 57, 60-3; Solomos 1989: 53-4).

The Parliamentary-Leper View

Such an account is not without its contradictory features. One of the most glaring is the schizophrenic portrayal of the undeniable evidence of the Wilson reaction to the loss of his Shadow Foreign secretary to a racialist campaign:

> Wilson moved quickly to respond to the Smethwick setback[...]with a spirited but largely ritualistic attack on Peter Griffiths on the first day of the new Parliament. He called upon Sir Alec (Douglas-Home) to repudiate the victor of Smethwick who 'until a further general election restores him to oblivion will serve his term as a parliamentary leper' (Hansard 3.11.1964: c.71; cited in Layton-Henry 1984: 59-60).

It is possible to challenge this interpretation of Wilson's attack on Griffiths as merely 'ritualistic'. It could be argued that this incident, when viewed in relation to subsequent pronouncements by Wilson and other Labour leaders, is most significant in revealing the idea of 'political racism' associated with Smethwick and the idea of racial language which informs that view. An important plank in the argument for the 'ritualistic' nature of the attack on Griffiths is how it is seen to accompany Labour's volt face over opposition to immigration controls (cf. Foot 1965: 184-194): 'though Harold Wilson referred to Griffiths as a 'parliamentary leper', non the less his victory solidified Labour's determination not to be 'soft' on the race question, as demonstrated in the heavily restrictionist 1965 Immigration Act' (Ben-Tovim and Gabriel 1982: 148).

This movement is conventionally accounted for in terms of the thesis of Labour's concession to the principles of pragmatism in the face of the electoral unpopularity of immigration. This movement - from principles to pragmatism - allows the condemnation of the Smethwick campaign to become 'merely ritualistic'. In this way, events appear to be motivated by political pragmatism; and principles are merely the public rhetoric which must accompany practical policy implementation (cf. Foot 1965; Katznelson 1976; Reeves 1983). So, in effect the 'electoral fears' perspective is organised around three linking elements: (i) the need to politically neutralise that factor which might lead to political instability; (ii) the subsequent 'volt face' of the Labour party' from opposition to controls to their advocation; (iii) the construction of an elite, bi-partisan consensus, designed to keep 'race' off the political agenda. In fact this syllogism rests upon the key assumption of the certain possibility of the misuse of party politics to exploit 'popular feeling' or 'popular racialism'. This is the lesson of Smethwick - the Griffiths campaign was successful because it succeeded in exploiting such innate popular feeling.

Political disagreement about the 'nature' of this feeling has formed the sub-plot or ideological foundation of postwar parliamentary and political debates, as our analysis in chapters 1, 3 and 4 has demonstrated. The relative positions adapted over this issue appear plainly distilled within the assertion Griffiths himself makes in the 1965 Race Relations Debate: 'The basic question is this: is it possible to legislate about people's feelings?' (Mr. Peter Griffiths (Smethwick) *Race Relations Bill - Second Reading*, 3 May 1965; c.1011). Here, as in the Smethwick reaction, racism is primarily about people's feelings. Such feelings are the natural property of people who, en mass, react to an unfamiliar experience (viz. mass immigration into their local community) and express this in forms of hostility. The politician, faced with this widespread reaction, rightly concludes that if this is what people feel and they then choose to express such a feeling in a racial idiom; then the politician does not have the right to condemn such usage. If he does this then he is not representing or acknowledging the feelings of his constituents. The logic of this stance is contained in Griffiths' defence of the infamous slogan which many suspect played a key role in securing the Smethwick local election success of the Conservatives: 'If you want a nigger neighbour, vote Labour':

> I should think this is a manifestation of the popular feeling. I would not condemn anyone who said that. I would say that is how people see the situation in Smethwick. I fully understand the feelings of the people who say it (Griffiths cited by Ivor Richards (Barons Court) in Hansard, *Expiring Laws Bill - Committee*, 17 November, 1964: c.309).

Here we have, plainly stated, the essence of Powellism; four years prior to its recognition.[15] Both Smethwick and Powellism are about a political relationship between politician and voters expressed through a racist reaction. This relationship is secured through the defensive and confirmatory language of the politician. Powellism is thus the working out of a logic well established by

Smethwick as it, in turn, rests on the activities and work of the 'black country' 'race' realists or 'populists': Gurden, Bell, Pannell and Osborne.[16] The approach begins by accepting racial hostility as a legitimate expression of a life-situation, as being grounded in a legitimate experience. Thus, if people feel hostility then this is the natural state that the politician and the legislators must work with. It is not up to the politician to pass judgement and say that what people think is wrong headed. A politicians' role is to represent such views and to give them an airing. This is the heart of the dilemma of Smethwick: the dilemma of racial language usage. Powell put this absolutely succinctly when he argued that he simply did not have the right to ignore the views of his constituent; or to substitute for those words his own.[17] The only qualification he makes is that he believes such views to be genuine and genuinely felt. Once this qualification has been satisfied then it is right and proper that such language should be allowed to speak for itself; hence the centrality of 'quotation' and *anecdotal evidence* to Powellism. Yet again the conceptual rehearsal for this type of delivery is made in advance of Powell's use of it. This politically defined relationship is also, significantly, the subject of a consistent rebuke by Labour politicians as an unacceptable use of a language racial incitement (see below).

The problem for Labour, in 1964, is that they do not have an alternative language to employ against this populist one. Their initial reaction is to deny the common existence of this language. Their subsequent reaction is to deflect the argument onto other causes. Racism is really a case of 'urban blight'[18] or something else, i.e. our working class constituents don't mean it, they know not what they say! It is out of this fear of the language of working class reaction to immigration that the language of PR2 arises: a language of condemnation of inter-party 'race' talk, driven by a desire to police, not the racial usage of the language of the electorate but that of the Right Honourable Members.

This metalanguage first makes its appearance in the savaging of Griffiths during the Prime Minister's Gracious Speech: the infamous 'parliamentary leper' incident. The next section will argue that this attack is informed by a theory of 'race' and racial language and that this theory can be traced and uncovered in the pattern of intra- and inter party discourse of the Labour leadership and contributors to debates in 1964 and 1965, in the wake of the shock of Smethwick.

A Politics Free from the Infection of Racialist Ideas: Wilson and the Campaign of the Labour leadership.

> People who are satisfied that they have eradicated from themselves racialist assumptions and reactions suppose[..].that they are now fully equipped to issue pronouncements about the racial situation: they are wholly mistaken. They are mistaken, not merely because they are almost certainly wrong in thinking themselves free from the infection of racialist ideas, but because they have as yet done no more than put themselves in a position from which they can begin to learn what they need to understand (M & A Dummett 1969: 25).

If we examine the political language employed over the issue of Smethwick and the Labour and Liberal articulated fear of a rise of 'race politics', it quickly becomes apparent that such language use is just not consistent with the orthodox interpretation, i.e. labour's pragmatic acceptance of the need to agree to legislate in conformity with anti-immigration feeling. As we have seen, the view of Smethwick as an outbreak of leprosy, while acknowledged as consistent with Wilson's earlier statements on the local campaign, is interpreted as 'ritualism' by political theorists and by a good deal of the politicians themselves. What can 'ritualism' mean, given this context? As we have already indicated, it refers to the idea that despite Wilson's outburst the Labour leadership must join the restrictionist lobby and be 'seen' to do so. Here, they are merely protecting their electoral interests against possible future damage over 'race'. At best the leper condemnation is rhetorical, a public flourish, provoked in part by Wilson's personal annoyance at the loss of his Foreign Secretary, which 'waves' in the direction of principles which Labour have now abandoned (and cannot afford to do other wise) in order to retain 'public face' over the defeat of Gordon-Walker.

Thus the apparently unshakeable consensus, held from Right to Left of the ideological spectrum, holds that Labour's 'behaviour' over 'race politics' is governed by electoral pragmatism and it goes no deeper than this. However, beyond the 'parliamentary leper' outburst, there are a number of similar uses of these metaphors of contagion as well as a strong degree of thematic and metaphorical consistency in such usage. Consider, for example, the following: 'Racialism is a disease rather than an accurate weapon. Once it starts spreading, it affects not only the people the disease is aimed at[...]but all inside our community' (Mr.John Fraser (Norwood) *Immigration and Race Relations* (Hansard), 6 December 1973: c.1562).

Can language be so innocent an instrument of political purpose as we are asked to believe here? Let us suggest, in order to seek its validation, the proposition that the purpose of the emergence and uses of this language is the attempt to control or 'police' the use of racial language statements. This appeal is made at two levels. Firstly to the party leadership. Tom Drieberg's attack on the Tory leadership, over failing to officially repudiate the member for Smethwick and his campaign, is a good example of this:

> The right hon. Gentlemen the Leader of the Opposition makes the correct noises about racial discrimination and so on, but when he is asked specifically to repudiate a Member of Parliament who has got into the House on the basis of one of the dirtiest and filthiest racialist campaigns ever conducted anywhere, even in Nazi Germany, he is too cowardly do so (*Expiring Laws Bill Committee*, 17 November, 1964: c.389).

Underneath this disturbing analogy is a conception of the danger of 'race' as an extremist state of feeling likely to be inherently conflictual and a cause of a conflict of passions and principles:

> [T]here is intense feeling about this whole subject of the racial tensions that may arise as a result of immigration. One ought, of course, to discuss these matters - or so we are told - in an unemotional, objective way but it is extremely difficult to do so. There are intense feelings on both sides. It is an issue from which one cannot exclude emotion altogether. There are the intense feelings of the racialists who organised the campaign for the hon. Member for Smethwick and who supported him - the intense feelings of hatred for someone whom they think congenitally inferior to themselves. These feelings arise[...]very largely from psychological insecurity (c.392).

It is Drieburg's judgement that: 'Peter Griffiths is young' and does not fully appreciate what he is doing. He is not fully able to appreciate: 'what is meant by racialism unless one has really lived through or seen for oneself something of its beastliness'(c.392). He refers to a Parliamentary visit to Buchenwald concentration camp: 'This was a searing and unforgettably horrible experience and it drove into one's mind and one's heart what racialism to the nth degree, as under Hitler, can mean, with the murder of 6 million Jews and all the other crimes' (c.392). And he adds, 'Those of us who were here in the war can also remember the racialism - this alien Nazi horror - even crept into this honourable House '(c.392). And, 'I say this[...]to try to explain the bitterness that so many of us have when a Member is brought there largely[..]on racialist votes and a racialist campaign' (c.392). Here racism is explicitly characterised, as in Wilson's comments, as the intrusion from outside of an 'alien' language that will pollute and infect the Commons. Here the social nature of 'race' as a political idea and its potential uses is employed to form a theory of racial language as having an inner dynamic that can affect its users to such a extent that racism can become widespread.

It is this fear of 'racial extremism' as an exacerbation of popular feeling, made possible by the nature of 'race' ideas, which exercises the thinking of Reginald Sorensen:

> We must realise that emotion in some areas has undoubtedly exacerbated a stupid, racial approach. Some hon. Members on this side of the committee, with the very best of intentions, at one time insufficiently appreciated that we were faced with certain difficulties that needed objective judgement rather than emotional generality (Sorensen, *Expiring Laws Bill Committee*, 17 November, 1964: c.330).

Mr Sorensen goes on to describe BNP graffiti: 'Keep Britain White'. Mr. Wilson of Truro reminds Sorensen that such activity is the result of a fringe 'crank society'. Sorensen's reply is unequivocal:

> [T]hat is what was once thought in Germany of a crank organisation there. What at one time was dismissed as a mere freak became in the end the evil despotism of that country and brought ruin to the world. That is what I am frightened of, because unfortunately the human mind can be conditioned and moulded, for good or ill (Sorensen, c.332).

Sorensen thus confirms the conception of racial language we have established: it is a form of argumentation and persuasion that does not observe the rules of argument or reason but rather appeals beyond or beneath the guards of a civilised society. Racism has the ability to: 'shape and mould the human mind'. Sorensen's argument attributes racism to cultural learning during childhood. This has the consequence of defining prejudice as external to politics.

> It is[...]the possibility of these cranks and freaks moulding, emotionally conditioning the human mind in sinister ways that when I saw (the BNP) letters[...]I felt anger that this decent, kindly community should have this poison injected into it. Who is to say that the same poison will not maliciously be injected into the veins of our common humanity elsewhere? (c.333).

And:

> When I went around during the last election one or two people here and there showed some colour prejudice. I tried to understand their prejudice. I tried to explain my position and to get them to transcend that automatic reaction

which I appreciate many people have at the mere sight of a coloured face. Sometimes people are so conditioned that they automatically react in that way (c.333).

The problem members should address, asserts Sorensen, is the way 'race' operates on *the emotional level*: 'One of the difficulties in the past has been that too many have been ready to give way to emotional impulses without fully appreciating objectively and dispassionately the very real and complex problems before them' (c.329). Sorensen makes a final impassioned appeal for 'decent men and women' to come together to 'eradicate any danger of this evil gaining strength in our midst' by those who would 'debase the human mind' (c.333).

Aubrey Wise, on the other hand, is, mischievously, able to turn the use of leprosy around on its definers by showing that, under the cover of this attempt to control racial language, they have conceded the need to appreciate the very 'feeling' of the electorate about this issue. This is the other meaning, the complete opposite of the one Labour emphasises, that is also contained in the idea of 'race' as a 'feeling state':

> Do I congratulate hon. and right hon. Members opposite on at last seeing sense on immigration, or do I sympathise with them on all having developed leprosy?[...]what the Smethwick electors did hardly justified an accusation of moral leprosy from the Prime Minister, particularly in the face of the Labour party's past record in that constituency of dealing with a problem which the constituents obviously felt was of great local moment. They wanted a Member who had studied their problem and had obviously shown some sense of understanding it (Mr. A.R. Wise (Rugby), *Expiring Laws Bill Committee*, 17 November, 1964: c.270-272).

What is perhaps not appreciated by either participant in this exchange is that the language of 'race', viewed as difficult and politically dangerous, is one developed by the 'race' populists, specifically Cyril Osborne:

> I recognise that this subject is political dynamite, and therefore I shall try to handle it with the same care and sense of responsibility that I should observe it were real dynamite[...]this problem, like real dynamite, will not cease to be dangerous by being ignored. Like real dynamite that accumulates in greater quantities, it could become increasingly dangerous. The size of the problem could become really serious and some foolishly applied or accidental spark could ignite the whole lot. We do our country a grave disservice by closing our eyes to what we know to be a very difficult but serious problem (Mr. Cyril

> Osborne (Louth) *Immigration Control* (Hansard) 5 December 1958: col. 1552).

This is one of Osborne's first attempts to get 'race' onto the Parliamentary agenda and it is significant that it is the form of words and the character of the issue which is at the centre of his thinking. Of course the nature of the 'race' idea is not pointing to the question of racism as a 'poison of the mind', as in Labour, but towards the problem of its 'combustibility' in terms of the feelings of the constituents who must 'endure it'. These are of course Osborne's racially defined 'Englishmen', who we have already met in our analysis of earlier debates.[19] The point of slippage here is that of the feelings of the indigenous and how this slides into the idea of 'race' itself as dynamite. In fact, the metaphorical identity between the idea of dynamite and disease can be reconciled at a pinch:

> In 1958, I was permitted to introduce a Private Member's Bill on this issue, and I then described the immigration problem as being like dynamite. Today, I think that it is considerably more dangerous. If I may say so without offence, to me it is like a cancer; the longer it is left, the more it will grow and the more difficult it will be to deal with and to heal (Cyril Osborne (Louth), *Control of Immigration*, (Hansard) 17 February 1961; c.1930-1).

The issue here, as we have already established, is how language usage reveals the process of 'race' erasure involved in the attempt to pose (black) immigration as a national issue. There is a searching around for the terms of its public formulation going on. Much of the framing idea of emotions/passions and feelings are already in place and obviously derive from earlier conceptual primitives or themes. Of interest here, from that prior debate, is the contribution of Labour mp. Harry Hyne (Accrington) and how the racism/anti-racism dynamic pulls ideologically at the centre of attempts to frame the 'concern':

> This is a difficult, delicate and not very pleasant subject to discuss[...]delicate, because anyone who raises it is immediately open to the suspicion of racialism or of arousing passions and prejudices which no one wants to arouse (H. Hyne, *Immigration Policy*, (Hansard) 3 April 1958; c.1415).

What holds this articulation at its centre is the understanding that, irrespective of ideological position, 'race' is inherently passion and prejudice arousing, and it this very nature of the thing that must be overcome if it is to be discussed. Of course recommendations made for restriction of the imputed 'cause' of this 'feeling' are, at this point, off stage.[20]

Labour's Language of Non-Race

It is not necessary, in acknowledging the significance of this language usage, in what it reveals about the party's psyche over 'race', to deny the validity of the dominant interpretation of Labour's post-Smethwick behaviour but rather the underlying motivations for it. It is within the consistency and meaning of the language articulated over Smethwick and the need for a centrally coordinated reaction, that a guiding idea of 'race' is established and increasingly, consistently applied. It is the political working out of the logic of this idea by the Labour leadership which allows us to see a degree of conceptual unity to the content of the leper outburst and the move to controls. However, such control is as much about endorsing black migrant exclusion as it is about the need to bring under political control that discourse able to politically articulate the idea of 'racial inferiority' through the increasingly self-conscious application of arguments about the 'cultural differences' of such migrants.[21]

This idea of 'race' then is one concerned with what we would now recognise as the politics of anti-racism i.e., the politics of the control of the uses and applications of ideas and practices associated with 'race' and racism.[22] Here we are asking that, rather than endorse a view of electoral pragmatism adopted out of competitive reaction or as a calculation of the unpopularity of the 'issue' with the electorate, we should consider the extent to which the public language and behaviour of Labour acknowledge and confirm an implicitly held theory of 'race'.

What is this theory of 'race' and how is it held by the Labour Cabinet? The first thing to acknowledge is that such a theory of 'race' is not explicitly held by Cabinet members. Rather evidence for its existence lies in the statements and comments made in public and Cabinet discussion. It is perfectly possible to posit the existence of a theory that governs or guides active group behaviour being 'transparent' to its members. Such a theory is only explicitly visible in the act of formulation, yet it appears unmistakable that such a theory gives continuity to the various statements, particularly from the arch pragmatists like Wilson, Crossman and Callaghan.[23] The theory of 'race' identified here is not racism, if by that we mean an ideological view of the inferiority or culturally determined differences of other groups; in this case, black migrants. Rather, we are referring to something like a theory in the modern usage of anti-racism: that is a view of the diagnoses and corrective action necessary to combat and defeat the reproduction of racist practices, procedures and philosophies (cf. Sarup 1989; Donald and Rattansi (eds) 1992). It is therefore a type of racialisation.

It is the keenly dispassionate eye of the visiting C.L.R. James who is able to reveal the unity of these ideas at the centre of the contagion metaphor:

> The Prime Minister in his first speech in the new House of Commons used a very striking phrase about the MP for Smethwick and his campaign. Mr. Wilson no doubt did this of set purpose. I inquired about the particular aim and was lectured by a very prominent anti-racialist in the Labour Party as to the full "significance" of the use of the word "leper". Leprosy, I was told, was a contagious disease (I let that pass), and Mr. Wilson was pointing out that there was a danger of this racial question spreading contagiously from Smethwick, or wherever it was allowed to develop, and corrupting the democratic traditions and practices of Great Britain: the phrase was a warning of what could happen, and the need for all member of parliament to be mobilised against it (James, *New Society* 1964: 5).

Of course, in the intervening thirty years, the meaning and application of the term anti-racism has undergone a transformation.[24] In the context of the 1960s anti-racism was an attempt to formulate and diagnose a response to the apparent and alarming growth of racism in the electorate and within the political field itself. To many Labour and Liberal politicians, Smethwick appeared the crack through which the flood would rush. It is this anti-racist approach that we should designate as PR2 because this view entailed the coming together of just these factors in an explosive cocktail. An historical summation must conclude that the theory of racism that informed this view was a dangerous and misleading one which has had a number of damaging consequences for the development of a politics of anti-racism in Britain.[25]

Viewed retrospectively, the impact of 'Smethwick' on Wilson and the Labour leadership is deep and disturbing. Paradoxically, something of the depth of penetration of the campaign can be gauged from Wilson's outburst in the House. The very fact that he chose to speak of this matter in that context confirms the connection, in his thinking, of the significance of the campaign as the importation of 'race' into the political arena. The leprosy metaphor extends this judgement to warn of the attack upon the system of politics and the relationship of the polity to the electorate which 'race' threatens to overturn.

> There have been those who did not scruple a year ago to play on issues of race and colour for squalid and ignoble political motives[...failure to act] might lead in a very short time to a social explosion in this country of the kind we have seen abroad. We cannot take the risk of allowing the democracy of this

country to become stained and tarnished with the taint of racialism or colour prejudice (Harold Wilson, *The Times* 29.9.1965)

How are Labour to achieve this lack of contamination of racial political language? Much of the heat, the reaction and the internal conflict of Labour over Smethwick can be gauged in the 1964 *Expiring Laws Continuation Debate* over the party's decision, along with some significant Tory Radicals, to support the 1962 exclusion, so bitterly contested by Gaitskell's party. As political commentators have pointed out, this policy shift is acknowledged in the comments of Wilson in 1963, but it is in the Expiring Laws Debate that the decision is publicly worked out through debate. It is no exaggeration to say that the debate is one dominated to a very large degree by the Smethwick result and the consequences of its political impact in relation to the treatment of immigration and the language of 'race'. Much of the focus of this debate is on the impact of and legitimate use of political language. For example, Mr.Ivor Richards argued that 'race', 'was clearly an issue which should have been raised and discussed. What we objected to during the election, and what we object to today, was not the raising of the matter but the way in which it was raised' (Mr. Ivor Richards (Barons Court) *Expiring Laws Bill - Committee*, 17 November 1964; c.307).

Mr. Selwyn Lloyd, Chairman of the Conservative *Race and Immigration Committee* and formative regional 'race realist', objects to the control of language central to the Labour line. He suggests that such a line has already been conceded by agreement with the 1962 Act. He criticises Labour for being at fault in not wanting to be held accountable to the electorate for firstly, not responding to 'race', and subsequently, wanting to suppress its debate any further: 'It is a very peculiar constitutional doctrine that an important, controversial Bill, fought over bitterly in this House, must not be mentioned during the ensuing General Election' (c.307).

Lloyd argues that when the Conservatives attempted to hold Labour to account for themselves in the constituencies, Labour entered a 'peculiar new phase[...]they denounced anyone who so much as mentioned the Bill or the problem in the country. They denounced them as racialists. It was nothing less than a gigantic smear campaign' (c.307). But for Richards it is Lloyds' language which is at fault; the language of regional race populism:

> The immigration problem is something which should be discussed in a calm, rational and helpful tone[...during the election] in London as well as in the Midlands the question of immigration was raised, not only in the form of sober discussion as to whether there should be control but in a "colour"

way[...]I know of people on the doorstep being told about immigration in that way, and Conservative canvassers told them. It is idle for right hon. and hon. Members opposite to deny that the issue of colour was raised in this way during the General Election, because it was raised (Richards, c.308-9).

This assertion then leads Richards, apparently reluctantly, into referring to *The Times*, 9 March 1964, coverage of the campaign of Peter Griffiths: 'I accept that this deals with Smethwick and I use it simply as an illustration of what seems to many of us on this side a dangerous attitude which may be growing up in British politics' (c.309). Richards justification for this judgement is Griffiths comment that: 'No racial group wanted integration: coexistence should be the aim'. He comments: 'I thought that this doctrine of separate and equal development on the part of both the coloured and white races had been overthrown in most civilised societies. It is not right and proper to see it raising its head in a British General Election in 1964' (c.309). Next Richards refers to the infamous slogan: "If you want a nigger neighbour, vote Labour" (cf. Foot 1965) and Griffiths' response to the effect that it was a manifestation of 'popular feeling': 'He is fully entitled to say that he understands their feelings, but it would be tragic if the British Election of 1964 went down in history as the first General Election in which colour was an issue: not immigration but colour' (c.309).

Here there is clearly the desire to separate emotions and feelings from the plain or objective language of immigration; to separate the irrationality of 'race' from the issue of immigration. This strand of argumentation, attempting to separate and separately define 'race' from immigration, so that the latter can be legislated for in the absence of hostility and passion, is at the heart of the mainstream acceptance of the very racial logic of Smethwick by the Labour leadership and the Liberal-Tories alike. It is on this basis that Richards appeals to the Opposition for an inter-party control of racial political language: 'How are we to try to integrate coloured people already in this country into our community?[...]the one way in which it will not be done is by using the sort of language certainly used by members of the Conservative party during the General Election' (c. 310).

Richards points to other examples of the Smethwick approach, very much honed down to the question of the use of language and the responsibility of the politician in trading in racial language. His example is the reported remarks on the 1964 Election campaign by the Conservative prospective candidate for Leyton (the seat the defeated Gordon-Walker is to fight for re-selection as Labour Foreign Secretary). Richards quotes Mr. Buxton:

"While I was canvassing many people complained about the immigration of coloureds. They do not resent coloured people as such, but they do object to the blacks coming off the banana boats and taking council houses that would be available for locals". If the Conservative candidate used those words, even if he was using them only to express the point of view of the electorate in that constituency, he was wrong to do so in those terms. Such language can only exacerbate a situation which may already be difficult (c. 310).

However, Mr. Richards grounds such an appeal upon the realist acknowledgement that 'immigration is a problem': 'Of course, problems arise from immigration - problems of housing, education and all other tremendous problems of injecting a coloured minority into already overcrowded areas' (c.308). Notice that it is not racial language and irrationality that is injected into the community; but rather the migrants themselves. Once such a position has been reached it is possible to begin to acknowledge further elements of the problem and how they impinge upon the politics of policy formation: 'It should be the aim of every member of the committee to see an abatement of any tension arising from a difference of culture or colour. If we subscribe to this end, we all have a duty to take this matter out of party politics' (Mr. Aubrey Jones (Birmingham, Hall Green) c.312).

It is the argument of the 'race' Liberals that the Conservatives deliberately ignore or rather expediently neglect the account of the contributory causes of the reaction and *react* only to the 'public reaction' itself. Such an attitude amounts to: 'There are these problems. We will not deal with them but we will put a complete stop on people coming into the country' (c.308). The element of 'realism' that is new in the positions of Liberal, Labour and Tory is the acknowledgement that, for whatever reasons, the social problems associated with immigration are caused by the sheer quantity of immigrants and cannot be solved except on the basis of an agreement of future severe restriction.

Against this position it is clear to see that Liberal Tories, such as Nigel Fisher, in outspoken alignment with Labour in 1962, had shifted much further to a 'realist' position than Labour by 1964. Fisher, a critic of the 1962 Bill as a 'colour bar', is now moved to argue:

> I believe now that a larger and an uncontrolled influx of coloured immigrants would be more damaging to race relations in this country and, therefore, in the end, to Commonwealth relations, too, than the smaller and controlled influx that we have under the Act. We must face the fact that a larger and uncontrolled entry now would create such feeling among our own people here that there might be serious repercussions. There might be very strong anti-

colour feeling, and possibly race riots and incidents of that kind, which[...]would have the worst possible effect upon race relations, both in Britain and outside it (Fisher c.358).

In fact, Fisher has performed a complete reversal of his position: 'whereas I opposed the [1962] Bill because I though that it would be bad for Commonwealth relations and also for race relations, paradoxically I now support the Act for the same reasons, because I think that, without it, the position would be worse' (c.358). In the course of this reversal Fisher concedes the main plank of the Conservative approach to the 1962 Bill: the potential size of the immigrant population free to come into Britain under the 'open door'. He admits that in opposing restriction he was thinking of the damage that would be done to the West Indies, rather than: 'of the much larger Asian countries of the Commonwealth and what would happen here if literally hundreds of thousands of Commonwealth citizens from India and Pakistan wanted to come to Britain' (c.358).

For Fisher a major part of the problem to be faced is that the problem is *now largely an Asian one*. He asserts that the figures suggest that, given the size of the back log, had controls not been introduced the numbers arising would have outstripped the countries ability to absorb them. 'That is a fact, and we all know it.' (c.359). In addition to numbers, there is also the problem of language: 'Most Indians and Pakistanis cannot speak our language, and it may be that control under the Act should now be extended to language control as well, because it is so much more difficult to assimilate people who cannot speak the language of their adopted country' (c.359). Fisher closes his speech specifically with reference to Smethwick: 'if hon. Members believe in and want good race relations[...]let us get away from the atmosphere generated by Smethwick. All that one can say about Smethwick is that it has exposed a problem which all of us, in our heart of hearts, know exists. It is an unfortunate problem. It is the problem really - and I think that we might as well admit it - of racial prejudice' (360). This 'real' problem requires a realist stance:

> It is unfortunate[...]it is un-Christian; and it is always denied by those who feel it; but it exists. I believe that it is our duty here not to allow it to become worse by taking up strong political attitudes ourselves, because if race once becomes an issue of party politics in this country, we are going to embark on a very dangerous and slippery slope (Fisher c.360-1).

The chiefly remarkable thing about this Liberal capitulation to the realists is that it is made on the basis that legislation, arrived at without reference to racial ideas or racial language, will not be racist and will furthermore prevent racism from becoming an element within politics. But how has this demarcation exercise been achieved? It has been made possible by moving some of the elements previously characterising the Right hand side onto the Left hand side; of taking on board the arguments of the racists by redefining them as political Commons'sense. This operation is legitimated at two levels. Firstly, by being able to assert how such 'realism' allows a clearer definition of the acceptable and unacceptable terms of the Race and Immigration Debate. This is the preservation of the liberal centre ground from extremism: 'The main thing of importance is to prevent the colour of people's skins becoming, directly or indirectly, for any reason, a party political issue in this country' (c.361). Such a distinction obviously does not apply to language. However, this limiting exercise allows a liberal minded reconciliation with ultimate goals: the solution on a world scale.

> If we fail to do the sort of things about which we have been talking today, if we allow racial bitterness to develop in Britain, which God forbid, we shall be creating not only a terrible and insoluble problem for our children and our grandchildren in this country but we shall be failing to take our contribution to the solution of the problem of race relations in the world (c.362).

This theme is taken up by Minister of Labour, Mr. R. J. Gunter, who asserts that the British need to 'give to the world' an example of how they can demonstrate a way of solving this 'deep and biting problem',

> We are all sinners. Do not anyone assume a holier than thou attitude. Let us conclude that no public man or woman in this country ought to do other than be most careful in the choice of his or her words about this problem. Everyone of us ought to have a proper regard[...]for the fact that any exacerbation of feeling in this country can very well have its repercussions elsewhere (Mr. R.J. Gunter c.381-2).

Here at the heart of the Liberal Commonwealth of Labour is the conception of racial language and the separation of racial commonsense and realism from the unreason of racial passions and feelings. Again it is the use of racial language which will enable the public articulation and entry of that racial passion into political debate. Such a potential flood will sweep away democracy and debate. It is this conceptual matrix which underpins the internal logic of the Tory front bench:

> I have known few other topics about which there has been more intense feeling among individual people. I have known few topics on which there has been a more clamant desire to feel that one's Member of Parliament was identified with one's own personal point of view. This is a subject about which there is strong feeling among individuals, particularly in the older parts of our big cities where people have lived all their lives and where they have seen the character of the neighbourhood change very rapidly. We always need to bear that personal aspect in mind when we are discussing this question (Sir Edwin Boyle (Birmingham, Handsworth) c. 375).

This narrative exercise is important in drawing the elements of racial idealism and realism together in a inter-party alliance that can allow political leadership:

> We must be careful not to confuse racialism with realism. I hope that I always condemn racialism as much as anyone. I can think of very few meaner actions than publicly identifying some vice, or disease, or bad social conditions with a particular racial group of community. I hope that all of us on this Committee will agree on that. However, at the same time, let us be realistic about this subject (Sir Edwin Boyle c.375).

Sir Edwin then quotes approvingly from Mrs Elseph Huxley's *Back Street New Worlds*: 'While race discrimination is out of fashion nowadays, quite a lot of citizens harbour doubts, fears and resentments they are, in the present climate of opinion, ashamed to admit.Those are the realities of the present situation' (c.375). However, against this he argues:

> It is a most encouraging feature of our national life today that so few people are prepared to say that they favour race discrimination. But doubts, fears and resentments are very strongly felt among people. Many people are conscious of a difference between how they feel and how they feel they ought to feel. Doubts and fear of this sort are widely felt in this country (c.375).

It is not just that we can already recognise the 'race' language of Commons'sense that has been so firmly established in debates; despite that fact that, as we have seen, a number of theorists have claimed its emergence in 1976! It is how this discourse of the 'genuine' and those experiencing (racial) 'fears' can only be reassured by prudent legislation aimed at the overall restriction of numbers. It is the linking of the discourse of the popular 'ordinary' member of the communities 'under strain' with the prospect of restriction of overall numbers that is the achievement of the discourse of 'race' in postwar debates.

This matter of immigration even at its present level, is causing a great deal of extreme unhappiness and a considerable amount of tension and difficulty. That is why I asked the Home Secretary[...]not to think in terms of just ideas and principles, but to realise that for the sake of social harmony and for the sake of solving our problems, bearing in mind the heavy level of concentration of immigration that we already have, it is bound to be necessary to continue strict control of immigration for the future. It is for this reason that my party greatly welcomes the fact that we are today more agreed on this principle than we might have dared to hope two or three years ago (Sir Edwin Boyle c.380).

The establishment of this moveable consensus is the result or effect of Labour's mobilisation of the discourse of leprosy and contagion, in that such a malady requires government action to contain and limit the damage to popular consciousness, since the level of racism in the population at large is a feature of open expression.

The Politics of Racial Language Usage

Why is it Labour who are so alarmed by the 'race' scenario; is it because it is their candidate that was brought down, or is it something more? The answer to this question lies in a consideration of the depth, and the contradictoriness, of Labour's fear of the emergent politics of racial extremism, announced by Smethwick but finding their apogee in the phenomenon of 'mass market' Powellism. We will explore the dimensions of this fear and the political language strategies to which it gives rise in specific detail. Firstly, let us turn to the larger question. Consider the following: 'the suggestion was made by the Home Secretary[...]that a grave situation had developed in the country at large, which was now trembling on a knife edge from which it could only be retrieved by an act of major surgery - the amputation of the cause of the infection' (Rose et al 1969: 613; cf. *Hansard*, vol. 759, c.662).

Here we can sense the politics of 'panic' in the language of *extremis*: of politics on the edge. Racial description becomes itself a bearer of racial typology and models of social pathology; metaphors of illness and contagion construct a sub-political mechanism and a class of victims who are open to infection. Coded here, but present, the nameless but numerous class of proletarians inhabiting 'the country'; as the class aspires, in the ideology of labourism, to the soul of 'the nation' (cf. Nairn 1971). Thus a politics of hypodermic injection, or stimulus response, conducted on an audience of passive victims of racial infection is countered by the surgical necessity to dispose not of the diseased limb or organ - but the unwitting bearers of the disease: 'the blacks'.

As we have already established, the idea of 'race' is sub-political not because, like values or bias it intervenes, distorts or clouds clear and reasoned - 'neutral' judgement ; but because it operates on those areas and locations of social consciousness and being that are beyond or outside of reason: feelings, passions, emotional states, etc. On the issue of immigration, opined Alan Watkins, 'people are scarcely rational' (New Statesman 26, April 1968); thus, the politics of immigration restriction delivered politics up to the darkness of the 'tribal mind', as the April editorial in *New Society* put it shortly after Powell's 1968 speeches. It is this concept that holds the logic in place. Racism is non-rational; not open to reasoned intervention. The solution is to get rid of the cause of such contagion - since it is not possible to do anything about it. Indeed it is dangerous simply because it does not advance by winning over minds but by clouding and distorting emotions and by raising and inflaming passions. The danger is that the malady will turn into an epidemic.

An interesting feature of this discourse is how the medical pathology metaphors shade into the idea of the threat of the non-literate. It is this class who are most susceptible to a form of communication which operates on non-rational lines; an appeal to prejudice and passions. Racial ideas are somehow able to work below the level of consciousness. Ideas which the sub-literate are susceptible to. Increasingly this metaphorical language stands in for the discussion of 'race', per se. It pre-structures the ideological field with a language of racism and more importantly, a language of anti-racism.

The contradiction at the heart of this political struggle within language is that popular racism comes out of a real process of response to working class articulated experience; whereas the language of Labourism attempt to deny it; then to deflect it to some other *misunderstood* causes: urban blight, deprivation, etc. Finally, the Labour cabinet attempt to curb the spread of the fungus by the administration of the medicine of restriction, which goes much further than even the Tories had contemplated (Rose et al 1969).

The contradictory nature of the need to confirm the grass roots of labour and yet deny racism is a discursive strategy of inherently problematic kind. For example, Home Secretary Callaghan, commenting on dockers and factory workers who had gone on strike in support of Enoch Powell, argues that they were: 'expressing in a demonstrative way disquiet which I knew they had had for a very long time' (*The Times*, 30 April 1968). At the Labour Party Conference, in October 1968, Chair Jennie Lee, spoke of: 'home grown primitives[...]barbaric gentlemen partial to violence' within the country, and concluded: 'What could give greater provocation to violence than the gospel of Enoch Powell? Back to the jungle, the weak to the wall, each man for himself, sacred white supremacy?' (*The Times*, 1st October, 1968; *IRR 'Newsletter'* October 1968: 367). On Powellism as political phenomenon: 'it would be a very grave mistake to underestimate the power of this kind of appeal, and a still greater mistake to think that only half-wits and layabouts were attracted by it' (IRR: 367). Wilson, in his party speech, repeatedly attacked the 'guru from Wolverhampton' and concluded: 'If ever there was a condemnation of the Opposition it is the fact that the virus of Powellism had taken so firm a hold at every level' (*The Times*, 2nd October, 1968). Wilson went on to confirm that the 'intolerant society would not be countenanced' despite the 'blood curdling language of the April speech'. Wilson again described Powellism as a 'very evil doctrine'. Whereas Fred Gregory, MP spoke of 'the cancer of racialism' (*The Times*, 4th October, 1968).

The great fear of Powell among the Labour leadership is redolent of the language of the 'Anti-Enoch letters' reviewed by Diana Spearman.[26] Spearman identified much of the letter comments as motivated by 'fears of Alf Garnett i.e., '(a) fear and distrust of ignorant and uneducated public opinion ran through the letters, a fear openly expressed in 160 of them.' Thus Powell was accused of 'Stirring up the fascist instincts of the least literate and intelligent section of the community' while 'your supporters are ignorant men who dislike social change'[...]'the Alf Garnetts of Great Britain support you, the educated elite do not'[...]'The British public thinks only with its passions'[...]'I beg you not to set yourself up as a leader of uneducated labourers' (Spearman, *IRR 'Newsletter'* June, 1968: 236).

It is necessary to locate this 'fear of the illiterate' and the language of emotions and passions within the politics of the Labour party leadership. Paul Foot has characterised the Labour party, at this time, as consisting of four 'wings' or tendencies: 'Radicals', like Gaitskell and the Fabians, almost indistinguishable from Liberal-Tories, with their understanding of economic needs and traditional hatred of racialism; the Left (like Silverman and Foot) standing for the 'brotherhood of man' and 'Commonwealth sentiment'; the Right (like Frank Tomney and Frank McLeavy) 'race populists'; and its 'practical' or 'rotten' centre (i.e., Soskice, Crossman, Edelman). Foot's argument was that Labour's opposition to restriction measures rested on a political alliance between the Radical and the Left: 'When the alliance[...]began to collapse after Gaitskell's death, the "rotten centre" yielded to restrictionist, xenophobic pressure from the "Right"' (*IRR 'Newsletter'*, October, 1965: 4-5).

What needs to be explained, in terms of the development of political language, is how Labour shifted to a view of 'race fears' as practical commonsense needing the support of immigration control. A Church Leader commentary from 1969 captures the essence of this shift: 'it was not emotional racism, but, in an overcrowded island, plain common sense' (IRR, *Newsletter*, February, 1969: 59).[27] It is the winning of the political battle over commonsense that establishes the ordinary discourse of racial commonsense and racial fears and their legitimate basis in the working class community. The Tory 'race' populists are so much more able to occupy this ground because for them it is an encroachment. Labour are supposed to be the 'natural' guardians of this political channel, this is there difficulty with Smethwick and Powellism.

Let us return to the 1964 Expiring Laws Bill to illustrate how this encroachment works:

> We are all, of course, against the colour bar. [Hon. Members: "Oh"] Are the real circumstances in relation to these clubs quite as they now appear? I stand in the Committee and say that I have some sympathy for the Midlands working men's clubs concerned[...]Indeed, the theory has always been that a club is an extension of the home (Mr. Geoffrey Lloyd, *Expiring Laws Bill - Committee*, 17 November 1964: c.304).

Mr. Lloyd quotes the General Secretary of the West Midlands' Branch of the Club and Institute Union: "We cannot have these people coming off a ship and walking straight into a working man's club", I link that point with the second statement which the Prime Minister made in his speech last night, when he referred to the importance of improving the standard of living in the Commonwealth countries so that no man would be driven here by the whip of poverty' (c.305). This seemingly 'wild card' appeal for cross party alignment is made explicit later on when he asserts:

> By world standards[...]the Midlands working man is a rich middle class man, and he attaches enormous importance to the standards which he has built up. Therefore, I feel that we must have some sympathy with him when he wishes to be a little careful, not necessarily on account of the colour of a man's skin but on account of the completely different approach a newcomer may have when he first arrives in this country (c.305).

Contained herein is the commonsense of the 'race relations' situation as established by the Conservative and Labour 'race' populists: that the problem of racialism is a misunderstanding of the 'commonsense reaction' that is likely to occur among simple working men and within English communities rooted in particular, class based traditions. The newcomers' habits and standards are bound to be different and often to be seen as lower. This only emphasises the great gap between the First and Third worlds and highlights the problem of managing the contact of large numbers when, for such MPs, what should be addressed is the economic drive of the standards of living in the countries of emigration.

Political articulation of the 'fears' of the working man are explicit and central to the *Race Relations Debate* of 1965, initiated by Labour and, in which, Peter Griffiths makes a notable contribution (c.1008-1015). But of more importance, in framing the fears of Labour and the working class, are Labour MPs, like John Binns (Keighley):

> There is in my constituency amongst the working class people a tremendous amount of resentment[...]I do not believe it has any real basis of racial hatred. It is possible that it is developing into a form of colour prejudice[...]but if it is developing into a form of colour prejudice we in this House must accept a great deal of responsibility for this[...]because for far too long we have prevaricated and dodged this issue[...]And now when we have accepted the need to control immigration[...]before these measures can start to bite we introduce this Bill (which) does nothing to remove the social problems which are the root cause of this resentment (John Binns (Keighley) c. 1004-5).

Binns' immediate political gut response is to off-load the problem onto the Conservatives, in a wildly populist swipe:

> This problem was created (by the Conservatives). It was during the 13 years of their rule that most of the immigration took place. I admit that the flood gates were wide open, but there is some evidence that during their period of office the flood of immigrants was deliberately directed towards these gates (c.1005).

This partisanship then shifts a gear into the grass roots populism of the Labour mp. faced with the local politics of working class 'racialism':

> Both sides of the House have some responsibility for the resentment felt by many of my constituents against coloured immigrants. I am afraid that under the Bill this resentment will be mistaken for racial prejudice and that some action will be taken against it under the criminal code. I do not believe that this resentment is racial prejudice. If it is not, what is it and what is its basis? I believe, with the hon. Member for Buckinghamshire, South (Mr. Ronald Bell), that its basis is just cold fear (c.1005).

Here we can see a natural alliance between populist Labour and the defenders of the 'whiteman's country', Bell, Osborne, et al. The common language they share is the language of racism and the working class community. This is also, as we have suggested and will demonstrate, the locus of classic Powellism.[28]

> In my constituency there are many working people who have not had any previous contact with coloured people and suddenly wake up and find large groups of coloured immigrants within their community. I speak of Asiatics and Pakistanis who cannot speak a word of English. They come straight from the tribal villages of Pakistan and their ideas of personal hygiene are absolutely different from ours[...]These fears within the British people are strengthened in a place like Bradford when they read of the big increase in the incidence of tuberculosis and other diseases, and when the working man buys his terraced cottage and finds that the cottage next door is suddenly sold to a Pakistani who fills it at the rate of six to a bedroom (c. 1005-6).

Here, quite unmistakably, the Brotherhood of Labour cedes ground to the interests of the indigenous and the pre-Powell plea for recognition within politics of the (i) validity of those who are confronted with the problem (ii) whose fears are justified and (iii) who are threatened with 'reverse discrimination'. Here is evidence, if it were needed, of the fear of Powellism (pre-Powell) among Labour. It is the Labour populists, faced with the experience of immigrant settlement, who articulate the racial fears of their constituents and their status as the victims of a situation created by the legislators. 'What will the Bill do to remove[...]the fears of my constituents? I do not believe that it will. In its present form it will only aggravate the fears, and because it is only the working-class people who have contact with these immigrants I am not sure that the argument of working class people that the Bill will discriminate against them is not true' (c.1006).

Here we have Powellism in embryo and the idea central to the populist articulation of the 'genuine feelings' of the working class who must endure the situation with the immigrants at first hand. This allows the appeal to the 'genuineness' of these sentiment and feelings and the need to recognise the *ordinary, decent constituent*. 'The greatest danger lies not in what the Bill will do, but in what it is thought that it will do. I am sure that every hon. Member must have had numerous letters, not just from extremists but from reasonable and sensible people who have said that they fear that this is the first step in the erosion of freedom of speech' (Mr. Peter Griffiths (Smethwick) *Race Relations Bill, Second Reading*, 3 May 1965, c.1012).

This allows the Conservatives to appropriate the populist language of 'the man in the street'. Significantly it is Labour who are seen to be with the 'highbrow liberals' over the 'race' issue. 'I am tired of the "Holier than thou" attitude and the wringing of hands by people who often know little of the problem, or, if they know it, deliberately close their eyes to it. It is a typical attitude in my constituency, where we had a candidate who spent his time preaching about discrimination and the colour bar and then returned at night to his carefully discriminating and carefully segregated headquarters' (Griffiths, c.1014).

The reference here by Griffiths, to the defeated 'elite' Labour candidate, former Shadow Foreign Secretary, Patrick Gordon-Walker, is indicative of how the politics of Labour, over 'race' and Immigration, are viewed as increasingly out of touch with 'real feeling' and 'real issues' affecting constituents. Thus 'race fears' take on a palpable life beyond their metaphors and become the basis of electoral address and local assessment of performance. Let us now return to the issue of the impact of this flavour of politics upon the Labour leadership.

Electoral Fears: Crossman and the Pragmatics of Racial Restriction

As we have seen, it is the perceived basic-incompatibility of the political system with 'racial thinking', belief or prejudice, which gives rise to the 'electoral fears' perspective. The fears are not actually for the fate of (good) 'race' relations' or even the status of 'race' as an explanatory concept, but rather the nature and present structure of the polity should a politics based on 'race' be allowed to flourish. The subsequent reportage of Labour's 'volt face'(cf. Foot 1965; Deakin 1969) or retreat into electoral pragmatism (Katznelson 1976) appears to confirm this interpretation, by the seemingly indisputable confirmation of concrete events i.e., the 1965 White Paper and the 1966 'bi-partisan' electoral campaign.

It is conventionally assumed that Crossman's candid diary entries for this period of the 1964-1970 Labour Government, provide sufficient insights into the rationale for such a strategy of attempted bi-partisanship through increasing 'immigrant' (i.e., 'black') restriction, to convince. The argument advanced there is that such a strategy is underpinned and made sense of in terms of a political expediency or pragmatism necessary to quell electoral reaction to 'Immigration' and 'race'.

The textual support for such an interpretation, often cited, but largely un-examined in any detail, is the Cabinet diary entry, recording and commentating on the 1965 Labour party White Paper which, according to commentary, 'scorched the Tories white trousers' in its severity and signalled the electoral turn around of the party from contestation to support for controls (cf. Rose et al 1969; Patterson 1965; Gabriel and Ben-Tovim 1982: 148).

A close textual analysis of this account (Crossman 1975: 299) reveals not only this dominant organising interpretation but another view which we may identify as: PR2. Such a view entails, as we have argued, a theory of 'race'; but the form it takes is as a theory of anti-racism or, more specifically, a theory for the correct treatment of the idea of 'race' within politics. Such a theory rests on the grounding assumption or belief that such a treatment must follow from the perceived 'nature' of the idea; that this belief stems from the history of racism to which the terms refers rather than something internal to the idea is resolved by funnelling one into the other. However the marked characteristic of this cleaning-up operation is that the term and the idea comes ready packaged and consequently absent of the history which has mysteriously been 'evacuated' from it.

Such a view is the organising element of the passage in providing the theory and logic by which such an electoral pragmatism makes sense. This argument is asserted despite the fact that the full dimensions of this theory remain hidden to their author and unacknowledged, and therefore substantially unrecognised, by the professional audience who received such a view as, proof positive, of Labour pragmatism over the 'race question'.

> This afternoon we had the statement on immigration and the publication of the White paper. This has been one of the most difficult and unpleasant jobs the Government has had to do. We have become illiberal and lowered the quotas at a time when we have an acute shortage of labour. No wonder all the weekend liberal papers have been bitterly attacking us. Nevertheless, I am convinced that if we hadn't done all this we would have been faced with certain electoral defeat in the West Midlands and the South-East. Politically, fear of immigration is the most powerful undertow today. Moreover, we had already abandoned the Gaitskell position when we renewed the Immigration Act, and any attempt now to resist demands for reduced quotas would have been fatal. We felt we had to out-trump the Tories by doing what they would have done and so transforming their policy into a bi-partisan policy. I fear we were right: and partly I think so because I am an old fashioned Zionist who believes that anti-semitism and racialism are endemic, that one has to deal with them by controlling immigration when it gets beyond a certain level (Crossman 1975: 299).

There are at least four points to note in this account of how Labour attempted to re-adjust its immigration policy to correspond with 'political reality'. Firstly, there is no logical or necessary correspondence between labour restriction from the 'new Commonwealth' and lack of demand: quite the contrary, such labour is being restricted at a time of 'acute shortage' of such. So here we see performed a curious inversion of 'truth' to social and political reality.[29]

Secondly, labour's main rationale for increasing Commonwealth labour restriction is its electoral popularity. In other words, such legislation corresponds to 'political realism', i.e., sustaining popular support by endorsing popular feeling on social issues such as 'immigration'. Thus Crossman states quite plainly that it is 'fear of immigration' not immigration itself which is the 'problem'. For realists, like Crossman, this means the government must respond to such fears by restricting the numbers coming in. It is an 'unpleasant job' because such exclusion goes against the humanist-liberalism 'realists' such as Crossman would like to espouse, were the government not subject to electoral and inter-party pressure to retain votes by supporting popular positions.

Thirdly, such arguments, in turn, conform closely to a political logic already in-place over the 'immigration' issue. In fact Labour have provided many of the planks of this construction of 'political reality' to which they are attempting to conform, by conceding in the 1963 Expiring Laws Debate the need for 'new commonwealth' (i.e. 'black') Immigration control at a time of acute and continuing demand for just such workers; and by abandoning the incontestable 'economic' arguments of Gaitskell and Patrick Gordon-Walker after the 1962 Debate and Gaitskell's death (cf. Foot 1965: 187-90).

Fourthly, it is endorsed by an appeal to the political logic of the consequences of bi-partisanship politicking. In other words Labour will remain electorally vulnerable i.e., unpopular and liable to lose public support to the extent that they do not concede to popular pressure over major socially defined issues like 'immigration'. So labour must attempt to anticipate the moves of the opposition over the issue and do it first. In this way they either neutralise a possible further raising of the stakes or they are able to steal the fire of the opposition by going further than their opponents. Such a strategy (a) enables you to maintain popularity with the electorate while, (b) preventing the opposition from employing the issue to political advantage; (c) prevents the issue from becoming a major party splitter (cf. Layton-Henry 1984: ch.4).

However, the 'bedrock' of this account of 'political expediency' and its necessary relationship to 'political reality' are not contained in a claim for the eternality of politics but that of the 'nature' of popular prejudice and/or racism and, most importantly, its likely relationship to political leadership. According to this view it is necessary to concede to the racist right not because they are correct in their assessment of the character or consequences of (black) 'immigration' but because of widespread racism among the working classes. It is the prejudices of the 'social wedge' upon which the traditional party support is founded, which is most problematic to successful leadership. This is because Crossman believes such prejudice to be endemic and eternal. If this is so, then, given the situation, any party is free to play the racist card and achieve a successful response.

Thus the 'political reality' to which the labour party or leadership must conform and, during his membership of the Cabinet was seen more and more to so do, is the need to bring about hard fought, piecemeal changes, often requiring individual ministerial ability, against the weight of existing reaction against such change. Gradual but definite change, within the context of liberal-democracy, must take place against a number of obstacles or 'eternals' which structure and support popular political conceptions; particularly among the most reactionary sections, the working class themselves. The effect of the unpacking of this logic is to endorse such racism, as to all practical intents and purposes, eternal and therefore as, ipso facto, the cause of itself i.e., it is the existence of racist belief among the working class which creates the risk scenario for a reforming, liberal minded party. To challenge such beliefs would be to risk the whole strategy of social reform over 'empty' principles.

The net effect of such logic is that the existence of racism is accounted for in terms of its object: New Commonwealth Immigration. Thus the problem is not indigenous British racism but too many commonwealth immigrants! In fact Crossman goes further and posits an eternal mechanism which rises and falls according to the level of 'immigration'. In other words the realist solution becomes, in effect, to keep 'immigration' to a minimum. This of course could be accounted for as a minor slippage, not germane to the realist position which is tactical. However, the evidence suggests that the 'practical' realist stance towards the politics of 'race' is underpinned and organised around an underlying 'racial consciousness': a racial consciousness structured around an in-principle acceptance of widespread racism as inevitable and endemic, which is itself supported by a theory of human nature which is central to the inter-party commonsense of the mainstream parties. This view can be summarised as: the eternality of racism is a function of the present constitution of human nature in society. The realist position then is merely to recognise that it is this grounding nature that the realist politician must work with. Surprisingly, the textual support for this argument can be found in Crossman:

> I believe that the differences which divide mankind are as strong as the universal principles which unite us. These differences are of course matters of race and culture which are, emotionally at least, as important as economics and self-interest[....]I believe that our main effort must be to control racial and cultural passions. We must be prepared to admit that our country has a very severe limit to its capacity for racial assimilation (Crossman 1975: 44).

What is Crossman arguing here?; that the stuff of racism is eternal, undoubtedly. But the overall sense of the passage is sustained by a number of conceptual oppositions: that people are divided by race and culture, differences which find expression in emotions, and in racial and cultural passions. However, set against these inevitable divisions are the existence of principles that can unite, can act as mechanisms of unity. But for this to work it is necessary to restrict that which would stir and animate such passions into politics: *other 'races'*. Here politics is a form of defence against the forces that animate difference and division on the modern world stage. Politics is the tool of reason against the play of 'racial' passions. The appeal to reason and the application of political reason is only possible after or when such racial passions have been curbed.

This stance is also present in Crossman's public 'face'; that is, his attempt to explain the political necessity of recourse to this kind of realism to the centre 'liberal' audience of *The Times*: 'Understanding the profusion of shrinking violets' (6.9.72): 'As a party, we are frequently faced with a potentially destructive conflict between our progressive principles and the prejudices of our working class voters' (Crossman 1972). Here, explicitly formulated, is the model of the relation of the party, guided by liberal principles, to the class it must lead to a more liberal society. The obstacles to this leadership are that the class exists and comes to consciousness in prejudice, in reaction. In one sense this is a traditional Labour Fabianism. In another sense it is not. The difference between Fabianism and Crossman's stance is one of realism. Faced with the task of leadership the Fabian seeks to educate the led. A realist, faced with such a challenge, capitulates to it, in the short term, in order in the long term to be in a position to 'win the day'.

> As progressives we were opposed to capital punishment, persecution of homosexuals and racial prejudice whereas as a large section of our working class supporters regard such ideas as poison. What they hate most is our softness on colour. It nearly cost us the election of 1964 - particularly in the West Midlands - and it was widely felt that our improved majority in 1966 was largely due to our new tough line on immigration control. That is why as a government we were panicked in the autumn of 1967 by top secret reports predicting a mass expulsion of Asians from East Africa and began to make contingency plans for legislation which we realized would have been declared unconstitutional in any country with a written constitution and a Supreme Court (Crossman 1972).

Firstly, it is dubious whether there are any marked similarities in these 'electoral poison' issues and therefore why they should be grouped together in this way.

That aside we have an argument that appears to make concrete the electoral fears invoked earlier: once the popular 'groundswell' has built up Crossman is able to argue that the Kenyan Asians Bill was a panic response to such opinion; here the crisis arises out of popular anxiety and presents the government of the day with a fait accompli.

The implausibility of this argument rest on both levels of its construction. If immigration, homosexuality and capital punishment are all electoral poison then why is it that it is only one of these issue that Labour must capitulate its principles to? The answer has to do with the popular feeling such issues are said to arouse. Here again it is only the popular feeling of colour prejudice that concerns Labour. How can we account for this? After all it is well known that the majority for capital punishment is incontestable, yet legislation revoking it has been supported despite repeated calls for a referendum by various self-appointed populists, newspapers and organizations.[30]

This strand of enquiry leaves unanswered the question of why immigration control is more significant an issue to sacrifice than capital punishment or gay rights? The components of the answer are suggested later:

> A parson can fill his church and an editor sell his newspaper by preaching principles which outrage majority opinion. A political leader can only do so if his party has no prospect of power. Mr Heath and Mr Wilson must leave to others the exhilaration of leaping far ahead of public opinion in order to educate it. In our two party system the political leader must recognise the strength of racial feeling and be very careful indeed not to go too far ahead of it (Crossman 1972).

We have now gone full circle. The reason, opines Crossman, that anti-immigration, anti-gays and capital punishment are the animators of majority opinion is because such opinion is formed by the force of cultural and 'racial feeling'. Faced with this 'fact' politicians must be circumspect. Does this then suggest that of the three concerns, it is racial passion that is the most serious ? Or is it of the three the only one not amenable to education? If this is so; if racial feeling represents a force that cannot be won but must be worked with: what sort of a political order and social relations does it suggest? Precisely a racial order. It is the only 'world view' that can be compatible with such a diagnosis.

But is such a conclusion inevitable? Is it not the case that the reason why Immigration is the most difficult popular feeling to deal with is because it has become the focus of politicians and political discourse? This suggests that the natural level of racial and cultural passions, rather than set by some universal primitive mechanism of present nature, is actually a function of political concern. This is not, as in Labour's travails, a universal state of reaction to shifts and changes in public opinion; it is the attempt to mould and re-work that opinion. Powellism, in the form of press and public agitation, by Sandys and Powell over the potentially 'massive influx' of Afro-asians, is what Labour are reacting to in 1968; not the massive groundswell of public opinion. They are reacting to the predictable response to a Powellist appeal because such a politics moves along the same grooves as their own attempt to go along with 'the public'.

For Crossman, a forthright attempt to go against such a momentum, to attempt to educate the masses, to lead them towards an enlightened liberalism would deliver the whole feast to the forces of Powellism: 'By treating the Kenya Asians as though they were white[...]Mr Heath and Mr Wilson[...]may win the praise of a substantial educated minority. But we would also create a bandwagon for Enoch Powell which might tempt him into leading that ultimate terror of British democracy: an authoritarian third party' (Crossman 1972).

Here revealed is a discourse, not of 'race', but of class. Here the politics of Labour is the politics of Fabianism: enlightened, educated leadership in the context of the reactionary and uneducated masses who, as a result, are vulnerable to the appeals of a Powellism. What has happened is that the Fabian strategy of intellectual and cultural leadership by the educated class has been 'interrupted' by the racial discourse of Powell. This nightmare scenario can be located quite explicitly in Crossman's frightened diary reaction to vintage Powellism in 1968: '*Saturday, April 27th*. There's no doubt how last week has got to be described. It was Powell week and we are still absolutely dominated by the effect of his Birmingham speech[...]The significance of his[...]speech[...]is that he has successfully appealed to the mass of the people over the heads of the Parliamentary leaders for the first time since Oswald Mosley, and in doing so he's stirred up the nearest thing to a mass movement since the 1930s' (Crossman 1977: 28-9). And also, even more specifically: 'Enoch is stimulating the real revolt of the masses. There he is with his 40-50,000 letters streaming in, the marches from the docks and from Smithfield, all part of a mass response to a very simple appeal, 'No more bloody immigrants in this country' (p. 29). The elements we have noted coalesce now into this comment:

> I should guess he miscalculated the extent of the popular appeal and has been slightly appalled by it[...]There have been amazing demonstrations outside while, inside, the Palace of Westminster is filled with awareness of this mass movement. Talk about plebiscitary democracy ! Here it is in action, making its impression direct on the Government[...]It has been the real Labour core, the

illiterate industrial proletariat who have turned up in strength and revolted against the literate (p.29).

Here, unmistakably invoked, is a manual proletariat who are illiterate, presumably in the cultural sense that they are ripe for emotional appeals to 'race' and nation, which the language of Powellism can articulate into frightening political action.

Conclusion

This chapter has argued that the political treatment of Smethwick has been insufficiently investigated, particularly its discursive impact upon 'race' debates taking place within Parliament, as well as within and between the major parties, particularly Labour. Our analysis of the reaction of Labour, both within and without Parliament, clearly shows the construction of a theory of racial language which, while produced to identify and protect politics from the misuse of the sentiments and emotions encoded within the politics of Smethwick and Powellism, has succeeded in allowing the further encroachment of their logic, by endorsing measures leading to restriction of the objects of such discourse: black migrants. The central theme here is the identification of racism with irrationalism and emotion mapped onto the fear of the inevitability of racism and the legitimacy of those expressing its sentiments at a grass roots level. In this way Smethwick and Powellism enable the further establishment of the discourse developed by the 'race populists' at the centre of legitimate politics, by accepting the logic of the explosive/corrosive effects of 'race' politics, and by denying the ability of public language to carry a discourse of intellectual contestation against it. In our final chapter we will go on to examine how these issues can be applied to illuminate the language and politics of Powellism.

6 Enoch's Island: Race, Nation and Authoritarianism in the Language and Politics of Powellism

This chapter is specifically concerned with the question of Powellism. Its purpose will be to address those questions left unanswered within our analysis of the theory of the New Racism and its application to Parliamentary Debates, particularly in the light of the inadequacies of that theory; substantive questions of the political impact and effect of Powellism as a political discourse on the politics of Immigration control and state policy, resulting in the regulation and/or stigmatisation of black people in Britain as a problematic and undesirable minority. What is significant about this racism is how Powell attempts to employ it within a political field characterised by a limited existing available discourse, and in a climate of repression of racial terminology and appeals to racial ideas. What this means is that Powell attempts to introduce a political discourse of racial articulation into an existing, quite developed political ideology of patriotism and conservative institutionalism. This is why Powellism appears to take a cultural and national form. However Powell fails, as have his previous fellow-travellers, the 'black country' racists, to win hegemony for a racial discourse of exclusionism; despite the fact that, overall, such a politics is successful in securing exclusion and stigmatisation of Britain's black population (although of course, this is achieved before the rise of Powellism). And this, despite the fact that Powell achieves a greater degree of sophistication in his discourse of racism and its articulation with the themes of patriotism, than they.

The chapter is organised into three broadly thematic sections. The first section addresses existing Political Studies accounts of Powellism as a discrete political phenomenon explicable via (i) the nature of 'race' politics as liable to populist agitation and (ii) the peculiarities of the man himself. It argues that this approach is broadly complimented by those that see the answer to the question of

Powellism as located within his unique biography and historical period, as reflected in the circumstances of the Conservative party during a protracted disengagement from the politics and ideology of Empire and domestic social imperialism (cf. Utley 1968; Roth 1970; Foot 1969).[1] Considerations of space mean we cannot pursue these arguments much beyond a thumb-nail outline. Against them we claim empirical and theoretical reasons for viewing Powellism as *a series of distinctive political interventions* taking place at intervals in the late 1960s, 1970s and mid 80s. It is a feature of Powellism as a political entity that such interventions become more public and media oriented but, despite this, such interventions are not *necessarily* similar in content or strategy.

This argument involves a recognition of the extent to which Powellism is a multi-dimensional entity, in terms of both its conceptual content, periodization and impact. This involves an appreciation of the changing meanings Powellism has acquired at different times, which reflect attempts to define and map it as a political discourse. How the content of Powellism has developed, mutated and changed and, in particular, how the internal thematic balance of issues or agendas has shifted over time. Such considerations must involve something like an intellectual history of Powell's political ideas; also how this content can be understand as a series of interventions spanning political time. Again for reasons of space we must decline the development of these areas beyond their utility to the argument advanced here.

The second section addresses the area we identify as absolutely central to any claim for the political significance of Powellism: its referential success as a populist political discourse that has apparently created its own constituency. This argument will be explored in relation to the way Powellism has re-articulated the conceptual-ideological terrain, mapped by the 'race populists', which has lead to Powell's success in winning a popular audience.[2] Any accounting of such 'ideological' success must involve the question of Powellism as an 'elite discourse', particularly in terms of the role and impact of this factor in providing the discursive mechanism that has enabled the construction of a 'popular/populist' articulation with its intra- and inter-class audiences.

The third section presents the central contestation informing the treatment of Powell within the book as a whole: that the Powellism of 'anti-immigration' is to be understood, not as a new cultural racism or nationalism, but as a political re-articulation of the signifieds of biological racism. This argument, drawing on the discourse centred methods of the book as a whole, employs a substantial textual analysis of the content of Powell's speeches and writings. Only Nairn has attempted anything like the depth of coverage upon which the analysis of this section is based.[3] On the basis of such analysis we will argue that the speeches and writings that constitute and inform Powell's anti-immigration politics, are derived and have their reference within, a finite number of ideological epistemes or 'units', such that: (i) Powellism is a (biologically reductionist 'old') racism; (ii) Powellism is a (nationalist) patriotism; (iii) Powellism is a variety of Conservative institutionalism and, (iv) Powellism is a political populism.[4] Each of these thematic units will be examined in turn, since it is only through a clear understanding of these elements, and their potential for significant political articulation, that the phenomenon of 'mass-market' Powellism can be adequately understood.

Such textual evidence will be employed to support the argument that Powellism was, during the period of its most dramatic political visibility, quite clearly a racism (and was certainly interpreted as such), despite the fact that, thematically and conceptually, the roots of Powellism lie in a theory of the nation (which is conceived as both an economic and political entity), a traditional patriotism and a Conservative institutionalism; all of which are conceptually articulated through a mystical and transcendental 'romantic nationalism' (cf. Powell 1965; 1969: 337-41).[5] In this respect, Enoch Powell's racism is almost entirely borrowed. The material upon which Powell worked lay close to hand and required no major innovatory terms. This is not to suggest that there is no originality to Powell's discourse; clearly there is much that is. However, Powell's elective role has been to push to a greater degree of sophistication the language politics of 'race' in the context of its discursive repression.

The distinctiveness of Powellism lies in the application of an elite political tone and public oratory to what was seen as a backstreet and wholly illegitimate issue. There is no doubt that, at times, Powell achieves a degree of political sophistication in his deployment of the subterranean force of the absent signifier of 'race', achieved through the successful politics of the euphemism. In this respect he brings a greater degree of skill and literary sensibility to the rhetoric of the racial politics of the absent signifier. However, much of this innovation arises from the discursive articulation of a populist politics of the nation (it would be an unwarranted assumption that Powell's patriotism is popular) that the utilisation of the 'race' and Immigration exclusion debate made possible, once freed from its traditional lower middle-class moorings and intellectual foundations within Empire administration theory and pre-war Tory social imperialism (cf. Utley 1968; Foot 1969; Nairn 1970).[6]

In order to clarify the distinctiveness of the argument advanced we must first address the received ambiguity in the understanding of the term Powellism, and the kinds of explanations that have been attached to it, so that we can go on to present the distinctive type of interpretation my research materials propose.

The Meaning(s) of Powellism

As far as the popular and received view are concerned, the term Powellism is almost uniquely associated with an obsessive and very strident form of anti-immigration politics and public oratory. Such a politics has been described as 'populist' (Hall 1979) and as demagoguery. The impact of the Powellism of 'race' on Immigration, Race Relations and Nationality legislation, to some theorists, is fundamental; it has quite literally shifted the terms of debate (Hall 1978; Schoen 1977; Solomos 1989). For others, Powellism is the indicator of a new kind of political relationship in British politics which is extremist and anti-centrist, anti-consensus and confrontational (Gamble 1974); above all it is ideological and consistently so (Phillips 1977; Nairn 1970).

The Powellism of 'race', nationality and restriction could be endorsed as a consistent working out and application of a distinctive 'world view' or 'structure of feeling' (Williams 1961: 64-88) which has achieved popular recognition and appeal across the cultural, political landscape of the working and middle class electorate (Schoen 1977). It is an empirical analysis and understanding of the nature of this relationship which sustains Schoen's view of the significance of Powellism. He goes so far as to define the 'Powellites' as likely to be 'male, middle-aged, working-class Conservatives living in the Midlands or the South of England' (1977: 195). It is this aspect, the kind of support that has sustained Powell, which Schoen refers to as Powellism:

> In as much as Powell has been a national politician, addressing himself beyond class or regional issues and often going beyond party itself, he did indeed succeed to an astonishing extent in building a cross-party, inter-regional, cross-class following, a more truly national constituency than that possessed by any of the parties (Schoen 1977: 195).[7]

Powellism is also the term given to a particular form of populist politics, where mass leadership is secured from above and directed towards some symbolic object. This involves the setting up, within the political discourse, of a relationship between audience, speaker and symbolic target to which legislation or government action is required, based on popular and widespread consent. The shorter version is populism, where a political leader will seize upon a 'popular' issue in the attempt to employ it as a mandate for consent to more conventional piecemeal and institutional measures. Often the gap between the former and the latter is considerably large. Populism has been a contested term (cf. Laclau 1977) but a usable definition has been offered:

> Populist movements are movements aimed at power for the benefit of the people as a whole which result from the reaction of those, usually intellectuals, alienated from the existing power structure, to the stresses of rapid economic, social, cultural or political change. These movements are characterised by a belief in a return to, or adaption of, more simple and traditional forms and values emanating from the people, particularly the more archaic sections of the people who are taken up to be the repository of virtue (*New Society*, 25 April 1968).

If we map this portmanteau definition of populism onto Powellism we find an interesting lack of fit. Powellism is a populism which aims at the consolidation and extension of elite power but on the basis of a return to a mythical relationship with tradition and the sentiments of the historical past; because only this will rescue the instinctive, non-democratic relationship between people and state exemplified in the ancient institution of Parliament. Powell certainly is an intellectual alienated from the existing power structure. But he views such a structure as a superficial excrescence, which has grown up on top of the essential seat of power: the 'Sovereign in Parliament'. Postwar governments have clung to the delusion of Empire grandeur, seizing upon the developing Commonwealth as a new supra-national body. Such un-realism has lead inevitably to the pursuit of inauthentic goals, most particularly, the financial support of a world military capability more fitting to a vanished Empire, as well as the fostering of inappropriate values and beliefs at home. Powell must therefore go against the existing establishment in order to restore, at some future date, the return of the old organic authority upon which the English nation is based.[8] The repository of this allegiance and ancient instinct for government by a minority i.e., those most able to instinctively comprehend the national will, are 'the people' of England. For the purposes of his Immigration speeches, such a role is taken up by the 'forgotten Englishman' of the inner city, who alone is possessed of the truth regarding what it happening in the 'areas most affected'.[9]

For many, the term Powellism simply refers to a particularly strident form of racial politics. This argument can be disputed on the grounds that, as we have already suggested: (i) it is quite possible to think of Powellism without 'race', even more damagingly (ii) it is possible to think of Powellism without Powell; and 'race politics' without either. This suggests that it is structural and political factors which are the most important in explaining the emergence and significance of Powellism; not the personality of Powell himself. However, the style of Powellism does owe a great deal to the man and the intellectual formation to which he was subject. Perhaps the dominant interpretation of Powellism is the view that it is uniquely determined by the biography and personality of Powell

(Utley 1968; Foot 1969, etc.); particularly through the impact of the personal and party trauma of loss of Empire and decolonisation. Let us briefly review this approach.

Powellism as Empire Blues

> *The capacity of the British for extricating themselves from empire with comparatively little trauma is a central, yet neglected, theme of modern history; it is best understood through the evolution of attitudes in that party which, up to 1900, had been most blatantly committed to the imperial cause* (Pugh 1985: 184).
> *The premise of Powellism is quite simply that the Indian Empire has been lost* (Utley 1968: 50).
> *The most glittering jewel of Empire died hard in Enoch Powell* (Foot 1969: 19).

It is indisputable that Powell was an Empire loyalist. All his biographers and interpreters note his profound love of India. Powell's posting there during the Second World War began a period of deep immersion into Indian society and culture, as refracted through the colonial experience of governing. It is Utley (1968) who reminds us that it was the Indian Empire that struck Powell as a momentous exercise in minority control of a 'distant and alien land' by means of the 'very penetration of Englishness' to the roots of that ancient society. This may strike us as an exaggeration but it also suggests something of the role of the ideology of *Englishness* in Powell's conception of the Empire and colonies. This 'fantastic structure', as he was later to call it, was created by the energies and skills of the 'adventurous and industrious' English and the prize of India was the greatest triumph of this phase of expansion and settlement.[10]

Thus, Powell came to political consciousness through the imperial vision of the Indian Empire and the English administration that 'ran it'. He experienced the loss of that Empire as a personal and party tragedy: realignment to a post-Empire party was a slow and painful process, accompanied by rear-guard action (Roth, 1970: 99-108). Foot (1969) views the shift from the party of Empire to postwar reconstructionism by the Tory hierarchy as a species of political cynicism, to which ideology furnished the rhetorical support. Here ideology is employed to cloak or conceal interests: once there was no interest for the British establishment in maintaining a military and civil role in Africa and the colonies then the quicker it could withdraw, under the banner of 'responsibility', the better. For Powell, this fundamental shift had to be conducted in ideological terms, through the reconciliation of ideas about the party and the nation. Foot (1969) argues that Powell's own intellectual disengagement and reconstruction of

Toryism, allowed the party a route. But, as Barker (1981) reminds us, what emerges within Powellism is not the pragmatic economic expansionism of the 'non-class', 'end of ideology' of Macmillanism but a fundamental re-think of the philosophical *premise* of Toryism itself; or at least the Toryism to which Powell had devoted his early political career and the time in India: the Toryism of Empire. Thus if Foot is right he is in the limited sense that what Powell supplied was an ideological route for the 'grass roots' and elements of the fundamentalist right. That is, Powell effectively supplied them with the terms and outlook of disengagement from Empire that could allow a form of reconciliation with a party and leadership profoundly out of sympathy with their political 'instincts' (cf. Barker, 1981: ch.3).

Powellism as Intellectual Biography

> *For over twenty years of my public life a large part of my thought and study has gone to advocacy of those self-regulating mechanisms which it has become customary to describe as 'the market'. In fact it was in this context that the expression 'Powellite' and 'Powellism' were current for years before something called 'race' reared its head in the political vocabulary* (Powell 1977: 8).

Phillips (1977) distinguishes three different meanings of the term Powellism: (i) that Powellism refers to a political ideology because Powell's 'political ideas[...]are seen as achieving sufficient depth and internal consistency to provide a more or less universal guide to political conduct' (p.99); (ii) that Powell's ideas are sufficiently distinguishable from the main parties to require a separate label; and (iii) to the extent that the term has been employed to 'describe the impact of Powell and his ideas on the electorate' (p.99).

Phillips can be read to suggests the term 'Powellism' is multidimensional and contradictory. It is quite categorically a political restatement of classical economic liberalism (Powell 1964); coupled with a limited form of selective public provision or state initiated intervention (Powell 1965; George and Wilding, 1976: ch.2). Powell is quite correct to assert that the term Powellism pre-dates his treatment of 'race'. It first becomes distinctive as an economic doctrine. This credo of market capitalism is combined with an old style Empire Toryism which is the source of Powell's nationalism. To this mixture we must add a grudging, utilitarian welfare policy (Powell 1966); and of course, Powell's anti-immigration populism.

In the early 1950s Powell laments the dissolution of Empire; up to the late 1950s he is deep within the turmoil of the inner crisis of the Conservative party disengaging from the idea of the 'party of Empire'. By the early 1960s, Powell is proposing the abandonment of policy 'sacred cows' if the party is to get of the opposition benches; from 1966-68 Powell puts a 'new model' Conservatism on the agenda. His interventions become increasingly more frequent, rising to an incredible media crescendo in April and November 1968, the period when Powell was Shadow Defence Minister.[11]

We can therefore conclude that the term Powellism is multi-dimensional, in terms of content, history and politics, and cannot simply be confined to the description of a particular kind of agitational politics of anti-immigration; to do so would be to miss the important contribution the rest of Powellism plays in the formation of that politics. Thus, Powellism is a generic term for the themes that structure the historically shifting, political and ideological discourse of Powell.

The Political and Ideological Impact of Powellism

In this section we will explore the conceptual and syntactic relations between racism and political language as they are revealed within the analysis of three areas we have identified as central to the explanation of Powellism as a form of political racialisation: (a) its *political impact* in terms of the penetration of the language and programme of Powellism into the official political culture and policy of the dominant parties (cf. Barker 1981; Miles and Phizacklea 1984; Gilroy 1987); (b) the nature of the *ideological transformation* achieved in the narrative formation of Powellism as political discourse (cf. Barker 1981; Seidel 1986a; Gilroy 1987a) and, (c) the *relations of signification* Powellism has achieved with its audiences and, therefore, its referential success (cf. Hall et al 1978; Smithies and Fiddick 1969).

A key point of entry into the debate about the politics of racial language usage and Powellism is the view, held by media commentators and academics alike, to the effect that Powell's language and 'speeches contained little that had not been previously said by Conservative MPs or was not Conservative Party policy' (Miles and Phizacklea 1984: 64). In one sense this is a statement of the obvious and yet it is quite misleading. It is, if we accept it at its value, entirely inconsistent with the arguments of the New Racism theorists whose whole case rests upon the notion of Powellism as a conceptual and rhetorical watershed in the use of racial political discourse. As we have already established, such a view treats the emergence of Powellism and the language that signifies that emergence as distinctive and unique in a way which is not consistent with the evidence.

However it would be equally wrong to reject any notion of the innovatory quality of Powellism. A finer, more weighted distinction is required:

> Other MPs had achieved 'political success' by their expression of the 'race'/immigration theme. What was different [about Powell] was the way in which these increasingly familiar elements were combined to produce an extremely articulate and logical expression of racism, whilst dispensing with much of the 'extreme' rhetoric of previous proponents of such views. Powell rarely made explicit use of the idea of 'race' and made no reference in his own words to 'coloured immigrants'. But he was able to submerge the idea of 'race' in a notion of Britishness, of nation. This was done by citing the views of the 'ordinary British citizen' expressed in conversation or letter in combination with his own reference to 'alien cultures'. The crude and inconsistent racism expressed in the factories, shopping centres and pubs was endorsed by a politician who had the authority of education, political office and a position in the Shadow Cabinet (Miles and Phizacklea 1984: 64).

This summary account, by Miles and Phizacklea, does suggest a more adequate framework. Yet it down plays that element most central to the interpretation of Powellism offered by the New (cultural) Racism writers: the innovatory terms offered by Powell that have some claim to 'newness'. If we add this element into the mixture we have the width of focus necessary to provide a sufficiently expansive but empirically anchored account of Powellism. As we have already suggested, such an account must involve three dimensions: (i) the political impact of Powellism on the politics of 'race' and immigration control'; (ii) the nature of the ideological transformation achieved in the narrative of Powellism as political discourse; and (iii) the relations of signification and referential success achieved with Powellism's audiences.

Area (i) is that claimed by conventional political-sociology which has consistently produced an account of Powellism as an aberration and oddity, to more recently: Powellism as a dramatic actor in the failure of 'race' politics to penetrate the 'hard core' of the political system (Layton-Henry and Rich (eds) 1986). What has begun to shift and transform in the meantime has been the conception of Powell's relationship to his audience: (iii). This movement has been one of movement from a position of mass manipulation of inarticulate sentiment and authoritarian emotion to a view of the 'fears' and 'concerns' of a working class electorate as a species of commonsense. This movement conceptually describes the movement from prejudice to 'populism'. The promise of the New Racism thesis was that it could offer an alternative to such approaches by concentrating exclusively upon the interior language of Powellism and the attempt to construct a popular racist commonsense with its audience. This project remained incomplete because the theorists asserted and assumed a relationship they could not sufficiently demonstrate.

What needs to be explained is how Powell, in the context of an existing development of a racialised account of the politics of New Commonwealth Immigration, which had made possible the codification of restrictive and exclusionary 'race' laws, was able to provide a more rigorous presentation of these themes and ideas through the careful narrative content and formulation of his speeches, with the result that he was able to succeed, when they had not been fully able, to make a: 'direct appeal to, and legitimation of, a part of working-class experience' (Miles and Phizacklea 1984: 64).

(i) *The Political Impact of Powellism*

While a number of treatments within a neo-liberal and neo-marxist analysis of the politics of 'race' in Britain have begun to assess the impact and significance of Powell (Layton-Henry and Rich 1986: introduction; Solomos 1989), much of this analysis is a belated recognition within political studies of the importance of Powellism as a phenomenon worthy of study, rather than an assessment of the terms of his political impact. Powellism, and the 'race politics' with which he is synonymous, were ignored for similar reasons: that they were populist diversions from the hard 'core' of mainstream national policy making. Studlar's influential treatment of 'race' politics as a form of 'elite autonomy' reinforced this view (Studlar 1980). What has changed is the view that ideologies play a central role in the construction of political issues and policy formation (cf. Edelman 1977; 1988). The recent work of Solomos has done more than anyone else to establish this in the case of 'race' in British politics (cf. Solomos 1986; 1988 and 1989).

It is not clear if there is a consensus among radical or liberal theorists about the impact of Powell. In some ways this reflects the ambiguity concerning the use and application of the concept of ideology to the politics of social policy formation. For example, to claim that Powell's interventions have set the terms of public debate about 'race relations' does not necessarily indicate any specific impact on policy formation and legislation. A recent historical survey has specifically traced Powell's impact on public policy discussion (Solomos 1989); however we cannot impute from this specific legislative changes. The only way this can be established is by (i) identifying Powell contributed clauses or specifying (ii) clauses reflecting Powell's specific ideas. In this respect all political and sociological theorists would argue that the pattern of immigration legislation, prior to and post-Powellism 1968-74, has been towards a tightening of the categories of inclusion and restriction of dependent entitlement and also the move towards a definition of nationality, which superficially appears to reflect Powell's ideas. However, against this, we must also consider the extent to which the pattern of restriction was already set upon this course, i.e., that such a pattern would have resulted even in the absence of Powellism?[12]

A resolution of this dilemma is possible upon the lines of inquiry we have already sketched i.e., Powell's impact can be considered in terms of the success of particular interventions: in 1968 over the Kenyan Asians and the Race Relations Bill; in his 1969 attack on the validity of the Registrar General's population estimates for the 'coloured birth rate'; his 1970 Election campaign and continued warnings and foreboding of 'numbers'; his 1971 Commons interventions to discredit the concept of 'patrial' and to widen the repatriation clause of the Conservative Immigration Bill; in 1972 over Britain's obligations to the Ugandan Asians; in 1973-4 in his anti-Common Market election campaign; in 1976, in leaking the Hawley Report, while alleging Home Office 'cover-up' of back-log of potential immigrants and illegal entry rackets; in 1981 with his renewed warnings of 'racial civil war' in Britain's inner cities and his much quoted rhetorical response to the Urban disorders of, 'You've seen nothing yet'; and his call for a test of nationality that would define those who belong to the British nation in the debate on the Conservative Nationality Bill; in 1985 over further Urban Disorders; in 1988 in his well publicised return to the themes of the 'rivers of blood.'[13] The question is whether such political interventions have shaped and determined the parameters of the 'race' debate and specifically the kinds of legislation and policy that has emerged from it?

This pattern of intervention cannot be assessed against the same criterion, because specific interventions where made in particular arenas and for different reasons. The most important single element to consider is that Powell's initial major intervention removed him from cabinet and therefore from a specific role in helping to frame and implement government legislation over Immigration and Race Relations, thereafter. His influence on such policy formation was subsequently conducted from outside of this arena and from 1974, from the 'political wilderness' of South Down. However, even if we take this period as a whole, what is particular noticeable is that much of the legislation initiated in this period is 'reactive' in terms of Powellism. The Labour Kenyan Asian Bill is a good example, as we have already argued. Although in 1972, over the Ugandan Asians, this sort of pressure was resisted by the Conservatives. This seems to be Powell's most effective form of intervention; given his structural position, outside of the cabinet and, after 1974, outside the ruling parties. Powell's other kind of influence was as a debate contributor and, most significantly, as a committee member of passed Bills. Most notable here is the 1971 Immigration Bill which Powell attacks for its 'racial' criterion and yet, in committee, presses for a widening of its repatriation measures. Powell's effect here has to be judged contradictory.[14]

Again, it is almost certainly the case that it is Powell's re-entry into the Immigration Debate, in 1976, and the leaking of Home Office reports that provides the motive force behind the Conservative approach to the Race Relations Debate, and the pushing for a further debate on Immigration in the same year. However, although Powell's influence is felt here, as we established in chapter 4, the majority of the Tories vote in support of the Bill. A similar assessment must accord to the 1981 Nationality Debate which, as we have suggested, is saturated and seems formed out of the central concerns of Powellism. But again, in debate, it is not to Powell's liking and he votes against it as a Bill; but for its amendment in Committee. In this instance, we can say that the Bill does establish criteria closer to Powellism than at any time previously. In the other areas of legislation and debate, Powellism must be judged a failure; over the EEC, despite finding alignment with Benn, Labour and substantial sections of the Left opposition to entry: 'I received a letter from Enoch Powell - now that was a surprise - congratulating me on my Common Market speech yesterday, 90 per cent of which he had agreed with' (The Benn Diaries, October 28th 1971; cited in The Guardian, 28 September 1988).[15]

But such 'populist' demands for a referendum leave the public unmoved and the political agenda shifts away from Powell's nationalist outcries against a European future. Echoes of this dilemma have reappeared in the attitude of Mrs. Thatcher within the politics of Europe and the post-Thatcher debacle within the Tory ranks which precipitated rumours of a realignment of Powell with the Tory Party (Daily Telegraph, November 1990).

Finally, Powell's interventions into the debate over the 'Urban disorders' certainly attempted a political racialisation. However, as Solomos has argued, this tendency was well in tow among the Thatcherites and had, by the time of the resurgence of such large scale unrest in 1985, become politically neutralised as a species of 'lower class' hooliganism and materialism driven by 'greed'. As then Home Secretary Hurd put it, 'it was not a cry for help but a cry for loot'. This linguistic transformation allowed the social authoritarian language of the 'new right' full play in creating a succession of images of 'irresponsible parents' ('where were your children last night?), 'looters' and 'vandals'. This is not to say that 'race' dose not play a metonymic role here by invoking the 'disorganised' (i.e., absent father) black family, allowing children to roam the inner city streets. But it is not a leading theme (cf. Solomos 1986; 1988: ch.6).

Powellism, Racism and Thatcherism

Relevant at this point is the issue of the relationship of Powell and Powellism to the contemporary New Right and Thatcherism.[16] Easily conflated here are the ideas and the impact of Powell and the New Right. Thus, it can be argued that just as the apparent contradiction at the heart of Powellism: that between free-market liberalism and authoritarian-nationalism, remains un-resolved, so Powell's influence highlights the contradictory wings of the New Right itself. Certainly the case can be made for the ideological formation of the New Right out of the anti-consensus, return to the market leadership of Powell in the mid to late sixties (cf. Gamble 1974: 115-122; Utley 1968; Cowling 1988). However, the limitations of such a perspective is how such midwifery can account for the Powell of 'race', of social authoritarianism, and the nation? As for example, a leading exponent of the view that Powellism beget Thatcherism, specifically defines such a movement as one jettisoning 'race':

> What is now called Thatcherism was originally known as Powellism: bitter tasting market economics sweetened and rendered palatable to the popular taste by great creamy dollops of nationalistic custard. In his case immigration control was the custard and it was a bit too rich for any but the strongest digestion. She was lucky to have the Falklands campaign handed to her on a plate, which did the same job more effectively, turning far fewer stomachs (Peregrine Worsethorne, *Sunday Telegraph*, 12 June 1983: in Edgar 1983: 39).

An inescapable component of Thatcherism has been its authoritarianism, particularly noticeable in the populist appeals made by the Thatcher regime in the wake of the inner city disorders and the Falklands' war (Edgar 1983; Hall 1982; Sivanandan 1982). However, while authoritarian values have comprised much of the rhetoric of Thatcherism, they have not translated themselves into specific policy initiatives on 'race'. This is particularly true of the Thatcherite stance on Nationality and Immigration. While Thatcher rose to prominence on an 'end immigration' ticket the Thatcher regime, despite overseeing the ratifying of the covertly racist British Nationality Act (1983), and a number of covert restrictionist measures and policies, involving the manipulation of Immigration rules,[17] were unable or unwilling to instigate any major 'new' legislation in line with such election promises.

The Nationality Bill, as we argued in chapter 5, owes its inception to a Labour party green paper. The Debate itself was certainly conducted in the presence of Powell, but the transformation of 'race and immigration' into

Nationality legislation is certainly one already under way within each of the major parties policy reviews, despite Labour's protestations to the contrary. In this respect, it is plausible to suggest that, despite Mrs. Thatcher's 'race'-populism, once elected to office the party evaded a fully racist theorisation of immigration and nationality; because such a populist policy is politically inflexible, especially when emergencies of principle arise (Layton-Henry 1984; Barker 1981: 26-7). Also Powell was always waiting in the wings to outplay whoever took up the populist line.

A particularly good example of these contradictions of political rhetoric and political reality, was the controversy over the 'Hong Kong Chinese', where the Thatcher cabinet was obliged to secure entry visas for a privileged minority of entrants against a right-wing rebellion led by Norman Tebbit and supported by Labour rebels (cf. The Times, Guardian, Independent, Telegraph and Mail, 4,5, 20th April, 1990).

(ii) *Powellism before Powell?: The Formation of the Anecdotal Racial Discourse of Powellism*

In the House of Commons Debate on Control of immigration (17 February 1961 (Hansard) vol. 634), a debate to which, like so many in the years of silence, Powell was a non-contributing attendee, we find a striking resemblance of narrative style, language and delivery to Powell's own later, much more deliberately constructed efforts:

> The point can best be summed up by what was said to me by a constituent of mine. He was the occupant of a house of which he had the statutory tenancy, and the house had been bought over his head by a Jamaican who wished to get him out. The man was a fairly humble railway worker, and he told me "Believe me, it is said that we hate the Jamaicans, but it is nothing to what they feel about us." That is the kind of thing that is occurring[....]The man of whom I spoke was a decent, honest sort of man who really had no such hatred at all, but who felt the result of what is happening in this way (Sir Hugh Lucas-Tooth, (Hendon, South) *Control of Immigration* 17th February 1961; c.1981).

Let us compare this anecdote with one of Powell's most (in)famous:

> A week or two ago I fell into conversation with a constituent, a middle-aged, quite ordinary man employed in one of our nationalised industries.[18] After a sentence or two about the weather, he suddenly said: 'If I had the money to go,

I wouldn't stay in this country.' I made some deprecatory reply, to the effect that even this government wouldn't last for ever; but he took no notice and continued: 'I have three children, all of them through grammar school and two of them married now, with family. I shan't be satisfied 'till I have see them all settled overseas. In this country in fifteen or twenty years time the black man will have the whip hand over the white man (*Birmingham Speech*, 20th April, 1968; in Powell, 1969: 281-2).

The conceptual structure and content of these anecdotes are remarkably similar.[19] Obviously Powell's is more literary and self-conscious, paying attention to accent, to the point of clipping words to create authenticity and distance. This allows him to 'quote' racial analogies that turn the received view of slavery and Empire, 'on its head'. These are the elements Powell has added; the attention to detail and 'authenticity' are required for the delivery of this speech to the national media. The supporting paragraph fixes Powell's preferred interpretation:

> Here is a decent, ordinary fellow-Englishman, who in broad daylight in my own town says to me, his Member of Parliament, that this country will not be worth living in for his children. I simply do not have the right to shrug my shoulders and think about something else (Powell 1969: 282).[20]

The language of the honest, decent, respectable, 'quite ordinary' Englishman invokes and constructs the validity of these 'tales', confirming upon their teller membership of that community that can share this 'feeling for the soul of the nation'.[21] As Behrens and Edmonds (1981) have pointed out, the characteristic markers of the 'race populists' are: (i) a duty to articulate the view of the ordinary English and (ii) to act as guardians of the national heritage and English institutions, that these relations are apparently expressive of. This sense of Englishness as symbolic birthright and identity conferred by an invoked collective identity and tradition, as our analysis of debates in chapter 3 has demonstrated, goes back to the mid and late 1950s. It is hardly surprising that this language usage travels in the other direction, post 1968 Powell:

> Some years ago I met a constituent who found himself and his family the last English person in a road otherwise totally occupied by immigrants. He said to me "What have I done to deserve it?"[...]I make no apology for the fact that this problem mainly concerns England and the big English cities. There are certain areas there where an Englishman may feel that he is a stranger in his own land. Nobody has told him who, or how, this happened, or what is the point, what is the aim, what sort of England will this be in 10, 20 or 30 years

time (Mr.John Stokes, (Halesowen and Stourbridge), *Race Relations Bill*, 4 March 1976: c.1643).

Here we have, well absorbed and perfectly recreated, an identifiable language of Powellism: the ordinary English, the street by street occupation, the invasion and cultural alienness which must lead to conflict; the situation moved beyond tolerance and the threat to the future, birthright and identity of the nation written into the private tragedies of the common people who populate the streets of England. The selection of specific terms: 'occupied'; the use of ordinary speech; the claim for 'authenticity'. As Barker has pointed out, such stories where common in the Daily Mail coverage of the 'great debate' on immigration (1981: 24-5) and suggest the widespread construction of a discourse of 'race' decisively influence by Powell's treatment of it.

There has been much coverage and debate about the 'truth', reliability, validity and representativeness of these anecdotal stories. As Ann Dummett pointed out, and others since, Powell's story was standard mythology to be heard in any pub in 1968 (cf. Foot 1969: 114). For example, Seabrook has recorded the new 'folk devil' of the declining Midland and industrial North: 'Packie Stan' (Seabrook 1970):

> There is a kind of folk ogre[...]a compound of all the least acceptable characteristics of the immigrants in the town, and whose name sounds like 'Packie Stan'. He kills goats and chickens in the back yard, his children pee on the flagstones, has a large family, and he depresses the price of property wherever he goes. He contrives to filch people's jobs and yet batten on Social Security at the same time. The police are on his side and he had been granted immunity from the laws of the land by the Race Relations Act (Seabrook 1971: 39).

Such a folk devil arises from the many anecdotal stories passed from mouth to mouth by people, identical in detail, and yet common to many different towns:

> Each time I was told [the] story, it was said to have originated in a different (and named) street in the town. Nobody could identify the protagonists. It was invariably told to the story-teller by a friend who personally knew the individuals concerned, but who remained always at one remove from the actual informant (1971: 39).

Seeking verification of the story by identification of the individual was likely to arouse resentment among tellers, 'because it looks as if you're doubting their word. It's simply a well known fact, that's all.' (p.40). Thus, Powell's refusal to give up names and addresses and the inability of certain major papers to find the people and situations depicted in his stories is in a greater sense irrelevant. What is important is the idea of 'typicality':

> He said that in any event he was not quoting the letter as evidence of the truth of what it stated. He was not quoting it as evidence because he did not need evidence; and he did not need evidence because what the letter said had happened was to his knowledge so typical as to be an established fact. He had used the letter as an illustration of what he knew to be true (Terry Coleman interview, *The Guardian*, 20th May 1970).

The point surely is made that Powell was quite able to construct a 'typical story', and was almost certainly, in the early years of immigrant settlement, to have been offered countless stories, concerning the 'blacks', that would have been 'typical' in this way,[22] in reflecting working class sense of 'loss of community', economic insecurity and racialised social antagonism. As Seabrook has argued, the feeling of acute loss of working class standards and community, forged in collective hardship and poverty, can result in various forms of fundamentalist reaction, one of them being 'racial extremism' (cf. Seabrook 1978).

Having established these connections it is surely predictable that the 'race populism' and the Parliamentary racism which we have recorded will exhibit a ubiquitously anecdotal form? At the centre of each piece of appeal on behalf of the beleaguered English, working class in 'our' major cities is an anecdote or story or reference to a conversation or letter. On top of this often a reference is made to a newspaper as verification of the validity or generality of the incident or sentiment. Such a reference is employed to indicate the source of the reality denied those not directly involved in the 'race experience'. Take, for example, the following:

> Hon. Members should see some of the things which go in Birmingham. They would then think that it was getting out of hand. Certainly the police have more than they can deal with[...]I am not saying that it is all crime, but I know of cases where the police have been so busy at certain times of night that there has been as much as an hour's delay after the making of a 999 call before they have been able to get out and settle these little brawls which take place, not only among coloured immigrants but certainly among immigrants[...]Most of the newspapers have been fairly honest about this issue. They have been more reliable and the Birmingham newspapers, the Birmingham Post, the Birmingham Mail and the Birmingham Despatch, have tried to be fair[...]We

> have had criticism from The Times and this is understandable. The Times is not sold in the areas of difficulty. The places where immigrants are now living are not the places where the Times is sold to any great extent. The Times is sold in areas where people never see immigrants and do not understand the problem (Mr. Harold Gurden, (Birmingham, Selly Oak), *Commonwealth Immigrants Bill - Second Reading*, 16 November 1961; c.737-8).

Compare this with Powell's 1976 Speeches:

> There are cities and areas in this country, some not many miles from this House, where assaults upon the police are matters of daily occurrence and where in daylight, let alone after dark, ordinary citizens are unwilling and afraid to go abroad. Day by day and at a mounting rate this transformation in actual outward behaviour is taking place in these cities[....]Occasionally there emerges something above the surface. I do not expect that Hon. Members saw the headline "50 police constables injured in Birmingham" as it appeared in the Birmingham Sunday Mercury of 16th May[...]or the most part, these cases go unreported except locally; but they are continuing and mounting and are very well known to those who live in the areas concerned and who see such areas being transformed beyond all recognition, from their own homes and their own country to places where it is a terror to be obliged to live (*Immigration and Emigration* (Hansard) May 24th 1976, c. 47: in Powell 1978: 161).

In its self-consciously defensive and incoherent way the earlier speech, from which our quoted fragment is taken, contains a striking number of the elements central to Powellism represented by the second extract; elements which Powell has appropriated, cleaned-up and re-fashioned for his 'race-war' speeches, particularly those delivered in 1968, 1969 and 1970. Central to such speeches is the stress on the 'reality' that can only be judged by those who actually experience contact with 'the immigrants', by virtue of their residence within the 'areas most affected'. From this source, Powell and the 'race populists' are able to fashion the discourse of the 'fears' and aspirations of the 'ordinary' Englishman, waking up to a multi-racial nightmare.[23]

Once Powell has claimed the idea of the community, become its defender, he can go on the initiative and begin to talk of the community as a site of war, a war of invasion and slow, street by street occupation. This logic can take him right to the heart of what Barker calls the New Racism: the idea of alien encampments in the heartlands of Britain. But now it is no longer the recognisable metaphors of the working class community but the mythic land of Blake: England's green and pleasant become unpleasant and overrun.

The decaying working class community is the central metaphor of the anecdotal story, strategically placed within the 'Rivers of Blood' speech, as Gilroy has noted:

> The anarchy generated by black settlement is counterposed to an image of England in which Britannia is portrayed as an old white woman, trapped and alone in the inner city. She is surrounded by blacks whose very blackness expresses not only the immediate threat they pose but the bleak inhumanity of urban decay (Gilroy 1987: 86).

The ability to articulate the idea of 'race and immigration' to the idea of urban change and decay is a central success of 'race' politics. Its beginnings lie in the debates taking place in the latter half of the 1950s and the early 1960s, as we have documented; 10 years or more before Powellism explodes. It is inescapable, as I have attempted to consistently argue, that Powellism has more continuity with these treatments then others have allowed.

(iii) *Powellism and Relations of Signification: Articulating the Audience of Popular Powellism.*

Let us consider this material from another angle now. There is embodied in these key speeches of Powellism the 'relations of signification' that have made Powellism one of the most popularly received and effective styles of political communication in postwar Britain. Powell is rivalled by no other single politician, especially over 'race'; in fact the audience for his other speeches and interventions has been made possible by this intervention (cf. Schoen 1977). The question this raises is: what is it about Powellism that enables it to construct a successful referential symbolic relationship with its audience?

Firstly, it must be pointed out that the existing literature on this aspect of Powellism is conceptually myopic. Particularly superficial and absurd is the conventionalist way in which many critics take Powell's Immigration and Nationality discourse as being an unproblematic popular appeal to working and lower middle class supporters. Schoen's account is representative here:

> Enoch Powell's immigration speeches from 1968 on are noteworthy because of his effort to go beyond the statistics and personalise the concern he felt about the problem. The former classics don was trying - and he is still the only front-ranking politician to have done so - to narrow the gap between elite and mass attitudes on this particularly emotive issue by showing that he saw the problem in the same way as the man in the street (Schoen 1977: 25).

Or consider the following:

> [T]here can be little doubt that he [Powell] expressed the real fears and anxieties of the white Englishman and woman. In doing so Powell put himself forward as a populist, one who understood the people, sympathized with their plight, and would represent them against that small minority, the elitist clique, which controlled the government and the means of communications and which cared not one whit for what the common man thought (Freeman 1979: 295-6).

Such accounts of the 'content' of Powell's speeches, and the kind of relationship he has managed to secure with popular audiences, are woefully inadequate. For example, to what extent can the language of Powellism be that of the 'man in the street'? It is quintessentially the essence of Powell that he is not the man in the street and certainly his language is a language that is far removed from that of his audience. Whatever the nature of the relationship Powell has managed to secure it is not one based on a shared language. What is important, as Miles and Phizacklea suggest, is that Powell has sought a relationship with a common audience. This is the essence of Powell's populism: that an elite, highbrow politician should seek to represent the interests of the common, 'quite ordinary English'. The secret of this relationship is deferential and absolutely in tune with the tenor of Conservative nationalism, on 'behalf' of the people (cf. Nairn 1970; 1981: 272-3). This relationship, and its preferred constituency, is an ideological achievement of Powell's language, which is able to invoke and then draw upon his audiences' concerns; as at the same time motivating them to a view which is his own. It is this ideological mechanism of popular articulation we need to examine. We will argue that the formation of Powellism, as a bona fide 'political racism', has been through its ability to articulate, to itself, the experience of 'race' and the 'inner city'; themes that have enabled it to fashion a 'populist' and popular commonsense which could: (a) achieve initial recognition; (b) mobilise existing images and symbols; (c) impose a racialised causal interpretation.[24]

With the exception of Seidel (1986a: 107-35) and the discussion of the 1968 and 1969 speeches by Barker (1981: 36-42), Gilroy (1987a: 85-88) and the more recent work of Mercer (1990; 1994) and Smith (1994) there has been an empirically limited attempt to produce an analysis of the content and forms of communication made possible by the discourse of Powellism that is able to provide: a deconstruction of its symbols, narrative codes and ideologies, as well as the overall significance of such discourses to the social forces and ideologies it has articulated.[25] The well documented evidence (Smithies and Fiddick 1969;

Seymour-Ure 1974: 99-136; Schoen 1977) of Powell's success in getting a 'recognition' response from his intended audience, does not, at the same time, verify the veracity of the 'content' of his speeches or the 'genuineness' of the response to it; in fact the logic is circular (cf. Rex 1970: 147-50). Too often the mainstream critique of Powell has centred upon the extent to which his account could be verified by the existence of the 'individuals' whose vignettes lent his 1968 speeches, in particular, the poignancy his classical illusions and pedantic turn of phrase, often lacked. The inability to discover the 'little old lady' 'alone' on a street 'taken-over' by immigrants or the 'lonely little white girl' in a class full of 'dark faces' (*Sunday Times*, 5 May 1968). More revealing of Powell's relationship to his audience is his assertion that the proof of the existence of the 'old lady' or the 'white girl' is less important than the belief that such a situation is 'typical'; or that his audience believe it to be typical (*Sunday Times*, 5.5.1968; *Times*, 6.5.1968; *Times*, 8.5.1968).[26]

The account or model of political discourse relied upon in most accounts of Powell's speeches is quite simply inadequate; not only in its lack of attention to the thematic content and composition of such speeches, but also the way in which such discourse actually produces meaning for its audiences. Such an 'ideological effect' is the complex result of an interplay of discursive grammatical rules by which meaning signification is achieved, and the class codes and orientations of its audience that allow this meaning to be communicated (cf. Hall 1980a: 128-38; Morley 1980a; 163-73; 1984: 104-17).[27]

No account of Powellism can be considered adequate which does not address this fundamental interplay. Such a criticism must pass to the heart of the primary inadequacy of accounts of Powellism as well as, for the most part, the analysis of politics and political communication itself; particularly because existing analyses and models are premised on reductionist, behavioural or positivist accounts of communication and meaning creation which operate with a knee-jerk, stimulus-response model of the political audience or a simplistic assumption of the essential correspondence between 'popular' appeals to a working class audience and the inevitable, if somewhat distasteful, reality of working class life, which allows 'feeling' or 'emotion' to be 'whipped-up' and used by the 'unscrupulous' politician or 'populist' agitator. This is not to suggest that feeling or emotion plays no part in such a communication process, but rather that such feeling and emotion form the raw material of the cultural and symbolic social imaginary that can be constructed in the interstitial space between public and private communication fields (cf. Cross and Keith (eds) 1993).[28]

A programmatic statement of the many dimensions and elements involved in the analysis of the relationship of political discourse to its social constituency has been offered by Steadman-Jones:

> Messages are sent to addresses. They are amended or recomposed, according to whom they are sent. Speakers address audiences, whom they conceive (or project) to be composed of a specific type of social being. Political discourses are addressed to particular constituencies, indeed at certain formative turning points are able to constitute or reconstitute such constituencies. There is an intimate connection between what is said and to whom. Yet it cannot be said that such a connection can be conceived in terms of a recognition of the pre-existence of the common social properties of the addressees. It should rather be thought of as the construction, successful or unsuccessful, of a possible representation of what such common properties might be (Steadman-Jones 1983: 23-4).

The process outlined by Steadman-Jones is entirely discursive; it operates in and through discourse. What is not emphasised sufficiently however is the role of the audience in the reception and interpretation of such imputed political communication (cf. Morley 1980a; 1980b; 1986). It may be that within this dimension are contained some elements of the extra-discursive environment against which such communication is made. Both Mattelart and Morley (1980b) have emphasised how communication depends upon reception culture and this itself is a complex function of class, gender, ethnicity, etc.

The pertinent question raised by Powell though is how a discourse that has no material or social basis in everyday working and lower middle class experience of social inequality, can articulate to itself a popular audience? Such a phenomenon has been termed populism (cf. Laclau 1977: 143-98; Mouffe 1979: 168-204; Hall 1980b; 1980c: 19-39) i.e., the attempt to win an audience to the maintenance of a social order that places them in the subordinate and unequal position of 'addressees'. Often such appeals take the form of requests for support for radical measures designed to protect the existing social order from libertarian forces which are seen to undermine traditional, legitimate authority and discipline (cf. Hall et al 1978; Hall 1979; 1988).

Much attention has been focused upon the perceived success of the discourses of the New Right, which disarticulate and rearticulate the traditional 'interests' of the subjects they 'hail': Powellism is a prime example of such a discourse; Thatcherism a celebrated one. Hall has applied the idea of populism to Mrs. Thatcher and also, to a more limited extent, Powellism (Hall 1978; 1979; Hall and Jacques (eds) 1983; 1988). It seems absolutely clear that such a concept is central to the achievement of Powellism in producing the kind of audience it has produced. However, as we have suggested, the likely basis of such a relationship is the elite recognition of a grievance which is of concern to the popular audience. As Steadman-Jones suggests, the success of such a mechanism depends upon the prior existence of a suitable 'social problem' or issue upon which to work: 'the almost definitional claim of political discourse is to be a response to a pre-existing need or demand. But in fact the primary motivation is to create and then orchestrate such a demand, to change the self-identification and behaviour of those addressed. The attempted relationship is prefigurative, not reflective' (Steadman-Jones 1983: 24).

Powellism quite clearly has a ready-made issue, whose ideological history has already been formed. The importance of such debates to our argument is how it indicates the necessary processes by which a language of 'populism' is able to disarticulate and transform the meanings of the social existents which compose and enclose the 'experience' of unequal positions within an asymmetrical social order. However, it does not follow that winning social narratives can eradicate all traces of such experience. Paradoxically, without the extra-discursivity of inequality, of social contradictions, then the language of Powellism or any other populist discourse, of right or left, could find no purchase at all. Here Steadman-Jones, strongly influenced by the followers of a theory of 'discursive-practices', bends the stick too far in the other direction in viewing discourse as responsible for its own conditions of existence. It is as ludicrous to say that the discourse of Powellism arose naturally from the social and material experience of postwar 'black' immigration, (finding it political voice in the champion of the working man, that high priest of free-market liberalism and anti-trade unionism, John Enoch Powell)[29] as it is to say that Powellism invented and created the contradictions inherent in the social-perception and experience of postwar, 'white' working class to the on-set of 'black' immigration into 'their' towns and communities (cf. Seabrook 1972; 1978).

Thus, the answer to the puzzle of the populism of Powell lies in the initial ability to connect with working class 'experience' and to validate such a view at the same moment as articulating it. The act of public articulation of this experience allows the 'experience' itself to be 'fixed' and defined so that it may serve the further purpose of the speaker. This effect is made possible by the structural relationship of the speaker to the audience. Once this channel has been opened then whatever is articulated through it becomes the utterance of its audience. This element is further reinforced by the public demonstration of the provision of this channel which is absolutely central to the claim of populism to provide a mouth-piece to those denied one. It is this element which marks the quintessential element of Powellism: because it is this central feature of populism which is first enlarged, and highlighted, and then given a particular twist by virtue of the Conservative patrician culture from which it emanates. It is surely one of the definitional elements of Powellism, as an unusual political discourse in British politics, that it self-consciously constructs a political relationship between itself and its audience (rather than employing that traditional, unspoken one of deferential genuflection to the populace). It is the construction of this channel which is vital to the success of the vision of immigration Powell will draw.

Thus, in Powell's first important anti-immigration speech at Walsall, he begins with a direct appeal to his 'preferred' constituency:

> There is a sense of hopelessness and helplessness which comes over persons who are trapped or imprisoned, when all their efforts to attract attention and assistance bring no response. This is the kind of feeling which you in Walsall and we in Wolverhampton are experiencing in the face of the continued flow of immigration into our towns *(Speech at the Annual Dinner of the Walsall South Conservative Association*, February 9th 1968: in Smithies and Fiddick, 1969: 19).[30]

The significant use of the 'we' and 'our' here are a deliberate attempt to appeal to and articulate such 'experience'. The purpose of such an articulation is to confirm the 'racial' nature of that 'experience' and 'feeling' while at the same time displacing the guilt associated with this unspoken, illicit connection. Once this has been established, it is possible to motivate that articulation to some political end. Powell's political project has been to attempt to do precisely this.

However, in order for Powell to achieve this he must introduce the other element that will define the structural parameters of this offered 'public' relationship. He does this through a skilful juxtaposition. The 'racial' image of the 'only white child in her class' is set against the image of Powell as Member of Parliament for Central Africa, because, Powell suggests the 'reality' of the lonely little white girl is as distant and incomprehensible as knowledge of Africa to the audience excluded from this experience. In this way two alternative racial images overlap each other; the second assigning significance to the first. While we are placed in the position of the bewildered 'colleague'. This inclusionary and exclusionary mechanism allows Powell to select and define his audience and they to recognise him. This is the second and most important link: the knowledge that Powell is on the side of the 'hopeless' and 'helpless' and suffering this process also. But the significance of this is that he is a politician; he does have a voice and therefore, through him, do they.

This relationship is further confirmed in the Birmingham and Eastbourne speeches, and has been reconfirmed since by many more. At first, Powell elevates this relationship to a national task of leadership: 'The supreme function of statesmanship is to provide against preventable evils[...]the discussion of future.[...]avoidable evils is the most unpopular and at the same time the most necessary occupation for the politician' (*Speech to the Annual General Meeting of the West Midlands Area, Conservative Political Centre*, April 20th 1968; in Smithies and Fiddick 1969: 35). But this serves the immediate purpose of allowing him to quote the views of the 'quite ordinary working man' and therefore to cement the relationship as the spokesman for the denied, for the 'forgotten' ordinary Englishman. Powell's other purpose is to articulate the plight of the minority to the future of the national majority and to see in this minority the 'soul' and essence of the nation.[31]

Powell returns to the metaphor of the oppressed minority when he wants to introduce the infamous 'letter' of the 'little old white lady' : 'The sense of being a persecuted minority which is growing among ordinary English people in the areas of the country which are affected is something that those without direct experience can hardly imagine. I am going to allow just one of those hundreds of people to speak for me' (Birmingham Speech: in Smithies and Fiddick 1969: 40-1). Here, in a remarkably self consciously way, the secret of the relationship is revealed. Later, of course, this beleaguered minority of long suffering English people will be under siege and invasion. We have already suggested how Powell is able to 'motivate' this interpretation.

These findings allow us to re-join and develop the central argument we have explored in the previous chapters concerning the conceptual relationship between racism and political language: in the case of Powell it is necessary to explore the ways in which ideas of, or social narratives about 'race', are taken up, developed and employed as political language. As this study has suggested, the location of an answer to an explanation of Powellism lies in the way in which Powell's construction of the social narrative of the significance of 'race' to his audience sets up a discursive relationship to the 'old racism' in a way that it is able to articulate it to a language of Englishness, patriotism and the nation which is threatened by a racial nightmare of cultural invasion and occupation. The 'old' themes of race are constituent elements of signification within this public political language form. But it is a carefully chosen public language that is able to invoke and articulate those themes and elements which provide a racial reading of the politics of 'black' migration.[32]

Our final section will support this analysis by returning to the argument about the ideological thematics of Powellism, and how the internal conceptual relations, and external political articulations, that result in the force of anti-immigration Powellism, can be understood as conceptual relations within the developing and mutating discourse of Powellism. This is particularly important when we attempt to account for the role of nationalism within mass-market Powellism and it relationship to the distinctive political discourse that is developed to support racist exclusion. It is this issue we turn to first.

Powellism, Racism and Nationalism: Crossing Boundaries

A notable feature of the major attempts to explain Powellism theoretically have, without exception, contained a central uncertainty or ambiguity as to the question of whether Powellism is best defined as a nationalist-racism or a racist-nationalism (cf. Nairn 1970; Hall et al 1978; Hall 1978). It is probably fair to say that such theorists agree on the notion that Powellism is principally a 'romantic-nationalism' which has, in the context of a perceived crisis of the political order, sought to employ popular racism as a vehicle for its articulation with a mass electorate (Nairn 1970; Hall et al 1978). One of the costs of this stance however is that such a racism has no distinctive content, *qua* racism; it is reduced, as Nairn succinctly puts it, to: 'Go home, wogs, and leave us in peace' (Nairn 1981: 259). For Barker, as we have seen, the New Racism, as articulated by Powell, is *all* about content. The inherent contradiction in Barker's exposition is that the discourse he identifies as racist is ostensibly one of nationalism (cf. Miles 1987).

My argument for the continuity of Powellism, with the discourse of the regional 'race' populists, involved the claim for the formation of a postwar Parliamentary commons'sense, which is definable as racism because of its relationship to the development of the discursive signifieds of what has been called the 'old' racism. However, Powellism is arguably one of the most explicit political articulations of nationalism in evidence in postwar British politics. The question that we now need to address is what is the relationship between Powell's nationalism and his political deployment of racism? It is simply not acceptable to argue that Powell merely employed racism to further his nationalist project, because such a view rests on the assumption that racism has no particular content of its own. Such a view ignores the centrality of Powell's speeches to the articulation of such racism. Clearly Powellism *is* a discursive phenomenon. At the same time, we have argued against the idea that we can simply redefine nationalist articulations as racism, as the New Racism writers are wont to do. But we must acknowledge the force of their argument that Powell does not employ the obvious signifiers of old racism. This, without doubt, is the central problem of the analysis of Powellism and its ideological significance. If we are to unravel the ideological thematics of Powellism then we must begin with this conceptual ambiguity.

Benedict Anderson, in the course of an extremely influential discussion of modern nationalism, has argued for the absolute conceptual dissimilarity of racism and nationalism:

> The fact of the matter is that nationalism think in terms of historical destinies, while racism dreams of eternal contaminations, transmitted from the origins of time through an endless sequence of loathsome copulations: outside history[....]The dreams of racism actually have their origin in ideologies of class rather than in those of nation: above all in claims to divinity among rulers and to 'blue' or 'white' blood and 'breeding' among aristocracies (Anderson 1983: 136).

In other words, the racism most characteristic of modernity is a discourse of biological and physiological reductionism, allied to science and subsequently to the maintenance of the asymmetrical relations of colonial empires, both at home and abroad.[33] Given the inherent confusion internal to the debate about the New Racism it is important to insist, as Anderson does, upon a core definition of the characteristic terms and imagery of the ideologies of racism and nationalism. Within the New Racism thesis there is a complete absence of discussion of the ideology of nationalism; while racism is confined to an outline of a doctrine. As we have established, the central difficulty with the identification of racism within political discourse is that virtually no postwar politician explicitly refers to the signifier of 'race' in political debate concerned with the exclusion of 'black' migrants. As we argued in chapter 1, the racialisation of immigration control debates takes place in a context characterised by the elite political erasure of the dominant 'race' signifier. What our proceeding analysis of Parliamentary debates has clearly shown is that postwar immigration control debates have been informed and made possible by the development of a language of post-'race' signification. The floating signifieds of 'race' have been articulated through the successful development of an ideological narrative of the social, which has successfully articulated such signifieds within the language of available discourse. In addition, we have established that Powellism has a great deal of continuity, rather than discontinuity, with such a political language form. However, this still leaves the question of Powell's nationalism un-addressed.

It is the specific quality of Powell's nationalism that we must identify if we are to understand in what ways it allows Powell to articulate and deploy a language of racism in the pursuit of his political aims. The following argument from Anderson is again useful to this end: 'In an age when it is common for progressive, cosmopolitan intellectuals (particularly in Europe?) to insist on the near-pathological character of nationalism, its roots in fear and hatred of the Other, and its affinities with racism, it is useful to remind ourselves that nations inspire love, and often profoundly self-sacrificing love' (Anderson 1983: 129).

While Anderson is certainly right to take Nairn to task for arguing that racism is largely politically derivative of nationalism and to insist that nationalisms are largely not malevolent in the insidious ways in which racisms are, Powellism is, as all theorists imperfectly identify, Nairn most of all, in some way an articulation of these contradictory elements into a reactionary political force. It is surely correct to argue that nations are imagined, as Powell insisted long before Anderson, but such inventions do not always belong to 'the people'. In the case of Powell's authoritarian nationalism of the 'parliamentary nation', the people are largely 'absent' from it (Nairn 1981: 269-7). Nairn is therefore correct to argue that racism supplies Powell with the popular impetus that an English nationalism cannot supply in British politics. It is the emergent social discourse of inner-city racism that supplies the signifieds of a potentially popular construction of post-colonial identity that Powellism requires to further his particular political project. Thus, what Nairn fails to appreciate is that the discourse of racism also takes a powerful narrative form, one that is reconstructed as 'home grown' in postwar Britain. And it is this populist political narrative of white-identity politics that Powell attempts to articulate in his 'earthquake' speeches, commencing in Birmingham in 1968.

The answer, therefore, to the peculiar phenomenon of Powellism as powerful postwar nationalist politics that seeks out the politics of anti-immigration as it means of articulation, is that the very success of that articulation depends upon the psychological and discursive integration of the emerging social discourse of racism with Powell's sentiments and values as a patriotic nationalist. Without this articulation Powellism would have remained as a peripheral discourse to the right of the Conservative party, under Heath. Thus we will argue that Powell's political deployment of the ideological force of racism, that which most commentators define as Powellism, is driven by a patriotic nationalism, which is both authoritarian and anti-democratic. It is not a nationalism of the people but an elite, institutional conservatism. Racist politics has been waged on behalf of the nation. The idea of the nation, although an 'imagined community', is located, for Powell, within the mythical and 'actual' institutions of British society, particularly Parliament. It is the combining of these elements that has produced the subversively odd phenomenon we have witnessed: the radical Conservative revolutionary. Let us substantiate these claims.

The Conceptual Content of Powellism

In this section we will argue, by reference to an extensive range of examples of content of Powell's speeches and writings, that: *(iv) Powellism is an old racism; (v) Powellism is a patriotism; (vi) Powellism is a Conservative institutionalism and, (vii) Powellism is a political populism.* We being with racism. We will offer a detailed deconstruction and analysis of the form of racism that Powell exemplifies. The textual treatment offered will claim to be the most thorough and wide ranging analysis of Powell's speeches and writings yet attempted. From this material we will argue that the Powellism of anti-immigration racism involves a complex discursive relationship and treatment of the erased signifieds of biological racism. This is because Powell's psychological and political treatment of this discursive phenomenon is complex. The account of this relationship offered by the New Racism theorist does not recognise this complexity because they believe that Powellism achieves a conceptual and political break from the discourse of old racism. We have argued that this is not possible because the old racism on which they confer doctrinal significance is itself a transformed discourse, but a discourse whose political success depends upon its capacity to articulate the power of the idea it conceals.

(iv) *Powellism is an (Old) Racism*

As we have already argued, there is ample evidence of the centrality of the 'old' racism to the formation, continuity and longevity of Powellism; and that, specifically, the discursive formation of Powellism has its ideological roots in the 'core' regional discourses of the 'black country' race populists.[34] In addition, empirical sources suggest that Powell's most prolific speech writing and interventions are those concerned with a limited set of racial epithetic themes and, further evidence suggests, that much of Powell's questions to Ministers and interventions within Parliament are in policy and issue areas which have traditionally been seen as the prerogative of old, biological grounded racists: (New Commonwealth) immigrant birth rate; dependants; foreign students; overstaying; and incidence of medical ailments and diseases, for example: small pox, TB, etc.[35]

This evidence should clearly establish the proposition that Powellism is a racism. However it is necessary to add the qualifying argument that this is because the content of his speeches are organised around themes and associations which form a conceptual and ideological bridge to the erased signifieds of old biologistic racist themes and, it has been the practical construction of this innovatory discourse which has led a number of theorists, mistakenly, to view Powellism as a distinctly new form of racism.

Our purpose here will be demonstrate, on the basis of wide ranging empirical evidence, how Powellism has been able, as a political discourse, to promote and express racism to an electorate in British politics. Firstly, the defining characteristic of this discourse has been its capacity to refer to and invoke the themes and images of an old, biologically grounded racism.[36] However it is evident that Powell has not simply espoused a biological account of 'race'. Indeed on a number of occasions he has rejected such a theory and, once or twice, he has subjected it to critical attack. The content of such attacks suggest, beyond intellectual gamesmanship, that Powell does not support such a theory. Indeed he suggests difference goes deeper than merely physiological variation.[37] In addition, historical evidence about Powell's thinking suggest he did not readily embrace such a theory.[38]

This suggests that Powell's 'turn to immigration' enters its racist phase at the point when Powell begins to engage with the themes that are already established in the transformations in racial public language arising from the political relationship between back and frontbench in Parliamentary Debates.[39] Powell's innovation is to develop and enlarge the content and scope of this language. He does this by discursively articulating a range of racialised signifieds within the space of 'erasure' of the 'race' signifier. This process is achieved within a language strategy that disclaims crude biological determinism while pushing the signifying function of the erased terms to their syntactic limits. Thus 'race' is read in the space of erasure by the function of that space and by the linguistic inversion of a repeated pattern of signifieds that intersect it. Such a language is linguistically sophisticated; recognisably 'elite' but populist in that it seeks to address the theme of 'race' through repeatedly pointing to the contradiction of its absence. Rarely is this challenge explicit; Powell's elite racism is always inferential. Often Powell explicitly rejects the signifier as inappropriate to the sentiment or 'structure of feeling' he wishes to share with his audiences. Once this space has been evacuated Powell can rearticulate it to the ideas of the nation and patriotism. Such an articulation allows him a defence against the charge of racism. Thus Powell appeals to a residuum of racist belief, present in the consciousness of his audience, on the basis of defence of the nation and culture.

Enoch's Island: Race, Nation and Authoritarianism in Powellism 219

But what inheres in the maintenance and defence of an indigenous culture is the myth of a bounded biological/ethnic community. Let us look at an example of Powellism that can illustrate the linguistic complexity of Powell's racism:

> [B]y no contrivance can the prospective size and distribution of our population of 'New Commonwealth ethnic origin'[...]prove otherwise than destructive of this nation. The basis of my conviction is neither genetic or eugenic; it is not racial, because I can never discover what 'race' means and I have never arranged my fellow men on a scale of merit according to their origins. The basis is political. It is the belief that the self-identification of each part with the whole is the one essential pre-condition of being a parliamentary nation, and that the massive shift in the composition of the population of the inner metropolis and of major towns and cities of England will produce[...]by the sheer inevitabilities of human nature in society, ever increasing and more dangerous alienation (Powell 1977: 5).

Contained herein are what some would argue are the terms of Powell's 'new racism'. A view that explicitly rejects a theory of biological classification as the basis of differential political treatment but, in the same breath, substitutes another kind of determinism (which some have defined as cultural); here simply 'human nature', is irrefutably a new kind of racial argument. Certainly it does not refer to or seek justification in a doctrine or a science of biology. The question is whether a political racism can be communicated in the absence of these ideas? What Powell achieves in this discourse is, firstly, to reject biologistic racism and then to suggest that if 'race' remains as an idea it does so in an ambiguous way: what its contemporary meaning and applications are now to be, is unclear.[40] He then shifts to a nationalist discourse of political integration. On the basis of this political calculus he asserts that the quantity and increase of an unspecified element of the 'inner metropolis' will inevitably produce a separation of groups and thus, implicitly, work against the mechanism that secures political homogeneity.

The question we are posed with at this point is: how is this a racism, at all?; since we know that Powell is communicating a racism to his audience in some fashion; how is it being achieved? It is not being done on the empirical basis of literally what Powell has said. Beyond the rejection of 'race' doctrine and the presentation of a theory of political homogeneity, the rest of the speech is vague and ambiguous. It could be argued that what Powell has achieved is to replace the idea of 'race' with that of a theory of human nature. This is Barker's argument. Simply that to be racist is to conform to the deepest instincts of a cultural group, particularly if that group is threatened. But this is a re-description of racism not a replacement of it. Rather what is taking place is that, semantically speaking, the meaning of Powell's discourse, and the reason why we know it is racist, is made and communicated within the process of social cognition; a 'moment' that is realised through a discursively achieved recognition, made possible by a linguistic chaining of referents to that dispersed, de-centred 'complex of ideas' called 'race' (cf.. Omi and Winant 1986: 68). Racial images and ideas that are so well established that they do not need to be voiced specifically to be 'known'. In another context, Hall has referred to such language games as 'inferential racism':

> By inferential racism I mean those apparently naturalized representations of events and situations relating to race, whether 'factual' or 'fictional', which have racist premises and propositions inscribed in them as a set of unquestioned assumptions. These enable racist statements to be formulated without ever bringing into awareness the racist predicates on which the statements are grounded (Hall 1981: 36).

Thus the characteristic feature of Powell's 'New Racism' is the sophisticated way in which it is able to refer to and invoke the images and ideas of the 'old racism'; and it is on this basis that racism can be communicated to an audience. This is because the existing 'relations of signification' allow this meaning, almost inevitably, to be generated. Thus, paradoxically, the 'old' racism, so called, is absolutely fundamental to Powellism as a successful political discourse. It quite literally provides the epistemic foundation upon which Powell can play a number of linguistic games with the 'hidden dimension' of 'race'; and he does this to great effect. Thus Powell's (so called) 'New Racism' is quite literally built up from a biological-basement to a sophisticated play of signifieds that conceal their signification. A signified cannot signify its signifier and yet that is what Powell appears to achieve. Neither can a signifier re-signify itself; for it is erased. Yet somehow signifieds appear to refer back to the space of their determination (cf. Laclau 1994). Through their discursive function and through the signification of the absence of 'race' the lack is nourished (cf. Derrida 1976; Zizeck 1989; 1990). Some theorists have referred to this aspect as the 'metonymic' quality of such language (Solomos and Back 1993: 24) suggesting that culture is the unit of metonymic substitution; thus 'race' is coded as culture.[41]

However, the conceptual complexity of this argument notwithstanding, the key empirical component, which can establish a clear conceptual relationship between Powell's discourse and the themes and ideas of the 'old racism', is the centrality of the 'numbers game' to Powell's argument, as well as the particular treatment he gives it. Upon this inferred racial basis he builds up a euphemistically complex political syllogism, composed of the following sub-units: (a) the 'numbers game' of present and projected 'coloured' birth rate; (b) social contact between whites and blacks; (c) deterministic elements of human nature, which make it inevitable that such contact will result in 'racial' violence'; (d) finally, that it is necessary to act in conformity with this 'understanding of the situation'. Let us examine each of these elements in turn in order to understand how they are synchronically ordered.

(a) *The 'Numbers Game'*

> *The scale of Commonwealth immigration into this country in the last twenty years - apart altogether from the nature of that immigration - is already in point of numbers out of all comparison greater than anything these islands have ever experienced before in a thousand years of their history* (Enoch Powell, *'Immigration' election speech at Wolverhampton*, 11th June 1970; Wood (ed) 1970: 97-8).
> *There are some circles in which it is not possible to talk about population figures without being abused for 'playing the number game'* (Enoch Powell, *Paper read to the Institute of Population Registration*, 1 May, 1970).

Powell's numbers game is played in 'simple terms and round figures'. It involves an equation between only two variables, 'the coloured and the rest'; the term coloured denoting 'New Commonwealth immigrants and their offspring'. The focus of the variables and figures is an examination of 'present and prospective' demographic trends i.e., 'natural increase' : 'births minus death' 'and migration, namely, net immigration of coloured and net emigration of the rest' (Powell 1972: 185-6). Such 'simple terms and round figures' are used in statistical presentations, such as the following:

> In 1969-70 the natural increase of coloured was on a conservative estimate about 50,000. This with a net immigration of 43,000 gave a total addition of 93,000. The natural increase of the rest was 185,000, which, after deducting a net emigration of 105,000 gave a total addition of 80,000. Thus the coloured population grew by 93,000 and the rest by only 80,000. Nor was there anything unusual about 1970: in 1969 the coloured population had grown by 103 000 and the rest by only 98,000 (*Speech to Conservative Supper Club, Smethwick* 8 September 1971, in: Powell 1972: 186).

Aside from official presentation, accompanying the release of a report; or public discussion of census data in Parliament, I cannot think of a single example of a public speech, delivered to a voluntarily assembled audience, which is like this speech of Powell's in its use of detailed statistics, statistical comparisons and models and demographic projections based on this; delivered, let us not forget, orally. It is also worth recalling that probably as much as fifty per cent of vintage Powellism, the Powellism of 'race fever' of the 1968-74 period, is a public recital and investigation of numbers, data bases, projections, calculations and criticisms of other 'official' data bases, projections, and calculations, etc. Yet it is clear, as Powell knows full well, what these innocently empirical facts are telling us: *that the rate of 'natural increase' of the black population is higher than that of the indigenous.*

Barker has argued that Powell virtually invented the political 'numbers game'. This is not quite true; others tried it out before him but nobody has taken it to the lengths that Powell has. His treatment of the issue is characteristically methodical and precise; logically consistent statements are made on the basis of the careful presentation of statistical data. The deployment of logic and weighted language is noticeably uncharacteristic of virtually all other political presentations and thus Powell is 'noticeable' for his oratory here, as elsewhere.[42] Yet, despite Powell's undoubted intellectual rigour, the formal sophistication, the nature of such speeches are quite suspect. Are the audiences who gathered to hear such calculations and projections admiring of the skill of its presentation? In Parliament such exercises were greeted with irritation and howls of derision. The comparison of audiences tells us something. Neither assembly could possibly follow closely the argument from numbers Powell has mounted; certainly not enough to be able to challenge it in any detail. Yet neither audience has wanted to. The reason are entirely dissimilar. This is because Powell's political audiences came to hear his public orations of demography as proof of their worst anxieties; their worst nightmares. Whereas his political opponents viewed it as a political incantation whose ostensible concern with numbers was merely the surface 'code' of a more sinister agenda.

Such popular speeches on 'new commonwealth' demography have been scathingly referred to by Deakin as Powell's '*black math*' (IRR: Newsletter 1969). This phrase nicely captures the element that is central to the significance of this subject. What is at the root of the calculations, disputation of trends, variables and tracing of the 'rate' of increase and decrease in 'indigenous' to immigrant populations, is the conviction that there are already too many 'coloured' in Britain. Those people that *know* this: 'need no statistics to tell them; they know, because they see and because they think' (Powell 1972: 184). The function of Powell's 'numbers game' for his audience is to confirm what they, *by virtue of experience*, already *know*. It is a feature of Powell's populist approach to Immigration that the people are always the primary repository of wisdom; the first to know and the last to be informed by those that should know. The secondary audience of such collective statistical airing are the political establishment and the media. It is this group that needs to be persuaded of the terrible portent of the swelling numbers of (formerly colonial) 'aliens'.

The political purpose of Powell's 'number game' is to present the statistical truth of 'what is happening' so that a wider audience can grasp it. In order to achieve this Powell has to take-on the official establishment view, particularly the Home Office, the Registrar General, Institute of Race Relations, etc. All of whom are, argues Powell, complicit in presenting the statistical phenomenon of coloured immigration as a 'transitory scare'. This involves Powell in the 'heroic struggle' of having to drag 'out one figure after another into the daylight' (Powell 1972: 184). These 'facts' are 'vitally important' because, argues Powell, the correct figures are not known or have been calculated incorrectly by official incompetence; or deliberately out of a misguided liberal sentiment to conceal the 'true extent' of the numbers involved. The purpose of Powell's politics is to put a meaning to the aggregation of totals and comparisons; not for the people who come to hear Powell but to challenge those in authority on behalf of the suffering, silent 'indigenous' majority:

> Do those who govern us know, or do they not, that one-tenth of the population of the metropolis itself and of other major cities and areas of England is coloured already? Do they know, or do they not, that in due course it will be not one-tenth, but a quarter, a third and even more?[...]Is that the future which they accept for this country on behalf of the British people, or is it not? (*Public Meeting of the Hampshire Monday Club, Southampton,* April 9th 1976: Powell 1978: 76-7).

It is the official refusal to acknowledge the racial crisis that these numbers portend that has 'sealed the conviction in the minds of millions of their fellow countrymen that those who govern neither know what is happening nor care what is to come after. It will not be forgotten. It will not be forgiven' (1978: 77). This, of course, is a theme already well developed by the 'race populists', who first apply it to their colleagues who refuse to acknowledge or comprehend the 'areas most affected' because of an attachment to an outmoded and idealist liberal view of Empire and Commonwealth. Powell merely drives this assertion to its ultimate consistency: the liberal-leaning fraction become the 'enemies within': 'On this subject, so vital to their future, the people of this country have been misled, cruelly and persistently, till one begins to wonder if the Foreign Office was the only department of state into which enemies of this country were infiltrated' (Powell in Stacey (ed) 1970: 98).

Here, Powell suggest the dimensions of a national political emergency of which 'cooking the immigration books' is only the tip of the iceberg. Some theorist have viewed this 'moral panic', in signalling the movement into 'political emergency', as more central to the political impact of Powellism as a discourse (Hall et al 1978; Hall 1978). If Powell's 'numbers game' is part of a more general argument, it is so in the sense stressed, throughout the book, of being a derivative of that central theme of British immigration control politics: *the massive influx of immigrants into an already overcrowded island*. The phrase 'numbers are of the essence' has become synonymous with that politics, in describing the central concern that unites the differing politics of the major parties. It is rivalled only by Hattersley's infamously 'clever syllogism'.[43] Powellism takes this debate into the next dimension because of the exhaustive thoroughness with which he embarks upon its public analysis.

In fact, this public examination of the question of numbers begins at Deal, in October 1967, when Powell raises the concern that, because of political exclusion 'hundreds of thousands of Asiatics' became eligible for UK passports, 'just like you and me' (Stacey (ed) 1970: 78). The significance of this political travail is clearly spelled out:

> The present inflow of 50,000 Commonwealth immigrants year is itself excessive, representing as it does a direct addition of half a million every ten years to our existing immigrant population. It is quite monstrous that an unforeseen loophole in legislation should be able to add another quarter of a million to that score without any control or limit whatsoever (Powell in Stacey (ed) 1970: 79).

In his Walsall speech, in February 1968, the half-million every ten years has become 'an additional million taken in every twenty years, or another two millions by the turn of the century' (p.80). Powell's innovation here is to pick up on and stress the additional *burden of dependants* of immigrants who further swell the numbers. Such dependants are mentioned as included on UK passports issued to Kenyan Asians in the Deal speech. In the Walsall one they become a critical focus in themselves:

> You here in Walsall, like us in Wolverhampton, are unable to provide school education for all of our children from the statutory age because of the continuing influx of immigrants. Yet the present law makes it impossible to

prevent some forty to fifty thousand actual or alleged dependants, mostly children of school age or below, from entering this country (p. 80).

In Powell's April 20th Birmingham speech, the problem of dependants is picked up again:

> It almost passes belief that at this moment twenty or thirty additional immigrant children are arriving from overseas in Wolverhampton alone every week - and that means fifteen or twenty additional families of a decade or two hence[...]We must be mad[...]as a nation to be admitting the annual inflow of some 50, 000 dependants, who are for the most part the material of the future growth of the immigrant descended population (Stacey (ed) 1970: 86).

Like the Walsall speech Powell again links this influx directly with its (alleged) 'impact upon the existing population':

> For reason which they could not comprehend[...]they found themselves made strangers in their own country. They found their wives unable to obtain hospital beds in childbirth, their children unable to obtain school places, their homes and neighbourhoods changed beyond recognition (p. 89).

Thus Powell's numbers game arises out of the mainstream Immigration Control debate. It adds a dimension of innovation to this debate by selecting for focus 'immigrant dependants' as an added, undocumented source of immigration. Wedded quite graphically to this is the absolute statement and support of the idea that immigration has been allowed to continue in certain areas at the direct cost and expense of its indigenous inhabitants. This discursive extension, while exhibiting continuity with mainstream discourse, moves Powellism into the domain of populist politics in seeking to connect and represent the interests of the politically subordinate. It thus represent, ironically, a move towards a racist model but in the direction not of a return to the 'race' populists but towards a racism pushed to partisan consistency from the very basis of centre ground politics: the concern with the volume of numbers as an impediment to cultural integration and as a possible source of social antagonism.[44]

As we have seen, the dominant discourse in mainstream debates is the discourse of numbers and the metaphor of the overcrowded island. However, internal to this discourse, is that of a conceptual trade-off between numbers and cultural character. At the heart of the 'numbers game' and the discourse of numbers, as we have illustrated in chapter 3, is a quantitative/qualitative dichotomy. This distinction is the one that pertains to Powell's distinction of 'numbers and alienness'. It is the idea of cultural alienness and non-assimilable which plays-off against numbers and the threat of the formation of unassimilated community blobs which the nation cannot swallow or absorb (cf. Lawrence 1982: 81).

Powell takes these themes and places them at the centre of his campaign speeches as a statistical and political problem of the precise calculation of the quantity of numbers in relation to alienness. Britain cannot absorb or take in more than a small amount of foreign bodies because otherwise she will cease to be the same culturally. This argument has been seen as quintessentially a 'new racism' but it is the almost tedious working out of the logic hidden within the syllogistic structure of the political commons' sense of Immigration Control Debates. What he adds to this debate is the idea that quantities of bodies of the same ethnic/national origin will assert an alienness of their own accord, quite apart from intention. What makes quantities of bodies in certain numbers a problem is that such quantities of 'difference' cannot be absorbed, assimilated; to all intents and purposes, hidden within the larger body. Unassimilated communities will form areas of alienness within the English national landscape: 'Whole areas, towns and parts of towns cross England will be occupied by different section of the immigrant and immigrant-descended population' (Powell in Stacey (ed) 1970: 85). Again there is an earlier pattern of presentation of this sort of claim, as for example the pioneering style of Osborne, who Powell has learned much from:

> [T]he overwhelming proportion of these immigrants stay in England[..]and they form on the map a new coloured city as big as Bedford, Chester, Colchester, Scunthorpe or Worcester. This cannot be allowed to go on indefinitely because in another ten, twenty or thirty years time the face of England would not be recognisable *(Control of Immigration* (Hansard) 17 February 1961; c.1932).

In fact, the language of the 'numbers game' can be traced back to the agitation around the Alien's Bill of 1905 and beyond (cf. Gainer 1972). Take, for example, the Comments of Major Evans-Gordon: 'Ten grains of arsenic in a thousand loaves would be unnoticeable and perfectly harmless[...]but the same amount put into one loaf would kill the whole family that partook of it' (cited in: Holmes 1991: 82-3). Gilroy quotes Lord Elton, an early campaigner against the *Unarmed Invasion* (1965), in a seminal 'numbers game' anecdote:

If it were known in my home village that the most reverend Primate that Lord Archbishop of Canterbury were coming to live there, we should undoubtedly ring a peel on the church bells. If it were known that five Archbishops were coming I should still expect to see my neighbours exchanging excited congratulations at the street corners. But if it were known that fifty Archbishops were coming there would be a riot (Lord Elton, *House of Lords Debate on Immigration Bill*, c.198-9; cited in: Gilroy 1987: 83).[45]

Such examples must suggest a degree of narrative theme and continuity in the ideological character of the numbers game and its political usage. Gilroy is surely right to point to the essence of this discourse of numbers as a conceptual opposition between the quantitative and qualitative but not that this polarity has shifted, in the language of Powellism, to the qualitative 'new' racism. What changes is the priority of the elements involved in the conjunction: 'The significance and consequence of an alien element introduced into a country or population are profoundly different according to whether that element is one per cent or 10 per cent' (*Speech at Birmingham* 20th April 1968: in Powell 1969: 283). Is this a major departure from the logic of Elton?

In this sense, Powellism has been the effect of driving a political wedge into the heart of the 'hidden logic' of the debate about numbers that has stood in for a debate about migration. The overwhelmingly negative element at the heart of the debate is capable of a *reductio absurdum*:

> The argument about numbers is unwinnable because however many you decide upon there will always be someone to campaign for less and others for whom one is too many[...]Even if new migrants are reduced to nil, the argument can be shifted to the numbers of dependants; when they are reduced it can be shifted to the question of illegal immigrants; when these are shown to be few in number it can be argued that the government is cooking the books. In the last analysis if you play the numbers game then black people already here and every black child born here is a problem and the discussion shifts to question of deportation (Moore 1975: 27).

Moore identifies here the logic of exposition that Powellism has amplified and addressed over the last thirty years or so. We have connected Powell to this mainstream 'race' debate. Previously we have identified the eugenicist undertow to the formation of the 1962 Act. Powell's treatment also has a racial undertow: it is the idea of racial demography or rather 'black birth rate'. The critical focus of Powell's gaze is upon the question of the extent to which the 'immigrant increase' will approximate to that of 'indigenous decrease'; or more precisely 'to a rate of increase at which their proportion to the total would remain static' *(Speech to London Rotary Club, Eastbourne*, 16th November 1968: in Powell 1969: 307). Powell's answer is abundantly clear: the rate of increase is already proportionately higher than that of the indigenous population. Two factors are allowing this 'massive' increase: continuing immigration of dependants and the 'natural' increase of births to 'New Commonwealth' mothers.

Powell has insisted, on a number of occasions, that this argument is not one concerned with the differential fertility rates of 'New Commonwealth' to indigenous mothers, but rather the overall increase of net immigration (which includes birth to new commonwealth mothers) to total population, minus outflow. But it is precisely this obsessive concern with the 'present and prospective' coloured birth rate that defines the terms of Powellism as most euphemistically racist.

The *racial imaginary*, as Anderson (1983) and Cohen (1988) argue, is fuelled by ideas of 'infections' and 'adulteration', and the decline in fecundity of the white 'race'. Powell's obsessive concern with the relative frequency and quantity of increase of coloured 'offspring' is, despite protestations to the contrary, a thinly disguised invocation of a subterranean white racial nightmare. Powell knows that differential racial birth rate is a collective signifier of racial divisions and an endlessly signifying chain of racial fantasies and nightmares by which the collective-unconscious of the dominant 'races' have pathologized their Others (cf. Fanon 1986). He does not need to say it; in fact he makes a virtue out of not saying it:

> You will[..]have noticed that I assume throughout no greater fecundity in the coloured than in the indigenous population. Yet, after all this, we are confronted with an Inner London, a Birmingham, a Wolverhampton [...]already destined to be almost one-fifth coloured (*Group 5 Young Conservative Conference, Scarborough*, January 1970: in Stacey (ed) 1970: 167).

Or:

> I think it may avoid misunderstanding if I make it absolutely clear that at no stage am I talking about birth rate. Indeed in the argument which I am about to advance I shall assume that the birth rate of the immigrant population is precisely the same as that of the indigenous population (*Expiring Laws Debate (Hansard)* November 1969: in Stacey (ed) 1970: 153-4).

However, as a caveat to such a measure, Powell does assume, for the purposes of 'model building' and generalisations of possible overall projections, that 'the proportion of any particular births - let us say *the proportion of coloured immigrant births*[..].must in due course become the proportion which that element of that population bear to total population' (1969: 154). What this means is that in a city 'like Wolverhampton', where over the last six years '25 per cent - 1 in 4 - of all births have been coloured immigrant births', if that proportion 'continued for a generation', as in the model, 'this would mean that inexorably that community was destined to be one-quarter coloured' (1969: 154). In addition, '[t]he proportion of the population which is established over twenty-five years [the length of a generation] is thereafter destined inexorably[...]to perpetuate itself' (p.155).

Here Powell's racial narrative has been achieved almost because of his protestations of non-racialism. His simple, apparently non-racial 'facts', 'illustrate the extent to which the composition of the future population is already determined' (p.155). Powell's discursive evasion of an explicit racial narrative allows him still to implant into the consciousness of his collective audience the idea of an expanding 'black' population, which because of their disproportionately great numbers, must continue to grow. Ironically, and deviously, the 'inexorable' perpetuation of this community is their 'natural increase' proportionate to the indigenous.

However, at the same time, Powell does want to argue quite specifically for the notion of differential birth-rate; but as an inevitable but unintended consequence of cultural difference. It is the size of the group, so evidently a 'foreign community', that means its birth rate and therefore rate of expansion will be greater than the indigenous society because such a group is not subject to the same social pressures to limit childbearing. Powell dismisses any claim that 'newness' or the age structures of the different populations might account for the different rates or that, over time, cultural assimilation will modify practices. For Powell, the numerical size of the group means that its cultural alienness will be the determining element in its future birth rate:

> I have no doubt that an immigrant element thoroughly absorbed into a host population does tend to have the same birth rate[...]But to suppose that the habits of the great mass of immigrants, living in their own communities, speaking their own languages and maintaining their native customs, will change appreciably in the next two or three decades is a supposition so grotesque that only those could make it who are determined not to admit what they know to be true or not to see what they fear (*Speech to London Rotary Club, Eastbourne*, 16th November 1968: in Stacey (ed) 1970: 106).

Why is the idea that habits and customs will change or modify in twenty or thirty years a 'supposition so grotesque'? Because Powell's argument depends on the opposite assertion? Because we must accept the determination of cultural behaviour as *absolute truth*. This commonsense understanding is available to use if we look and take cognisance of our fears which are telling us the truth about 'cultures'. Certainly once *they* are a certain size this process will be absolutely determined and predictable. Unabsorbed populations form, inevitably, alien communities; become 'wedges' and 'implants' and areas of settlement; sites of invasion and implantation. The process is inexorably driven by a deterministic, cultural fatalism: 'in Wolverhampton, in Smethwick, in Birmingham, people see with their own eyes what they dread, the transformation during their own lifetime or, if they are already old, during their children's, of towns, cities and areas that they know into alien territory' (*Speech to Conservative Supper Club, Smethwick,* 8th September, 1971; in Powell 1972: 184).

The language of transformation of towns into 'alien territory' is an achieved discourse but it is also a euphemistic device for the connotation of the urban 'whitemare' of American inner city ghettos and the 'tragedy' occurring, *over the Atlantic*. But a moments reflection will reveal that this 'tragedy' was, in actuality, that the Civil Rights movement of, and in support of the liberation of, disenfranchised blacks led to urban disorder and violence against the state. Therefore this is a conservative discourse of social control and its central metaphor is the poor, aggressive and segregated black. This image of the black urban poor is what Barthes (1973) calls 'myth': historical symbols and imagery bled of its connotative meaning into which myth inserts itself as ideology. 'When it becomes form, the meaning leaves its contingency behind; it empties itself, it becomes impoverished, history evaporates, only the letter remains[...]the meaning loses its value, but keeps its life, from which the form of the myth will draw its nourishment.' (p.117-8). Powell performs essentially the same operation in order that he may borrow the 'haunting tragedy' metaphor without the rest of the historical baggage. In order to do this he must remove the historical actors from the drama; active participants must become passive elements (cf. Trew 1979a; Sykes 1985). Thus the blacks who come to occupy the former places of the homogenous, do so according to the forces of human nature, in the absence of legislation. We will illustrate this point below.

The other discursive neutralization Powell must perform is to turn the black, especially the 'West Indian' black, into a foreigner. He must emphasise above all the absolute dissimilarity of the stranger. No matter that this ignores the cultural hegemony of the West and, in particular, the educational system of the colonial satellites that inculcated the very Tory values of Sovereign, Church and State as the 'dominant culture' of the Caribbean (Hiro 1973; 1990). He needs them to be strangers; to embody, as a group, absolute differences of culture and behaviour so that the idea of 'race' can be carried as a sort of hidden code or narrative within the process of cultural adaption. Of course, no surprise, that Powell chooses to view cultural adaption as 'integration' i.e., 'to become for all practical purposes indistinguishable from[..]other members' (Powell: *Birmingham Speech*: in Stacey (ed) 1970: 92). What gives this difference its sharp political edge is the idea that the Commonwealth is no longer one that belongs to Britain; therefore any prior relationship of culture, of politics etc., is forgotten[46] and all that remains is the 'pure fact' of mass immigration:

> Of the great multitude, numbering already two million, of West Indians and Asians in England, it is no more true to day that England is their country than it would be to say that the West Indies, or Pakistan, or India are our country. In these great numbers they are, and remain, alien here as we would be in Kingston or in Delhi; indeed, with the growth of concentrated numbers, the alienness grows (Powell: in Stacey (ed) 1970: 92).

Even here, in this apparently characteristic 'new racist' argument, we find the same development of the conceptual dichotomy of numbers and alienness upon which debates from the late 1950s have been founded. Powell's political innovation within this discourse is, firstly, to stress that the size and concentration of immigrant communities means that they are culturally insulated from those forces aimed at their integration; and secondly, that such communities, foreign enclaves within the state, will, as a consequence, begin to think and act as separate interest groups with different demands to that of the majority. To believe otherwise is to give credence to the dangerous delusion of the idea of 'integration' which, given the absolute numbers of the 'relevant' population, is an impossibility. The logic of this argument can only endure if we accept that the indigenous are somehow a unity with no difference of interest or demand to divide them. This assumption operates upon an inferential model of ethnic homogeneity and national belonging which requires little or no political interpretation. We will return to this point below.

(b) *Social Contact Between Whites and Blacks*

If the newcomers are not, for all practical purposes, swallowed up by the host numbers; if they remain visible or recognisable as a body then that must create a problem of 'race relations' i.e., produce, by dint of numbers, a conflict situation between the host society and the visibly new group. Once a 'race relations' situation has been created then this requires some sort of special provision or effort from the hosts and the formation of interests by the incoming group which will either divert resources or become the source of grievance. The logic of this process is self generating and sets in train the forces of divided community and political conflict: 'these growing concentrations in the inner cities and the industrial conurbations [creates] the disruption of the homogeneous "we", which forms the essential basis of parliamentary democracy and therefore of our liberties, is now approaching the point at which the political mechanics of a "divided community"[...]take charge and begin to operate autonomously' (*Speech to Public Meeting of the Hampshire Monday Club*, Southampton, April 9 1976: Powell 1978: 165).

Having reached this stage the problem of Immigration is only solvable at the political level. Powellism has been about the recognition of these tendencies and a warning about their inevitable consequences for the nature of British politics and the unity of the nation upon which its historical character and continuity depend. Here we prefigure Powell's Conservative institutionalism and the belief that the continuity of British identity and nationhood depends upon a 'racial'/ethnic instinct for Parliamentary government, which mysteriously *knows* the desires of its patriae. A foreign element would create an 'alien wedge' who would be allocated seats on a racial basis and undermine the ethnic consent that embodies the historical authoritarianism of the English state:

> The next stage is reached when the wedge effect is transferred from the electorate to the legislature itself. For 5 per cent of the total population, a proportion probably reached already but in any case not far off, the quota of Members of Parliament, if once the notion of quota is accepted would be some 32 Members in a House of Commons of 635[...]I need not follow the analysis further in order to demonstrate how parliamentary democracy disintegrates when the national homogeneity of the electorate is broken down by a large and sharp alteration in the composition of the population (Powell 1978: 166).

Consistently in his Immigration speeches Powell depicts 'the blacks' as having no identity outside of their mass presence as: 'alien wedges', 'enemies within' or as 'encampments', 'implants', involved in an inexorable process of street by street invasion and occupation of what was once familiar territory, but now rendered 'foreign' by its 'occupation' 'ceas(ing) to be part of Britain' in anything but a 'geographical sense'. The theme that becomes dominant, from the mid seventies onwards, is very much the *'enemy within'*; not the problem of the numbers coming in, but the significance of the problem of the alien cultural character of this immigrant population now in 'occupation' in areas across Britain:

> [G]iven a massive alien population accepted as permanently resident, especially if that population is predominantly Asian, immigration has become a consequence and not a cause in its own right *(Speech to the Surrey Branch of the Monday Club, Croydon* October 4th 1976; in Powell 1978: 162).
>
> [T]he growth in size of those implants has not slowed down but is rapidly rising: 140,000 a year is the present rate of increase, from outside and by reproduction, of the New Commonwealth population in Britain *(Speech at Public Meeting of Hampshire Monday Club*, April 9th 1976; in Powell 1978: 165).

The use of the adjective 'implants' here seems deliberately intended to remove agency and humanity from the migrants (cf. Sykes 1985). The use of the word 'reproduction' is significant for this purpose also: it creates a sense of determination and distance. We find ourselves observing a mass process, happening seemingly without human volition. For these are not people that have actively chosen to migrate; it is an invasion of bodies of encampments, of lumps and clots. They do not settle, move in; they occupy, dislodge, replace; and they do it, inexorably, street by street, as if to some pre-ordained end-game. Here we have migration and settlement as military invasion and encampment of hostile battalions. Take Powell's infamous 'Enemies Within' speech at Northfield, Birmingham, 13th June:

> When we think of an enemy, we still visualize him in the shape of armoured divisions, or squadron of aircrafts, or packs of sub-marines. But a nation's existence is not always threatened in the same way. The future of Britain is as much at risk now as in the years when Imperial Germany was building dreadnoughts, or Nazism rearming. Indeed the danger is greater today, just because the enemy is invisible or disguised, so that his preparations and advances go on hardly observed (Powell: in Wood (ed) 1970: 104).

Powell uses not only the military take-over, occupation and inhuman process metaphors but also an insidious version of the immigrant-host model (the 'pathology of a society that is being eaten alive; for this is a branch of medicine where the clinical material is abundant and the symptoms richly documented' *(Hampshire Monday Club Speech, Southampton*, April 9 1976: in Powell 1978: 165) but explicitly transformed into the parasite - host model: 'the recognised presence of an alien and particularly an Asian population exerts an irresistible gravitational pull which nothing can counteract. One way or another the mass attracts to itself the means of its increase: the invasion and penetration of the host body continues by its own momentum, and no barriers or obstacles will be effective' (p. 163).

The narrative consistency and dynamic of these themes is towards the inescapable delineation of a deterministic factor which lies beyond the explanatory purchase of the groups involved in this inevitable, inexorably determined conflict. On such a scale the migration of a culturally alien group will be determined en masse such that they must and are motivated to act as they do because they cannot do otherwise. We will now examine this underlying element.

(c) *Deterministic Elements in Human Nature*

The question of the inhuman process metaphors Powell uses can lead us into a focus on the elements that renders such an account deterministic and therefore pseudo-racial in argumentation (cf. Rex 1983: 159).[47] What is most notably an innovatory technique, and a 'knowing' one, is Powell's defence of his claims for 'racial' conflict as determined by factors beyond the control of participants; and his concern with the 'dangers' of a process that makes both 'parasite and host' victims of something neither can do anything about. 'The truth is that both the indigenous and the immigrant population will alike be the victims, and the unintending victims, of forces created by the circumstances which we have allowed and continue to allow to develop and which we show no intention of ever endeavouring to reverse' (*Speech to Stretford Young Conservatives*, January 21 1977: in Powell 1978: 169)

The forces working are do with human nature, as it is. Not as radical and liberal legislators would like it to be.[48] Thus the protagonists will find themselves in dispute and moved towards violence, inexorably, because they cannot do otherwise. The determinism is not in the process, i.e. it is not global-capitalism that drives bodies around the globe setting indigenous labour against the 'fear' of the newcomers; but human nature asserting itself. This is how Powell is able to criticise 'race relations' talk as 'twaddle' because it is looking at the process in individual morality terms and ignoring 'human difference'. From a dismissal of 'race relations' Powell is able to move to an implicit idea of human difference as deeper and more profound than 'race'.

> It is impossible to begin to understand the way in which those forces operate if the discussion is conducted, as race relations always are discussed, in terms of moral imperatives and the attitudes of individuals - like and dislike, good will

and ill will (*Speech to Stretford Young Conservatives*, January 21 1977: in Powell 1978: 169).[49]

This allows Powell to ridicule and undermine the denial that the symbols of racial difference are the *activator* of the reaction to the presence of the 'blacks':

> I do not see how it can be other than deeply insulting to describe a Jew as that man with a different shaped nose from mine, or a Zambian as that man with a different sort of hair from mine, or a Chinese as that man with narrower eyes and a yellower pigment than mine. To reduce all the deep-seated differences between the various nations, societies and tribes of mankind to some external physical attribute in this way is to commit the grossest indignity and disrespect to human nature itself (Powell 1978: 168).

Here the fundamental differences between cultural and national groups are seen as infinitely deep and deterministic. This is how Powell can talk of the way in which difference asserts itself, as of nature, and begins to act accordingly. Large cultural groups cannot mix; cannot share the same territory or cultural homeland. Here we have the suggestion of a pseudo-biological theory like that we encountered in the ideas of Barker (1981). For Powell, to locate this fundamental difference at the level of biology is to commit oneself to crudity. He never says what it is: the '*sin qua non*'; but it is an inevitability. What conclusion can we draw, he asks, if these forces inexorably must assert themselves?; if people must form cultural and national wholes based on this determination? Are we not speaking of 'race'? As we have argued, Powell studiously avoids the language of 'race' and points to its crudity and association with Hitlerism, bad science and IQism. Yet recently he has taken to referring to the English as a 'race' (cf. *Independent*, 23.4.1988).

If it wasn't for the fact that Powell has tried not to use it, to disparage it, and to seek to identify the factors that operate in the space, or site of erasure, the word had formally occupied,[50] we would have to acknowledge that he has achieved, to a certain extent, a critical use of the term. Certainly he is able to harness its associations and significatory cultural power without having to defend the ideological baggage that inevitably is carried with the explicit use of the concept.[51] However, in achieving this discursive operation, and by seeking to develop a description which proceeds on the basis of old racist associations, Powell has not created a New Racism, simply because he has not sought to replace the old association with an entirely new one. It is surely the most misrecognised feature of the New Racism that without recognition of the 'old racism' no understanding of the 'new' can take place. It is the submerged, the suppressed, the alluded to term which alone supplies the 'factor x'; the element which is 'protean' and 'inexorable'. It is the effect of this 'absent-presence' which allows Powellism to operate:

> This debate, these regulations and the whole discussion of immigration in the literal sense is conditioned by something that is hardly ever mentioned in these debates. The major premise of the arguments remains unspoken. We debate under the presence of a cloud, to the existence and presence of which hardly anyone ever draws attention. We have these debates and we engage in this legislation only because of the present and prospective composition of the population of England in one particular respect[...]It is because of what we know about the present composition of the population and what we have reason to know about its future that we engage in feverish discussion of an extra thousand or more entering or being prevented from entering this country year by year (Powell, *Immigration Rules* (Hansard) 10 March 1980; c.1040-1).

Powell is able to make this extraordinary statement, much to the consternation of his colleagues and opponents, because of the previous establishment of the negative association of 'the blacks' with immigration and immigration with 'race'. Such a series of links are well in place before the projected emergence of the New Racism in 1968: in this sense the materials of the discourse of Powellism are made prior to its emergence. The fact that Powellism operates the fault-lines of the 'race'/immigration syllogism of public discourse is most convincingly demonstrated by his 'knowing' exploitation of these contradictions:

> It is a matter of much more than semantic importance[...]that we have no appropriate word to describe that element in the population. We call it "the immigrant population"; but that is increasingly inapplicable, for increasingly that population consists of those who have not immigrated into the United Kingdom. So, from that difficulty, we take refuge in colour, and refer to the "coloured population" or to "the blacks"; but we know perfectly well how unsatisfactory that is. After all we are all coloured. "Coloured" in that context is a mere euphemism that betrays our embarrassment and difficulty of expression. As for the word "black", I will only say that no one who has ever served in India[...]could ever bring himself to use that term[...]In these circumstances, to imagine that by these rules or any others one can bring, in the Conservative Party's terminology[...]"a clear end to immigration", is totally absurd; for if there is a settled population of this magnitude, it is idle to imagine that its recruitment will not continue (Powell c.1041-3).

It is speeches such as these which become a regular feature of Powell's interventions, especially within the House of Commons, which drive many hon. Members to demand from Powell that he 'says what he means'; or simply to admit that he is racist. Of course Powell will not acquiesce to such demands. Powellism as a language strategy is about this very thing; of creating a political phenomenon out of the inadequate language of 'race'. A feature of this language is how Powell insists that he employs the term 'recruitment' as 'an entirely neutral word' (c.1043). As Barker (1981) noted in the use of the word 'dislodge'; Powell chooses to use process metaphors that describe an event taking place by dint of a determination which guide and inexorably move human behaviour in a pre-determined direction. The only specific negative idea he links this with is that of military manoeuvres. Recruitment here is to a faction or group; but this military staging metaphor must become, through the working out of these determinations, an open war involving active violence and fanning of grievances in a divided community.

From at least 1976 onwards Powell explicitly talks of the consequences of New Commonwealth *occupation* as civil-war very much upon the lines of the model of Northern Ireland: 'The disruption of the homogenous "we", which forms the essential basis of parliamentary democracy and therefore of our liberties, is now approaching the point at which the political mechanics of "divided community" (if I may borrow terminology from jargon devised to describe the Ulster scene) take charge and begin to operate autonomously' (*Speech to Hampshire Monday Club*, April 9th 1976: in Powell 1978: 165). Once he has framed this image of the divided community of opposed forces and interests he can develop it:

> Where a community is divided, grievance is for practical purposes inexhaustible. When violence is injected[...]there begins an escalating competition to discover grievance and to remove it. The materials lie ready to hand in a multiplicity of agencies with a vested interest[...]in the process of discovering grievances and demanding their removal[...]Hand in hand with the exploitation of grievances goes the equally counterproductive process which will no doubt, as usual, be called the "search for a political solution" (Powell 1978: 165)

The rationale and invoked referent and reality is Northern Ireland, made explicit in the phrase 'political solution'; and by the absurd claim that such inexorable conflict will lead to armed struggle: 'With communities which are so divided nothing can prevent the injection of explosives and firearms with the escalating and self-augmenting consequences which we know perfectly well from experiences of other places within the United Kingdom..' (*Immigration and Emigration* (Hansard) May 24th 1976; c. 47: in Powell 1978: 161). Here it is self evidently clear that Powell borrows the images of Ulster to stand in for those of 'race conflict', and yet he supplies us with very little concrete evidence of the factors that are supposed to motivate this escalation to civil war. Thus the inevitability supposedly written into the rapid escalation of community conflict and violence can only be achieved if the 'race conflict' metaphor is doing the work for that of the 'divided community' of Ulster. Once again 'race' is inferentially motivated to its meanings through images of other things.

Powell does an essentially similar job of discursive dis-articulation of the themes of racism and urban deprivation. What is most surprising about this is that such terms already connotate: 'the blacks'. Powell begins, in the mid seventies, to realise that he must seek to disarticulate these themes if he is not to suggest that the problems of racism and the inner city are in some part due to material conditions.[52] Such an interpretation is anathema to Powell's whole argument because it might suggest that greater provision could overt the 'race war'. Thus he fulminates:

> [T]he fallacy of supposing that the consequences that are apprehended from the massive substitution, in various parts of the country, for the indigenous population of a population from overseas are[...]due to what is called physical deprivation, poverty, and so on[...]It is a fallacy[...]to link as cause and effect what is in modern parlance called, very dangerously, deprivation with the dangers of the large and growing alien wedge[...]in this country[...]The central point is that the dangers which all apprehend from that thing which has happened to this country in the last generation are not caused by material deprivation and cannot be removed by ending it (*Race Relations Bill* (Hansard) July 8th 1976, c.1663; in Powell 1978: 163-4).

Here Powell attempts to completely disarticulate the theme of 'race' from that of deprivation by suppressing the thematic connection of 'race' to inequality and that theme to inner city run down. This is self consciously done at the expense of the power of that weight of ideological work done by the 'race' populists and popular media debate throughout the 1950s.[53] Powell does this because he knows that to admit even the possibility of the connection will have the consequence of (i) inviting claims of 'old' racism and much more importantly (ii) offering a means of material solution to the worst excess of such a posited relationship. Powell cannot allow that anti-immigrant feeling and the potential antagonism of black against white might be a simple reflex of social deprivation and could therefore be alleviated by ending such deprivation, since the unity of purpose on which his national consciousness depends requires the conflict to be irresolvable. Absurdly, his narrative strategy to circumvent this association is to attempt to construct an image of the inner city composed of, or featuring, middle class victorian housing within respectable neighbourhoods, struggling in genteel poverty and circumstances.

> When I reflect upon that transformation[...]which took place over a quarter of a century in the town in Staffordshire of which I represented one part, it is not primarily of the relatively restricted rundown central areas that I think. I think of the streets of middle-class and lower middle-class occupation, the long streets of 1880, 1890 and 1900 housing which, during those two decades, ceased to be occupied by the indigenous population and were occupied[...]by the newcomers (*Race Relations Bill* (Hansard) July 8th 1976, c. 1663.: in Powell 1978: 164).

So both the indigenous and the foreigner 'occupy' housing. The difference is that with the arrival of the 'newcomers' is introduced *that* element: the deterministic behaviour of large groups of a similar origin. As such a group grows the problem becomes enlarged and cannot now be solved by alleviation of social or economic measures. Such an argument seems a long way from the urban squalor, crime, vice and disorder of the earlier 'race' populists and yet the argument has not really moved very far; what has changed is that the determining element still plays a central role but it no longer can be spoken of in quite the same way as before. Its political speech must be that of a troubled silence. As Rex has put it, 'So the argument changes its ground, and will change it again, as soon as it appears to be finally pinned down' (Rex 1970: 148).[54]

(d) *Political Requirement to Act in Conformity with the 'Understanding of the Situation'*

It must now be self-evident that Powell's deeply held conviction that mass immigration of alien nationals is incompatible with what he takes to be the existing traditional relationships which constitute the political nation, motivate the discursive political narrative he has constructed. All the protracted raking over hoary old stories, anecdotes and embers of old racist mythology and enmity from the run down streets of the racial inner city, and latterly, the analogical deployment of the metaphors of Ulster, are driven by this political judgement. Logically, therefore, Powell must call for repatriation; since nothing short of the removal of this element will stop it expanding and creating offspring very alien to the way of life and government of the indigenous English. The contradiction of Powellism, and a leverage point on the hidden racism that best establishes the political terms of Powell's projection of incompatibility and inter-ethnic conflict, is that Powell is unable to explicitly call for forced repatriation. Often during the course of debates Powell has been interrupted by Government and Opposition speakers who have demanded that he state his solution to such an inexorable catalogue of doomed inevitability; Powell's response has always been to return to his warnings of the *'inexorable doubling and trebling of the relevant population'* and the fact that the people would not and could not endure it, etc.

In November 1968, in his Eastbourne speech Powell does, explicitly call for the setting up of a Ministry of Repatriation:

> The resettlement of a substantial proportion of the Commonwealth immigrants in Britain is not beyond the resources and abilities of this country, if it is undertaken as a national duty[...]It ought to be, and it could be, organized now on the scale which the urgency of the situation demands, preferably under a special Ministry of Repatriation or other authority charged with concentrating on this task (*Speech to London Rotary Club, Eastbourne*, 16 November, 1968: in Powell, 1969: 313).

To call for large scale voluntary repatriation assumes that there is a considerably widespread will among migrants to leave Britain (*New Society*, 2 October 1969). This is why Powell insists upon the development of voluntary, assisted repatriation; that such a factor would tip the balance in the desired direction: net outflow. It has been pointed out that by late 1968, with the calls by Powell for the setting up of a Ministry of Repatriation, the only difference between Powellism and the extreme right wing and fascist fringe was the word *'voluntary'* (Walker, 1977: 113).

However, Powell's discussion of this area of logically concomitant policy is informed by the idea that it is, and can be, consensual because the logic of the *rightness* of the solution flows out of the nature of the group incompatibility of the situation; which the participants *ought* to be able to recognise. Faced with no significant evidence of action, either by the government or of popular groundswell support, Powell seeks to locate the lack of outcry to the situation as one, dependent upon *alerting the sleeping giant of English nationalism* which, when under most danger, is most unaware:

> The English nation have their own peculiar faults. One of them is that strange passivity in the face of danger[...]which has more than once in our history lured observers into false conclusions[...]about the underlying intentions and

the true determinations of our people (*Eastbourne Speech*: in Powell 1969: 313).

This allows him to put off the inevitable point at which it will be too late to act;[55] simply because the nation and the national consciousness will have not been sufficiently awoken to the dangers. Principally this is because they are being misled about the figures, and thus by projection, the future composition of the society, by a liberal intelligentsia which is blind; and by a foreign office which has been infiltrated by those who aim at the destruction of England as 'it is known or could be imagined'[56] by the ethnically homogenous. Thus the balance of attending upon racial disaster is perpetually trembling on a knife edge. A situation against which the addition of one or two more numbers or implants might shift the weight irrevocably against the indigenous:

> [Y]ou may be surprised that I have discussed t[he] future almost wholly in numerical terms, and in numerical terms related to these immediate years. If so, you should not be surprised: numbers are of the essence, and the scale still trembles between descending on one side or the other irretrievably *(Speech to Southall Chamber of Commerce, Centre Airport Hotel, Middlesex*, 4 November 1971; in Powell 1972: 206).

But the blame for this situation does not go to the people but to the establishment to the extent that it is unable to act in conformity with the 'deep instincts' of preservation of the nation. In this respect, Powell's oratory and ventriloquism, on behalf of the people, suggests that by intoning the instinctive demand of the audience (even in the absence of consciousness of it) he is not asking the people to act but for the government to act in their 'interests'. A popular outcry would tip the balance towards government intervention. This is why Powell speaks to the state 'on behalf' of the best instincts of the many. Inevitably, the situation, although open to action, is fraught with danger; dangers on the model of the American experience should something not be done to prevent the inevitable increase in the cultural and ethnic materials accumulating:

> The explosive which will blow us asunder is there and the fuse is burning, but the fuse is shorter than had been supposed. The transformation which I referred to earlier as being without even a remote parallel in our own history, the occupation of the hearts of this metropolis and of towns across England by a coloured population amounting to millions, this before long will be past denying (*Speech to Carshalton and Banstead Young Conservatives*, 15 February 1971: in Powell 1972: 198).

Here the racial time-bomb ticks away and it is only Powell who is able to see it for what it is. It is Powell's duty as a prophet of 'race' doom to let the people know and, in a curious way, to point out to the establishment the error of their ways. Powell says that he is forced to do this; to speak the plain truth about whether anything can be done or not. Mercifully, of course, something can be done; the nation can be awakened in time; the government will listen to the 'real voice of the people' and will act; and the danger will be averted.

> The power of decision is still in our hands, and that power is a power over numbers; but it is a power which grows weaker as each year goes by and which, once lost, is never to be had again[....]Those who say 'it is too late', those who say 'nothing could be done now', are not realists but the victims of propaganda. It is not too late; there is still time; but with every passing month and year the opportunity seeps away - for ever (*Speech to Southall Chamber of Commerce, Centre Airport Hotel, Middlesex*, 4 November, 1971: in Powell, 1972: 207, 189).

Such textual evidence suggests there is a formal difference between the two demands: Powell speaks of 'massive, albeit, voluntary repatriation'. This is less a grammatical caveat than a menace. Logically it is concomitant on the assumption that voluntary repatriation would be 'massive'. Powell, consistent with the terms of his own ideology, believes this to be the case, but the evidence is less than convincing; despite the considerable help press coverage has afforded Powell (cf. *The Times*, 1969).

One of the contradictions of Powell's alignment with racism is that he cannot logically extricate himself from the attribution of inhumanity required in any 'planned movement of population' (Powell 1978: 172). In 1976 Powell addressed himself specifically to the costing of this voluntary population movement in the form of passage and incentives; presented as a form of 'reverse overseas development aid', via the transfer of skills of the immigrant and *immigrant descended* population to their country of origin' (*Speech to Surrey Branch of the Monday Club, Croydon*, October 4 1976: Powell 1978: 172-4). Such detailed consideration is unique in postwar 'race' debate within the formal political arena and it must be concluded that such discourse finally does align Powell with the language of the fascist right.

(e) *Powellism is a Patriotism*

> *Nationhood is a baffling thing; for it is wholly subjective. They are a nation who think they are, there is no other definition* (Speech delivered at Londonderry, January 15, 1971; Powell 1972: 165).

> *It would be true to say that all the major causes in politics to which I have devoted myself in the last twenty years and more have grown for me out of two convictions: that the nation is the one social unit which, on the secular plane at least, provides a satisfying frame of reference for men's individual hopes and ambitions; and that the only nation I can recognise as my own is that defined by allegiance to the Crown in parliament or, alternatively stated, that which voluntarily, cheerfully and instinctively recognises the authority of Parliament as exclusive and supreme. Subjects apparently the most diverse are for me aspects or applications of a central dedication to these beliefs* (Powell 1977: 4).

It was my argument earlier that Powell's political racism is almost entirely borrowed. However this dramatic statement has had to be modified in the light of empirical evidence of how the semantics of Powell's intervention into the 'race' debate have involved a strategic dis-articulation and use of biologistic or fundamentalist racial belief. At the same time we have maintained that to reject the role of such a discourse is to remove the basis upon which popular Powellism has been constructed. Powell has worked with those very themes and issue that define the terrain of the old racism but he has done so with a mixture of declaratory partisanship: identifying racially opposed groups, as well as the development of a relatively sophisticated linguistic strategy able to neutralise, disguise or displace the formal association of such interventions with racial criteria. This, it must be emphasised, has not prevented him from being condemned as racist, a point often overlooked. However this argument still leaves the question of Powell's nationalism unaddressed.

It was my argument that it was Powell's nationalism or patriotism which motivates his intervention into the 'race' debate. Powell takes up the discourse of racism in search of a popular politics of the nation. However in the pursuit of such objectives there is a linguistic transformation of the two types of discourse. While it is evident that Powell is most concerned with developing politically a euphemistically organised or de-racialised discourse; in the course of this linguistic operation he does borrow and import themes and ideas from his nationalist discourse. We can more clearly appreciate these factors by closely examining the content of that discourse.

This section will show quite clearly that, contra the New Racism thesis, Powell's discourse of the nation and his racialised account of Immigration are clearly distinguishable. One does not masquerade as the other. However, a close examination of Powell's nationalism will reveal that Powell's conception of the nation does contain a notion of ethnicity that can be racialised. Powell quite clearly has recognised this and has quite deliberately chosen to disarticulate such a potential motivation. However, more recently, he has chosen, surprisingly perhaps, to acknowledge it and define it quite specifically as 'race'. We can quite clearly see this shift in strategic thinking within Powellism across the distance of the following two statements:

> 'It so happens I never talk about race. Indeed, I do not know what race is.' Mr.Powell said that he had never got a clear answer, for instance, to the question about whether Englishmen and Welshmen were of the same race. 'Race', he said, was a 'four-letter word which is substituted for what I do talk about - a subject which affects the future of this part of the country and of many parts of the country' (*Times election report, Halesowen,* June 5th. (6.6.70).

> "English" is an adjective which denotes a language. "English" is an adjective which denotes the inhabitants of a country. "English" is an adjective which denotes a particular people or, not to be mealy-mouthed, a particular race (Enoch Powell, *Independent*, 23.4.1988).

In the first quotation Powell is playing his characteristic 'euphemistics' game: firstly he satirises the meaning(s) and confusion surrounding 'race'; what lies unspoken is that 'race' is troublesome precisely because it has a pejorative history, hence the repression and confusion involved in its usage. Powell capitalises quite deliberately upon this 'suppressed' meaning. By talking about *New Commonwealth Immigration* instead of 'race' and by attributing the use of the term to others - liberal critics - he is able to borrow the 'subterranean' force of the absent signified by denying ownership of the signifier: it is not 'I' who use the term 'race' but *'they'*. The second speech however is a speech about nationalism; a nationalism that Powell sees under threat, and here the English have finally been understood to be a 'race' again. In one sense Powell's conception of 'race' has not changed. He believes it to be the description of a culturally bounded national community. But something has shifted; 'race' in the late 1980s has been re-won for a nationalist discourse. It means, as John Casey has put it, 'a feeling for persons of one's own kind' (Casey 1982: 25).

Enoch's Dream: The Patriotic Nation

If there is a key to the 'incredible patchwork of nostrums'[57] that has been Powellism it is probably the idea of patriotism. Certainly Powell himself seems to think so (Powell 1977: 4). It is Powell's deeply held conviction of 'the nation' as an historically bounded community, symbolised by the institutional features of English antiquity, to which all true Englishmen *(sic)* instinctively feel a sense of identity and belonging. It is this belief which affords Powell emotional and intellectual insulation against, amongst other things, and most significantly for us, the accusation of racism and demagoguery. An intellectually buttressed patriotic sentiment appears to initiate, underscore and provides ultimate justification for many of the political interventions, and types of political issues, Powell has taken up: the capitalist nation, post empire; anti-immigration and national survival; the European Community and the preservation of 'parliamentary sovereignty'; Ulster loyalism and the defence of those who belong to the Union; the 'racial' crisis at the heart of British politics as symptomatic of the failure of the liberal intelligentsia to lead Britain after the demise of Empire.

The evidence of major speeches, particularly those delivered to the Royal Society of St. George from the early 1960s to the late 1980s, demonstrate that Powell has, in the sense stressed by Fanon (1985) and Anderson (1983), a deep affection for his country (Powell 1965: ch.13; 1969: ch.14; *Independent*, 23 April, 1988). It is probably better to call this motivating sentiment of Powellism, patriotism: profound love and devotion towards one's country (Powell 1978: ch.1, 5, 12). For Powell, such devotion takes the form of reverence and the expression of sentiment towards the idea of the 'nation as the object of loyalty and affection' (Ritchie, *Introduction* to Powell 1978: 2). Powell is not a nationalist, in his own terms or in the terms of someone like Nairn (1970), because his conception of the nation is not one that eulogises 'the people' but rather the nation as an unbroken institutional and historical tradition.[58]

Unlike the Third World nationalism, so eloquently spoken of by Anderson, for Powell the love of the nation does not extend to a course of national liberation by 'the people' or even one on their behalf. The conservative nation is not to be realised through revolution but through reaction and consolidation. For Powell the nation is imagined as splendid, but in the sense of the unique creation of the 'slow alchemy' of the centuries and the guided purpose of the mythical English. The historical institutions and practices of the ancient British state and society are fetishized as the symbols of the unity of the English as a people. It is in this sense that the nation is *imagined* as a collectivity.

If patriotism is the motivating sentiment and justification of Powellism, the nation is its political-ideological centre: the symbolic and institutional repository for the sentiments and allegiance of the patriae. In actuality, both a composite being, an aggregation of economic actors, and by a collective will, an 'imagined community' since, '(t)he life of nations, no less than that of men, is lived largely in the imagination' (*Speech at Trinity College, Dublin* 13th November 1964: in Powell 1965: 137). However, the character of this imagining, as Nairn has argued, is entirely *conservative*. A species of conservatism that inhabits the peculiar institutions and conventions of an ancient political order, long since trapped within the entrails of its Imperial adventure, the pursuit of which it preferred to those of its domestic interests; hence protracted and acute decline of Britain has accompanied every government beyond the boom years of postwar expansion and reconstruction (cf. Nairn 1981; passim). And it is the ideological crisis that has accompanied this decline that Powellism both addresses and constructs.

Empire Myths and Neo-nationalism

Nairn has claimed that Powell's 1964 speech at Trinty College, Dublin on the *illusion* of Empire 'is easily the most interesting comment on imperialism by a Conservative spokesman this century' (Nairn 1981: 266). It is within this speech that Powell constructs the influential idea of the nation as an imaginary.[59] This collective imaginary is composed of shared myths. Such 'myth making' is the true purpose of national history. Such a narrational activity has little to do with objective judgement: *history is myth*. 'Our imagination[...]works under the influence of the received mythology. So we make for ourselves a fictitious history which corresponds to our favourite myths and reinforces them' (*Speech at Trinity College, Dublin* 13th November 1964: in Powell 1969: 325).

The nation deems a 'true' interpretation to be an expression of collective sentiment rather than idealist thought. 'So what I am saying is that a nation lives by its myths. What those myths are, matters immensely to its happiness, success or failure. The greatest task of the statesman is to offer his people good myths and to save them from harmful myths' (p.325). In the course of his 1961 speech to the *Royal Society of St.George* Powell offers his most revealing myth:

> Herodotus relates how the Athenians, returning to their city after it had been sacked and burnt by Xerxes and the Persian army, were astonished to find, alive and flourishing in the midst of the blackened ruins, the sacred olive tree, the native symbol of their country. So we today at the heart of a vanished

empire, amid the fragments of demolished glory, seem to find, like one of her own oak trees, standing and growing, the sap still rising from her ancient roots to meet the spring, England herself *(Speech to Royal Society of St. George*, 22nd April 1961: in Powell 1969: 337-8).

Within the form of borrowed Greek tragedy Powell here constructs the myth of England as an essence that proceeded Empire and yet remained untouched by it. Thus, its undeniable demise, and the documented evidence of the tremendous personal impact this 'reality' had upon Powell's personal sense of identity, can leave its core somehow essentially unaffected and untouched. Incredibly Powell can claim that 'England[...]underwent no organic change as the mistress of a world empire. [Thus] the continuity of her existence was unbroken when the looser connections which had linked her with distant continents and strange races fell away' (p. 338).

Such an intellectual about-face suggests the dimensions of a deep psychological wounding which intellectual construction has built over; although we cannot pursue this enquiry here (cf. Roth 1970). It accords with the view of Empire as a possession acquired 'in an absence of mind' which is intellectually threadbare and suggests the magnitude of importance of political myth for Powell's philosophical ontology. Once again, Barthes' (1973: 117-8) account of the 'moment' when myth becomes ideology seems wholly appropriate here. The ideological significance of such a transformation is that, of course, it enables such an essence to remain, untouched and untroubled, after the 'imperial delusion' of a now vanished Empire passes like some malignant weather-front that obscures the contours of the land below. Such an unspoiled, pure originary can then form the basis of a new 'authentic' flowering of the nation. This is, as Mercer has argued, a 'textual strategy' (1994: 307). And yet despite, or perhaps because of the seeking after a formal elegance of rhetorical style, and the pedantic attention to speech construction, Powellism is a sublime wish fulfilment: a right wing fantasy of the most laughable kind. As Nairn has eloquently stated, Powell's England is a strange 'Disney-like[...]world where the Saxon ploughs his fields and the sun sets to strains by Vaughan Williams' (Nairn 1981: 262); or a sort of Sunday Magazine reader's almanac, as in Powell's description of a: 'marvellous land, so sweetly mixed of opposites in climate that all the seasons of the year appear there in their greatest perfection; of the fields amid which [the English] built their halls, their cottages, their churches, and where the same blackthorn showered its petals upon them as upon us; they would tell us, surely, of the rivers, the hills, and of the island coasts of England' (*Speech to the Royal Society of St. George*, 22nd April 1961: in Powell 1969: 339).

This 'Disney-like English world' that Powell inhabits is itself the escapist illusion, inflected with the tone and images of an 'abstract upper-class kitsch' of Houseman and the Georgian poets, and thus, the cultural expression of a stagnant class culture.[60] The political institutions and exercise of power in Powell's England, like that concatenated into the *Biography of the Nation* (1955) or the absurdly fetishized, *Great Parliamentary Occasions* (1957), is a schoolboy's history, hermetically sealed in novelty glass. Such a speech takes the form of a eulogy spoken by the ancient English through the mouth of the living in that unique tongue, invented by the English: 'the tongue made for telling truth in' (Powell, 1969: 339). What would the English tell us? 'They would tell us of a palace near the great city which the Romans built at a ford of the River Thames, a palace with many chambers and one lofty hall, with angel faces painted on the hammer beams, to which men resorted out of all England to speak on behalf of their fellows' (p.339).

Powellism is an impossible conservative fantasy of consent to a species of authoritarian rule by a cultured elite who instinctively know the hopes and desire of their fellow Englishmen. It is the mysterious essence of 'Englishness' written into the very institutions of England that ensures collective consent. Whenever Powell is dealing with power and subordination of the polity to it, he is at his most mystical: institutional power and consent to its exercise is contained within the symbolic paraphernalia of the 'Kingship of England'. It is only the symbolic power of these objects, from a noble past, that can 'claim the allegiance of all the English'. Here allegiance is an organic element, because evolved through a slow, historical chemistry, infusing the relationship of the English to their rulers. Monarch is fused with parliament; parliament expresses the fellowship of the English:

> [T]he unity of England, effortless and unconstrained, which accepts the unlimited supremacy of Crown in Parliament so naturally as not to be aware of it; the homogeneity of England, so profound and embracing that the countries and the regions make it a hobby to discover their differences[...]the continuity of England, which has brought this unity and this homogeneity about by the slow alchemy of centuries (Powell 1969: 339-40).

This continuity is bound up, implicitly, with an unspoken sense of ethnicity which, though historically hybrid, has formed a unity within the recognisable 'interior' of English national life:

> [T]he unbroken life of the English nation over a thousand years and more is a phenomenon unique in history, the production of a specific set of

circumstances like those which in biology are supposed to start by chance a new line of evolution. Institutions which elsewhere are recent and artificial creations, appear in England almost as works of nature, spontaneous and unquestioned. The deepest instinct of the Englishman[...]is for continuity: he never acts more freely nor innovates more boldly than when he most is conscious of conserving or even of reacting (1969: 40).

Here the ideology of conservatism as 'a settled view of human nature and society' is inflected at nodal points by the trace of ethnicity and pseudo-biological inferences of the 'gene-pool' of the English. Culture expresses and constructs 'race'. Central to this narrative of origins and identity is the discourse of the 'island race' (cf. Barnett 1982; Miles 1987) and the organicist metaphors of gardens, seedbeds and the ghosts of nature's blueprint or geno-type. It is out of the history of this:

[C]ontinuous life of a united people in its island home springs, as from the soil of England, all that is peculiar in the gifts and the achievements of the English nation, its laws, its literature, its freedom, its self discipline. All its impact on the outer world - in earlier colonies, in later pax Britannica, in government and law giving, in commerce and in thought - has flowed from impulses generated here[...]The stock that received all these grafts is English, the sap that rises through it to the extremities rises from roots in English earth, the earth of England's history (1969: 40).

In 1988 Powell returned to the Royal Society of St.George, Birmingham Branch, to speak again on behalf of English Folk:

It has been well remarked that societies depend for existence upon the mutual recognition of their members, because that implies a shared introspection."He thinks as I do , he wants what I want, because I recognise that he is also an Englishman"[...I]n 1688 Englishmen recognised that they were all of one mind. That singular happiness of the English is their gift of being governed with their consent[...]The essential ingredient of that consent is the implicit assumption of a common identity which overrides differences of mere opinion, the blood[...]that is proverbially thicker than water (*Speech given to the Royal Society of St.George, Birmingham Branch*, 22 April 1988).

In the late 1980s Powell is willing to import his racialised narratives of the black community into his patriotic eulogies, as euphemistically and elliptically here: 'for 20 years now the English have been assured that they must be governed at home by the sufferance of those who not only visibly do not share with them a common identity but are to be encouraged to maintain and intensify their difference' (Powell, 22 April 1988). Here 'race' is signified by skin colour and equated with cultural identity and difference.

The test of 'race' on the Tory backbench is cultural absolutism and subservience to an enforced homogeneity. The cost of such a levelling patriotism 'does not come easily and is not to be had cheaply' (ibid). In the 1980s the question of the national survival of the English depends upon their collective assertion of difference:

> When politicians and preachers attempt to frighten or cajole the English into pretending away the distinction between themselves and the people of other nations and other origins, they are engaged in undermining the foundation upon which democratic government by consent and a peaceable and civilised society in this country are supported (Powell, *Speech* 22 April 1988).

As Solomos (1989) has argued, Powellism has two themes : (i) the cultural threat of immigration and (ii) loss of instinct of the nation. These are combined in Powellite exposition in terms of the fears that the moral and political fabric of British society is being hollowed out by 'enemies within' and that, political non-recognition of this will lead to the demise of the British as a nation.

> [P]arliamentary democracy disintegrates when the national homogeneity of the electorate is broken down by a large and sharp alteration in the composition of the population. While the institutions and liberties on which British liberty depends are being progressively surrendered to the European superstate, the forces which will sap and destroy them from within are allowed to accumulate unchecked (*Speech to Hampshire Monday Club, Southampton*, April 9 1976: in Powell 1978: 166).

Could it be that the eternal sap that lubricates the island essence of the British is drying up? If we eschew a reading of the historical echo of the weakening of racial stock and blood, it is unmistakable that Powell must posit an ethnic root to the possibility of unity. The implicit theme, located at the heart of this conception, is the racial nature of the relationship that gives political unity: ethnicity must be politically unified.

Democracy is made to mean here something quite narrow; not characterised by the compromise of difference but the idea of politics being harmonious and acceptable, if ethnically narrow. The unity of the English as a consensual nation is a fantasy that can only be asserted in the face of the threat of racial dilution, the hidden narrative of Powell's numbers game. Although Powell has been known to ridicule the validity of the term 'race' he finds, in his later

1980s speeches, a conceptual reconciliation with the term: 'we shall never disentangle, identify and measure the various sources which, since neolithic times or earlier, have contributed to the gene pool of the English people' (p.166).

Powell suggests elsewhere (Coleman 1982) that the 'genius' of English democracy is within the idea of the Parliamentary nation. This is not a conception of democracy but of dictatorship or authoritarian rule by virtue of a mystical tune into the instincts of the people, and this relationship is to be evoked and secured by speaking the language of Church and State (cf. Casey 1982). This leads us, quite nicely, into the idea of Powellism as a Conservative institutionalism.

(f) *Powellism is a Conservative Institutionalism*

> *It is difficult to exaggerate the degree of Powell's symbol-fetishism. He literally worships, every sacred icon of the great conservative past* (Nairn 1981: 271).

As we have established, for Powell, the nation is constructed in the imagination. Such imagining occurs in circumstances and institutional settings, within tradition and arrangements handed down from the past, that provide the mental furniture of that imagining (Powell 1977: 2). For Powell the parliamentary nation is an ancient institution, peculiarly English and alive in the symbols and mysticism of the past; within traditions, customs and folk-lore lie the authentic roots of English society (Powell 1969: 337-41). The defence of the nation is therefore a defence of an ancient political institution and form of political allegiance. The soul of old England haunts the chambers of Parliament (cf. Nairn 1970; Barnett 1982; Powell and Wallis 1968).

Powell's Conservative political formation has been based upon the assumption that Westminster was 'the place not of Parliament but of monarchy, the place where the hallowed dust of the Plantagenets still exercised symbolic power' which gives it an 'indispensable centrality to the life of the nation' (Powell 1977: 4). Powell quite clearly believes that the nation is imagined but such imagining depends upon the symbolic materials to hand. In the case of England, ancient symbols and institutions abound and form a sort of 'fifth dimension', accessible only in the national 'corporate' imagination by which the Englishman is able to find himself, especially since: 'Self-identification [is] the touchstone of nationhood' (p.5)

At the centre of such imagining is the pinnacle of English antiquity: the 'Sovereign Parliament', whose symbolic power arises from the sense that such an institution was the product of an historic agreement between monarchy and people in a bloodless, *Glorious Revolution* (cf. Powell and Worsethorne (ITV:

2.7.1988). This mythology is the stuff from which Powell is able to derive the idea of the Parliamentary Nation as pre-democratic political form. It is this ancient institution that provokes the instinctive focus of the 'self-identification' of the English which is the guarantee of nationhood.

We can illustrate the importance of Powell's devotion to an essentially mystical view of (imputed) Conservative institutions within three significant debates in which he has intervened. The first of these is the 1953 *Royal Titles Bill* Debate (Hansard, 3rd March, cols. 240-8) to which Powell made, what Foot describes as, an 'angry' intervention. The debate, whose purpose was to ratify the change in the Queen's titles, made necessary by the transition in status of the monarch from that of Empire to a 'new commonwealth' of nations, brought into being by the 1948 Nationality Act, was not seen as particularly important or controversial. Powell was still a relative novice MP at this point and a constructive speech in such a context could have quietly furthered his career. But, as it turned out, Powell's speech was far from the safe speech of a novice but amounted to an impassioned lament for the dissolution of the power of the Crown over the former dominions of the Empire.

What is chiefly remarkable about the speech is how Powell tests the validity of contemporary changes and ideas against the imputed veracity of the abstract principles of Crown and Monarchy. His reasons for doing this are that he views such principles as primary to the maintenance of the power of the Crown in (the English) Parliament. Powell protests against the introduction of an implicit principle of the Act, the potential divisibility of the Crown, which would mean that the 'Unity of the Crown' had been abandoned. Any changes in the title of the form of address of the Monarch are tantamount to the 'divisibility of the Crown' i.e., a radical departure from the historical unity that has characterised and defined the rule of the crown:

> [B]y successive Acts of Union the three kingdoms of England, Ireland and Scotland, each with their separate historical origins, were merged into one. There was one realm over which was the 'Imperial Crown of the United Kingdom of Great Britain and Ireland and territories'[...]With this unity of the realm achieved by the Act of Union there grew up the British Empire; and the unity of that Empire was equivalent to that unity of that realm (*Royal Titles Bill* (Hansard) 3rd March, 1953: in Powell 1969: 254).

Note how Powell derives an historical judgement from an abstract principle. This is a magnified element of Powell's method of historical mythologizing. It may be, as Powell insists, all history is myth but here such a myth defines the events and their meanings. For Powell, the meaning of national life and the history of nations unfolds according to a kernel or core of abstract values or principles upon which the peculiar institutions are organically grafted. Hence, historical complexity can, at any moment in time, be *reduced* to these elements. Given this we should not be surprised to find that Powell dates the 'dissolution of imperial unity of the Crown over the dominions' to the 1948 Nationality Act:

> The British Nationality Act 1948 removed the status of 'subject of the King' as the basis of British nationality, and substituted for allegiance to the Crown the concept of a number[...]of separate citizenship combined by statutes. The British Nationality Act 1948 thus brought about an immense constitutional revolution, an entire alteration of the basis of our subject hood and nationality, and since the fact of allegiance to the Crown was the uniting element of the whole Empire and Commonwealth it brought about a corresponding revolution in the nature of the unity of Her majesty's dominions (Powell 1969: 255-6).

Here Powell clearly confirms the view that historical events not only proceed from abstract principles but that changes in such principles can allow events to occur. Thus, the move to independence of former colonies of the Crown is seen as a *consequence* of the 1948 Act, which made it possible for 'any of those territories to throw off their allegiance without any consequential result' (p. 256). This latter assertion suggests that continuing adherence to allegiance in statute would have held the British Empire together, as well as implying that such a principle could justifiably be defended by force. Here, plainly, Powell in the early 1950s, was an Empire and colonies sabre-rattler of the most pedantic kind, and quite out of step with the leadership of his party. For Powell, changes in the Queen's title amounted to 'the suppression of the word "British" from the description both of her Majesty's territories outside the United Kingdom and of the Commonwealth'; as such it revealed 'an abject desire to eliminate the expression "British" ' (p.255). Powell wants to know the reason why this 'teeming womb of Royal Kings, as the dying Gaunt called it, wishes now to be anonymous' (p.255). Consequently the term 'Head of Commonwealth' is a Sham 'which we have invented to blind ourselves to the reality of the position' (p.258). The consequences of allowing the 'divisibility of the Crown' are that 'we' will, 'sink into anonymity and cancel the word "British" from our titles' (p.258). Against this disillusion of Britain, Powell offers up the Empire loyalist vision of the unity of Colonial rule, concatenated into a formula:

> I assert that the essence of unity, whether it be in a close-knit country or in a loosely-knit federation, is that all the parts recognise that in certain circumstances they would sacrifice themselves to the interests of the whole. It is this instinctive recognition of being parts of the whole[...]that constitutes unity. Unless there is some instinctive deliberate determination, there is no unity. There may be an alliance. We may have an alliance between two sovereigns Powers for the pursuit of common interest[...]but that is not unity. That is not the maintenance or the creation of any such entity as we imply by the name 'Empire' or 'Commonwealth' (p. 257).

This is characteristic Empire loyalist writing in its unconscious elision of the interests of the British as equivalent to that of the 'common interest'. Acts of domination become acts of union and unification. Such a mythical history must face a hard reality with the vastly accelerating decolonisation of the territories of which it was composed. At the close of this argument Powell gets nasty: 'the underlying evil of this is that we are doing it for the sake not of our friends but of those who are not our friends. We are doing this for the sake of those to whom the very names "Britain" and "British" are repugnant' (p.258). Evidently, those who no longer wish to be subordinate imperial partners in the British glory have turned against the Sovereign.

The Commonwealth and Queen 'Row'

Thirty years later, as The Times noted (Home News, 23.1.1984) and Powell himself, by referring to the 1953 debate (Powell, *The Times* 26.1.1984), Powell was still engaged in this argument (cf. Times, Irish Times, Morning Star, Guardian, Sunday Telegraph, 21, 22, 23.1.1984). Two speeches, reveal this in particular, the first delivered on the subject of the Queen's Christmas message to the Commonwealth, and the second, a response to the furore caused by the first, published in *The Times* (26.1.1984).

Newspaper editorial and leader coverage interpreted the speech as a rebuke directed at the Queen and her ministerial advisers for preferring the 'interests and affairs of other continents and countries' and the prejudices and opinions of a new and 'vociferous minority of newcomers'; evidently a coded reference to 'new commonwealth' settlers and descendants. The leaders suggested Powell was critical of the Queen's speech for its bias, because of an alleged anti-racist message it carried and for pandering to minority prejudices.

In fact, like much of Powell's writing on constitutional issues, it is prose encased in a grammatical sobriety and exactness which is apt to conceal the political venom which drives it. But in these speeches Powell invokes the legal and symbolic framework of sovereignty and unity and directs it at the Queen and towards the construction of a position the complete opposite of the one advocated in 1953. Instead of arguing for the lost unity of the Crown and dominions he argues for absolute severing of relations between the dominions and the Crown. Thus the previous speech and intervention is a public lament for the loss of relations; the latter an invective for the failure to slough of such relations. Both appeal to the legitimacy of symbols and protocols of sovereignty and the Crown. A principle governs the logic of both positions. This principle is the conception of *allegiance*. In the Royal Titles Bill intervention Powell bemoans the watering-down and dissolution of the terms of allegiance replaced by the idea of association; such a change will lead to the dissolution of the Empire. His later interpretation, reflected in his Queen and Commonwealth interventions, is a cold fury to be done with any sort of relationship short of allegiance.

As Anthony Barnett has pointed out, this concept of allegiance refers to an almost feudal conception of rule (Barnett 1982: 32). It is not simply consent to authority, it is a kind of offering up of duty to the power of the authority of the Crown; giving oneself over to duty under the Crown. This is what is at the root of Powell's lament and invective. Nothing short of allegiance (read: subservience) will do. In fact this sort of invective is also present in the early intervention. Also the target of this invective is the same: those who do not show the proper respect for the authority in Parliament of the Crown.

This un-democratic, authoritarian statism is at the heart of Powell's conception of the English nation and the power of the institutions that compose it; a view which informs his rejection of parliamentary democracy and advocacy of the parliamentary-nation.: 'I slightly bridle, when the word "democracy" is applied to the United Kingdom. Instead of that. I say: We are a Parliamentary nation[...]We have institutions, which you can't separate from us and who we are' (*Terry Coleman Interview*, Guardian 15.06.1982). This is how the Sovereign is the embodiment of the people and the national ideologue can speak 'for the nation'. This is the basis on which Powell can write a 'biography' of the nation as if it were a living, sentient thing. This internal narrative theme of Powellism can reveal connections in the development of Powellism as a political discourse, linking the themes of the 1953 debate; the Commonwealth row and, also, the 1981 Nationality Debate, where the concept of allegiance takes on a central ideological role. Let us explore this connection.

Powell and the 1981 Nationality Debate: Testing Allegiance and Defining Belonging

> *Patriotism is to have a nation to die for and to be glad to die for it - all the days of one's life* (Powell 1977: 8).

The concept of allegiance we have identified is also, arguably, the ideological 'deep structure' of Tory backbench support for the Government's 1981 Nationality Bill; and is therefore consistent with our theme of ideological language alliance between back and frontbenchers upon which racial Parliamentary language and legislation has been developed. The 1981 Debate is both a continuation and culmination of this pattern. The importance of the theme of allegiance is signalled early by Powell's interruption of the Home Secretary's (Willie Whitelaw) presentation of the Bill to inquire, 'What will be the rights and duties - the content of citizenship - for the people in the category that the right hon. Gentlemen has just been speaking of?' (*British Nationality Bill*, 28 January, 1981: c.936).

Powell's gripe with the Bill is that the basis of nationality and citizenship, 'Is not wholly birth within the allegiance, nor is it wholly descent: it is a combination of the two' (c.966). He argues that the flaw in the drafting of the Bill is that the government dare not base nationality on the indigenous tradition: 'jus soli'(the test of soil); or that of the European: 'jus sanguinis' (the test of blood); it mixes the two. The reason for this, predictably, is because of the 'change in the composition of the population' within Britain. All was well, '[a]s long as those born within the realm were likely to be relatively homogeneous' (c.166-7). This political problem of the lack of homogeneity of the nation is for Powell, and for most of the backbench, traceable to the previous Nationality Act which allowed immigration into the country on a massive and unforeseen scale, creating a population whose allegiance is suspect. Why is this allegiance suspect? It is in the nature of numbers and cultures and the formation of communities that the answer lies. People are able to take up citizenship without any obligation to the nation and since there is no longer a homogenous society, automatic allegiance can no longer be assured. Thus an adequate nationality Bill must build into itself a 'test of allegiance'.[61] The import of such a 'test' is outlined by Powell:

> [T]he House is being invited to consider a new status, that of British citizens, without any clear concept of what are the fundamental rights and duties that will correspond to it. By fundamental rights and duties I mean the right to enter or leave the realm at will and the right of the franchise; but I mean also

the right - it is as well a duty and a privilege - of serving the nation - in peace and particularly - the ultimate test of nationality - in war (c.966).

The meaning of this is quite clear: that an adequate test of eligibility for inclusion within nationhood must be to give up ones' life for the nation. Allegiance here is ultimate devotion to the nation. The inference is, of course, that many would not be prepared to be *this* loyal. It comes as no surprise that *'they'* are more likely, geographically speaking, to originate from outside of the allegiance:

> There is an immense quantity of dual citizenship in the United Kingdom at present, an immense range of possession of dual citizenship, dormant or otherwise. Is dual citizenship really compatible with nationality? Is it really compatible with the inherent obligations and implications of allegiance that lie at the foundation of national status and nationhood? (c.966).

As we have seen, such a relationship should be natural or mystical and *if* the population was historically homogenous then this allegiance would not be questioned. This is why the subject of allegiance is such a serious test of loyalty because it is the quality of inclusion upon which the persistence of the nation ultimately depends.

> [A]llegiance is the very essence of nationhood, there is no meaning in nationhood without allegiance. Nationhood means that a man stands to one nation, to one loyalty, against all others[...]I do not believe that the attempt[...]in the Bill to combine birth within the territory with a certain limitation upon descent has satisfied the true test of allegiance (c.967).

The future continuity and identity of the nation cannot be left in the hands of possible internal traitors or the indifference of those who are culturally and historically incompatible with the nation. Here, as we have previously suggested, Powell's problem with the terms of definition of nationality is that it is too wide: it is too inclusionary, as was the patrial clause in the Conservative 1971 Immigration Bill (which was bitterly contested by Powell and Labour rebels through Committee).[62]

Powell's ideas and central ideological theme are supported, echoed and addressed by the Conservative backbenchers: 'allegiance towards a country is one of the most important factors in one's being[...]If we wish to retain our sense of cohesion as a nation, we must return to the concept of allegiance' (Mr. Nick Budgen, (Wolverhampton, South-West) c.1003-4).

The underlying *real-politick* of this stance is a virulent attack upon the traitors of the cultural-nation, those who do not feel themselves to belong and who owe allegiance to some other country. The political metaphor of this state is that of: dual nationality:

> [I]f they wish to enjoy the benefit and shoulder the obligations of British citizenship, they should owe allegiance to no other country[...]It follows from that that I believe that something must be done to abolish the idea of dual nationality[...]One of the best ways for the new immigrant community to demonstrate its adherence to this country is to say "I have given up my citizenship of Pakistan or Bangladesh. In the event of the United Kingdom declaring war upon Pakistan, I am prepared to fight with the British Forces against Pakistan." What better way could there be of demonstrating that this was home? What better way could there be of demonstrating that they were British Black people? (c.1004).

Of course Powell would not and could not countenance this sort of argument. The very deterministic nature of the situation means that the notion that there could be more than a handful of foreigners is misguided: there cannot be a 'black British' group in Powell's homogenous nation. Such a situation requires legislation to remove those incompatible with the nation. Hence his hostility to all political appeals for the 'ethnic vote', to 'black conservatives' and to the idea that those born outside of the terms of the allegiance can belong. Thus, once again, Powell's politics are primary in setting the broad parameters of the Debate but are incompatible with the specific political objectives which become the divisive 1981 Nationality Bill and it clauses; resulting in the requirement that Citizens of the Commonwealth renounce their citizenship of country of origin and become 'British' again; or remain subject to the anomalies of holding a passport that identifies them as culturally alien (Cohen 1981). Here the language of cultural incompatibility and repatriation finds a real-politick among those whose support for the Bill is strategic; a sort of staging post to the ultimate goal: 'I believe that the Government should have given consideration to requiring citizens here with dual citizenship to exercise a choice within a convenient period as to whether they wish to opt for British citizenship or another country's citizenship. I do not believe that one can have divided loyalties. I do not believe that one can be loyal to more than one country at once' (Mr. K. Harvey Proctor (Basildon) c.996).

(g) Powellism is a Political Populism

> *[B]y word and letter, from all parts of the country, a tide, which rose and fell but never ceased, of encouragement and reassurance has flowed in to me from strangers, from the general public, from the ordinary people of this country; for the instinct of fairness is one of the deep and characteristic instincts of this nation* ('Vote Tory' 1970 Election speech at Wolverhampton, 16th June: in Wood (ed) 1970: 121).

> *The power, the near magic of Mr.Powell cannot be denied; he makes people listen. The atmosphere of the meeting was fervent, revivalist[...]Powellism in the West Midlands, begins to take on the attributes of a movement* (Peter Jenkins, The Times Election report from Smethwick, 5.6.70).

Thus, paradoxically, Powellism is also a populism; despite the impression that such a political orientation seems to go against the philosophical content of Powellism as an authoritarianism. The answer to this apparent dilemma is that Powellism became an attempted mass-based populism because Powell believes that contemporary political life has been characterised by an increasing denial of the meaning and responsibilities of nationhood, i.e., an increasing political denial of the central role of national sentiment within historical British society (cf. Powell 1972; 1977; 1978; Casey 1982). Such a dangerous and disturbing tendency has required Powell to adopt means necessary to find director ways of articulating, what he believes to be, its authentic voice (Powell 1971; 1972; 1973a; 1977; 1978). Through populism Powell hopes to be able to invoke and 'bring to life' the usually *supine* English nationalism that he knows exists in the hearts and instincts of 'the people'. It is this authentic English voice and the patriotism of nation and 'belonging' that Powell is fuelled to 'make active' in contemporary politics. He feels he needs to embark on this mission, as Nairn has argued, because it is only this demonstration of unity and homogeneity that can 'stop the rot'. The nation is under threat and in danger from powerful and insidious forces, not only from without but *within* the political territory. The attempt to deny this relationship or to attempt to substitute for it another one; or to destroy it altogether, comprise the contemporary British crisis, a state of affairs which Powell has most consistently thematized as a racial crisis (Powell 1965: ch.13; 1969: ch.14; 1972: 9, 10, 11; 1978: passim). But, as we have seen, Powell's deployment of 'race' is deeply disputed and open to contradictory arguments. What I have taken to be the sufficient internal coherence of the most influential of these, at least in the ways it has been taken up by others, is that Powellism has enabled the racialisation of the cultural definition of the nation: such that a euphemistically informed language of culture, community and nation could replace the old biologism of old racism. The crucial assumption here is that this language was successful in redefining the sensibilities of its preferred political audience. This point is, unfortunately, regularly confused with the question of Powell's popularity.

Powellism *really* was popular with a good cross section of his British political audience. But such popularity, consistent with the argument we have sought to advance, depends upon the recognition of the concept of 'race' as a non-transformed signifier. We have supported this reading through textual analysis but we can also support it by application to the empirical data about Powell's popularity.

The singular most remarkable and significant thing about Powell's use of 'race' within the politics of Immigration and postwar Toryism is just how popular it has made him (cf. Studlar 1974; King and Wood 1975; Harrington 1974). Powell was genuinely popular among sections of the electorate of the late 1960s, 1970s and 1980s. However the evidence overwhelmingly suggests that Powell's popularity rest on his specific dissenting view towards Immigration policy where Powell was able, in a series of dramatic speeches, to create the effect of a massive policy difference between himself and the party leadership of both Labour and Conservatives. This popularity as a political dissenter of high rank has not generalised itself across other Powellite issues; despite the fact that Powell has specifically developed such themes, by attempting to articulate the signifieds of the absent signifier of 'race', across them.

It is no exaggeration to state that Powell became a contender for the leadership of the Conservative party on the basis of his racial populism. Prior to his excursion into this arena he was unknown or mistrusted by the public as a right-wing 'free-market' extremist. Gallop poll surveys, designed to elicit public support, as measured by percentage of population and estimated ranking for a possible Tory leadership contest, clearly illustrate this interpretation; thus in December 1964 Powell had 0% support; in November 1965, 6% ranked him 6; January 1967, 13% ranked him 6; January 1969, 33% ranked him 2 and October 1969, 36% ranked him 1. On the basis of this data Phillips can assert, 'From a position of not being mentioned as a possible leading member of a Conservative government in December 1964, he had become first choice by October 1969' (Phillips 1977: 122). More specifically Phillips has claimed that it was Powell's April 'River of Blood' speech that resulted in his rise to prominence within the electorate: 'In a Gallop Poll conducted just before this speech only 1 per cent of a sample survey mentioned Powell as a replacement for Heath. In the month following he was the choice of 24 per cent of another sample and was ranked first. During the Ugandan Asians conflict in 1973 he was once again the prime ministerial choice of about a quarter of the population' (pp.124-5).

Schoen (1977, also Johnson and Schoen 1976) deepens this judgement with an impressive array of data ranging over Powell's political career, arguing that his periods of greatest popularity came when he was popularly associated 'in the public mind' with the Immigration issue (1968-74) and against the prevailing government and elite view. That this identification with the issue of 'race and immigration' achieved a formidable mobilisation among sections of the electorate seems clear but his personal popularity also carried over into a measurable political effect for which ever political party Powell endorsed, after his (in)famous rejection of the Conservatives, and endorsement of Labour, in 1974 (Douglas and Schoen 1976: 170; Schoen 1977: ch.8).

Although Powell, in many ways, was able to define the 'race' and immigration issue as a popular theme, simply because of the kind of media attention he achieved, he lost Conservative voters in the 1973-4 period by advocating support for Labour over the question of National Sovereignty but gained Labour supporters. Thus, Douglas and Schoen summarise, Powell's 'support remained strongly linked to the race issue - he reached his peak popularity during the Ugandan Asian controversy in early 1973, with roughly one quarter of the electorate wanting to see him as Prime Minister, five years after his initial Birmingham outburst' (1976: 170). Thus Powell's politics was publicly formed through association with the 'race and immigration' issue and this element allowed Powell a basis of personal popularity within a good cross section of the electorate. This potential personal political effect was often decisive in General Elections between 1968 and 1976 (the date of the study) but could be generalised to the 1980s i.e., up to the point of Powell's defeat at Southdown (due to growing contradictions, ideologically within the Ulster Unionists). This personal political effect was achieved because of Powell's populist stance outside of the main parties over the issue of the public politics of 'race' and the way in which Powell's stance was one of principled engagement in a period of generalised disillusionment i.e., *partisan dealignment*, with consensus politics of the social democratic variety and the two party elite hegemony of ideas.

Enoch became a 'man of the people' over 'race' and put himself against the existing political establishment; popularly seen as a stance against the liberal elite. The paradox of this, as we have suggested, is that he remains wedded to the idea of an elite social order and a deferential relationship between leaders and populace and, as our analysis indicates, this sort of relationship is at the heart of his populism. When he asks the popular masses to support him he is asking for an instinctive assent to leadership, via the national instincts, in line with a view of authority and allegiance to the nation i.e. the Conservative political establishment. It would be a grave mistake to assume that Powell's anti-establishment means a policy of abolition of the establishment rather than its reform. What Powell most desires is a return to the mythical, instinctive traditions and allegiances of nationhood (as part of the reclamation of some mythical English past) but coupled with a (market) economic realism.

There can be little doubt that Powell's nationalism, once recovered from his writings and interventions, is an exclusionary, authoritarian discourse that requires 'cultural subjects' to fill the positions of allegiance. There can also be little doubt that very few would share his 'febrile' poetics of longing for the nation. What is clear is that Powell's populism rests upon his attempt to yoke the floating signifieds of 'race' to nation. His audiences responded to the old signifiers of 'race' , and this allowed the possibility of the political transformation involved in a 'new' discourse of cultural belonging to the nation. It is also the case that Powellism appeared to define the politics of 'race and immigration' because of the mediated effect (Seymour-Ure 1974) of an elite, cabinet politician going popular over 'race'. In this respect, despite our textual analysis of the deep structure of Powell's speeches and writings, his words cannot have been easily accessible to the audiences that supported him. It is likely that interpretations of the meanings of speeches relied on the mediation of national television and fleet street editors. This fact, in itself, means that the Powell effect was not absolutely rooted in the discursive content of his speeches but his conjunctural positioning around issues which already had a great deal of ideological power, but which Powell's feverish political energy certainly helped to drive forward, once he had established a public-political constituency.

Conclusion

This final chapter has mounted a wide ranging argument involving a general theoretical proposition and synthesis of findings indicated in previous chapters. It has specifically applied the debate about racism and political language to the content and ideological significance of Powellism as a political discourse. This has involved posing the central question raised and treated in various ways by the book: is Powellism a 'new' or 'old' racism? Or is in fact Powellism a nationalism? We have argued the case that Powellism is a sophsiticated political articualtion of old racism that is grafted on to an existing body of discourse that perhaps has more claim to the term Powellism.

We have demonstrated the use and articulation of racism within Powell's political discourse in two ways: Firstly, by demonstrating the continuity of conceptual relations of Powell to other varieties of political 'race' populism, as we have argued in various ways in previous chapters. This argument has become, in the process of enunciation, quite explicit in this chapter. Secondly, we have cited a great deal of textual evidence to show Powell's conceptual foundations within and articulation of, a set of old biologistic racist themes, which have concerned and dominated his stance and speeches on immigration control. In addition, we have identified and attempted to show the relationship between this politically prominent element to the other elements of Powellism, namely: patriotism and political authoritarianism. Finally, we have argued that, although these elements are separate to racism and, in point of fact, prior to racism, Powell has found means of articulation of them politically, and this tendency has become more prominent as time has passed and the Powell project, to the extent that it has had a discernible political momentum and purpose, has foundered.

Conclusion

What has this book tried to do? It has presented a critical and extended engagement with the theory and evidence informing the New Racism thesis. On the basis of this engagement it has offered a modified version of the thesis; one that is able to account for the growth and development of a language of public/political racism in postwar Britain. In addition we have identified the anecdotal form of such racism as its most salient feature. We have suggested that explaining the anecdotal form of such a public language is the key to understanding the success of such a racism. This is so on two counts. Firstly, in terms of explaining the ideological power of postwar racist discourse i.e. its ability to connect home with its audience. Secondly in terms of its success in hegemonizing the political field through the development of a Parliamentary commons' sense.

The explanation for these phenomenon lies in the way in which the development of the anecdotal discourse of a local politics of neighbourhood, community and territory has allowed the communication of racism in a form that has been afforded a degree of political legitimacy. This is the secret of the Smethwick phenomenon and Powellism. They are important moments in the development of this political language form and the construction of its audience. The construction of widespread working class support for a conservative politics of anti immigration is that such a politics has managed to articulate existing signifieds of racism within an emergent narrative of neighbourhood nationalism and social decay. But we have importantly shown that this discourse is one that is developed from at least the mid 1950s onwards and is the key to the political success of the 1962 Commonwealth Immigrants restriction Bill.

We have sought support for our argument both theoretically and empirically. Theoretically we have engaged with those theorists that have offered an account of the significance and development of a postwar political racism. We have identified such theories as those of the New Racism approach, a sociological tradition of theorising, and a Marxist political economy informed approach.

Through a sustained engagement with these approaches we have sought to critically employ the arguments and concepts of post structuralist and post modernist theorists in order to offer a synthesis that can advance the debate.

In debating the merits of these approaches we argued, in chapter 2, that the phenomenon identified by the New Racism writers had been anticipated and formed an important moment in the development of sociological theorising about racism in postwar Britain, but a moment that was never fully engaged. The most important theoretical legacy of this approach was the concept of racialisation, developed by Banton (1977) to explain the historical process whereby a domestic racial theory was disseminated into an imperial and colonial context; a process identified as racialisation. Despite the fact that Banton has argued that the postwar context has seen the development of a political process of deracialisation he, at the same time, argued that the concept of 'race' was employed by politicians to make sense of postwar migration to Britain (1980).

Reeves gave this concept a harder analytical edge by showing how the political language of parliamentary debates could be seen to be subject to a process of deracialisation (1983). But such a process was far from a welcome one. On the contrary, political language employed to exclude negatively evaluated populations had been subject to a process of sanitary coding and public cleansing, and this served to conceal political intentions and motives. This was, as guilty politicians imperfectly realised, because a deracialized discourse could more effectively evade the condemnation of racism and yet achieve the exclusion such politicians required. The weaknesses of this approach were that Reeves took the context of racial hostility entirely for granted in his study. In other words he did not show how the process of deracialisation actively involved a discursive process of re-racialization. The fact that politicians were able to communicate a politics of exclusion to a partisan audience did not occur easily or simply in the context of the absence of racial discourse. The absent space of 'race' was filled increasingly by the development of a post-'race' signification which rearticulated old racisms to a new socially exclusionary language.

Reeves' approach echoed the pragmatism of political studies scholars, such as Studlar (1980), who have argued that elite politicians acquiesced to populist issues out of self interest or for reasons of political survival. The flaw in such studies was built into its assumptions; assumptions apparently validated by the available empirical evidence. Firstly, such studies viewed 'race politics' as an element outside of party politics but very much *inside* political audiences. However, as we indicated in chapter 1, recent Marxist influenced work on the postwar state and racialisation has clearly shown that the political elite already held a deeply racialized view of incoming black migrants when their substantive numbers were very meagre (cf. Harris 1987). This view of the influence of the secret state, we argued in chapter 1, needed to be complimented with the liberal political histiography of Layton-Henry and others (1984; 1992) that recorded the enormous ideological force of the campaign of backbench 'race' activists on the eventual formation of official legislation.

The value of the Marxist approaches of Miles, Carter, Harris and Joshi is that the political process of racialisation was placed within a wider economic and social process, involving the differential political treatment of migrants within the framework of global capitalist migration and capital accumulation. Central to such a model was the activities of the political state and the contradictory currents of inclusion and exclusion based on the need to regulate and control labour supply within the capitalist economy. However, the central dilemma of such an approach was the role of ideology in structuring the actions and processes of the state and state elite. Our major criticism of this approach was that the concept of racism as an ideology informing a process of racialisation of groups, according to racial criteria, was not more closely identified with the political languages through which it was realised within internal and public debates. We traced such deficiencies to the economistic framework employed as the basis for such arguments, as well as deficiencies in the theory of ideology itself. In continuing to support an epistemologically defined account of racism as an ideology the approach had to view racism as a structurally reproduced concealment of the consciousness of agents within capitalism of the economic processes informing the inclusion and exclusion of groups. This approach did not afford ideology enough autonomy, especially in recognising the need theoretically to show how ideology must be realised in a discursive form by such agents, and this crucially depends upon being able to analytically reveal the discursive process by which racialisation may or may not be achieved in a given context. Secondly, the approach operated with a view of racism as a doctrine of inferiority sanctioned by scientific discourse. Such a view of racism as a historically situated discourse made it difficult to apply to different political contexts in terms of the language actually employed by politicians and the role such language formation played in the wider economic and social context of postwar Britain.

Here, we argued that the New Racism approach served to highlight the centrality of racism to political processes occurring in the domestic politics of postwar Britain by showing how discursive ideologies were operating and what political purposes they served. Here the work of Hall (1988) and the Race and Politics Group (1982) was important in offering an account of the discourse of 'race' as a nodal point in the development of a politics of the new right, exemplified by the impact of Powellism, and finding its institutional form in the rise of Thatcherism. Although the account of the New Racism and Thatcherism are theoretically incompatible in many respects both approaches sought to apply a more sophisticated neo-Gramscian analysis to the politics of 'race' in postwar Britain. A central concept here was that of commonsense (Gramsci 1971). These writers argued that a new political commonsense had been formed out of the signifieds of the post-imperial racism of Powellism and the New right, and that this newly emergent discourse had allowed the formation of an emergent hegemony of the political field. The concept of hegemony is important here in supplying a more adequate framework for understanding how the political audience and state could be articulated within a discourse of incorporation which allowed leadership by a new historical bloc of forces in the context of post imperial decline and restructuring.

The point of suture we sought to open regarding the New Racism thesis was that concerning the claim for a break or rupture in the epistemology of contemporary racism, occurring between Powell and what proceeds him, in particular, Griffiths. We argued that this confused a number of claims. Firstly, that we can identify a discourse of the old racism operating prior to the emergence of the New Racism. But the New Racism writers have provided no evidence of this. Therefore it becomes difficult to sustain a periodization of the shift from a biological to a cultural racism. At the same time we argued that historical evidence supported the view that old racism is hegemonic up to the period of the Second World War. It is in the postwar period that we see the development of New Racism. However the emergence of this New Racism had to be understood through the complex formation of factors that form the particular political and social context of discursive reformation and political change.

What we have claimed is that a new discourse of racism emerges in postwar Britain from the late 1940s onwards, one that is decisively stimulated and shaped by political, ideological and social forces. Such forces form the social and political superstructure of repression of racial languages in the public sphere. The immediate object of such political repression is the defeat of nazism in central Europe but its other repressed dimension is the empire and colonial relations that have sustained Britain's imperial role and sense of national identity prior to the Second World War.

Postwar British politics is one conducted in the context of decolonisation and Pax Americana. The language and ideology of colonial relations cannot occupy the front region of political rationality, particularly one in a new world order of global markets and the emergence of a common market of nations. It is the fact of this social and political repression which creates the context for the emergence of the political form of racial discourse and the source of its explosive political and popular force. The paradox is this: while the master signifier of 'race' is expunged from public space its signifieds proliferate. The impetus for this proliferation is the development of a dedicated campaign by marginalised backbench elements of the Conservative and Labour parties. A marginalised political rump dedicated to the retention of Africa and latterly the expulsion of ex-colonials from postwar British soil.

It is the existence of this ideological complex that provides the discursive primitives that allow the development of postwar language of the social and political significance of Englishness as an identity politics rooted in an ideological discourse of the social. The early development of an anecdotal discourse of political and public racism is one that identifies immigration through the metaphors of disease and contagion and through social and moral decay. Here the activities of particular MPs and orators becomes important in the development of this discursive form. Cyril Osborne, Harold Gurden, in alliance with the Labour MPs, such as Harry Hyne. It has been our argument that the Powellism of immigration is borrowed from these pioneering styles. However, we also argued that such a complex political phenomenon as Powellism cannot be simply borrowed. This is because Powellism is a pre-existing political discourse, one centred by market economics and a patriotic nationalism and Toryism, a voice out of favour in the administrative and interventionist governments of the postwar consensus. Powell employs 'race' not out of a conviction of racism but one of nationalism. His speeches and writings attempt a sophisticated account of area, region, neighbourhood and community that is being changed irrevocably by immigration of culturally foreign groups. The New Racism writers argued that this language of cultural incompatibility was a sophisticated racism by which Powell could evade the political censor. However we have contended that Powell's ability to achieve a recognition effect within his audience depends upon the recoding of 'race' being *decoded* by its audience.

The key to the New Racism argument is the idea that the problem of new commonwealth immigration cannot be voiced within the context of liberal tolerance and that such a repressive liberal establishment can only be contested by a language of commonsense feeling; feeling that only those in the areas affected by immigration can voice. But, as we have shown, it is the politics of Smethwick which decisively develops this politics of neighbourhood and 'race' realism. Smethwick is therefore crucial to the formation of both the content and tactics of the New Racism politics. However a critical distinction is important here. Smethwick politics were rooted in the local politics of the town, achieving national political recognition through Griffiths' infamous 1964 victory; Powellism was a politics of the centre, a national not a local politics. The success of Powellism has been the ability of Powellism to play elite sophisticated games with the discourse of post-'race' signification, and articulate this linguistic complexity to a language of the local and the territorial, but to recognise in both the powerful sense of loss of identity that the denial of postwar British racial superiority accorded.

Notes

Preface

1   The debate about the New Racism emerges in British sociology in the early 1980s (Barker 1981; CCCS Race and Politics Group 1982) but the concept has subsequently been addressed in the context of debates about the resurgence of ideological racism in Europe, cf. Balibar (1991) and developments in France, in particular: Wieviorka (1994: 173-88; 1995: 42-5). Any theoretical assessment of the concept must acknowledge the important ideas of Taguieff, whose key books are still (sadly) not available in an English translation. The object of my analysis here is postwar British political discourse, and there are important differences in the meaning and deployment of terms in, say, the British and French context. But this should not lead to theoretical insularity or the abdication of responsibility of scholars to seek out and highlight common strategies and tactics among the ideological racists in both the European and British contexts.

2   The initial research was funded under ESRC Research Award: A004228724087, based at the Centre for Research into Ethnic Relations, University of Warwick. The completed study was submitted for Ph.D within the Department of Politics and Sociology, Birckbeck College, University of London in 1996.

3   The death of Powell, after a period of illness, occurred when this book was going to press. The subsequent discussion by leading politicians and media commentators as to whether Powell was a racist or an ultra-nationalist deserves analysis (see Brown *forthcoming*), however this issue is dealt with in detail in ch.6. The important relationship between Powell and the media in the structuring of the public debate about 'immigration' has been examined elsewhere (Brown 1988) and will be the subject of a forthcoming article.

4   A critical history of the debate has yet to be written (but see Brown 1997). My description emphasises the continuities between earlier sociological definitions and approaches to the problem of political languages and the expression/concealment of racism, as for example Reeves, and more recent approaches, such as van Dijk and the critical linguistic approaches associated with the journal *Discourse & Society*.

5   Such a claim is for the political project of Thatcherism. As Smith (1994: 36) argues '[t]o the extent that a project achieves hegemonic status, it appears that virtually any problem can be resolved within its framework'. Such a view is part of a neo-Gramscian hegemony as naturalization (as opposed to domination) theory, where the organisation of consent within a new political bloc is achieved through the re-articulation of weakened traditional social elements and ideologies. I am not concerned to assess the relationship of Powellism to Thatcherism, critical to this

account, but rather the evidence for the significance of the 'content' of Powellism to the moment of re-articulation.

6   The discursive history I trace in my research is from 1956-7 until 1988. But the discursive phenomenon I am concerned with is a postwar phenomenon whose 'conceptual primitives' are articulated from the late 1940s onwards.

7   The Gramscian term commonsense is central to the claims of the New Racism thesis. The assumption is that commonsense is the dominant ideology, sedimented into a common register, so that ideological meanings are bottom-up rather than top-down. Barker's account of the New Racism offers a particular claim about the making of a new commonsense and how this is achieved. The critical point in such accounts is the moment of 're-articulation', since this involves a reconstruction of the relationship between the dominant and the subordinate, initiated from the political realm as a discursive event. Hall's account of Thatcherism offers a sophisticated account of this process. See also Smith 1994.

8   The evidential basis of the New Racism is examined in my unpublished Ph.D. thesis, *Racism and Political Language: the impact of Smethwick and Powellism on the formation of a political racism in postwar Britain, 1957-1988*, Department of Politics and Sociology, Birkbeck College, University of London, 1997.

9   In point of fact it is the discourse of criminality that Gilroy views as central to the representation of the black presence in Britain. Powellism initiates a shift to a discourse, not of criminality, but legality, as the ultimate symbol of nationality.

10 Barker actually claims a new or re-worked biological discourse informs the New Racism (see Brown 1997: ch.2). The claim for state racism is not substantiated by engagement with state theory or with actual pieces of legislation (see ch.4).

11 Mercer, for example, while developing an argument from Hall's account of Powellism (Hall 1978; 1979), claims Powell's speeches on English nationalism and the Empire as 'myth' provide the *reversible-connecting* factor whereby 'race' can be re-coded as culture (1994: 307). Mercer claims this as a 'textualist-strategy': 'Powellism encoded a racist vision of English cultural identity, not in the illegitimate language of biologizing racism, but through literary and rhetorical moves that enabled the dissemination of its discourse across the political spectrum, to the point where it became legitimised by being gradually instituted in commonsense and in state policies' (1994: 307). A 'profound shift' or 'radical break from previous discourses on race' is also claimed by Smith (1994: 54) but such an account of the New Racism is developed within a sophisticated defence of hegemony as *naturalization* in which the success of Thatcherism's re-coding of 'race' inform the achievement of a hegemonic project (1994: ch.1). While Smith's discussion of the success of the New Racism is in terms of a post-structuralist (mis)identification claim (which privileges 'form' over 'content') the moment of re-articulation is carefully defined in terms of a moment of social 'un-fixity' where 'new articulations

borrow from and re-work various traditional frameworks so that they already appear to be somewhat familiar' (1994: 6).

12 For Lawrence (see ch. 2) racist commonsense in Britain is the product of centuries of sedimentation of images and ideologies of 'blacks' which are re-worked. This is certainly not a claim for a new biological-reductionism, as in Barker, but the articulation of a cultural language of crisis with popular racist ideologies.

13 Here Barker is conflating two elements (i) the unspoken prohibition on 'race talk' in public (itself symptomatic of the amnesia of empire (cf. Hall 1978: 25; Smith 1994:131-40) and (ii) postwar popular feeling against Nazism, which made it difficult for the Far Right to employ 'race' explicitly in attempted political projects. Barker's argument is that the achievement of a new 'race talk' in politics offers a popular politics that can articulate racist meanings. Importantly this argument is based on the view that people would not arrive at a racist (theorized) account of immigration without the discourse (theory) of the New Racism. Importantly the New Racism should be viewed 'not as an appeal to commonsense, but as a struggle to create a new commonsense' (1981: 22). Whereas Lawrence argues the new commonsense racist ideologies are popular 'because they intersect with and re-organise the common-sense racism of the white working and other classes' (1981: 4). The latter view is actually more consistent wit the arguments that I would view as the precursors of the New racism thesis, for example, the Dummett's account of 'crypto-racism' (1969); although neither Barker or the CCCS writers acknowledge or appear aware of earlier sociological or political studies approaches.

14 Other writers, prior to the new racism debate, argue that it is the liberal prohibition on 'race' in public space that allows Powellism the impact it does achieve by finding its way though the official silence. Powell is of course able to turn this silence into a conspiracy of the liberals against the best interests of the people (cf. Dummett and Dummett 1969; Seymour-Ure 1974; Braham 1982: 279-82).

15 Layton-Henry (1992: 72-3) identifies the anti-immigration Backbenchers, drawn from the ranks of both Labour and the Tories, as: Cyril Osborne (Louth), Norman Pannell (Kirkdale), Martin Lindsey (Solihull), Harold Gurden (Selly Oak), John Hynd (Attercliffe), Harry Hyne (Accrington), George Rogers (N. Kensington), Albert Evans (S.W. Islington) and James Harrison (Nottingham W.) I make the argument for their authorship of the New Racism in Brown (1997) and here. Layton-Henry (1984: ch.3) provides an important account of the Campaign for Immigration Controls.

16 In fact the New Racism theorists completely ignore all Parliamentary Debates prior to 1968; as they ignore all Debates taking place between 1968 and 1976 (Barker) and between 1968 and 1981 (Lawrence and CCCS). It seems outrageous that such an influential theory as the NR is based on such a narrow and unrepresentative selection of Debates and statements. See Brown 1997: ch.4.

17 This period covers the Parliamentary impact of the Backbench exclusion campaign, up to and including the intervention of Powell, and Powell's defeat as candidate for South Down.

18 The New Racism thesis rests on the validity of the claim for an epistemological break between the old and the new racism. But the NR writers are complicit in accepting this distinction from the New Racists themselves. Quite simply the evidence does not support this distinction since 'old racism' can be found post Powell and the new racism, prior to the break. See Brown 1997 and Ch.3, 4 and 6.

19 That is, not only is their a public political prohibition on mentioning or referring to the concept of 'race' but their is no basis for making an argument. 'Race' is under erasure and the political establishment has no agreed language in which to conduct a debate.

20 There is no satisfactory treatment in studies of postwar political racism of this notion. Theoretically Derrida's conception suggests something of the sense in which 'race' is present in its absence (absent presence) but how such an absence is articulated is at the heart of the fierce theoretical controversies surrounding the political implications of the attempt to combine post-structuralism and neo-Gramscism, cf. Barrett (1991) Smith (1994).

21 The term 'conceptual' or 'discursive primitives' is an important element in the neo-Faucaltian approach to the signifying frames or elements of articulation by which 'similar elements are articulated differently' at moments of discursive shift (see Foucault 1972: 37-8; Omi and Winant 1986: 64; Said 1978: 1-4; West 1982: 47-68; Goldberg 1990: 295-318).

22 The definition of racism as doctrine of hierarchy and inferiority, sanctioned by bad science, is a political act of prohibition (Benedict 1983; Barzun 1965; Miles 1989). In some instances, for example the case of Benedict, it is a social-scientific critique of the illegitimate uses of biological science. More generally the definition of racism as a doctrine of inequality allows the detached significations, by which racism has been made and remade historically, a route back to the erased space occupied by the prohibited notion. Banton's (1983) argument that racism should be defined as racial typology theory and assigned an epistemic moment in the development of biological thought allows in the *new racisms* of Griffiths and Powell (cf. the debate between Banton and Rex in: Zubaida (ed) (1970).

23 Actually the title of Coates and Silburn's study was *Poverty: The Forgotten Englishmen* (1972) (Harmondsworth: Penguin). I am indebted to the perceptive remarks of Joshi and Carter: 'They were the poor and unorganised, trapped in the decaying "inner city" areas of declining capital investment [...] invisible to politicians, the intelligentsia and large sections of the labour movement. It was to these invisible communities that the first post-war black immigrants were driven, to disappear from view in much the same way as their powerless, white working-class neighbours [....] For the white working class in the inner-city areas, a black presence brought a sharp

awareness that things had changed, an awareness of the loss of community and their own sense of failure, of being left behind in the competitive struggle to live in the same streets as the people over whom 'they' had once ruled' (1984: 67-8). Much of the material informing this view can be found in Seabrook's pioneering explorations (1971; 1978).

24 This quotation could be supported by many more examples. See Brown 1997 and references: 1958a; 1958b; 1961a; 1961b; 1961c; 1964; 1965.

25 Guillaumin's argument is that a discursive field can shift and mutate under an apparently stable signifier, so that the referentiality and function of the signifier changes. The reply to the New Racist argument has to be that the period of drift or transformation takes place post-1945 and involves the engagement with and political development of the changing relations of representation informing post colonial societies and their former subjects. As Balibar argues, 'The new racism is a racism of the era of decolonization, of the reversal of population movements between the old colonies and the old metropolises, and the division of humanity within a single political space' (1991: 21).

26 I am of course referring to the International Socialists and subsequently the Socialist Workers' Party. This political connection also links in Martin Barker, see his note in Preface (1981; see also p. 38; 1979: 2-3).

27 The research I conducted involved detailed content and textual analysis of all Immigration, Race Relations and Nationality Debates occurring in the period 1957-88 as well as all Powell's speeches and writings during this period.

28 Chapter 4 exemplifies this methodological approach by taking the specific claims of Barker and Gilroy, examined in chapter 2, at the level of theoretical consistency and subjects them to an empirical and comparative analysis of validity. It does so by re-positioning, for example, the Immigration Debate of 1976 within the broader context of Labour initiated Race Relations Debates taking place during that year. Here again the seeking out of a wider context for the production and development of ideological narrative styles is exemplified.

29 For a discussion of the term 'race politics' in relation to the phenomenon of Smethwick and Powellism, see especially chapter 5.

1 The Erasure of Race in Public Space

1 Solomos (1986d) provides a thorough overview of neo-marxist approaches that combine an account of migration and the state within a framework which attempts to reconcile the political-economic category of class with that of the ideological category of 'race'. This review is extended to suggest post-marxist directions in Cashmore (ed) 1994. Subsequently Solomos and Back have constructed a

chronology of theoretical moments within the analysis of contemporary racism which suggests that post-marxist approaches are now at the leading edge of analysis (cf. Solomos and Back 1993; see also note 1., ch.2).

2   Neo-Marxist perspectives such as Miles (1982) and CCCS: Race & Politics (1982) attacked the sociology of 'race relations' because it was seen to reify and reproduce an essentially ideological category (Miles) or political commonsense (CCCS).

3   Hall has developed this position, summarised in the introduction to his (1988) collected essays on Thatcherism and the Left, in trying to reconcile certain elements of a Marxist theorisation of ideology with Gramscism and its reconstruction within the discourse-theoretical approach of Laclau (1977; 1994) and Mouffe (1979) and Laclau and Mouffe (1985; 1987).

4   Hodge and Kress (1979) actually call their book 'Language as Ideology' thereby clearly indicating the distinctive emphasis of their argument, that it is through the form of language that ideology is given social existence in the structuring of social relations. However Kress and Hodge's approach and that of their co-workers Fowler et al (1979) depends upon the application of a methodology concerned with the analysis of grammar and syntactic structures. Despite the fact that they arrive at a determinism of ideology at the level of grammar structures and their homological relations to unequal social power structures, they specifically concentrate on the way in which language and text construction achieves ideology. See also their revision of this view in 'Social Semiotics'(1985).

5   See note 20 under Preface.

6   The term is of course borrowed from Marx by Claus Offe, Habermas, etc., and poses in perhaps too topographic a way the notion of the relationship between phenomenal forms and essences. Hidden in the metaphor is the mechanism of representation: of how, at the symbolic and referential level, a sign can stand in for a substance, prior to or beyond it. The problem this poses for the idea of 'race' is that it is, in one very clear sense, a falsity or error of thought quite literally without substance. With the discrediting of the scientific formation that defined the existence of 'races' we effectively have an absence or point of 'erasure', in the Derridean sense, in the semantic space where 'race' used to be. Surely this is what is indicated by placing the term in parenthesis ? Therefore when we examine the phenomenon of political racism are we examining the re-articulation of an empty signifier? If the answer to this is yes, then what does it signify or more importantly: how does it signify? See for example Laclau 'Why Do Empty Signifiers Matter To Politics ?' (1994).

7   This is a point of inestimable importance and perhaps the single most significant one in understanding the role of 'race' as public and political signifier of subterranean force in the politics of postwar Britain and the language of national identity, post empire. Its subterranean force does not flow from its putative connection to the sub-political unconscious or the authoritarian personality syndrome, but from its

undiminished signifying power in expressing group difference and inherence, in imagining exclusion and creating inclusion (cf. Smith 1994).

8 Given that racialisation approaches define racialisation as discourse that employs a racial category (cf. Reeves 1983).

9 This argument is derived from the general assertion, made in the preface, that the postwar discourse of racism is socially referential, in that it speaks to and about the social as its foundational logic and this is the source of its persuasiveness.

10 This point will be developed more fully in chapter 3.

11 The reason for the extraordinary persistence of the racial signifier is that it was never tied to one signified. The racism as doctrine view assumes this because it abstracts the intellectual kernel of this as doctrine. But we cannot fully deduce the ideology of racism from the terms of doctrine. The problem of the ideal type *scientific racism* is that it cannot get us close enough, for example, to the material imposition of scientific positivism upon subaltern populations. But racism was also, at the same moment, cultural, intellectual, philosophic, religious, etc. Once we have grasped this view of historical racism then we must acknowledge that we can no longer examine racism as a thing-in-itself but, as Terry Collits has argued, 'as a dense system of ideological practices over time entwined with history, language, gender and class relations, and problems of representation and interpretation' (Collits 1994: 64). Thus racist claims carry their own epistemologies and cannot simply be critiqued from the stand point of an appeal to science, but rather must be examined in terms of their textual strategies and in terms of the referential claims they attempt. The analysis of ideology must address itself to this problem.

12 For Miles the important point is that a racialised politics conceals the role of the state and the role of migrant labour in late capitalism.

13 Miles develops a persuasive account of ideology as both 'textual' and 'practically adequate' (1989: 80-2). This negative conception of ideology is one derived from the debate about Marx's ideas by Sayer (1979), Larrain (1979) and Geras (1976).

14 The recent edited collection of essays by Harris and James (ed) (1993) revisits the period in a defiantly political-economic fashion, arguing for a political-economic theory of racial categorisation where 'race' enters not only into the determination of how class is 'lived', experienced or 'fought through', but in how 'class' itself is constituted (p.4).

15 We have sketched out the broad parameters of this debate in the preface, see also Solomos 1989.

16 Paradoxically semiotic accounts of representation would argue that representation is the opposite i.e. the putting into concrete form (the signifier) of an abstract, ideological concept.

17 For a discussion of Halliday see Kress and Hodge (1979; 1981); Hodge and Kress (1985).

18 This is not to suggest that the political construction of 'race' occurs in this historically brief period or the period 1957-1988. Such a precise chronology refers to the period of documents studied. Such a study has been undertaken upon the assumption that this periodization will, on examination, reveal something of the dramatic visibility and linguistic transformation of the historically constructed discourse of racism, which the events of Smethwick reveal and illuminate. Obviously the development of such a discourse has a longer historical formation. See below for the development of this point.

19 This is an apparently obvious finding of a content analysis of the IRR Newsletter and the national press and yet it does not form a significant part of existing commentary. See the development of this argument in chapter 3.

20 Although, as we shall argue, all such discourses are discourses of racialisation.

21 It is interesting that Reeves' study, appearing in 1983, makes no mention or acknowledgement of the New Racism or the work of the Race and Politics Collective: CCCS (1982). It is important to state that Reeves does not consider the discrepancy we have noted between either the new racism and classical doctrine or between the latter and expressions of old racism. On this basis we will assert that, contra Reeves, there is ample evidence of old racism in parliamentary debates, cf. chapter 3.

22 To analyse the effects of legislation as a measure of political intent is to lay oneself open to the counter-charge that such 'effects' are an unintended outcome of otherwise well intended instruments. As for example,

> Whatever the intentions of the Government - and I do not suggest that they are actuated by colour prejudice - the fact is that the Bill's whole impact falls upon the coloured immigrants from the Asian and West Indian countries of the Commonwealth (Mr. Nigel Fisher (Surbiton) *Commonwealth Immigrants Bill*, 16 November, 1961: 779).

> My right hon. Friend said that this was not racialist legislation. It may not be racialist in intention, but it will certainly be racialist in effect (Sir D. Foot, (Hansard) *Commonwealth Immigrants Bill*, 27 February, 1968: 1271).

Conversely, it can be argued that political discourse is merely the rhetorical support of cynical or irrational legislation intended to appease the irrational and the hostile who wish to have it imposed i.e., playing the 'race' card: 'there is no shred of evidence that the Government have even seriously tried to [...]make a proper inquiry into the nature of this problem. They have yielded to the crudest clamour, "Keep them out" ' (Mr. Hugh Gaitskell (Leeds, South) *Commonwealth Immigrants Bill*, 16 November, 1961: 801).

23 The theoretical dilemma within which Reeves' work is situated is allegiance to a sociological perspective which is unwilling to acknowledge the existence of racist argumentation in the absence of racial categories.

24 There is no extant review and critique of this area as it informs the debate about racism and postwar migration (but see Miles 1989). Rather different theorists draw upon different traditions and theories of ideology, sometimes quite implicitly. Useful general discussion of the theoretical debates which form the intellectual backdrop to these issues can be found in Eagleton (1991) Barrett (1991) and Larrain (1994).

25 This distinction concerns the extent to which users of the concept endorse a broadly social scientific or post-modernist position qua concepts. Thus Miles argues that 'race' is an ideology because it can be characterised as a particular form of discourse that functions to represent: 'human beings, in a distorted and misleading manner[...]Such a concept presumes an alternative epistemological position, from the occupancy of which it is possible to demonstrate the falsity of the discourse defined as ideology, a position that is identified[...]as science' (1989: 42). This position could be contrasted with relativists (Feyerabend 1978) conventionalists (Kuhn 1970); and post-modernists (Lyotard 1984). Marxism has become (fatally?) characterised as an authoritarian, eurocentric 'grand narrative'.

26 A distinction pertinent to the application of the concept of ideology to the debate about 'race science' and rationality is that between 'genuine' science and pseudo-science offered by radical-liberal critics of scientific racism such as Chase (1977). The problem for Marxism is to disentangle a reflexive/realist science from a political dogma. Ideology is, as Miles acknowledges, a contested concept and for much the same reasons as those involved in the contemporary critique of the usefulness of the concept of racism. As we established at the outset of our discussion of Reeves and Miles, both approaches depend upon a prior epistemological position: that scientific objectivity can be drawn upon. In the case of Miles it becomes inherently critical given that racist statements are to be identified by their falsity or concealment of the actual (cf. 1989; passim). Despite this it must be said that Miles present an admirable defence of his approach (op cit, 79-84).

27 Much of the weight of British domestic and colonial racism can be identified with Eugenicism and the idea of the reduction of cultural factors and behaviour to deterministic gene prints. Thus the core of racism is a biological reductionism. It is useful to introduce the distinction between Core racism and Secondary racisms; the former refers to the natural or biologic grounding of 'races' in the bio-gene-plasm; thus correctly speaking the ideology of 'race' [the system of social marks: Guillaumin] is a 'biological-fiction' (Fuss 1989: 92; cited in Winant 1994: 286) or ideological-narrative; secondary racisms, the social discourses made possible upon the materiality of this 'episteme'.

28 This unexamined political discourse of 'political racism' forms the focus of chapter 5.

29 As I demonstrate in chapters 4 and 6, characteristically, 'new racial' arguments tend to reveal their derivation from prior old racists positions or accompany such assertions. This is particularly the case with the so called 'new right' and absolutely the case with Powell.

30 I deal with the specific claims of the New Racism thesis in chapters 2 and 4. A recent study of the emergence of the discourse of the New Right (Smith 1994) examines Powellism as 'demonisation of the other' in the period 1968-72. Mercer (1994) makes similar Hallesque claims, although interestingly, citing the formation of the discursive logic of Powellism in the late 1950s early 1960s; but arriving at similar conclusions about its significance.

31 See note 29.

32 These very significant points of discursive articulation are examined in textual and historical detail in chapters 3, 4, 5 and 6.

33 Thus the problem of racism is the problem of the decipherment of racist expressions in the sense that racism is a phenomenon that is recorded or apprehended as statement, speech, language, etc. Social science has tended to accept a psychological model of such as expressive of inner irrationality or turmoil. Racism is a modern irrationality, etc. A textual model that might foreground the content of racist expression had little chance of growth given the lack of interest in the rational content of a basically irrational phenomenon. Thus the problem of postwar political racism for sociology is to identify how that racism has been achieved. The secret of it lies in the mystery of the post-'race' as doctrine signifier and how it has articulated itself through the production of parliamentary discourse. In order to comprehend this we must view racism itself as a type of language. It's not that racism is in the language as a sort of invading force or virus but rather that political racisms are realised through the reality signifying power of public language. Much of the postwar production of racial discourse simply went unnoticed by sociologists. It wasn't until the rise of Powellism in the wake of Smethwick that they were forced to take it seriously.

34 This discourse is analysed in some detail in chapter 3.

35 The metaphors of dynamite, combustion, explosion etc., are common here and are highlighted in chapter 3. These metaphors are also common to journalism in the early 1960s as my survey of the IRR newsletter indicates.

36 At the centre of this view is the pervasive idea that racism is to be understood as a doctrine, derived from a taxonomy involving a moral hierarchy of 'types', which arose in a formative period in Victorian scientific thinking. This whole intellectual formation has subsequently been discredited as 'bad' or biased science which has served to justify colonial exploitation and empire building, finding its ultimate historical expression, for some, in the nazi 'race hygiene' programme and the holocaust. Despite the moral force of this argument I believe that its analytical kernel

is deficient and should be abandoned. One of the reasons for this is plainly political; the view of racism as attributable to a discredited doctrine allows today's 'new racists' and cultural absolutists to claim that their desire for national homogeneity does not involve a doctrinaire commitment to group superiority or claims for hierarchy but simply a recognition of cultural difference. However, the political contradictions run much deeper than this. Along with the discrediting of the 'race' as doctrine notion there has arisen a view that to hold to such a notion is to be deeply irrational or psychologically disturbed. This view very largely derives from the UNESCO interventions which attempted to discredit the notion of 'race' as biological fact of science and to characterise this whole strand of disreputable thinking in western science as a 'dangerous myth', one that had lead to the aberration of the 'final solution'. As one commentator has put it, such a belief could not be seen to be rational. The recent intellectual interventions of Bauman and others have begun to challenge this view by arguing that the holocaust, far from being a departure or some sort of historical anachronism, is more likely to be the pinnacle of application of the techniques and culture of modernity: 'The Holocaust was born and executed in our modern rational society, at the high stage of our civilisation and at the peak of human cultural achievement, and for this reason it is a problem of that society, civilisation and culture' (Bauman 1989: x). Nevertheless, the UNESCO intervention has had an immense subterranean impact. Firstly it announced a political prohibition on the connection between notions of 'race' and mass electoral politics. To politicise 'race' was to invoke the spectre of nazism. This rupture between the idea of 'race' and its public expression has pathologised it as a sub-political contagion likely to appeal to the illiterate and the emotionally unstable. At the heart of this sort of view is a 'mass society' derived audience composed at its core by Adorno's authoritarian personality types, ripe for fascism. This moral and intellectual attack upon the doctrine of 'race' and the signalling of its potential mass electoral appeal, had the effect of creating the liberal/ humanitarian commitment to its political expungement rather than contestation and critique.

2   Back to the Future: The New Racism Revisited

1   It is necessary, formally, to distinguish between this debate and the more recent claims for a 'neo' European Racism by Sivanandan (1988), Balibar (1991) and others. I am not concerned with this debate in this chapter although the account of the transition from 'biological' to 'cultural' stereotypes evident in the current anti-muslim/guestworker discourse described by Balibar and the distinction proposed by Taguieff (1990) between *inegalitarian* and *differentialist* racisms are pertinent to the conceptual focus of the British debate about the 'new' racism. In this respect I endorse the argument advanced by Wieviorka (1994: 182-3) concerning the conceptual opposition and articulation of the 'two logics' of racism, although I do not fully support the 'grand mutation' framework in which he places these distinctions.

2   Solomos and Back (1993), in a recent summary of developments suggest that, 'the theoretical engagements of the early 1980s cannot adequately conceptualise racism in the 1990s. The political struggles that underscored these debates have moved on.

In many ways the turn towards the conceptualisation of culturally defined racisms and the politics of identity has been led by the political events of the late eighties[...]The controversy over the publication of Salman Rushdie's book *The Satanic Verses* has provided a warning that the politics of culture cannot be appreciated within the conceptual language of the 1980s' (p.20). Central to Solomos and Back's account is the periodization of research into three phases: (i) Race Relations sociology (ii) Neo-Marxist racism analysis and (iii) new cultural politics. Certainly the title of Bob Miles' recent collection of essays, *Racism After 'Race Relations'* suggests he is still firmly in phase ii. It remains an open question whether Solomos and Backs' comments to the effect that 'in the context of the complex forms of identity politics the semantics of race cannot be confined to the politics of regulation' (Miles 1989)'(ibid), means that there is any space left for such an approach? Certainly if one takes a critical historical perspective, as Miles certainly endorses, the complex cultural and ideological dimensions of the politics of regulation mean that it has never simply been an exercise in forms of economistic reduction. In one sense Solomos and Back (1993) are quite correct to assert that the changing theoretical debate about the analysis of racism is driven by contemporary political shifts in the politics of racism which has, since the late 70s, been driven decisively by the 'new' Right. However it is also the case that shifts in the emergence and influence of new theories are themselves a function of political project construction, such as the influence of post-structuralism upon the current trajectory of neo-gramscism in Britain, which is the most defined politics of anti-racism on the current Left political scene.

3   Chapter 4 will subject these specific claims for transformation of conceptual content and political periodization to empirical scrutiny by examining, in detail, the relevant debates, post 1968.

4   Gill Seidel (1986) identifies the emergence of the 'new right' politics of (nation and) culture as Right-Gramscism to which the development of Left Gramscism, centred on the 'radical-democratic' discourse analysis advocated by Laclau and Mouffe (1985), is a model.

5   A particularly nagging example from Mercer (1994) is the following: 'Powellism encoded a racist vision of English cultural identity, not in the illegitimate language of biologizing racism, but through literary and rhetorical moves that enabled the dissemination of its discourse across the political spectrum, to the point where it became legitimized by being gradually instituted in common sense and state policies' (307). This is the culmination of an argument that advocates a reading of Powell as pivoting around the 'Enemies Within' speech of 1970 and the empire myths speeches of 1964. It claims, in cultural studies mode, that legislative changes are achieved through literary and rhetorical moves initiated by Powell. For a comparative view see Smith (1994), in terms of their use of the concept of 'new racism' and political language. See also note 6.

6   This point has not registered upon those that enthusiastically embraced the term (e.g. CCCS: Race and Politics Group 1982). It is my argument that 'The New Racism' was

read politically, particularly in the use of the earlier chapters, while the connection to Hume and the internal logic and methodology of sociobiology were conveniently ignored. This misreading was reinforced, if not initiated by the superficial compatibility of the concept with that of the development of Stuart Hall's account of Thatcherism and 'race' as a moral panic. Barker has recently disassociated himself from this analysis (cf. Barker 1992: 81-100) which lends support to this interpretation.

7   This paper is the one Banton delivers to the 1969 BSA conference on Race and Sociology (cf. Zubaida, 1970). For a more recent comment on aspects of this debate see Banton (1991).

8   Both Hall and CCCS re-define racism as an ideological articulation of political forces involved in the official definition of a 'crisis of hegemony' in their respective accounts of the crisis of the state/ruling bloc in 1970s Britain. We will examine this analysis below.

9   Within sociology 'race' has been theorised as a doctrine, as an ideology and as a syndrome of ideas particular to western science. This debate is the necessary basis of any revision of the use of the concept (cf. Miles, 1989; 1993).

10 My evidence for this claim is presented in detail in chapters 4 and 6.

11 A more recent version of such a debate has been engaged by Goldberg and Appia (cf. Goldberg (ed) 1990). But see my reconstruction of Barker's argument below and note 20.

12 This discursive process is not as straight forward as Banton would like us to believe, in that the term 'race' was most often absent from such debates in any explicit sense. Such remarks must be seen as facetious, given the acrimony concerning the extent to which Banton felt unable to attribute racism to the remarks of 'race populists' like Powell and Griffiths, specifically because of an absence of the 'idea of 'race' in what they said.

13 As Nairn comments on Foot (1969) over a similar kind of functional argument, 'very much more has changed than the scapegoat itself' (Nairn 1981: 257).

14 A good example of this is Miles' reconstruction of the discursive emergence of the concept of racism in the context of an intellectual attack upon nazism (1989: 42-50). This historical reconstruction is offered in support of a claim for its retention value as a concept with which to engage in *ideology critique* (cf. Marx and Engels, 1970 (orig. 1844-5).

15 See the analysis of the content of Powell's speeches and writings in Chapter 6.

16 In fact, Rex has made a number of theoretical contestations of the ideological debate and, in particular, Powellism (cf. 1973: ch.9). Indeed Rex's intellectual history

traverses that of Powell's at certain points, not least initially in terms of the 'review' in which the Powellism of immigration can be said to be launched; that of Rex and Moore's *Race, Community and Conflict* (1967) by Powell in the Daily Telegraph!

17   If we abandon the theoretical debate about the 'narrow' meaning of racism as a concept in preference for the political uses of it we run the risk of (i) accepting the logic of the new racists themselves and (ii) evacuating racism of any continuity as a concept we can recognise in political debate. I believe the most appropriate response to this dilemma, posed by the work of Miles particularly (1989 and 1993), is to seek to identity not the role of 'race' as an ideology in terms of a 'truth claim' but rather to identify the logic characteristic of racism as a reductionist argument. This is the essential of Barker's approach despite the fact that he neither grounds it securely in previous research or theoretical analysis.

18   Despite some strange lapses and a stubbornly Weberian orientation to the construction of a 'race relations' sociology, Rex does not deserve the vilification heaped upon him by, in particular, Lawrence (1981; 1982). See earlier versions of this attack in Sivanandan and Bourne (1980) and Gilroy (1980). If anybody has moved to a 'new racist' position it is more probably Banton.

19   This argument has already been advanced in the preface and will form the essential framework of adequacy for the 'new racism' thesis.

20   See chapters 5 & 6.

21   I believe that this formulation is more consistent than the case actually offered by the New Racism theorists, i.e. it is the best possible formulation of the range of their arguments, despite the fact that they provide little support for the positions they make claims for, in particular, i & ii.

22   It is important to note that much of the evidence for the widespread acceptance of the discourse of the 'new right' is within a narrow range of quality 'right wing' tabloids and political commentators of the 'new right' variety. Given the colonisation of the press that accompanied the rise of Mrs. Thatcher (cf. Murray 1986) it is hardly surprising that such issues and formulations found their way into that self-referencing circle of so called 'public debate'. This points to the problem of the theory of commonsense, for which see below.

23   cf. the ideas of Reeves (1983), discussed in chapter 1, which although produced in the early 1980s, made no reference to or acknowledgement of Barker or CCCS.

24   The title and theme of the early essay is 'Racism - the new inheritors' (1979) and it is this sense Barker wishes to emphasise.

25   This connection is suggested in an unsupported remark about the idea that racism has never been about the superiority/inferiority dichotomy, but a grounding reductionist problematic organised around an idea of instinctivism (1981: 4). This

assertion is picked up again at the close of the discussion of Hume's philosophy of the 'passions' (instinctivism), ch.4:

> Hume asserted a basis in instincts for national hostilities and racial separation. He has that directly in common with the new Tory racists from Powell to Thatcher. The question is whether there is a basis in biology for such assertions. It has normally been though that the part biology has played in the emergence of racism has had to do with the promulgation of pseudo-scientific ideas of 'pure race', 'racial blood', 'Aryan type' and so on. As I have suggested earlier, I think this notion may be a rewriting of the history of racism[...]I suspect that far more effective as a theoretical carrier of racism is a theory of the relations between groups. There is a hidden history of theories of the relations between groups, or nations, or races, all of which arrive at the conclusion that the reactions of hostility, the wish to exclude, the prejudices and hatreds towards those judged to be different, are instinctual, innate and accord with the laws of nature (p.76).

It seems unmistakable that Barker is suggesting that the history of racism has been misunderstood by scholars and that underpinning formulations of local theories of blood, types, strains etc., is a more fundamental theorization of 'innateness'. This distinction is contained in Barker's opposition between the terms *classificatory* racism and *motivational* racism, the latter referring to a more fundamental theory of group relations. It is this conceptual matrix which is being re-theorised in modern biology (cf. Barker 1983; Rose 1979).

26   For a version of 'new racism' that does, see Seidel (1986) and CCCS: Race and Politics Group (1982) and Gilroy (1987).

27   It may be that this is the overall argument that the 'new racism' seeks to promote but evidently Barker believed the connections to be more self evident than they actually are. In addition, the book and the concept have been read as a political intervention, particularly by CCCS (1982), concentrating most attention on the first few chapters on Toryism, rather than the account of Hume or the analysis of ethology and sociobiology.

28   Gilroy employs the defence of culture arguments to suggest that such is the defining characteristic of British racisms (cf. 1987). As I argue in chapters 4 and 6, it is not clear how such a view can be compatible with the idea of the 'new racism'.

29   See also the development of the concept of 'ethnos' as a function of the political articulation of ethnicity/nation in Anthias (1990).

30   In other words the defining characteristic of Conservative ideology is its disavowal that it is ideology! Conservative ideology is conceived as the articulation of the 'organic', the 'commonsense' of the community, the collective sentiment of the nation, etc. This disavowal can be traced to the construction of an (elite) nationalist project in the polemics of Burke (cf. Nairn 1970; 1981). For an alternative interpretation of some interest see Rich (1986).

31 As well as a misreading of Gamble, op cit, p.2.

32 Surely it is the job of ideology to secure the 'rationality gap' or legitimation 'factor of cohesion' in an increasingly globalised, anti-national economy? (cf. Habermas 1974; Hall and Jacques (ed) 1989). Nationalism and racism are thus local elements of ideology within a global system of corporate economics? (cf. Miles and Solomos 1987; Giddens 1991; Sklair 1991).

33 We will argue in chapters 3 and 4 that this kind of appeal is not in the least new although its use by Frontbench spokesmen, like Whitelaw, does demonstrate a major accommodation to the forces of Powellism.

34 Although, as we have already seen, these claims are not always clearly made and are often internal to the exposition rather than the explicit framing of the argument.

35 It is evident that the relationship between commonsense fears and the new Conservative political commonsense is very central to the validity of the thesis and yet there is no attempt to discuss empirical evidence or prior research findings concerning the content of popular 'fears' (as for example, Miles and Phizacklea (ed) 1979). The question surely posed here, but unrecognised by Barker, is the relationship between the existing commonsense held by people and the discourse of the 'old racism'?

36 This is surely the distinction operating in Barker's idea that people are not racist since their experience is 'close to themselves'? Racism is an ideology: a system for organising that experience and making it mean something particular? There is a theoretical anti-racism loaded into this assumption: that racism is a function of political construction. It seems to me that this is essentially correct except that it would be wholly unrealistic to expect that, by 1968, most peoples' perceptions of 'the blacks' were not severely racialised.

37 This notion is grounded in the massive exposition of the idea of late postwar British politics of the 1970s as a full blown crisis of the ruling bloc, with the breakdown of the postwar consensus, signified by the emergence of a series of 'moral panics' and 'folk devils' which are seen to symbolically menace the state and social authority, resulting in the need for the control apparatus to seek more authoritarian forms of suppression of social forces outside of the state (cf. Hall et al 1978; CCCS 1982: ch.1).

38 Here Lawrence re-works Hall's re-working of Gramsci's idea of sedimentation that 'doesn't leave an inventory'. See the discussion of the notion of commonsense racism in Brewer (1984). A criticism of Lawrence's argument is that it fails to provide an account of how ideologies both sediment and transform their meanings. Ironically perhaps such a view undermines the idea of a *new* (cultural) racism.

39 The politics of this analysis have been distinctively developed by Gilroy (cf. 1987; 1993).

3 **Racism and Parliamentary Discourse (I): 1957-68**

1 This period of examination is not meant to indicate inclusivity of claims for the emergence of the idea of 'race' within Parliamentary Debates; other studies show quite clearly its provenance to exchanges from the early 1950s, cf. Miles and Phizacklea (1984). Rather the study examines this period in detail in order to trace the formation of official/public language leading up to the 1961 Bill.

2 Such statements are made on the basis of the critique we presented in chapter 1, concerning the important contribution of Reeves (1983).

3 This point refers to the contradictory elements found within our exploration of the thesis in chapter 2.

4 Here we suggest that idea, presented in the chapter I, that racism exists within British society as a popular discourse that is composed of a finite number of elements that reflect and record the various discourses of the Other that have characterised, historically the relations between the English and their colonial and imperial 'subjects'. What defines this discourse is its provenance within a biological-reductionism, despite the fact that it now takes many forms.

5 In fact the claim made in the 1961 Debate was for the Bill as a 'colour bar' that would enshrine and reflect colour prejudice. See below.

6 Although it should be emphasised that, as chapter 2 has demonstrated, such an idea is quite vague and imprecise and is not, as it stands, operationalizable as far as detailed research goes; the existence of the concept is shadowy and it certainly cannot act as a comparative variable in any kind of model at present.

7 The difficulty with this judgement is that it is confirmation of one element and not all elements composing the complex interplay that emerges within the produced legislation of the 1961 Bill. Many currents are at work here, not least of which is a secret or covert construction and, ad hoc implementation, of sentiments and judgements amounting to a full blown advocacy of controls which can be teased out of Cabinet committee and working party papers from the late 1940s, as recent radical scholars, such as Carter, Joshi (1984) and Harris (1987) have shown. This work is an important correlative to the ideological construction of the period leading to legislation as one of *laissez faire* which many blame Deakin for (IRR 1969; 1970) but which was, let us remember, also shared by radical black writers like A. Sivanandan (cf. 1976; 1982: passim).

8 The backbench populists referred to here are the group of 'race realists' we identified in the introduction: Osborne, Gurden, Pannell, etc.

9   As our comments above, note 7, must indicate such scholarly work is of paramount importance in the developing history of this period (for a summary of the uses to which such work can be put see Solomos 1989). Its impact can already be gauged by the screening of the BBC2 programme 'Britain's Post war immigration Policy: Racism or Realism?' *Time Watch* 5th April 1994.

10 At the very least we have here (to employ unfashionable Althusserian language) two temporal levels unfolding according to their own inner dynamic, whose historical interplay needs to be documented and worked through. This is both a theoretical observation and a methodological principle of investigation. It is such a task that should most appropriately employ, in addition to a political economy framework, 'discourse analysis'.

11 Powell, for example, exercises specific effects upon the latter Bills in Committee stage, particularly the 1971 Bill. See chapters 5 and 6 for discussion of this point.

12 This point will be developed further below.

13 The ideological themes structuring the 1961 Debate were derived as generalised because they were significantly dispersed within the overall text, having multiple entries within the detailed content analysis conducted. Although the detailed textual analysis in this chapter employs a conventional parenthetical reference, it's validity claims rest upon the cumulative detail of the 'close reading' achieved and the textual exposition made of this detail.

14 Here we are referring to the idea of the 'Public Sphere' wherein theorists have identified a *public discourse of 'race'* without really specifying how, and by means of which channels, it has become possible and how it has been reproduced and sustained. Evidently it is constructed by media technologies and narratives but the literature on the construction of media racism is not able to provide a sufficient rationale for the construction and reproduction of this sphere (cf. Hartmann and Husband 1974; Hall 1978; 1981). For a bibliography see Downing (1985). van Dijk's recent work (1988; 1990) attempts to argue for a general model of the reproduction of elite racial discourse.

15 While chapter 4 will cover aspects of the Debates taking place in 1968; 1969; 1971; 1973; 1976; 1979; 1980; 1981; 1983; 1985 and 1987.

16 Although obviously the division of debates by chapter means that different aspects of the debate about Powellism and the NR will be dealt with. This chapter will concentrate on beginning to suggest the extent of the evidence of the conceptual connection of classic Powell, 1968-74, to the earlier language and presentation of the 'race' populists. Obviously this contestation will follow on from the leading arguments of this chapter to the effect that the language of debate is explicitly racist and that the continuity of this language, as it transmutates from backbench to front, is clearly evident.

288 *Political Languages of Race and the Politics of Exclusion*

17   Eugenicist discourse can be found in prior parliamentary debates, such as that of the 1905 Aliens Restriction Bill, cf. Gainer 1972. For a discussion of the significance of the Eugenicist project, in terms of its social class basis and the wider continuity of discourse of 'social-biology' and as a Society for Social and Political Reform within Britain, see the excellent Mazumdar (1992), esp. Intr. & Ch.1.

18   These sources are good on mapping the context of the debate but their coverage of the content of the debate exemplifies my criticism above.

19   As further analysis will substantiate this is a central, if not *the* central ideological-motif of Immigration Debates over a period of thirty years.

20   There is an argument for continuity of imagery and mobilisation of political language concerning Central European refugees, particularly in British Conservative discourse over this issue (cf. *Guardian*, Winter 1992). Unfortunately we cannot pursue this point further here.

21   i.e., such a field of ideologically-significatory discourses are well established as the bedrock of debate, as our analysis of the debates in the period 1957-61 will substantiate. A substantive source of imagery which confirms this 'reading' is the *IRR: Newsletter's* coverage of national and provincial press reporting, 1960-9. Segal (1967) is good on the contrast between local and national coverage. The standard source is, of course, Hartmann and Husband (1974) but this study is dominated by Powellism.

22   It may be the case that Powell, 'on race', *came from nowhere* but Powellism, as we shall show, did not.

23   One of the key questions of the 'biography as explanation' school of thinkers on Powell is why the long period of silence on Immigration, considering that it was the 'principle if not the only local issue of importance', as Powell later argued? After all, it is well know that Cyril Osborne invited Powell to join his anti-immigration pressure group early on but Powell kept his distance. Foot cites Powell as suggesting that 'race' was 'a monkey to caught more softly' meaning that it was only through legislative changes in citizenship that progress could be made. The idea that nationality and citizenship are central to Powell's thinking on 'race' is one deserving of consideration but this alone does not explain the adoption of the political means Powell sought and the language he employed in the service of this project. It will be our argument in chapter 6 that this period of silence was a very important period of gestation of the language of Powellism and that such a language was one learned from the Conservative backbenchers during these debates.

24   See our discussion of the national-political impact of Smethwick in chapter 5 and, in particular, the extensive use of the neglected 1964 *Expiring Laws Debate*.

25   See chapters 4 and 6 for a discussion of the basis upon which, as this quotation indicates, the 1981 *Nationality Bill Debate* could be as viewed as an Immigration Bill by another name.

26   See for example tabloid press construction of the 1987 Visa Panic (*Sun, Mail, Express and Star*, October 15, 16th 1986).

27   This argument is elaborated in chapter 4 and 6, passim.

28   This theme occurs in Powell's speeches at Deal and Birmingham in 1968 and is, as we shall argue in chapter 6, integral to an understanding of the dynamics and significance of Powellism as a political force.

29   It is Hall et al (1978) who quote Fanon to the effect that every dominant class or group finds in the substance of its inferiors the stuff of nightmares.

30   In point of fact this is a peculiarly 'English' racism in the tone and the language employed, particularly in the context of the city and the imagery of squalor, overcrowding and moral turpitude which characterises so much social authoritarian commentary on the 'racial' poor, including, surprisingly perhaps, Engels:

> The Milesian deposits all garbage and filth before his house door here, as he was accustomed to do at home, and so accumulates the pools and dirt-heaps which disfigures the working people's quarters and poison the air[...]At home in his mud-cabin there was only one room for all domestic purposes; more than one room his family does not need in England. So the custom of crowding many persons into a single room, now so universal, has been chiefly implanted by the Irish immigration (F.W.Engels, *The Conditions of the Working Class in England* (English ed. 1892); Hobsbawm, 1982: 124; see also, pp. 122-5).

31   The thematic continuity to the discourse of Powellism is surely unmistakable here. Such observations form the basis of my argument, conducted in chapter 6, to the effect that Powellism is an 'old racism' in terms of a demonstrable continuity of shared metaphors; imaginary worlds realised through a defended and shared language of 'race' and culture.

32   This suggests, qua the New Racism Debate, that 'race' is likely to be expressed as a social imaginary and that this usage is closely intertwined with a biologically informed class discourse of social inferiority. Thus 'race' significations are coded according to political climates and tactics (cf. Edgar 1981). This would be a much more reasonable position for the NR theorists to take.

33   In this regard see also my critical appraisal of Gilroy's (1987) arguments concerning the periodization of this conceptual shift in discursive imagery and its relationship to the formation and success of a politics of anti-immigration in chapters 4 and 6. In fact Gilroy's argument about the significance of Powellism very largely turns on a

shift in the terms of legality as a privileged metaphor for nationhood. I contest this argument elsewhere.

34   I follow Layton-Henry (1992: 73) in identifying the member for Accrington as Harry Hyne and not, as Hansard records, Hynd. The confusion is with the member for Attercliffe, Mr. John Hynd, also a Labour backbench restrictionist.

35   Of course this is exactly the kind of unsubstantiated reasoning that Butler produces in the 1961 Debate!

36   The effectiveness of such claims did not go unnoticed by tabloid editors, one of the most infamous of these is the *Daily Express* headline 'A Million Chinese Can Arrive Here Next Week If They Want To' (cited in Seymour-Ure 1974: 118).

37   However it is much too convenient to dismiss these early interventions as transparently racist. Certainly the core is composed of the old racism. But the structure of these debates is more subtle and complex than this sort of blanket description allows in positing a point of break or transition in what appears a complex field of change and continuity, within the inter-discursive context of debates and press and media coverage. A specific textual contestation will be made of the argument of Gilroy and Barker in chapters 4 and 6.

38   The imputation of 'racial hygiene' propels the association forward (cf. Rose 1982); although it is perhaps more appropriate, in the British context, to locate the discourse of the unfit within the Eugenics movement and the class discourse of the problem of pauperism and class differential fertility (cf. Mazumador 1994).

39   This is the problem identified in the analysis of the NR by Barker but, as we can see, this conceptual dilemma is one that can be extended backwards through successive debates in the postwar period. The point most pertinent here is that generalisations should not be made on limited empirical data.

40   A particular perverse example of this practice of spurious quotation is that of Harold Gurden's (Osborne's chief ally in the 1961 Debate) exposure of 'letter' sent 'to the editor of the Trinidad Guardian' 'by a West Indian' (Bally Seer, from Port-of-Spain, c.741) which is quoted as follows:

> We are very clever at diplomacy. We extract millions of dollars from Britain and America and we don't even have to show appreciation. We are 'independent' now[...]we get our schooling and technical know-how from Britain, Canada and America, yet we are anti-British and anti-American. We breed like flies, and don't have to bother with marriage and responsibility for the kids. We send thousand of our offspring to Britain; mostly unskilled and many criminals. Britain takes them all without restriction, we expect her to take them. We don't want her people here[...]We send fruit and other produce to Britain and get better prices than other countries. When we want something more, we yell 'Colonialism', 'Imperialism' and threaten Communism. We blow a lot of froth about ancient

slavery and exploitation and of our working people, and they cheer us. We send out ministers (loaded with spending money) all over the world to mix and talk with important statesman and they return puffed up with good ideas which they call their own. We have a 'culture' to sell to the world. Our people make a hell of racket on oil drums and beat lumps of iron. We concoct what we call Calypsos which many people consider utter drivel and often dirty[...]Britain is our 'sucker' and we do not expect her to join any Common Market or in any way help herself (to help us more). We want the British people to take on double austerity at this time, while we keep our high salaries and comforts[...]We are anti-everything European and don't want those foreigners to come here unless they are very rich (*Commonwealth Immigrants Bill*, 16 November 1961; c.740-1).

Gurden's justification for this 'quotation' is to assert: 'I have been challenged, but the opinions I have expressed are nothing like as severe as those expressed by this coloured person.' (c.741). It appears to slip the conceptual logic of the presentation of his case that such a letter is itself constructed to support the very view he wishes it to reflect upon; like Powell's letter, a document is used as evidence of an underlying 'reality' to which it supposedly gives us access. Yet such a reality is pre-given and requires no work to give it life. The hunch that such a letter is a fabrication as Powell's little old ladies' is perhaps to miss the point that what should be focused on here are the materials that allow the construction of a post-colonial racial narrative which is able to re-position the ex-colonial powers as no longer obligated or connected to their former satellites. This is the central element of the narrative of Powell, Osborne and most of the 'race' populists alike.

41   See the use of this metaphor as a symbolic encapsulation of the discourse of anti-immigration within Parliamentary Debates by Miles and Phizacklea, *White Man's Country* (1984; passim).

42   How different is this 'old' racist sentiment to that of the NR of Palmer (ed) (1986); Scruton, Honeyford, etc.?; or indeed, 1980s Powellism?

43   Again, another discursive feature thought to be exclusive to the transformation in terms wrought by Powellism.

44   As I pointed out in note 34 the Member for Accrington was Mr. H. Hyne, not Hynd, as Hornsby-Smith attributes here. Mr. Hyne is also the MP who could, without fear of fact or fairness, assert: 'Is the hon. Gentlemen aware that many Pakistanis get out of their country by saying that they are going on a pilgrimage to Mecca but that the pilgrimage finishes in this country'? (*Oral Answers: Business of the House, India & Pakistan*, 15 May 1958: c.612).

4   Racism and Parliamentary Discourse (II): 1968-88

1   See the preface and especially chapter 3.

2   This claim will be examined, as it specifically relates to Powellism rather than the New Racism (NR), in chapter 6. Obviously, as we established in chapter 2, both Barker, Gilroy and the CCCS collective subsume Powellism within the NR, although not in quite the same way or to the same extent.

3   The book referred to is, of course, *The New Racism* (1981).

4   The question of a biological justificatory argument is not dealt with in this chapter. Again this issue is central to the examination of the NR thesis *as theory*, in chapter 2; and to the question of whether Powellism is a racism, in chapter 6.

5   Despite this claim, Gilroy does not in fact apply this rigour to his own analysis of Powell, confining his attentions to the April 1968, 'Rivers of Blood' speech (1987: 85-8).

6   Race Relations Debates, resulting in the *1976 Race Relations Act*, took place on 4th March *(Hansard, vol.906, Feb.23 - March 5th: c.1547 - 1670)* and 8th July, 1976 *(Hansard vol.914, June 28th - July 8th, 1975-6; c.1627-1968)*.

7   The debates in question are: *British Nationality Bill - Second Reading, January 28 1981, cols. 935-1047 (Hansard) Fifth Series, vol.997)*; *British Nationality Bill (Committee), 2 June 1981, cols. 795-898 (Sixth series, vol 5)*; *British Nationality Bill (Committee), 3 June 1981, cols. 931-1028 (Sixth series, vol.5)* and *British Nationality Bill (Committee), 4 June 1981, cols. 1091-1194 (Sixth Series, vol.,5)*.

8   Despite Powell's April and November speeches, and their tremendous impact on the 1968 Race Relations Debate and the political agenda, Powell does not enter into official debate until the winter of 1969, during an Expiring Laws Debate.

9   The Debates in question are those taking place prior to 1976, i.e. 1968, 1971, 1973; and those after, 1979, 1980, 1981 and 1983.

10 See below and chapter 6.

11 It is self-evident that Powell's ability to frame and direct legislation is severely curtailed after his exit from the Conservative Shadow Cabinet, despite the fact that it is only this moment that allows the political formation of the constituency able to respond to a populist politics of 'race'. And, arguably, Powell's role in the 1970 Election campaign, which gives the Tories the chance to direct such populism towards legislation. For a fuller discussion of these points see chapter 6.

12 He makes a single interjection, and this in the form of the supply of a point of information. See below.

13 As we established in chapter 2, it is this claim that distinguishes the NR thesis: that *since 1968 there has been a transformation in the conceptual logic of Parliamentary language on Immigration and Race Relations*.

14 Bell's consistent resistance to any kind of Race Relations legislation is a philosophical contestation of the negative, as opposed to positive, value of the term 'discrimination' which Bell, in anticipation of the newer 'New Right', lauds as the height of the culturally civilised and English. To discriminate is to make a value judgement i.e., to mobilise values. See below.

15 *Political and Economic Planning* (PEP) carried out extensive surveys of the level and kind of discrimination occurring in Britain in the periods, 1966-7, resulting in the publication of the first report, W.W. Daniel (1968) *Racial Discrimination in England*. The evidence from this survey certainly influenced Labour's drafting of the 1968 *Race Relations Bill*, despite the draconian Kenyan Asians Bill. The second PEP survey took place in the period, 1972-5 and culminated in the publication of a Government White Paper on discrimination in 1975. The subsequent Race Relations Bill was published on 3rd February 1976 (cf. Layton-Henry 1992: ch.3).

16 See the astoundingly pragmatic recording of this quotation by Layton-Henry (1992: 36) as evidence of political 'tolerance'.

17 The defence of the English is a key definer of the 'black country' 'race' populists. See, for example, the detailed analysis of 1961 Commonwealth Immigrants Bill Debate in chapter 3. The discursive construction of the 'folk-archetype' the 'Forgotten Englishman' is a key feature of continuity in the debates of the late 1950s, early sixties and seventies. This 'fundamentalist' conception is common to debates taking place in 1958, 1959,1960 and 1961 (see for example, chapter 3); as it is to the discourse of, for example, John Stokes in debates taking place in 1976 and 1981. See below.

18 I have deliberately paraphrased Whitelaw's argument as cited by Barker from the *Immigration Debate* of the 7th, 'Many genuine people, entirely free from any racial prejudice, want reassurance' (c.971; cited in Barker 1981: 14).

19 For a full exploration of this point see chapter 6.

20 See the discussion in chapter 2.

21 Although this concept is situated within an analysis of the 1960s, initially by Cohen (1973), and describes the construction and uses of contemporary 'youth' folk devils; extended by Hall et al to the racialising of 'mugging' (Hall et al 1978). However it seems legitimate to apply this concept *retrospectively*, (as Barker does, over another issue: Screen violence), for the late 1950s (cf. Barker (ed) 1984).

22 This concept belongs to another Debate entirely and one which Barker has twice made a decisive public intervention into cf. 1984 (ed) and the *BBC2 Late Show*, May 1994.

23 This is consistent with our discussion of the evidence of elite acceptance of the underlying racist logic of the social construction of the Immigration 'problem', in the

late 1950s and early 1960s. See the discussion of this in chapter 3 and the idea of the gradual emergence of a public language of 'race' within Official Debates.

24 Actually Powell does speak in the Immigration Debate, by providing a point of information, see below. But beyond this his role is formally 'silent' but influential. Barker, of course, is curiously silent about this. Powell's glowering 'silence' in the face of the effects of Powellism in the press and media confirms our point that, of the three Debates taking place during this year, the March and July *Race Relations Debates* are the most significant. Powell's active contribution to these are a confirmation of this.

25 This speech is another very good example of what is central to the argument for Powellism as a racism: the way in which it is able to refer to existing racial imagery and ideas and to articulate such ideologies within an inferential and symbolic narrative of racial crisis. See my discussion of this point within the argument that *'Powellism is an (old) racism'*, chapter 6.

26 It has been a consistent element of Powellism as well as the 'new' and 'old' right that a person, thoroughly absorbed, could 'pass' as English but only if the number of such is very limited. See, in particular, the anecdotal formulation of this argument by Harvey Proctor in the 1981 Debate below (*cf. British Nationality Bill, Second Reading, 28 January 1981; col. 999*).

27 Solomos, a more circumspect user of the concept, identifies two prominent themes within Powellism, (i) the rapid-growth of the black population and (ii) the threat such a magnitude of aliens poses to the unity or homogeneity of the social and cultural fabric of British society (cf. 1989: 124). The first is evidently, biological; the second, cultural. Importantly perhaps historical analysis of ideology shows that cultural exclusionary discourse, in the service of protecting the Nation, is a characteristic of the 'old' right, between the wars (cf. Weber 1986).

28 That is they are silent about the direct thread of continuity to biologistic politics contained within this metaphor. Such an insight is passed over in a superficial treatment of a conceptual transition in Barker, between the biological and the pseudo biological-cultural; and in Gilroy, the quantitative and the qualitative. But see chapter 6 for a fuller discussion of this point.

29 See the absurd return to the 'numbers game' in Powell's preface to Russell Lewis' (1988) critique of: *'Anti-racism: a mania exposed'*!

30 For comparison see Lawrence 1982; and Gilroy 1987: 45.

31 The point of disputation is whether this language is 'new' or relies on the 'old' to 'motivate' its effect?

32 For an argument about the periodization of Powellism see chapter 6.

33   For a discussion of the impact of Ulster politics on Powell's 'Ideological Imaginary' see chapter 6.

34   Repatriation is not a distinctively new claim and the degree to which it rests upon (new racist) cultural incompatibility is debatable. See chapter 6.

35   It is my argument, in chapter 3, that this theme is the dominant one throughout the late 1950s and early 1960s and its centrality remains evident right up to the 1981 Nationality Debate.

36   Solomos (1990) makes an ambiguous argument about shifts in the NR. However, these claims are based on an acceptance of the ascendancy of the cultural argument. Such a position still side-steps the question of what the claim for the NR amounts to. As chapter 6 makes clear, it is the conceptual relationship to the 'old racism', within political language narratives, which is of crucial importance; and it is this that provides the greatest difficulty to the new cultural theorists. As for the specific content of speeches in support of new 'racial' realism, there is, in the detail of prior Parliamentary Debates, ample evidence to show this not to be a new phenomenon. See for example, Patterson's (1969) discussion of the pressure exerted on Labour by the Conservatives in the 1964-6 period, under the slogan 'one in - one out' and the need to create the right climate of trust for those most affected, i.e. the Forgotten Englishman.

37   'Race' has certainly been a key theme in the 'New Right' assault upon those institutions that have been seen as under the ideological grip of the ('new') Left: Education, Local Government and Labour Politics. An historical alliance forged between Liberal anti-racism and Marxism in the 1970s has been seen as a specific focus of attack, where anti-racism has become a Marxist encrypted witch hunt; a sort of surrogate for a failed revolution among the rest of the proletariat. See, in particular, the attack upon A. Sivanandan in Palmer (ed) 1986.

38   Language statements in support of *point of view* constitute reality signifying systems. It follows from our arguments in the preface that racial language usage is to be viewed in this way rather than as a species of irrationalism. This argument is developed throughout the book but its politics are best treated in chapters 1 and 5. See Wetherell and Potter's stimulating discussion of 'interpretative repertoires' (1992: 89-93) of which my phrase plagiarises.

39   A 'reading' of the IQ debate would do best to locate it within a contestation of the roots of differential achievement within structural social inequality. In this context hereditarian arguments abound and the issue is a perennial one for a pro-privilege faction of educational de-reformers. More recent episodes in the right-wing fundamentalist counter attack upon educational reform are referred to in the Palmer edited: *Anti-Racism: an assault on education and value* (1986). See also Rattansi (ed) (1992: 11-48) and Sarup (1986) for a Left response.

40   Again, it is a characteristic of New Right discourse to present complex social issues, for example, those involving racism, as simple morality dilemmas involving the issues of free choice and the right of individuals to discriminate. This ideological strategy has been largely successful in test cases involving the rejection of local school placements on racial grounds, where the forces of anti-racism are seen as a form of ideological tyranny 'against the people'. For example the story of 'Katrice' *(Daily Telegraph* 19th October 1991).

41   See the discussion of this example as part of a comparative analysis of the *content* of the 'new' and the 'old' racism in chapter 6.

42   As chapter 6 will show, Stoke's narrative style is one very dependent upon that of Powellism and that of populist newspaper editorial styles of the late 1970s. Chapter 6 traces the development and continuity of this narrative style and its prominence within debates taking place in 1958, 1959, 1960 and 1961; and the similarity of such to the content of backbench contributions by Stokes & Co. in 1976, 1981, etc.

43   See the tracing of this theme, particularly within the innovative and formative contributions of 'race' populist, (Sir) Cyril Osborne, in chapter 3.

44   It is a truism of sorts to say that 'race' is no longer explicitly mentioned and, of course, this is a distinguishing characteristic of the NR; however (i) this is not strictly true as, for example, in the previous referred example of the relationship of Stokes to Osborne; not only do both theorists anchor their concerns within the ideological Englishman and the protection of the character of England but also they define that community as a 'race' and contrast it with the blacks as a different 'race' with different culture and customs, particularly religious practices. See below for quotations in this respect; and, (ii) although there is a shift away from a Eugenicist discourse that characterises the late 1950s debates, as chapter 3 has shown, especially in terms of the idea of breeding, it is not true to characterise the early debates as explicitly employing the term 'race' since all postwar debates exhibit the language taboo of 'race'; and this is the central characteristic of Parliamentary Debates about 'race' in the postwar period, as we have tried to argue throughout.

45   It is relevant to mention that some NR writers explicitly foreground the slide to old racism as characteristic of the NR, for example, Seidel (1986); while CCCS: Race and Politics (1982) point to the inability of the self styled 'new racists' to maintain the language of the new, i.e. they slip into the old. Barker tends to maintain the idea that the slide is made by the receptors of the discourse; while politicians, when challenged, tend to slide in the opposite direction, i.e. to closure. These ideas are very similar to Reeves' 'sanitary coding' (1983). What is central to the language transformation claims is the replacement of 'race' with 'nation'. This issue is best taken up in chapter 6, but it is interesting that arguments for the subsumption of racism within nationalism (Nairn 1970; Hall 1978 et al and Barker 1981) suppress, in practice, the specificity of racism (Nairn 1970; Hall 1978) or nationalism itself (Barker 1981). Interestingly, in contesting Anderson's (1983: 136) separation of the content and 'intent' of racism and nationalism, Gilroy argues for the 'simultaneous

Notes 297

biological and cultural' character of British racism (1987: 45). It is not clear how this assertion sits in relation to the claim for the 'linguistic' emergence of a 'new (cultural) racism' (op cit, 85-90); or in what ways it can be claimed that the 1981 Nationality Bill can therefore be the corollary of this 'conceptual shift'. This slippage is reproduced by Anthias and Yuval-Davis (1992: 45, 57) in their treatment of the comparative claims of Barker, Gilroy and Miles over the character of the new/old racism. But see chapters 2 and 6.

46   For a discussion of this (racist) Commons' sense as central to the analysis of 'political racism', see chapter 5.

47   The Committee sat on the 8th July, 1976. See note 6. above.

48   Press cuttings from the period show a massive exposure of the issue and Powell's leaking of the report is a media 'event'. Also there are ample references to this 'climate' and the report within debates.

49   There quite simply is a lack of empirical support for the notion of a conceptual 'break' involving the emergence of a NR distinctive from that of the 'old'.

50   See the introduction to chapter 3.

51   The relationship between (ideologies of) 'race' and vote is not a simple one and yet it has been treated as such or ignored by the vast majority of psephologist and sociologists of politics (cf. Solomos, 1986). But see the recent discussion of this by Smith (1994) in terms of 'hegemony theory' and the idea of 'normalization' achieved through 're-coding'.

52   See the contributions of those Labour members who contested the 1961 Bill. References in chapter 3.

53   The 1994 Conference is a case in point, where a beleaguered Tory party at the polls allowed the venomous right to offer up a gamut of 'folk devils' for the assembled to bay for blood and to hail a 'back to basics' philosophy.

54   See, in particular, chapter 3, where the 'idle', 'unfit' and 'unemployable' *dregs of the Commonwealth* press in ever greater numbers at ports of entry.

55   For a discussion of these episodes of 'moral panic' see, for example, Hartmann and Husband (1974) and Braham (1982).

56   cf. Layton-Henry, (1992: 56-61) for an analysis of the impact of the second PEP report upon Labour in this period. See also note 12 above.

57   This phenomenon I define as a species of 'political racism', the genealogy of which is explored in chapter 5.

58 Chapter 1 suggested the strong historical, political and conceptual relationship between racism and prejudice and the impact on political analysis of racism as (i) a species of individual irrationalism likely to reside in (ii) those of an authoritarian personality and (iii) the socially inferior. This argument must be fully developed elsewhere.

59 This clear conceptual division blurs in practice between Labour populists, who share a more broadly Tory view and Tory liberals who share a more Labour view. See more detailed discussion of this in chapter 5.

60 See my argument in chapter 3 that it is the establishment of these central, iconic themes and significations by the peripheral 'race' populists that establishes the conceptual larder upon which, increasingly, the centre and Front bench will draw as 'race' passes into the mainstream language of Parliamentary Debate. This transformation of 'race' signification is necessary given the postwar context of debate and absolutely dependent upon the ideological work achieved by this small group of activists.

61 See chapter 6 for detailed discussion of Powell's contribution to this debate and the elements of difference with Tory backbench Powellites.

62 Labour are usually more eager to contest racism within legislation when in opposition. When in power they have produced some of the most stringent and restrictionist measures of any government in Western Europe. But see the analysis in chapter 5.

63 The Liberals are also of the belief that a non-racist Nationality Bill is possible, one that should involve 'a positive assertion of what nationality and citizenship mean' (Mr.David Steel, c.958).

64 This is somewhat of an exaggeration because the theme of numbers like 'race' is never far from the surface of backbench Tory support not to bob up above the ideological water line, as for example, Ivor Stanbrook (cf. C. 983, 984-5) mentions both in his contribution to the debate in the midst of an apparent display of the virtues of the NR.

65 A more detailed textual analysis of the content of these speeches is conducted in chapter 6.

66 This view of nationality is decidedly of the old kind and very much part of Powell's thinking. Such a view is reconfirmed in Powell's collections of essays on Church, Morality and State in *No Easy Answers* (1973b) and *Wrestling with the Angel* (1977). See chapter 6 for a discussion of the content and significance of these 'sermons'.

67 See note 16 above.

68   As we have already argued, if what is revealed in such a slippage is the notion of the 'old racism' then the NR is not as new as it is claimed to be. See in particular Seidel in Levitas (ed) 1986); as well as on right-Gramscism and the relationship of Powell to the Scruton lead 'authoritarians'.

69   Harold Gurden, MP for the Birmingham constituency of Halesowen, provided the essential ideological basis for the appeal on behalf of the local area and inhabitants 'most affected'. See chapter 3 for detailed coverage of the content of Gurden's speeches.

5   Smethwick and the Rise of a 'Political Racism'

1   The discourse surrounding the idea of 'playing the 'race' card needs much more detailed textual analysis of, in particular, party elite debate and the conception of the power of 'race' discourse than we can fully engage with here. However, see the development of this area below.

2   See the sections on Race Politics below.

3   Media research tends to suggest that in the early sixties it was local press coverage which anticipated the populist 'race' language style of the national tabloids in the 1970s. In the late fifties and early sixties the majority of 'race' coverage occurred in the colonial/de-colonisation context (cf. Segal 1967; IRR 'newsletter', 1960-9; Hartmann and Husband 1974). This area needs a great deal more research but it is evident that the binary thematics of the early politics of 'race' localism, an intense concatenation upon the local of the 'old' language and concerns of empire and Africa, is consistent with existing reporting categories and editorial policies.

4   This is what a 'close reading' of Foot delivers, despite the fact that Foot does not offer this category of the 'social imaginary' which I derive from the writings of Cornelius Castoriadis (cf. Thompson 1984: ch1). The theoretical issues informing the role of racism as a projected social imaginary are explored in chapter 6.

5   The evidence of the Griffith's campaign clearly shows the very close conceptual connections to the 'old racist' discourse of Gurden, Pannell and Osborne.

6   This economic rationalist discourse was one derived from Gaitskell and Gordon-Walkers' principled defence of the market mechanism regulating the level of immigration into the economy. In the context of dealing with the intertwining of 'race' and the social problem discourse of the inner city the term 'Urban blight' is Labour's preferred explanation. For a discussion of the development of this term as reflective of Labour's ineffective and contradictory understanding of the politics of the racialised inner city, under Wilson, see Wilson (1971; Benn 1987; Crossman 1975; Rex 1977).

7   A content analysis of the ten year period covered in the 'Newsletter', (1960-9) reveals the widespread usage of this 'race' vocabulary. 'Race' is variously said to 'simmer', 'spread' 'infect', etc.

8   It has been our previous argument, in chapter 1, that anti-racism is one side of a 'race' discourse that is both 'race'-positive and 'race'-negative. We will develop this concept as it relates to the debate about the language and politics of Smethwick, although the connections to be made to the debate about the decline of anti-racism as a political project must remain mute.

9   The speeches made during this period are some of the most infamous and vivid in British political history, including his Birmingham 'river Tiber' speech, Eastbourne 'toad beneath the harrow' follow up and the 1970 Election 'enemies within' doom and thunder at Northfield. These speeches and their language, as well as the considerable number of 'numbers' game' speeches from this period are analysed in detail in chapter 6. See also the debate about the periodization of Powellism in chapter 6.

10 Despite the fact that the reasons for this and the character of the elite are different in the accounts offered. As for example Studlar (1980) argues that populism by the elite over a non-party issue has allowed a politics of 'race' to be managed which does not damage major party interests; the elite has acquiesced to popular appeals. Whereas Bulpitt (1986) argues that the marginalisation of 'race' away from the political agenda is due to the 'state craft' of the elite who have kept the issue at a distance and thereby controlled its populist potential. This echoes the arguments of Katznelson's (1976) 'buffer institutions' thesis, where colonial style quangos are employed to keep 'race' away from mainstream debate and legislation.

11 The theoretical elements and discussion surrounding a discourse theoretical approach to this area have already been outlined in the preface, and within the discussion in chapter 1, and will not be repeated here.

12 See note 8.

13 The Survey, 'a sort of unofficial national commission' into the empirical detail and impact of immigration into British society, was conceived on the scale and purpose as that produced by G. Mydral's 'An American Dilemma' (1944).

14 This is quite clearly the discourse of the 'race' card and offers us an implicit theory of the relationship between politicians and their electorate into which nasty racism intrudes. This discourse will be revealed as we examine its discursive proliferation within, particularly, the internal party discourse of Labour.

15 For the argument that Powellism is most clearly defined in terms of the political relationship it endorses and extends see chapter 6.

16 Let us not also forget Labour 'race' rebels and populists who are quite active in the early formation of this tendency within British politics. This fact is now

acknowledged by commentators such as Layton-Henry (1992); see the preface and chapter 1.

17 In fact, of course, Powell does exactly that; being careful to place in parenthesis the racist and colonial 'isms' such as 'the blackman will have the whip hand over the white', 'grinning piccaninnies' who 'no only one word of English', 'racialist', etc. On top of this proletarian substructure Powell builds an elaborate superstructure of nationhood, belonging and cultural exclusionism. But it is held in place by the articulation of working class racism at the most basic level of received imagery of 'the blacks'. See chapter 6 for an exploration of this argument and its connection to the other aspects of Powellism.

18 For this concept see Note 6.

19 See especially the debate contributions discussed in chapter 3.

20 The Warwick based research into public records, referred to in the preface and chapter 1, clearly indicates what a number of scholars had already suspected: that right from the outset, the political elite viewed immigration from the commonwealth as 'unwelcome' and 'to be discouraged' because of the 'stock' of the people coming into Britain and because of their 'cultural incompatibility' and the 'race relations' problems that would ensue from their 'presence' (cf. Johshi and Carter 1984; and Harris 1987).

21 As we may recall, Barker (1981) argues that Griffiths' discourse is halfway between the 'old' and the 'new' racism. See this argument in chapter 3 and its critique in chapter 6.

22 As far as I am aware a history of Left Anti-racism has yet to be written, although a number of acerbic caricatures in semi-academic, academic and tabloid variety have appeared in the 1980s (cf. Brown 1984; Flew (ed) 1984a; 1984b).

23 Foot (1965) characterises these three as part of Labour's rotten centre; who, in alliance with the (racist) populist right wing, Tomney, etc., carried the vote for anti-immigration after the demise of Gaitskell.

24 And apparently in the 1990s, a terminal decline?

25 See the analysis of Sivanandan (1985a); Gilroy (1987b); and Donald and Rattansi (eds)(1992). Anti-racism, post-Honeyford and Dewsbury, and more recently, Rushdie, cannot entertain simplistic formulas. An effective engagement with racism must involve an engagement with racial language and the appeal of racist consciousness and conversational idioms. The Ridley affair surely reaffirms this? Here there is a marked correspondence between senior cabinet Minster and the sentiments of 'the people'.

26 See the discussion of Spearman's study in chapter 2.

27 I am certain Barker would claim this as an instance of the 'new racism' but in terms of the analysis we have presented it very definitely forms part of the developing discourse of 'race' negative and 'race' positive language of political debate.

28 See the discussion of this in chapter 6.

29 As we have seen, this was Gaitskell and Gordon-Walkers' position: immigrant labour 'supply' was always a perfect market response to labour demand.

30 *The Sun* has consistently run a poll in support of various Private Member's Bills to re-introduce capital punishment.

6 Enoch's Island: Race, Nation and Authoritarianism in the Language and Politics of Popular Powellism

1 It is surely indisputable that the 'idea of Empire' and of the shift in the meaning of this in the politics and thought of Powellism is absolutely central to the diagnosis of Powellism as species of political ideology. See especially Foot (1969). For an inspirational 'cultural' and political critique of Powellism, along these lines, see Nairn 1970; 1973; 1981.

2 We have already explored at some depth the character and personnel of the populists, both Tory and Labour in chapters 1 and 3.

3 Nairn's sources are extensive and historical; most importantly he looks at Powell's 'other' speeches, i.e. not just the one or two (in)famous ones.

4 But see also Powell's very self-conscious sermons on Patriotism, War and Christianity, etc. in *No Easy Answers* (1973b) and *Wrestling With The Angel* (1977).

5 Although echoes of this discourse remain in key speeches. The most obvious usage here is the imagery and language of the April 1968 speech: whiphand, piccaninnies, etc. But it also creeps into more recent speeches, as for example, Powell's objection to the social usage of the term 'black', by an appeal to the idea that it would be abhorrent 'to anyone who has served in India.' This social imagery and 'structure of feeling' is absolutely central to Powell's personal and political formation.

6 Schoen's (1977) impressive analysis of voting data patterns appears to confirm this. See also Johnson and Schoen (1976).

7 Here is the locus of Powell's authoritarianism, which surfaces most pointedly in his contributions to the *Nationality Bill Debate* 1981, and is a key component of Powellism, as we shall show.

8 The ideology of the forgotten Englishman was discussed in chapter 4 and is brought to a thematic conclusion here.

9   This 'boy's own' adventure story of expansion and exportation of Englishness across the globe, is central to Powell as an ideologue, see below: (b) Powellism is Patriotism and (c) Powellism is a Conservative Institutionalism.

10 This is Powell's last Ministerial Portfolio before his ejection from the Shadow Cabinet. The ejection itself comes at the point of culmination of a period of very critical speeches being delivered by Powell, particularly on defence. A subsidiary question here, covered by Utley, is why Powell was given the shadow defence brief during this period given his 'radical views' on the need to reduce military capability in line with a Little England policy?

11 I owe an off the cuff remark to the effect of whether there could be a Powellism without Powell, to Harry Goulbourne, who I met very briefly at the ESRC Unit at Warwick in the winter of 1987.

12 It has become a legend that Powell spoke of 'rivers' of blood rather than 'the river Tiber foaming with much blood' in the same way that people misquote certain popularised lines from Shakespeare (the original of which remains unread) such as the 'graveyard scene' from Hamlet.

13 A number of commentators have pointed to the hypocrisy of Powell exposing the hidden racism of proposed Tory legislation. But although this appears inconsistent in one sense it is not in respect of (i) the style of logical exposition Powell believes he brings to his analysis and (ii) support for his overall strategic objective to push for legislation more likely to exclude than include, patrial or otherwise. See also chapter 1.

14 See the Guardian serialisation of the Benn Diaries which were edited apparently to highlight the 1970 clash with Powell and subsequent agreement over Europe. See also Benn (1979: ch.4).

15 The terms of this question cannot be pursued as far as examining the 'new right' and its specific connections to Powellism. Although aspects of this question are indicated as they are relevant to the argument of the book. Seidel (1986) and Deakin (ed) (1989) map some of these connections.

16 I am reminded of the covert behaviour of a previous Tory regime by Carter, Harris and Joshi (1984; 1987). It could be argued that these interventions are enough to qualify as state racism, but it is the lack of ideological commitment to racism that is most marked, when it is the attention to such ideological-formation that has characterised the claim for the ascendancy of the New Right and Thatcherism.

17 The phrase 'one of our nationalised industries' is an obvious and ironic signifier of a 'natural' Labour supporter. The incongruity of falling into conversation with 'one of these fellows' is wildly improbable and suggests, as Gilroy has noted, 'precise calculation'.

18 The linguistic, narrational and shared metaphors form an essential continuity here that links: Powell, Gurden, Osborne and Stokes, old right and new right; old racism and new.

19 Foot's (1969) biting satire on this stance reveals its specious logic,

> Let us suppose for a moment that an ordinary decent fellow-Englishman were to approach Powell in the streets of Wolverhampton and suggest to him that the capitalist system was so intolerable that Britain in a few years time would not be worth living in. Would Powell feel duty bound to retail that message to his next meeting?[...]The truth is that Powell would reject the man's complaint, because he disagrees with it (113).

20 Of course the idea that there is an inner essence is a peculiarly nationalist one, although there is disagreement about the ontological status of such imaginings (cf. Nairn 1981; Anderson 1983; Smith 1988; 1989).

21 Foot goes further in providing evidence, culled from the Fascist press, very formally resembling the structure and content of Powell's 'little old white lady' letter: 'Some elderly women were nearly in tears as they revealed how Indians were blocking drains with stagnant refuse, threatening them when they protested, urinating and excreting in the streets' *Southall Resident's Association* report in the BNP's *Combat*, Jan/March, 1964. And in the *National Socialist* we find the following 'survey' findings: 'Among the mass of evidence that has been put before us by white victims of these methods, we have for instance photographs showing human excreta deposited by blacks outside the door of a white woman's flat in London as part of a campaign to get rid of her' (cited in Foot 1969: 114-5).

22 Such accounts have been seized upon as evidence of the transformation in discourse. Again there is considerable evidence for continuity.

23 In other words, the achievement of Powellism has been to find ways and to innovate ways of suggesting that the missing factor in various social problem scenarios is the factor of 'race'. In this sense Powell has attempted to racialize social and political reality and to point to an 'end game' of racial civil war arising out of such analysis.

24 Exceptions to this blanket criticism are the work of Sykes (1985; 1988) and Kress (1983; 1985) and Trew (1985). However, while the theoretical and methodological approaches of such authors are exemplary as textual analysis, the material analysed remains limited and dated. See, for example, Sykes' analysis of Powell's 1968 speeches (1985); or in a related vein Kress & Trew's (1985) analysis of South African 'race riot' headlines.

25 We find ourselves returning to an instinctive idea of truth here; it is verified by the genuine instincts of the ordinary and the many; it is the typicality of a narrative that provides its proof claims not its empirical status.

26 Morley's most recent work is a good example of a pioneer project to place the question of reception at the centre of research into the politics of communication and is indicative of a shift in social theory currently away from textuality; a textuality exemplified in the work of Hall and others in offering theoretical insights into the politics of Conservative hegemony (cf. Hall 1988).

27 In this sense images and identities of 'race' and place, and time, are inscribed and interpolated between the material and the imaginary.

28 Such features make all the more remarkable the 'success' of Powell among lower middle class and working class electors (cf. Schoen 1977).

29 All pg. refs. to Powell's Walsall, Birmingham and Eastbourne speeches in this section, as well as the interview with David Frost, are to the compilation by Smithies and Fiddick (1969) rather than Powell's own *Freedom & Reality* (1969), because the former preserves the chronological sequence of the speeches as delivered, as well as providing a much better commentary and footnotes arising from points made and contested in the speeches.

30 See note 19.

31 In other words, old racism is signified via the new; visible momentarily and then disguised. Its meanings and associations are carried in the social and political usage as part of the relations of signification by which the history of 'race' has come to be recognised.

32 See chapter two.

33 'Phrenology', argues Peter Fryer (1984: 171), 'justified empire-building'.

34 We have already met the 'race populists' in chapter 3, who, of course do not all emanate from the Midlands.

35 cf. Hansard, General Index - Sessions, 1967-8, vol.771;1969-70, vol.802; 1971-2, vol.844; 1972-3, vol.862; 1973-4, vol.869; 1974-5, vol.900; 1975-6, vol.920; 1976-7, vol.937; 1978-9, vol.966; 1979-80, vol. 9930.

36 The evidence of the majority of Powell's supporters suggests an overwhelming utilisation of the language of the 'old racism' (cf. Spearman 1968).

37 For Powell this 'deeper' level is cultural. This historically ingrained, slow alchemy of cultural formation provides the fundamental difference between groups. To call this 'race' is to misunderstand its profundity. See below.

38 On the Frost show (1969) Powell rejects the idea of racial inferiority as a basis for policy or ethical considerations, as he had done earlier in his political career. For Foot (1969) Powell's turn to immigration control on the basis of cultural

incompatibility is a betrayal of these public principals; Powell has committed 'weasel words'. However, Foot is guilty of running the difference between culture and 'race' together; whereas in Powell it is their articulation and changing relationship that is important. See below.

39   The process of the gradual construction and emergence of a public language of 'race' occupied our analysis in chapters 3 and 4.

40   Mercer has gone as far as to suggest that race is a signifier without or in search of a signified (cf. 1990).

41   Metonymic substitution usually involves the substitution of a part for the whole. Thus if culture is a code for 'race' it can only be if the code exists as a component of a prior associative system of signification of 'race'. Metonymy is achieved through chains of signification. Therefore it may be that it is, on the contrary, not the 'new racism' that is drawn too wide but the 'old racism' that is drawn too narrowly?

42   In their commentary accompanying Powell's blockbuster speeches of 1968-70, Smithies and Fiddick admire Powell's ability to use 'English': 'Beneath the classical exterior lies a feeling for the guts of the English language that Aneurin Bevan himself would recognise' (Smithies and Fiddick 1969: 15).

43   'Integration without control is impossible, but control without integration is indefensible' (Hansard, vol.709, cols.378-85).

44   As will be recalled these are the central themes of the 1962 Immigration Control Bill, as presented by Butler and the Conservatives.

45   In fact Powell quotes this anecdote verbatim in his Eastbourne speech (cf. Smithies and Fiddick 1969: 68).

46   It is Stuart Hall who coins the phrase 'historical amnesia' when he argues that: 'the development of an indigenous British racism in the postwar period begins with the profound historical forgetfulness - what I want to call the loss of historical memory, a kind of historical amnesia, a decisive mental repression - which has overtaken the British people about race and empire since the 1950s' (Hall 1978: 25).

47   We return once again to Barker's 'pseudo-biological' claim, see chapter 2.

48   Of course most of this group of misguided ideologists and dithering liberals are simply lacking in commonsense, such as the Bishop who 'pulls the bedclothes over his head' in the Birmingham speech; or they are actively engaged in promoting a society that will finish-off England for good.

49   Of course, as we have argued, Powell is quite correct in his judgement here!

50 Current controversies within neo-gramscism have centred not around Derrida but Post-Sassurean semiotics. Thus Laclua speaks of 'empty signifiers'. While Mercer (1992: 435-6) re-employs Volosinov, seemingly unaware of the Formalist/ Structuralist binarism, to speak of the multi-accentuality of the sign and the articulation of racial identity through difference. Central to these arguments is the advancing notion that previously negative terrain can be re-articulated, can be made to mean something else. Mercer, for example, advances the term 'black' and then turns to Powell's re-articulation of 'race', claiming a similar re-articulation. Hall (1989; 1990) is more cautious, seeing the signifier 'race' as still implicated in older relations of signification. It is clear that my argument refuses this logic. However a fuller contestation of these positions must be advanced elsewhere.

51 Researching the connections historically between ideas of 'race' deprivation, immorality and contagion is difficult because there is a complex usage which mixes moral condemnation with empirical description and biological determinism, etc. It is this complex of social pathology thinking which I identify as the old (biological) racism in chapter 3.

52 See my remarks about Labour's 'urban blight' theory in chapter 5.

53 This is a genuinely contradictory aspect of Powellism.

54 Rex is condemning here the ideology driven project to search out and quantify those factors best able to support the project of innateness that has gripped scientific and political thought in the West since the enlightenment.

55 In the case of recognising the fool hardiness of European entry the cut-off line is infinitely malleable!

56 Of course this phrase works both ways and could include a multi-ethnic future as well as not. See for example the absolutely inspirational *'A Touch of The Tar Brush'* John Akomfrah's impassioned critique of Powellism, through the life-histories of the mixed-race communities of Liverpool 8 (BBC2 *Think Of England* series: 21/2/1991).

57 This eloquent phrase is characteristically Nairn's.

58 See Powell's idea of the 'parliamentary nation' below.

59 The idea of the nation as an imagined community is advocated as intellectually respectable for left theory by Anderson (1983). But, as Mercer has argued, Powell discovered this in 1964 (but see Nairn 1970). Powell's contribution to the cultural debate on the nation and identity politics is now seriously acknowledged by both Hall (1992) and Bhaba (1990).

60 It is impossible to do justice to Nairn's (1970 and 1981) marvellous invocation of Powell's cultural belonging and class position.

61 A version of this test was infamously advocated by Norman Tebbitt.

62 This unholy alliance is clearly documented in press coverage of the 1971 Immigration Bill through Committee where Powell, with the support of Labour and the Left and Right of his own party and a Liberal, defeats the concept of patriality in committee stage (Report, *Guardian*, 17.4.71).

Bibliography

Abrams, M. (1969) 'Colour and Citizenship': letter *New Society*: 371-2.

Aitken, I. (1968) 'Mr Heath dismisses Mr Powell for 'racialist speech' *Guardian* 22 April.

Allen, S. (1971) 'Race and the Economy: Some Aspects of the Position of Non-Indigenous Labour' *Race* XIII (2).

Allen, S., Macey, M. (1990) 'Race and Ethnicity in the European Context' *British Journal of Sociology* September 41 (3): 375-93.

Allport, G.W. (1954) *The Nature of Prejudice* New York: Doubleday Anchor.

Anderson, B. (1983) *Imagined Communities: reflections on the Origin and Spread of Nationalism* London: Verso.

Anthias, F. (1990) 'Race and class revisited - conceptualising race and racisms' *Sociological Review* February 38 (1): 19-42.

Anthias, F. (1992) 'Connecting Race and Ethnic Phenomena' *Sociology* 26:421-438

Anthias, F., Yuval-Davis N. (1992) *Racialised Boundaries: Race, nation, colour and class and the anti-racist struggle* London: Routledge.

Ascherson, N. (1988) 'Making a saint of Enoch Powell' *Sunday Observer* 24 April.

Bagley, C. (1969) 'Coloured Neighbours' *New Society* 7 August: 213-4.

Balibar, E. (1991a) 'Es Gibt Keinen Staat un Europa: Racism and Politics in Europe Today' *New Left Review* 186 March: 5-19.

Balibar, E. (1991b) 'Is There A 'Neo-Racism' ? in: Balibar, E., Wallerstein, I. (eds) *Race, Nation, Class: Ambiguous Identities* London: Verso: 17-28.

Balibar, E. (1991c) 'Racism and Nationalism' in: Balibar, E., Wallerstein, I. (eds) *Race, Nation, Class: Ambiguous Identities* London: Verso: 37-67.

Balibar, E., Wallerstein, I. (eds) *Race, Nation, Class: Ambiguous Identities* London: Verso.

Ball, W., Solomos, J. (eds) *Race and Local Politics* London: Macmillan.

Banton, M. (1966) 'Race as a Social Category' *Race* VIII (1): 1-16.

Banton, M. (1969) 'What Do We Mean By "Racism" ?' *New Society* 10 April: 651-654.

Banton, M. (1970) 'The Concept of Racism' in: Zubaida (ed) *Race and Racialism* London: Tavistock.

Banton, M. (1977) *The Idea of Race* London: Tavistock.

Banton, M. (1979) 'It's Our Country' in: Phizacklea, A., Miles, R. (eds) *Racism and Political Action in Britain* London: Routledge and Kegan Paul: 223-246.

Banton, M. (1980) 'The Idiom of Race: A Critique of Presentism' *Research in Race and Ethnic Relations* 2: 21-42.

Banton, M. (1983) *Racial and Ethnic Competition* Cambridge University Press.
Banton, M. (1985) *Promoting Racial Harmony* Cambridge University Press.
Banton, M. (1987) *Racial Theories* Cambridge University Press.
Banton, M. (1988) *Racial Consciousness* London: Longman.
Banton, M. (1991) 'The Race Relations Problematic' *British Journal of Sociology* 42 (1): 115-30.
Banton, M., Harwood, J. (1975) *The Concept of Race* Newton Abbot: David & Charles.
Barker, M. (1979) 'Racism - The New Inheritors' *Radical Philosophy*: 21: 2-17.
Barker, M. (1981) *The New Racism: Conservatives and the Ideology of the Tribe* London: Junction Books.
Barker, M. (1982) 'Biology and Ideology: the Uses of Reductionism' in: Rose, S.(ed) *Against Biological Determinism* London: Alison and Busby: 9-29.
Barker, M. (1983a) 'Sociobiology and Ideology: The Unfinished Trajectory' *Krisis* (Amsterdam) 12: 28-53.
Barker, M. (1983b) 'Empiricism and Racism' *Radical Philosophy* 33: 6-15.
Barker, M. (1984) (ed) *The Video Nasties: Freedom and Censorship in the Media* London: Pluto.
Barker, M. (1992) 'Stuart Hall: Policing the Crisis' in: Barker, M., Beezer, A.(eds) *Reading Into Cultural Studies* London: Routledge: 81-100.
Barker, M., Beezer, A. (1983) 'The language of racism - an examination of Lord Scarman's Report on the Brixton riots' *International Socialism* 2 (18) Winter: 108-25.
Barker, M., Beezer, A. (1992) (eds) *Reading Into Cultural Studies* London: Routledge.
Barnett, A. (1982) *Iron Britannia: Why Parliament Waged its Falklands War* London: Allison and Busby.
Barnett, A. (1989) 'After Nationalism' in: Samuel, R. (ed) *Patriotism vol.I:History and Politics* London: Routledge: 140-55.
Barrett, M. (1991) *The Politics of Truth: From Marx to Foucault* Cambridge: Polity.
Barthes, R. (1973) *Mythologies* London: Paladin.
Bauman, Z. (1991) *Modernity and the Holocaust* Oxford: Polity Press.
Bauman, Z. (1992) *Intimations of Postmodernity* London: Routledge.
Behrens, R., Edmonds, J. (1981) 'Kippers, Kittens and Kipper Boxes: Conservative Populists and Race Relations' *Political Quarterly* 52 (3) July-September: 342-8.
Bell, R. (1968) 'Jenkins drops a back-door bombshell' *Sunday Express* 14 April.
Benn, T. (1979) *Arguments For Socialism* Harmondsworth: Penguin.
Benn, T. (1987) *Out Of The Wilderness: Diaries 1963-67* London: Arrow Books.
Benn, T. (1981) 'Britain as a colony' *New Socialist* Sept/Oct: 58-62.
Benton, T. (1984) *The Rise and Fall of Structural Marxism: Althusser and his influence* London: Macmillan.

Ben-Tovim, G. (1978) 'The Struggle Against Racism: Theoretical and Strategic Perspectives' *Marxism Today* July: 203-13.

Ben-Tovim, G., Gabriel, J. (1979) 'The Politics of Race in Britain: a Review of the Major Trends and of the Recent Literature' *Sage Race Relations Abstracts* 4(4): 1-56.

Benyon, J.,Solomos, J. (eds) (1987) *The Roots of Urban Unrest* Oxford: Pergamon Press.

Berkeley, H. (1977) *The Odyssey of Enoch: A Political Memoir* London: Hamish Hamilton.

Bhat, A., Carr-Hill, R., Ohri, S. (1988) *Radical Statistics Race Group: Britain's Black Population; A New Perspective* 2nd edn. Aldershot: Gower.

Billig, M. (1978a) 'Patterns of racism: interviews with National Front members' *Race & Class* XX (2) Autumn: 161-79.

Billig, M. (1978b) *Fascists: a social psychological view of the National Front* London: Academic Press.

Blondel, J. (1963) *Voters, Parties and Leaders* Harmondsworth: London.

Borthwick, R. (1988) 'The Floor of the House' in: Ryle, M., Richards, P.G., (eds) *The Commons Under Scrutiny* London: Routledge: 53-75.

Boyd, F. (1969) 'Workers' Friend' *Guardian* 24 April.

Boyson, R. (1978) *Centre Forward: A Radical Conservative Programme* London: Temple Smith.

Braham, P. (1982) 'How the Media Report Race' in: Gurevitch, M., Bennett, T., Curran, J., Woollacott, J. (eds) *Culture, Society and the Media* London: Methuen: 268-286.

Braham P., Rattansi, A., Skellington, R. (eds) *Racism and Antiracism: Inequalities, Opportunities and Policies* Sage: Open University.

Brewer, J. D. (1983) 'Competing understandings of common sense understanding: a brief comment on common sense racism' *British Journal of Sociology* XXXV (1): 66-74.

Brier, A., Axford, B. (1975) 'The Theme of race in British social science and political research' in: I.Crewe (ed) *The Politics of Race* London: Croom Helm: 3-25.

Brown, A. (1985) 'Power Plus Prejudice' *The Spectator* 22 June: 15-16.

Brown, A. (1985) Trials of Honeyford: problems in multicultural education London: *Centre for Policy Studies.*

Brown, A.R. (1986) 'Race', Politics and the British State: a comparative critique of A. Sivanandan' *Unpublished Dissertation, Department of Humanities, University of West of England.*

Brown, A.R. (1996) 'The Anniversary Enoch Press: the impact of Powellism on media 'race' reporting' *Unpublished Paper, Department of Sociology, Bath Spa University College.*

Brown, A.R. (1997) Racism and Political Language: the impact of Smethwick and Powellism on the formation of a political racism in Britain, 1957-88. *Ph.D*

Thesis, Department of Politics and Sociology, Birkbeck College, University of London.
Brown, A.R. (1997) 'Language, Power and Resisting Racist Discourse' *Paper given at the BSA Conference: Power and Resistance, York University, 7-10 April 1997.*
Brown, C. (1984) *Black and White Britain: the third PSI survey* London: Heinemann.
Bulpitt, J. (1986) 'Continuity, Autonomy and Peripheralisation: the Anatomy of the Centre's Race Statecraft in England' in: Layton-Henry, Z., Rich, P.B. (eds) *Race, Government and Politics in Britain* London: Macmillan: 17-44.
Burns, T. (1977) 'The Organization of Public Opinion' in: Curran, J., Gurevitch, M., Woollacott, J. (eds) *Mass Communication and Society* London: Open University/ Edward Arnold: 44-69.
Burgess, T. (1973) 'Figures in the void' *New Society* 11 October.
Butler, D., Kavanagh, D. (1974) *The British General Election of February 1974* London: Macmillan.
Butler, D., Kavanagh, D. (1975) *The British General Election of October 1974* London: Macmillan.
Butler, D.E., King, A. (1964) *The British General Election of 1964* London: Macmillan.
Butler, Lord (1971) *The Art of the possible* Harmondsworth: Penguin.
Butt, R. (1981) 'The evil mischief makers who are so quick to brand us all as 'white racists' ' *Daily Mail* July 10: 6-7.
Butt, R. (1986) 'English Teaching As Racism' *The Times* 1 May p.16.
Butterworth, E. (1967) 'The smallpox outbreak and the British press' *Race* 7 (4): 347-64.
Butterworth, E., Weir, D. (eds) (1972) *Social Problems Of Modern Britain* Suffolk: Fontana.
CCCS: Race & Politics Group (1982) *The Empire Strikes Back: Race and racism in 70s Britain* London: Hutchinson.
Callaghan, J. (1987) *Time and Chance* London: William Collins.
Carter, B. Harris, C., Joshi, S. (1987) 'The 1951 - 55 Conservative government and the racialisation of black immigration' *Policy Papers in Ethnic Relations no. 11*, University of Warwick: Centre for Research in Ethnic Relations.
Carter, B., Joshi, S. (1984) 'The Role of Labour in the Creation of a Racist Britain' *Race & Class* 25 (3): 53-70.
Casey, J. (1982) 'One nation: the politics of race' *The Salisbury Review* Autumn: 23-8.
Cashmore, E. (ed) (1994) *Dictionary of Race and Ethnic Relations* London: Routledge.
Castles, S., Kosack, G. (1973) *Immigrant Workers and Class Structure* Cambridge University Press.
Chase, A. (1977) *The Legacy of Malthus* New York: Alfred Knopf.

Clarke, J., Critcher, C., Jefferson, T., Lambert, J. (1974) 'The Selection of Evidence & the Avoidance of Racialism: a Critique of the Parliamentary Select Committee on Race Relations and Immigration' *New Community* III (3) Summer: 172-192.

Cohen, G.A. (1988) 'Anti-Anti-Racism': Letter *London Review of Books* 3 March 10 (5).

Cohen, P. (1988) 'The Perversions of Inheritance: Studies in the Making of Multi-Racist Britain' in: Cohen, P., Bains, Harwant, S. (eds) *Multi-Racist Britain* London: Macmillan: 9-118.

Cohen, S. (1981, 2nd.ed). *Folk Devils and Moral Panics* Oxford: Basil Blackwell.

Cohen, S. (1981) *The Thin End of the White Wedge: The new Nationality Laws - Second Class Citizenship and the Welfare State* Manchester Law Centre.

Coleman, T. (1970) 'The Word According to Enoch' *Guardian* 20 May.

Coleman, T. (1982) 'The Age of Enoch' *Guardian* 15 June.

Collits, T. (1994) 'Theorizing Racism' in: Tiffin, C., Lawson, A. (eds) *De-Scribing Empire: Post-Colonialism and Textuality* London: Routledge: 61-84.

Comas, J. (1956) 'Racial Myths' in: *UNESCO: The Race Question in Modern Science* Paris: Unesco): 11-53.

Commission for Racial Equality (1978) *Five Views of Multi-Racial Britain* London: CRE.

Connerton, P. (ed) (1976) *Critical Sociology: Selected Readings* Harmondsworth: Penguin.

Conservative, A. (1964) 'From the Years of Protest to the Year of Disasters' *The Times* 1 April, p.11.

Conservative, A. (1964) 'Patriotism Based on Reality Not on Dreams' *The Times* 2 April, p.13.

Conservative, A. (1964) 'The Field Where the Biggest Failures Lie' *The Times* 3 April, p.13.

Cosgrave, P. (1989) *The Lives of Enoch Powell* London: Bodley Head.

Cowling, M. (ed) (1978) *Conservative Essays* London: Cassell.

Crick, B. (1969a) 'In Defence of Patriotism' *The Observer* 16 February.

Crick, B. (1969b) 'The New Meaning of Tolerance' *The Observer* 13 July.

Critcher, C., Parker, M., Sondhi, R. (1975) *Race in the Provincial Press: A Case Study of Five West Midlands Newspapers* UNESCO: CCCS University of Birmingham, November.

Cross, M., Keith, M. (1993) (eds) *Racism, the City and the State* London: Routledge.

Crossman, R. (1975) *Diaries of a Cabinet Minister, vol.1: Minister of Housing 1964-66* London: Hamish Hamilton & Jonathan Cape.

Crossman, R. (1976) *Diaries of a Cabinet Minister, vol.2: Lord President of the Council and Leader of the House of Commons 1966-68* London: Hamish Hamilton and Jonathan Cape.

Crossman, R. (1977) *Diaries of a Cabinet Minister, vol.3: Secretary of State for Social Services 1968-70* London: Hamish Hamilton and Jonathan Cape.

Cunningham, H. (1981) 'The Language of Patriotism, 1750-1914' *History Workshop* 12, Autumn: 8-33.

Dahrendorf, R. (1982) *On Britain* London: British Broadcasting Corporation.

Daniel, W.W. (1968) *Racial Discrimination in England* Harmondsworth: Penguin.

Dant, T. (1991) *Knowledge, Ideology and Discourse: A Sociological Perspective* London: Routledge.

Deakin, N. (ed) (1965) *Colour and the British Electorate* London: Pall Mall Press.

Deakin, N. (1966) 'The 1966 General Election' *IRR: Newsletter* April: 2-10.

Deakin, N. (1968) 'The Politics of the Commonwealth Immigrants Bill' *Political Quarterly* 391: 24-45.

Deakin, N. (1970a) *Colour, Citizenship and British Society* London: Panther.

Deakin, N. (1970b) 'Race, the Politicians, and Public Opinion: A Case Study' in: Zubaida, S. (ed) *Race and Racialism* London: Tavistock: 127-49.

Deakin, N. (1989) (ed) *The New Right: Image and Reality* London: Runneymede Trust.

Deakin, N., Bourne, J. (1970) 'Powell, and the Minorities, and the 1970 Election' *Political Quarterly* vol.41: 399-415.

Deakin, N., Lawrence, D., Silvey, J., Lelohe, M.J., (1966) 'Colour and the 1966 General Election' *Race* VIII (1): 17-42.

Dean, M. (1970) 'Alabama Staffs.' *Guardian* 6 February.

Derrida, J. (1976) *Of Grammatology* Baltimore and London: John Hopkins University.

Derrida, J. (1978) *Writing and Difference* London: Routledge.

van Dijk, T. (1985a) (ed) *Handbook of Discourse Analysis, vol.4: Discourse Analysis and Society* London: Academic Press.

van Dijk, T. (1985b) (ed) *Discourse and Communication: new approaches to the analysis of mass media, discourse and communications* Berlin: Walter de Gruyter.

van Dijk, T. (1987) *Communicating Racism: Ethnic Prejudice in Thought and Talk* Newbury Park CA: Sage.

van Dijk, T. (1990) 'Discourse and Society: a new journal for a new research focus' *Discourse & Society vol.1* (1): 5-16.

van Dijk, T. (1991) *Racism and the Press* London: Routledge.

van Dijk, T. (1993) *Elite Discourse and Racism* London: Sage.

van Dijk, T. (1995) 'Discourse Semantics and Ideology' *Discourse and Society*: 6(2): 243-289.

DiKotter, F. (1992) *The Discourse of Race in Modern China* London: Hurst & Co.

Donald, J., Rattansi, A. (1992) (eds) *Race, Culture and Difference* Milton Keynes: Open University Press.

Downing, J. (1975) 'The (Balanced) White View' in: Husband, C. (ed) *White Media & Black Britain* London: Arrow Books: 90-137.
Downing, J. (1985)'Coillons....Shryned in a Hogges Toord': British News Media Discourse on 'Race" in: Dijk, T. van (ed) *Discourse and Communication* Berlin: Walter de Gruyter: 295-323.
Drake, St. C. (1955) 'The "Colour Problem" in Britain: A Study in Social Definitions' *Sociological Review* 3 (2): 197-217.
Dresser, M. (1986) *Black and White On the Buses: The 1963 Colour Bar Dispute in Bristol* Bristol Broadsides.
Drewry, G. (1988, 3rd. rev). 'Legislation' in: Ryle, M., Richards, P. (eds) *The Commons Under Scrutiny* London: Routledge: 120-40.
Duffield, M.R. (1984) 'New Racism....New Realism: Two Sides of the Same Coin' *Radical Philosophy* 37 Summer: 29-34.
Dummett, A. (1973) *A Portrait of English Racism* Harmondsworth: Penguin.
Dummett, A. (1988a) 'Anti-Anti-Racism': Letter *London Review of Books* 7 January 10 (1).
Dummett, A. (1988b) 'Anti-Anti-Racism': Letter *London Review of Books* 3 March 10 (5).
Dummett, M. (1974) 'Prejudice Reinforced' *Guardian* 28 February.
Dummett. M. & Dummett, A. (1969) 'The Role of Government in Britain's Racial Crisis' in: Donnelly, L. (ed) *Justice First* London: Sheed and Ward: 25-78.
Eagleton, T. (1991) *Ideology: an introduction* London: Verso.
Eccleshall, R. (1990) 'The Nature of Conservatism' *Social Studies* Review September: 2-5.
Edelman, M. (1977) Political Language: words that succeed and policies that fail New York: Academic Press.
Edelman, M. (1988) *Constructing the Political Spectacle* London: University of Chicago Press.
Edgar, D. (1977) 'Racism, Fascism and the Politics of the National Front' *Race & Class* 19 (2): 111-31.
Edgar, D. (1981) 'Reagan's Hidden Agenda: Racism and the New American Right' *Race & Class* XXII (3): 221-38.
Edgar, D. (1983) 'Bitter Harvest' *New Socialist* September/October: 19-24.
Edgar, D. (1987) 'Dreams of the Volk' *New Socialist* January: 18-21.
Elton, Lord (1965) *The Unarmed Invasion* London: Godfrey Bles.
Evans, H. (1971) 'A Positive Policy' in: *Race and the Press* London: Runnymede Trust: 42-53.
Express, Daily (1988) (leader) 25 April.
Eysenck, H.J., Kamin, L. (1981) *Intelligence: The Battle for the Mind* London: Pan.
Fanon, F. (1985) *The Wretched of the Earth* Harmondsworth: Penguin.
Fanon, F. (1986) *Black Skin, White Masks* London: Pluto.

Feyerabend, P. (1978) *Against Method: Outline of an Anarchist Theory of Science* Cambridge: Cambridge University Press.
Fielding, N. (1981) *The National Front* London: Routledge and Kegan Paul.
Fields, B. J. (1990) 'Slavery, Race and Ideology in the United States of America' *New Left Review* 181 May/June: 95-118.
Flew, A. (1984a) *Education, Race and Revolution* London: Centre for Policy Studies.
Flew, A. (1984b) 'The Race Relations Industry' *Salisbury Review* Winter: 24-7.
Flew, A. (1986a) 'Three Concepts of Racism' *Salisbury Review* 5 January: 2-6.
Flew, A. (1986b) 'Darker Shades of Racism' *The Times* 21 August p.10.
Foot, M. (1986) 'Enoch Powell' in: *Loyalists and Loners* London: William Collins: 185-192.
Foot, P. (1965) *Immigration and Race in British Politics* Harmondsworth: Penguin.
Foot, P. (1969) *The Rise of Enoch Powell* Harmondsworth: Penguin.
Forgacs, D. (1989) 'Gramsci and Marxism in Britain' *New Left Review* 176 July-August: 70-88.
Foucault, M. (1971) 'Orders of Discourse' *Social Science Information* 10 (2): 730.
Foucault, M. (1972) *The Archaeology of Knowledge* London: Tavistock.
Foucault, M. (1974) *The Order of Things: An Archaeology of the Human Sciences* New York: Vintage Books.
Foucault, M. (1977) *Discipline and Punish* London: Allen Lane.
Foucault, M. (1978) 'Politics and the Study of Discourse' *Ideology and Consciousness* 3 Spring: 7-26.
Foucault, M. (1979) *The History of Sexuality, vol. 1: An introduction* London: Allen Lane.
Foucault, M. (1980) *Power/ Knowledge* Brighton: Harvester Press.
Foucault, M. (1984) *The Foucault Reader*, P. Rabinow (ed): Harmondsworth: Penguin.
Fountain, N. (1968) 'The Monday Club' *New Society* 25 April.
Fountain, N. (1969) 'The Front' *New Society* 3 April: 513-4.
Fowler, R. (1991) *Language in the News* London: Routledge.
Fowler, R., Hodge, B., Kress, G., Trew, T. (1979) *Language and Control* London: Routledge and Kegan Paul.
Frankenberg, R. (1993) *White Women, Race Matters: The Social Construction of Whiteness* Routledge: University of Minnesota Press.
Freedman, C. (1983/4) 'Overdeterminations: On Black Marxism in Britain' *Social Text* 8: 142-50.
Freeman, G. (1979) *Immigrant Labour and Racial Conflict in Industrial Societies* Princeton University Press.
Fryer, P. (1984) *Staying Power: A History of Black People in Britain* London: Pluto.

Fuss, D. (1989) *Essentially Speaking: Feminism, Nature and Difference* New York: Routledge.
Gabriel, J., Ben-Tovim, G. (1979) 'Marxism & the Concept of Racism' *Economy and Society* 8 (3) August: 118-54.
Gainer, B. (1972) *The Alien Invasion: the origins of the Aliens Act of 1905* London: Heinemann.
Gamble, A. (1974) *The Conservative Nation* London: Routledge and Kegan Paul.
Gamble, A. (1991) The End of Thatcherism? *Social Studies Review* January: 86-91.
Gellner, E. (1983) *Nations and Nationalism* Oxford: Basil Blackwell.
Gellner, E. (1994) *Encounter With Nationalism* Oxford: Blackwell.
George, V., Wilding, P. (1976) *Ideology and Social Welfare* London: Routledge & Kegan Paul.
Geras, N. (1976) 'Marx and the Critique of Political Economy' in: Blackburn, R. (ed) *Ideology in Social Science: Readings in Critical Social Theory* Fontana: 284-305.
Geras, N. (1987) 'Post-Marxism?' *New Left Review* 163 May/June: 40-82.
Gilman, S. (1992) 'Black Bodies: White Bodies: Towards an Iconography of Female Sexuality in Late Nineteenth Century Art, Medicine and Literature' in : Donald, J., Rattansi, A. (eds) *'Race', Culture and Difference* London: Sage.
Gilroy, P. (1982) Review of the 'New Racism' by M. Barker(1981) *Race & Class* XX IV: 1: 95-6.
Gilroy, P. (1987a) *There Ain't No Black in the Union Jack* London: Hutchinson.
Gilroy, P. (1987b) *Problems in Anti-racist Strategy* London: Runnymede Trust.
Gilroy, P. (1990) 'One Nation under a Groove: The Cultural Politics of Racism in Britain' in: Goldberg, D.T. (ed) *Anatomy of Racism* Minneapolis: University of Minnesota Press: 263-82.
Gilroy, P., Lawrence, E. (1988) 'Two-Tone Britain: White and Black Youth and the Politics of Anti-Racism' in: Cohen, P., Bains, H.S. (eds) *Multi-Racist Britain* London: Macmillan: 121-155.
Gimson, A. (1988) 'Enoch Powell, midwife to the spirit of the nation' *Independent* 19 April.
Glass, R. (1960) *Newcomers: West Indians in London* London: Allen and Unwin.
Goldberg, B., Greer, C. (1990) 'American Visions, Ethnic dreams: Public Ethnicity and the Sociological Imagination' *Sage Race Relations Abstracts* 15 (1) February: 5-60.
Goldberg, D.T. (1990) 'The Social Formation of Racist Discourse' in: Goldberg, D.T. (ed) *Anatomy Of Racism* Minneapolis: University of Minnesota Press: 295-318.
Goldberg, D.T. (1992) 'The Semantics of Race' *Ethnic & Racial Studies* 15 (4): 543-69.
Goldberg, D.T. (1993a) 'Polluting the Body Politic' in: Cross, M., Keith, M. (eds) *Race, the City and the State* London: Routledge: 45-60.

Goldberg, D.T (1993b) *Racist Culture* Oxford: Blackwell.
Gordon, P. (1986) *Racial Violence and Harassment* London: Runnymede Trust.
Gordon, P. (1987) 'Visas and the British Press' *Race & Class* 28 (3): 76-80.
Gordon, P. (1989) *Citizenship For Some: Race and government policy 1979-1989* London: Runneymede Trust.
Gordon, P., Klug, F. (1986) *New Right/ New Racism* London: Searchlight.
Gorer, G. (1966) 'The Host Society' in: *Colour in Britain* London: British Broadcasting Corporation: 43-57.
Gott, R. (1989) 'Little Englanders' in: Samuel, R. (ed) *Patriotism, vol.I: History & Politics* London: Routledge: 90-102.
Grainger, J.H. (1986) *Patriotisms: Britain 1900-1939* London: Routledge & Kegan Paul.
Gray, R. (1982) 'Left Holding the Flag' *Marxism Today* November: 22-7.
Green, A.D. (1979) 'On the Political Economy of Black Labour and the Racial Structuring of the Working Class in England' *Race Series (SP: 62)* C.C.C.S. Stencilled Occasional Paper.
Griffith, J.A.G., Henderson, J., Usborne, M., Wood, D. (1960) *Coloured Immigrants in Britain* London: Oxford University Press.
Griffiths, P. (1966) *A Question of Colour* London: Leslie Frewin.
Guardian, The (1969) 'The Auction of Prejudice' (editorial) 27 January.
Guardian, The (1970) 'A multiracial Britain' (editorial) 1 June.
Guardian, The (1988) 'Rivers of no return' (editorial) 20 April, p.18.
Guillaumin, C. (1995) *Racism, Sexism, Power and Ideology* Routledge: London.
Habermas, J. (1970) 'Systematically Distorted Communication' *Inquiry* vol. 13: 205-18.
Habermas, J. (1973) 'What Does Crisis Mean Today ? Legitimation Problems in Late Capitalism' *Social Research* vol.40: Winter: 643-667.
Habermas, J. (1976) *Legitimation Crisis* London: Heinemann.
Hall, S. (1973) 'The Structured Communication of Events' *Occasional Stencilled Papers* CCCS: University of Birmingham, October.
Hall, S. (1978) 'Racism & Reaction' in: Commission for Racial Equality: *Five Views of Multi-racial Britain* London: Commission for Racial Equality: 23-35.
Hall, S. (1980a) 'Encoding/decoding' in: CCCS: *Culture, Media, Language: Working Papers in Cultural Studies*, 1972-79 London: Hutchinson: 128-38.
Hall, S. (1980b) 'Race, Articulation and Societies Structured in Dominance' in: *UNESCO: Sociological Theories: Race and Colonialism* Paris: UNESCO: 305-45.
Hall, S. (1980c) 'Popular-Democratic vs Authoritarian Populism: two ways of 'Taking Democracy Seriously' in: Hunt, A. (ed) *Socialism and Democracy* London: Lawrence and Wishart: 157-185.
Hall, S. (1981) 'The Whites of Their Eyes: Racist Ideologies and the Media' in: Bridges, G., Brunt, R. (eds) *Silver Linings: Some Strategies for the Eighties* London: Lawrence & Wishart: 28-52.

Hall, S. (1982) 'The Empire Strikes Back' *New Socialist* July/August.
Hall, S. (1985a) 'Cold Comfort Farm' *New Socialist* November: 10-12.
Hall, S. (1985b) 'Authoritarian Populism: a Reply' *New Left Review* 151: 115-24.
Hall, S. (1988) *The Hard Road to Renewal: Thatcherism and the Crisis of the Left* London: Verso.
Hall, S. (1992a)'New Ethnicities' in Donald, J., Rattansi, A. (eds) *Race, Culture and Difference* London: Sage: 252-60.
Hall, S. (1992b)'What is this "black" in Black Popular Culture ?' in: Dent, G. (ed) *Black Popular Culture* Seattle: Bay Press: 21-33.
Hall, S. Lumley, B., McLennan, G. (1978) 'Politics and Ideology: Gramsci' in: *CCCS: On Ideology* London: Hutchinson: 45-76.
Hall, S. Critcher, C. Jefferson, T. Clarke, J., Roberts, B. (1978) *Policing the Crisis: Mugging, the State & Law & Order* London: Macmillan.
Hall, S., Jacques, M. (eds) (1983) *The Politics of Thatcherism* London: Lawrence and Wishart.
Hall, S., Jacques, M. (eds) (1989) *New Times: the Changing Face of politics in the 1990s* London: Lawrence and Wishart.
Halsey, A.H. (1970) 'Race Relations: the lines to think on' *New Society* 19 March: 472-4.
Hamilton-Dunn, J. (1977) 'The Language and Myths of the New Right' *New Society* 5 May: 225-6.
Hardy, J. (1991) 'Playing the race card' *The Guardian* 23/4 November.
Harre, R. (1985) 'Persuasion and Manipulation' in: Dijk, T. van (ed) *Discourse & Communication* Berlin: Walter de Gruyter: 126-42.
Harris, C. (1987) 'British Capitalism, Migration and Relative Surplus Population' *Migration* 1 (1): 47-90.
Harris, C. (1991) 'Configurations of racism: the Civil Service, 1945-60' *Race & Class* 33 (1): 1-30.
Harris, C., James, W. (eds) (1993) *Into Babylon: The West Indian Experience In Britain* London: Verso.
Hartley-Brewer, M. (1965) 'Smethwick' in: Deakin, N. (ed) *Colour and the British Electorate 1964: Six Case Studies* London: Pall Mall Press: 77-105.
Hartmann, P., Husband, C. (1974) *Racism and the Mass Media* London: Davis-Poynter.
Hastie, T. (1981) 'Why Pay for an 'Industry' that Grows Fat on Racial Discord?' *Daily Telegraph* 30 March.
Hastie, T. (1987) 'With A View to a Riot' *The Times* 2 April p. 14.
Hattersley, R. (1988) 'Why rivers of blood do not foam through Britain' *Guardian* 9 April 1988.
Hattersley, R. (1988) 'Different traditions enrich a community' *The Independent* 23 April p.3.
Heater, D. (1983) 'Organisation of the Political Unit' in: *Contemporary Political Ideas* Essex: Longman: 103-35.

Hill, D. (1991) 'The Patriot Game' *Weekend Guardian* 9-10 February: 4-6.
Hindell, K. (1965) 'The Genesis of the Race Relations Bill' *Political Quarterly* 36: 390-405.
Hiro, D. (1973) *Black British, White British* Harmondsworth: Penguin.
Hiro, D. (1990) (2nd ed) *Black British, White British* Harmondsworth: Penguin.
Hirst, P. (1976) *Problems and Advances in the Theory of Ideology* Cambridge University Communist Party.
Hirst, P. (1977) 'Economic Classes and Politics' in: Hunt, A. (ed) *Class and Class Structure* London: Lawrence & Wishart: 125-154.
Hirst, P. (1979) *On Law and Ideology* London: Macmillan.
Hobsbawm, E.J. (1969) 'The limits of nationalism' *New Society* 2 October, p. 523.
Hobsbawm, E.J. (1977) 'Some reflections on 'The Break-up of Britain'' *New Left Review* 105: 3-25.
Hobsbawm, E.J. (1982) 'Looking towards 2000: the politics of decline' *New Society* 7 October: 8-12.
Hodge, R., Kress, G. (1979) *Language As Ideology* London: Routledge and Kegan Paul.
Hodge, R., Kress, G. (1993) (2nd.ed) *Language As Ideology* London: Routledge.
Holland, P. (1981) 'The New Cross fire and the popular press' *Multi-Racial Education* 9:3: 61-80.
Holmes, C. (1988) *John Bull's Island: Immigration and British Society, 1871-1971* London: Macmillan.
Holmes, C. (1991) *A Tolerant Country? Immigrants, Refugees and Minorities in Britain* London: Faber and Faber.
Honeyford, R. (1982) 'Multiracial myths?' *Times Educational Supplement* 9 November.
Honeyford, R. (1983) 'Multi-ethnic intolerance' *Salisbury Review Summer*: 12-13.
Honeyford, R. (1984) 'Education and Race - an Alternative View' *Salisbury Review* Winter: 30-32.
Honeyford, R. (1988a) 'Anti-Anti-Racism': Letter *London Review of Books* 7 January 10 (1).
Honeyford, R. (1988b) *Integration or Disintegration?: Towards a Non-racist society* London: Claridge Press.
Hoogvelt, A. (1969) 'Ethnocentrism, Authoritarianism, and Powellism' *Race* 11 July: 1-12.
Horowitz, D. (1970) 'The British Conservatives and the Racial Issue in the Debate on Decolonization' *Race* XII 2: 169-87.
House of Commons Official Report (1958a) 'Immigration Policy' *Parliamentary Debates* (Hansard) 3 April: 1415-1426.
House of Commons Official Report (1958b) 'Immigration (Control)' *Hansard* 5 December: 1552-1597.
House of Commons Official Report (1959)'Immigration From the Commonwealth' *Hansard* 17 November: 1121-1130.

House of Commons Official Report (1961a) 'Control of Immigration' *Hansard vol. 634* 17 February: 1929-2024 (vol.634).

House of Commons Official Report (1961b) 'Immigration' *Hansard, vol.645* 1 August: 1319-1331.

House of Commons Official Report (1961c) 'Commonwealth Immigrants Bill - Second Reading' *Hansard* 16 November: 687-823.

House of Commons Official Report (1964) 'Expiring Laws Bill - Committee' *Hansard* 17 November: 228-397.

House of Commons Official Report (1965) 'Race Relations Bill - Second Reading' *Hansard* 3 May: 926-1059.

House of Commons Official Report (1968a) 'Commonwealth Immigration' *Hansard* 23 February: 659-667.

House of Commons Official Report (1968b) 'Commonwealth Immigrants Bill - Second Reading' *Hansard* 27 February: 1241-1367.

House of Commons Official Report (1968c) 'Commonwealth Immigrants Bill' (Committee) *Hansard* (759) 28 February: 1421-1712.

House of Commons Official Report (1968d) 'Race Relations Bill - Second Reading' *Hansard* (763) 23 April: 53174.

House of Commons Official Report (1971) 'Immigration Bill - Second Reading' *Hansard* (813) 8 March: 42-178.

House of Commons Official Report (1973) 'Immigration and Race Relations' *Hansard* 6 December: 1469-1582.

House of Commons Official Report (1976a) 'Race Relations Bill - Second Reading' *Hansard* (906) 4 March: 1547-1670.

House of Commons Official Report (1976b) 'Immigration' *Hansard* 5 July: 964-1094.

House of Commons Official Report (1976c) 'Race Relations Bill' *Hansard* 8 July: 1627-1968.

House of Commons Official Report (1979) 'Immigration' *Hansard* (975) 4 December: 253-382.

House of Commons Official Report (1980) 'Immigration Rules' *Hansard* 10 March: 1011-1104.

House of Commons Official Report (1981a) 'British Nationality Bill - Second Reading' *Hansard* (997) January 28: 935-1047.

House of Commons Official Report (1981b) 'British Nationality Bill' (Committee) *Hansard Sixth Series* (5) 2 June: 795-898.

House of Commons Official Report (1981c) 'British Nationality Bill' (Committee), *Hansard Sixth Series* (5) 3 June: 931-1028.

House of Commons Official Report (1981d) 'British Nationality Bill' (Committee) *Hansard Sixth Series* (5) 4 June: 1091-1194.

House of Commons Official Report (1983) 'Immigration' *Hansard* 15 February: 178-228.

Howe, S. (1989) 'Labour Patriotism, 1939-83' in: Samuel, R. (ed) *Patriotism, vol.I: History and Politics* London: Routledge: 127-55.

Humphry, D., Ward, M. (1974) *Passports and Politics* Harmondsworth: Penguin.

Husband, C. (ed) (1975) *White Media, Black Britain: a critical look at the role of the media in race relations today* London: Arrow Books.

Husband, C. (1987) (ed) 2nd. edn) *'Race' in Britain: continuity and change* London: Hutchinson.

Husband, C. (1987) 'British Racisms: the Construction of racist ideologies' in: Husband, C. (ed) *'Race' in Britain: continuity and change* London: Hutchinson: 319-31.

Husbands, C.T. (1983) *Racial Exclusionism and the City* London: Allen and Unwin.

Husbands, C.T. (1985) 'Comparative Perspectives On Political Racism: The Significance of the Urban Context' *Paper presented to the Conference on Racial Minorities, Economic Restructuring and Urban Decline, Centre for Research in Ethnic Relations*, University of Warwick, 18-20 Sept. 1985.

Husbands, C.T. (1994) 'They Must Obey Our Laws!: Political Debate about Muslim Assimilability in Great Britain, France and the Netherlands' in: Hargreaves, A., Leaman, J. (eds) *Racism, Ethnicity and Politics in Contemporary Europe* Aldershot: Edward Elgar: 115-30.

Hutchinson, G. (1973) 'The National Front's growing challenge to Mr Heath' *The Times* 31 May.

Hymes, D. (1974) *Foundations in Sociolinguistics: An Ethnographic Approach* London: Tavistock.

Independent, The (1988) 'Rivers of Complacency' Editorial 25 April.

Institute of Economic Affairs (ed) (1964) *Rebirth of Britain London*: Pan Books.

Institute of Economic Affairs (ed) (1970) *Economic Issues in Immigration* London: IEA.

Institute of Race Relations: 'Newsletter' 1960-9 IRR: London.

Institute of Race Relations (1965) 'A Race Relations Cycle ?' *Newsletter*, March: 2-3.

James, C.L.R. (1964) 'Race: An alternative view' *New Society* 10 December.

James, W. (1989) 'The making of black identities' in: Samuel, R. (ed) *Patriotism, vol.II: Minorities and Outsiders* London: Routledge: 230-55.

Jameson, F. (1972) *The Prison-House Of Language: A Critical Account of Structuralism and Russian Formalism* New Jersey: Princeton University Press.

Jenkins, P. (1970) 'Enoch goes pop' *Sunday Times* 5 June.

Jessop, B. (1982) *The Capitalist State: Marxist Theories and Methods* Oxford: Martin Robertson.

Jessop, B., Bonnett, K., Bromley, S., Ling, T. (1984) 'Authoritarian Populism, Two Nations and Thatcherism' *New Left Review* 147: 32-60.

Jessop, B., Bonnett, K., Bromley, S., Ling, T. (1985) 'Thatcherism and the Politics of Hegemony: a reply to Stuart Hall' *New Left Review* 153: 87-101.

Jessop, B., Bonnett, K., Bromley, S., Ling, T. (1988) *Thatcherism: A Tale of Two Nations* Cambridge: Polity Press.
Jessop, B., Bonnett, K., Bromley, S. (1990) 'Farewell to Thatcherism? Neo-Liberalism and 'New Times" *New Left Review* 179 Jan/Feb: 81-102.
Johnson, R.W., Schoen, D. (1976) 'The "Powell effect": or how one man can win' *New Society* 22 July: 168-72.
Jones, C. (1971) 'Immigrants and the News' in: *Race and the Press* London: Runnymede Trust: 13-20.
Jowell, R. Witherspoon, S., Brook, L. (1989) *British Social Attitudes: Special International Report* (6th) Social and Community Planning Research, Aldershot: Gower.
Junor, P. (1983) *Margaret Thatcher: Wife. Mother. Politician* London: Sidgwick and Jackson.
Kamin, L. J. (1974) 'Psychology and the Immigrant' in: *The Science and Politics of I.Q.* Harmondsworth: Penguin: 30-51.
Katznelson, I. (1976) *Black Men, White Cities: Race, Politics and Migration in the United States 1900-30, and Britain, 1948-68* University of Chicago Press.
Kaufman, G. (1965) 'Dutch Auction on Immigrants' *New Statesman* vol. LXX: 1791.
Kavanagh, D. (1988) 'Ideology in British Politics' *Teaching Politics* Autumn: 2-7.
Keegan, W. (1986) 'New Right Theories and the Politicians' in: Deakin, N. (ed) *The New Right: image and reality* London: Runneymede Trust: 45-50.
Kerridge, R. (1982) 'A letter to Enoch Powell' *The Spectator* 10 July: 13-14.
Kettle, M., Hodges, L. (1982) *Uprising !* London: Pan Books.
King, A. (1965) 'New Stirrings on the Right' *New Society* 14 October: 7-11.
King, R., Wood, M. (1975) 'The support for Enoch Powell' in: Crewe, I. (ed) *The Politics of race* London: Croom Helm: 239-62.
Kitching, G. (1985) 'Nationalism: the instrumental passion', *Capital and Class* Spring: 98-116.
Klien, R. (1965) 'The apocryphal Book of Enoch' *New Society* 22 July: 24-5.
Knowles, C. (1992) *Race, Discourse and Labourism* London: Routledge.
Kress, G. (1983) 'Linguistic and Ideological Transformations in News Reporting' in: Davis, H., Walton, P. (ed) *Language, Image, Media* Oxford: Basil Blackwell: 120-38.
Kress, G. (1985) 'Ideological Structures in Discourse' in: Dijk, T. van, (ed) *Handbook of Discourse Analysis, vol.4* London: Academic Press: 27-42.
Kress, G., Hodge, R. (1988) *Social Semiotics* London: Routledge.
Laclau, E. (1977) 'Towards A Theory of Populism' in: *Politics and Ideology in Marxist Theory* London: New Left Books: 143-98.
Laclau, E. (1994) 'Why Do Empty Signifiers Matter To Politics?' in: Weeks, J.(ed) *The Lesser Evil and the Greater Good: the Theory and Politics of Social Diversity* London: Rivers Oram Press.
Laclau, E., Mouffe, C. (1985) *Hegemony and Socialist Strategy* London: Verso.

Laclau, E., Mouffe, C. (1987) 'Post-Marxism Without Apologies' *New Left Review* 166 November/ December: 79-106.
Lambert, A. (1988) 'Are Blacks to Blame for Prejudice?' *The Independent* 29 October p.15.
Lapping, B. (1969) 'The Liberal Hour' *New Society* 10 July: 65-6.
Larrain, J. (1979) *The Concept of Ideology* London: Hutchinson.
Larrain, J. (1983) *Marxism and Ideology* London: Macmillan.
Larrain, J. (1994) 'The Postmodern Critique of Ideology' *Sociological Review*: 289-314.
Lawrence, D. (1969a) 'Race relations' (letter) *New Society* 21 August.
Lawrence, D. (1969b) 'Colour and Citizenship': (letter) *New Society* 11 September: 408.
Lawrence, D. (1974) *Black Migrants: White Natives* Cambridge University Press.
Lawrence, D. (1978/9) 'Prejudice, politics and race' *New Community* 7 (1): 44-55.
Lawrence, E. (1981) 'White Sociology, Black Struggle' *Multiracial Education* Summer 9 (3): 3-17.
Lawrence, E. (1982) 'Just Plain Commonsense: the Roots of Racism' in: CCCS: Race & Politics Group *The Empire Strikes Back: race and racism in 70s Britain* London: Hutchinson: 47-94.
Layton-Henry, Z. (1980) 'Immigration' in: Z.Layton-Henry (ed) *Conservative Party Politics* London: Macmillan.
Layton-Henry, Z. (1984) *The Politics of Race in Britain* London: Allen & Unwin.
Layton-Henry, Z. (1992)*The Politics of Immigration* London: Macmillan.
Layton-Henry, Z., Rich, P. (1986) (eds) *Race, Government and Politics in Britain* London: Macmillan.
Layton-Henry, Z., Taylor, S. (1977) 'Race at the Polls' *New Society* 25 August: 392.
Lee, B. (1969) 'Enoch Powell's Language' *New Society* 23 January p. 119.
Lenin, V.I. (1977) *Selected Works 2* Moscow: Progress Publishers.
Lester, A., Bindman, G. (1972) *Race and Law* Harmondsworth: Penguin.
Levin, B. (1973) 'Putting our worst fears in black and white' *The Times*.
Levin, B. (1984) 'Would you buy another scare from this man?' *The Times* 5 October.
Levitas, R. (ed) (1986) *The Ideology of the New Right* London: Polity Press.
Lewis, R. (1979) *Enoch Powell: Principle in Politics* London: Cassell.
Lewis, R. (1988) *Anti-racism: A Mania Exposed* London: Quartet Books.
Leys, C. (1986) *Politics in Britain* London: Verso.
Leys, C. (1990) 'Still a Question of Hegemony' *New Left Review* 181 May/ June: 119-128.
Little, A., Kohler, D. (1977) 'Do we hate blacks?' *New Society:* 184-5.
Lyotard, J-F. (1984) *The Postmodern Condition: A Report On Knowledge* Manchester: Manchester University Press.
Macmillan, H. (1973) *At the End of the Day* London: Macmillan.

Mail, Daily (1988) 'Powell twenty years after' *Editorial* 23 April.
Marsh, A. (1976) 'Who hates the blacks?' *New Society* 23 September: 649-52.
Marx, K. (1983) *Capital: a critique of Political Economy*, vol. 1 London: Lawrence & Wishart.
Marx, K. (1982) *Capital: a critique of Political Economy, vol. 1* New Left Review/ Penguin: Harmondsworth.
Marx, K., Engels, F. (1970) *The German Ideology, Part One* London: Lawrence and Wishart.
Marx, K., Engels, F. (1978) *Articles On Britain* Moscow: Progress Publishers.
Marx, K., Engels, F. (1982) *Selected Correspondence* Moscow: Progress Publishers.
Mason, D. (1994) 'On the Dangers of Disconnecting Race and Racism' *Sociology* 28 (4): 845-858.
Mason, P. (1969a) 'Foreword: April, 1968' in: Patterson, S. *Immigration and Race Relations in Britain 1960-1967* London: Oxford University Press: v-vi.
Mason, P. (1969b) 'A Democratic Dilemma: Consensus and Leadership' *Race* X 4: 493-503.
Maude, A., Powell, J. E. (1955) *Biography of A Nation* London: John Baker.
Mazumdar, P.M.H. (1992) *Eugenics, Human Genetics and Human Failings: The Eugenics Society, its sources and its critics in Britain* London: Routledge.
Mercer, K. (1990) *Powellism: Race, Politics and Discourse* unpublished Ph.D, University of London, Goldsmith's College.
Mercer, K. (1992) '1968: Periodising Politics and Identity' in: Grossberg, L., Nelson, T., Treichler, P. (eds) *Cultural Studies* New York: Routledge
Mercer, K. (1994) *Welcome To The Jungle: New Positions in Black Cultural Studies* Routledge: London.
Messina, T. (1985) 'Race and Party Competition in Britain' Parliamentary Affairs 38 (4): 423-36.
Miles, R. (1982) *Racism and Migrant Labour* London: Routledge.
Miles, R. (1984a) 'Marxism versus the sociology of "race relations"?' *Ethnic and Racial Studies* (7) 2 April: 217-237.
Miles, R. (1984b) 'The Riots of 1958: The Ideological Construction of "Race Relations"?' *Immigrants and Minorities* 3 (3): 252-752.
Miles, R. (1987) 'Recent Marxist Theories of Nationalism and the Issue of Racism' *British Journal of Sociology* 38 (1): 24-43.
Miles, R. (1988a) 'Beyond the 'Race' Concept: The Reproduction of Racism in England' in: M. de Lepervanche, Bottomley, G. (eds) *The Cultural Construction of Race* Sydney: Sydney Association for Studies in Society and Culture.
Miles, R. (1988b) 'Racism, Marxism, and British Politics' *Economy and Society* 17 (3) August: 428-460.
Miles, R. (1989) Racism London: Routledge.

Miles, R. (1990) 'Racism, Ideology and Disadvantage' *Social Studies Review* (5) 4 March: 148-151.
Miles, R. (1993) *Racism after 'race relations'* London: Routledge.
Miles, R. (1994) 'Explaining Racism in Contemporary Europe' in: Rattansi, A., Westwood S. (eds) *Racism, Modernity and Identity* Cambridge: Polity: 189-221.
Miles, R., Phizacklea, A. (eds) (1979) *Racism and Political Action in Britain* London: Routledge and Kegan Paul.
Miles, R., Phizacklea, A. (1984) *White Man's Country: Racism in British Politics* London: Pluto Press.
Miles, R., Solomos, J. (1987) 'Migration and the State in Britain: a Historical Overview' in: C. Husband (ed) *'Race' in Britain, 2nd* ed. London: Hutchinson: 75-110.
Milner, D. (1975) *Children and Race* Harmondsworth: Penguin.
Minogue, K. (1988) 'This Talk of Racism is Nonsense' *Sunday Telegraph* 24 April.
Mirror, Daily (1970) 'Who Are The British? 3 March 1970.
Mirror, Sunday (1988) 'Race for Equality' 24 April.
Montagu, A. (1963) *Race, Science and Humanity* Princeton New Jersey: Van Nostrand.
Montagu, A. (1964a) *Man's Most Dangerous Myth: the fallacy of Race* Cleveland & New York: Meridian Books.
Montagu, A. (1964b) (ed) *The Concept of Race* New York: Free Press.
Montagu, A. (1972) (ed) *Statement On Race: UNESCO* London: Oxford University Press.
Moore, R. (1975) *Racism and Black Resistance in Britain* London: Pluto Press.
Morley, D. (1980a) 'Texts, readers, subjects' in: *CCCS: Culture, Media, Language: Working Papers in Cultural Studies, 1972-79* London: Hutchinson: 163-73.
Morley, D. (1980b) *The 'Nationwide' Audience* London: British Film Institute.
Morley, D. (1984) 'Cultural transformations: the politics of resistance' in: Davis, H., Walton, P. (eds) *Culture, Media, Language* Oxford: Basil Blackwell: 104-17.
Morley, D. (1986) *Family Television*.
Morley, D., Chen, K-S. (eds) (1996) *Stuart Hall: Critical Dialogues in Cultural Studies* London: Routledge.
Mouffe, C. (1979) (ed) *Gramsci and Marxist Theory* London: Lawrence and Wishart.
Mouzelis, N. (1988) 'Marxism or Post-Marxism?' *New Left Review* 167 January/February: 107-123.
Murray, N. (1986) 'Anti-Racists and other Demons: the Press and Ideology in Thatcher's Britain' *Race and Class* 28 (3): 31-19.

Nairn, T. (1970) 'Enoch Powell: the New Right' *New Left Review* 61 May-June: 3-27.
Nairn, T. (1971) 'British Nationalism and the EEC' *New Left Review* 69 September-October: 3-28.
Nairn, T. (1973) *The Left Against Europe ?* Harmondsworth: Penguin.
Nairn, T. (1979) 'The Future of Britain's Crisis' *New Left Review* 114 January-April: 43-69.
Nairn, T. (1981) (2nd edn) *The Break-Up of Britain* London: Verso.
New Society (1965) 'John Bean Naked' *Editorial* 5 August p.3.
New Society (1967) 'The Indo-Afro-Britons' *Editorial* 16 November: 691-2.
New Society (1968a) 'Mass-market Powell' *Editorial* 25 April p. 588.
New Society (1968b) 'Is the working class really racialist?' 2 May.
New Statesman (1968a) 'Keep Britain Civilised' *Editorial* 26 April.
New Statesman (1968b) 'The widow of Wolverhampton finds something nasty in her letter box' *Cartoon* May 3rd.
Nikolinakos, M. (1973) 'Notes on an Economic Theory of Racism' *Race* 14:4.
Nikolinakos, M. (1975) 'Notes Towards A General Theory of Migration in Late Capitalism' *Race and Class* XVII (1).
Norton, P. (1988, rev.ed) 'Opposition to Government' in: Ryle, M., Richards, P. (eds) *The Commons Under Scrutiny* London: Routledge: 99-119.
Observer, The (1968) 'Fears Behind White Workers' Backlash: Stop Shouting, Start Talking' *Editorial* 28 April.
Observer, The (1975) 'The time-bomb of race' *Editorial* 14 September.
Omi, M., Winant, H. (1986) *Racial Formation in the United States: From the 1960 to the 1980s* New York: Routledge and Kegan Paul.
Open University (1982) *Race and British Society* Milton Keynes: Open University Press.
Osborne, C. (1958a) 'India & Pakistan' *Oral Answers Hansard* 15 May: 611-12.
Osborne, C. (1958b) 'Queen's Speech - Debate on the Address' *Hansard Parliamentary Debates* 29 October: 194-204.
Page, R. (1977) 'To Nature, Race is Not a Dirty Word' *Daily Telegraph* 3 February.
Palmer, F. (1985) 'Countering Racism' Letter: *The Times* 18 May, p.9.
Palmer, F. (ed) (1986) *Anti-racism - An Assault on Education and Value* London: Sherwood Press.
Palmer, F. (1988) 'Anti-Anti-Racism': Letter *London Review of Books* March 3rd 10 (5).
Pannell, N., Brockway, F. (1965) *Immigration: What is the Answer?* London: Routledge and Kegan Paul.
Parekh, B. (1987) 'The "new right" and the politics of nationhood' in: Deakin, N. (ed) *The New Right: Image and Reality* London: Runnymede Trust: 33-44.
Park, R. (1950) *Race and Culture* New York: Free Press.
Patterson, S. (1963) *Dark Strangers* Harmondsworth: Penguin.

Patterson, S. (1969) *Immigration and Race Relations in Britain 1960-1967* London: Oxford University Press.

Pearson, G. (1976) 'Paki-bashing' in a North-East Lancashire cotton town: a case study and its history' in: Mungham, G., Pearson, G. (eds) *Working Class Youth Culture* London: Routledge and Kegan Paul: 48-81.

Phillips, K. (1977) 'The Meaning of Powellism' in: Nugent, N., King, R. (eds) *The British Right* Farnborough: Saxon House.

Phizacklea, A., Miles, R. (1980) *Labour and Racism* London: Routledge and Kegan Paul.

Pilkington, E. (1988) *Beyond the Mother Country: West Indians and the Notting Hill White Riots* London: I.B.Tauris.

Pocock, G. (1990) 'Nation, Community, Devolution and Sovereignty' *Political Quarterly* 61 (3) July-Sept: 318-27.

Pocock, J.G.A. (1972) *Politics, Language and Time* London: Methuen.

Pollock, F. (1955) 'Empirical Research into Public Opinion' in: Connerton, P. (ed) (1976) *Critical Sociology* Harmondsworth: Penguin: 225-36.

Porter, A.N., Stockwell, A.J. (1988) *British Imperial Policy and Decolonization 1938-64 vol.1, 1938-51* London: Macmillan.

Powell, J. Enoch (1960) *Great Parliamentary Occasions* London: Pall Mall Books.

Powell, J. Enoch (1964a) 'Chacun A Son Gout' *New Society* 16 January: 24-5.

Powell, J. Enoch (1964b) 'The Irresistible Market' *New Society* 6 February: 12-13.

Powell, J. Enoch (1965) *A Nation Not Afraid* London: B.T. Batsford.

Powell, J. Enoch (1966) *A New Look at Medicine and Politics* London: Pitman Medical Publishing Company.

Powell, J. Enoch (1969) *Freedom and Reality* London: B.T.Batsford.

Powell, J. Enoch (1970) *Income Tax at 4/3 in the £* (ed. Lejeune, A.) London: Tom Stacey.

Powell, J. Enoch (1971) *The Common Market: The Case Against* Kingswood Surrey: Elliot Right Way Books.

Powell, J. Enoch (1972) *Still to Decide* London: B.T.Batsford.

Powell, J. Enoch (1973a) *The Common Market: Renegotiate or Come Out* Kingswood, Surrey: Elliot Right Way Books.

Powell, J. Enoch (1973b) *No Easy Answers* London: Sheldon Press.

Powell, J. Enoch (1977) *Wrestling With the Angel* London: Sheldon Press.

Powell, J. Enoch (1978) *A Nation or No Nation ?: Six Years in British Politics* (ed. Ritchie, R.) London: B.T.Batsford.

Powell, J. Enoch (1981) 'Brixton (Disturbances)' *Hansard* 13th April col. 25.

Powell, J. Enoch (1981) 'Disturbances (Southall and Liverpool)' *Hansard* 6 July, col. 26.

Powell, J. Enoch (1981) 'Why I See Hope in These Riots' *The Sun* July 13, p.7.

Powell, J. Enoch (1981) 'Civil Disturbances': debate. *Hansard vol.8*, 16 July: 1411-1417.

Powell, J. Enoch (1981) 'The spectre of a Britain that has lost its claim to be a nation' *Guardian* 9 November.
Powell, J. Enoch (1984) 'What Commonwealth?' *The Times* 26 January.
Powell, J. Enoch (1985) 'Urban Disturbances' *Hansard, vol. 84*: 375-6.
Powell, J. Enoch (1987) 'Some Text-Book Definitions' *The Salisbury Review* September 1987: 65-7.
Powell, J. Enoch (1988) 'Fears that have not changed' *The Times* 19 April.
Powell, J. Enoch (1988)'Patriotism is not to be had cheaply' *The Independent* 23 April p.3.
Powell, J. Enoch (1964-1991) National Press cuttings: speeches, reports, articles and editorials.
Powell, J.E., Wallis, K. (1968) *The House of Lords in the Middle Ages: A History of the English House of Lords to 1540* London: Weidenfeld and Nicolson.
Pugh, M. (1985) *The Tories and the People, 1880-1935* Oxford: Basil Blackwell.
Rabstein, M. (1981) 'The Empire Strikes Back: Why Britain Needs National Liberation' in Bridges, G., Brunt, R. (eds) *Silver Linings: Strategies for the Eighties* London: Lawrence and Wishart: 87-100.
Rattansi, A. (1994) "'Western' Racisms, Ethnicities and Identities in a 'Postmodern' Frame' in: Rattansi, A., Westwood S. (eds) *Racism, Modernity and Identity* Cambridge: Polity.
Rattansi A., Westwood S. (eds) (1994) *Racism, Modernity and Identity: On the Western Front* Cambridge: Polity.
Reeves, F. (1983) *British Racial Discourse* Cambridge: Cambridge University Press.
Rex, J. (1969) 'Racism': Letter. *New Society* 17 April, p. 610.
Rex, J. (1970) 'The Concept of Race in Sociological Theory' in: Zubaida, S. (ed) *Race & Racialism* London: Tavistock: 35-55.
Rex, J. (1972) 'Nature versus Nurture: The Significance of the Revived Debate' in: Richardson, K. Spears, D., Richard, M. (eds) *Race, Culture and Intelligence* Harmondsworth: Penguin, : 167-178.
Rex, J. (1973) *Race, Colonialism and the City* London: Routledge and Kegan Paul.
Rex, J. (1983) *Race Relations in Sociological Theory* 2nd edn. London: Routledge.
Rex, J., Mason, D. (eds) (1986) *Theories of Race and Ethnic Relations* Cambridge: Cambridge University Press.
Rex, J., Moore, R. (1967) *Race, Community and Conflict* London: Oxford University Press.
Rex, J., Tomlinson, S. (1979) *Colonial Immigrants in a British City: A Class Analysis* London: Routledge and Kegan Paul.
Ricoeur, P. (1976; orig 1965) 'Hermeneutics: Restoration of Meaning or Reduction of Illusion' in: Connerton, P. (ed) *Critical Sociology* Harmondsworth: Penguin: 194-203.

Rich, P. (1986a) *Race and Empire in British Politics* Cambridge: Cambridge University Press.
Rich, P. (1986b) 'Conservative Ideology and Race in Modern British Politics' in: Layton-Henry, Z. and Rich, P. (eds) *Race, Government and Politics in Britain* London: Macmillan: 45-72.
Rich, P. (1987) 'The Politics of 'race relations' in Britain and the West' in: Jackson, P. (ed) *Race and Racism: essays in Social Geography* London: Allen and Unwin: 95-118.
Rich, P. (1989) Review of 'Racism' (R.Miles) *New Community* 16 (1) October: 166-8.
Richardson, J., Lambert, J. (1985) *The Sociology of Race Relations* Ormskirk: Causeway.
Richmond, A. (1954) *Colour Prejudice in Britain: A Study of West Indian Workers in Liverpool, 1942-51* London: Routledge and Kegan Paul.
Richmond, A. (1955) *The Colour Problem* Harmondsworth: Penguin.
Richmond, A. (1970) 'Housing and Racial Attitudes in Bristol' *Race* XII (1).
Richmond, A. (1973) *Migration and Race Relations in an English* City London: Oxford University Press.
Rose, E.J.B. and Associates (1969) *Colour and Citizenship: A Report on British Race Relations* London: Oxford University Press.
Rose, N. (1977) 'Fetishism and Ideology: a review of theoretical problems' *Ideology and Consciousness* Autumn (2): 27-54.
Rose, S. (1976) 'The IQ racket from Galton to Jensen' in: Rose, H., Rose, S. (eds) *The Political Economy of Science* London: Macmillan.
Rose, S. Kamin, L., Lewontin, R.C. (1984) *Not in Our Genes: Biology, Ideology and Human Nature* Harmondsworth: Penguin.
Roth, A. (1970) *Enoch Powell: Tory Tribune* London: Macdonald.
Rown, J. (1969) 'Race Relations' :Letter *New Society* 14 August, p. 262.
Rush, M., Althoff, P. (1971) *An Introduction to Political Sociology* London: Thomas Nelson.
Rushdie, S. (1982) 'The new empire within Britain' *New Society* 9 December: 417-19.
Ryan, A. (1986) 'Roger Scruton and Neo-Conservatism' in: Deakin, N. (ed) *The New Right: Image and reality* London: Runneymede Trust: 23-31.
Ryle, M., Richards, P. (eds) (1988) rev.ed. *The Commons Under Scrutiny* London: Routledge.
Samuel, R. (ed) (1989a) *Patriotism: the Making and Unmaking of British National Identity, vol I: History and Politics* London: Routledge.
Samuel, R. (ed) (1989b) *vol, II: Minorities and Outsiders* London: Routledge.
Samuel, R. (ed) (1989c) *vol, III: National Fictions* London: Routledge.
Samuel, R. (1989d) 'Introduction: exciting to be English' in: Samuel, R. (ed) *Patriotism, vol I: History and Politics* London: Routledge: xviii-ixvii.

Samuel, R. (1989e) 'The Little Platoons' in: Samuel, R. (ed) *Patriotism, vol II: Minorities & Outsiders* London: Routledge: viii-xxxix.
Sarup, M. (1986) *The Politics of Multiracial Education* London: Routledge.
Satzewich, V. (1991) *Racism and the Incorporation of Foreign Labour: Farm Labour Migration to Canada Since 1945* London and New York: Routledge.
Sayer, D. (1979) *Marx's Method: Ideology, Science and Critique in 'Capital'* Brighton: Harvester Press.
Schoen, D.E. (1977) *Enoch Powell and the Powellites* London: Macmillan.
Scruton, R. (1980) *The Meaning of Conservatism* Harmondsworth: Penguin.
Scruton, R. (1984) 'The Enemy in the Classroom' *The Times* 22 May.
Scruton, R. (1985a) 'Where Blacks Would be at Home' *The Times* 5 March, p. 14.
Scruton, R. (1985b) 'Who Will Cure this Social Disease?' *The Times* 8 November, p. 14.
Scruton, R. (1986a) 'Public Money Muzzlers' *The Times* 25 March: 12.
Scruton, R. (1986b) 'Subversives From the Suburbs' *The Times* 11 November: 20.
Scruton, R. (1988) 'Anti-Anti-Racism': Letter *London Review of Books* 7 January 10 (1).
Seabrook, J. (1970) 'Packie Stan' *New Society* 23 April, p. 395.
Seabrook, J. (1971) *City Close-Up* London: Allen Lane.
Seabrook, J. (1978) *What Went Wrong? Working People and the Ideals of the Labour Movement* London: Victor Gollancz.
Searle, C. (1989) *Your daily dose: racism and the Sun* London: Campaign for Press & Broadcasting Freedom.
Segal, R. (1967) *The Race War: the world wide conflict of races* Harmondsworth: Penguin.
Seidel, G. (1985) 'Political Discourse Analysis' in: Dijk, T. van, (ed) *Handbook of Discourse Analysis, vol.4* London: Academic Press: 43-60.
Seidel, G. (1986a) 'Culture, Nation and 'Race' in the British and French New Right' in: Levitas, R. (ed) *The Ideology of the New Right* Oxford: Polity Press: 107-135.
Seidel, G. (1986b) *The Holocaust Denial: Antisemitism, Racism and the New Right* Leeds: Beyond the Pale Collective.
Seidel, G. (1988a) (ed) *The Nature of the Right: A Feminist Analysis of Order Patterns* Amsterdam: John Benjamins.
Seidel, G. (1988b) 'The British New Right's "Enemy Within": The Antiracists' in: Smitherman-Donaldson, G., Dijk, T. van, (eds) *Discourse and Discrimination* Detroit: Wayne State University: 131-143.
Seidel, G. (1990) 'Thank God I Said No to AIDS': on the changing discourse of AIDS in Uganda' *Discourse and Society* 1 (1): 61-84.
Seymour-Ure, C. (1974) *The Political impact of Mass media* London: Constable.
Shils, E. (1975) *Center and Periphery: Essays in Macrosociology* Chicago: Chicago University Press.

Simon, B. (1978) *Intelligence, Psychology, Education: A Marxist Critique* 2nd ed. London: Lawrence and Wishart.

Singham, A.W. (1964) 'Immigration and the Election' in: Butler, D.E., King, A. *The British General Election of 1964* London: Macmillan: 360-8.

Sivanandan, A. (1974) *Race and Resistance: the IRR story* London: Race Today.

Sivanandan, A. (1976) 'Race, Class and the State: the Black experience in Britain' *Race & Class* XVII (4) Spring.

Sivanandan, A. (1982) *A Different Hunger: Writings on Black Resistance* London: Pluto Press.

Sivanandan, A. (1985a) 'RAT and the Degradation of Black Struggle' *Race & Class* XXVI (4) Spring: 1-33.

Sivanandan, A. (1985b) 'Britain's Gulags' *New Socialist* November: 13-15.

Sivanandan, A. (1988) 'The New Racism' *New Statesman and Society* 4 November: 8-9.

Sivanandan, A. (1989) 'UK Commentary: Racism 1992' *Race and Class* 30 (3) January-March: 85-90.

Sivanandan, A. (1990) 'All that melts into air is solid: the hokum of New Times' *Race and Class* 31 (3):1-30.

Skillen, T. (1985) 'Discourse Fever: Post-Marxist Modes of Production' in: Edgley, R. and Osborne, R. (eds) *Radical Philosophy Reader* London: Verso: 325-336.

Sklair, L. (1991) *The Sociology of the Global System* Brighton: Harvester-Wheatsheaf.

Small, S. (1994) *Racialised Barriers : the black experience in the United States and England in the 1980s* London: Routledge.

Smart, B. (1985) *Michel Foucault* London: Routledge.

Smith, A.D. (1979) *Nationalism in the Twentieth Century* Oxford: Martin Robertson.

Smith, A.D. (1988) 'The myth of the "Modern Nation" and the myths of nations' *Ethnic and Racial Studies* 11 (1) January: 1-26.

Smith, A.D. (1989) 'The Origins of Nations' *Ethnic and Racial Studies* 12 (3) July: 340-67.

Smith, A-M. (1994) *New Right Discourse On Race and Sexuality* Cambridge: Cambridge University Press.

Smith, D. (1974) 'Theorizing as Ideology' in: Turner, R. (ed) *Ethnomethodology* Harmondsworth: Penguin: 41-44.

Smith, S.J. (1989) *The Politics of Race and Residence* Cambridge: Polity Press.

Smith, S.J. (1993) 'Residential Segregation and the Politics of Racialization' in: Cross, M, Keith, M. (eds) *Racism, the City and the State* London: Routledge: 128-43.

Smitherman-Donaldson, G., Dijk, T. van (eds) (1988) *Discourse and Discrimination* Detroit: Wayne State University Press.

Smithies, B., Fiddick, P. (1969) *Enoch Powell on Immigration* London: Sphere Books.

Sofer, A. (1985) 'Race: Making Sure Nobody Loses' *The Times* 22 April.
Solomos, J. (1983) 'The Politics of Black Youth Unemployment: A Critical Analysis of Official Ideologies and Policies' *Working Papers on Ethnic Relations no.20* SSRC: Research Unit on Ethnic Relations, University of Aston in Birmingham.
Solomos, J. (1985) 'Problems, but whose problems? The social construction of black youth unemployment and state policies' *Journal of Social Policy* 14 (4): 527-54.
Solomos, J. (1986a) 'Trends in the Political Analysis of Racism' *Political Studies* XXXIV: 313-324.
Solomos, J. (1986b) 'Political Language and Violent Protest: ideological and policy responses to the 1981-1985 riots' *Youth and Policy* 18: 12-24.
Solomos, J. (1986c) 'Riots, Urban Protest and Social Policy: The Interplay of Reform & Social Control' *Policy Paper in Ethnic Relations no. 7*, Centre for Research in Ethnic Relations, University of Warwick, December.
Solomos, J. (1986d) 'Varieties of Marxist Conceptions of 'race', class and the State: a Critical analysis, in: Rex, J., Mason, D. (eds) *Theories of Race and Ethnic Relations* Cambridge University Press: 84-109.
Solomos, J. (1988) *Black Youth, Racism and the State* Cambridge: Cambridge University Press.
Solomos, J. (1989) *Race and Racism in Contemporary Britain* London: Macmillan.
Solomos, J. (1990) 'Changing Forms of Racial Discourse' *Social Studies Review* November: 74-8.
Solomos, J., Back, L. (1991) 'The Politics of Race and social Change in Birmingham: Historical Pattern and Contemporary Trends' *Research Papers No.1*, Department of Politics and Sociology, Birkbeck College, University of London, no.1 March.
Solomos, J., Back, L. (1993) 'Doing Research, Writing Politics: the dilemmas of political intervention in research on racism' *Unpublished paper*.
Solomos, J., Back, L. (1994) 'Conceptualising Racisms: Social Theory, Politics and Research' *Sociology* 28 (1) February: 143-61.
Sparks, C. (1985) 'Labour & Imperialism' *International Socialism* 2 (26) Spring: 1-14.
Spearman, D. (1968) 'Enoch Powell's Postbag' *New Society* 9th May: 4-6.
Stacey, T. (ed) (1970) *Immigration and Enoch Powell* London: Tom Stacey.
Statesman, New (1969) 'The Old Tory Adam' Profile: review 10 October.
Steadman-Jones, G. (1983) *Languages of Class: Studies in English Working Class History* Cambridge: Cambridge University Press.
Stokes, G. (1986) 'How is Nationalism Related to Capitalism? A Review Article' *Society For Comparative Study of Society & History*: 591-8.
Studlar, D. T. (1974) 'Political culture and racial policy in Britain' *Patterns of Prejudice* 8 (3): 7-12.

Studlar, D. T. (1980) 'Elite responsiveness or elite autonomy?: British immigration policy reconsidered' *Ethnic and Racial Studies* 3 (2) April: 207-223.

Studlar, D. T. (1985) "Waiting for the Catastrophe': Race and the Political Agenda in Britain' *Patterns of Prejudice* 19 (1): 3-15.

Sykes, M. (1985) 'Discrimination in Discourse' in: Dijk, T. van *Handbook of Discourse Analysis, vol.4* London: Academic Press: 83-101.

Sykes, M. (1988) 'From "Rights" to "Needs": Official Discourse and the "Welfarization" of Race' in: Smitherman-Donaldson, G., Dijk, T. van (eds) (1988) *Discourse and Discrimination* Detroit: Wayne State University Press: 176-205.

Taguieff, P-A. (1990) 'The new cultural racism in France' *Telos*, 83: 109-22.

Taylor, S. (1977) 'The National Front: backlash or bootboys ?' *New Society* 11 August: 283-4.

Taylor, S. (1982) *The National Front in English Politics* London: Macmillan.

Telegraph, The Daily (1988) 'A tolerant nation' *Editorial* 19 April.

Thompson, J.B. (1984) *Studies in the Theory of Ideology* Cambridge: Polity Press.

Tinker, H. (1977) *Race, Conflict and the International Order: From Empire to United Nations* London: Macmillan.

Times, The (1965) 'The Dark Million - 1: Local Councils Left Holding the Immigration Baby' January 18th.

Times, The (1984) 'Queen and Commonwealth' *Editorial* 6 February.

Times, The (1988) 'Mr Powell's Prophesy' *Editorial* 22 April.

Times, Sunday (1970) 'Playing the Numbers Game: Race and Immigration' *Leader* 15th March.

Times, Sunday (1973) 'Transforming the politics of race' *Editorial* 29 April.

Trew, T. (1979a) 'Theory and ideology at work' in: Fowler, R. Hodge, B. Kress, G., Trew, T. *Language and Control* London: Routledge and Kegan Paul: 94-116.

Trew, T. (1979b) 'What the papers say': linguistic variation and ideological difference' in: Fowler, R. Hodge, B. Kress, G., Trew, T. *Language and Control* London: Routledge and Kegan Paul: 117-56.

Troyna, B. (1981) *Public Awareness and the Media* London: Commission for Racial Equality.

Troyna, B. (1982) 'Reporting the National Front' in Husband, C. (ed) *'Race' in Britain: continuity and change* London: Hutchinson.

Troyna, B. (1986) 'The Controversy Surrounding Raymond Honeyford' *Social Studies Review* March: 19-22.

Tweedie, J. (1976) 'Colour blind' *The Guardian* July 12, p. 7.

UK Commentary (1976) 'Race and the Press' *Race and Class* XVIII (1) :69-71.

UK Commentary (1990) 'Europe for the Europeans: East End for the East Enders' *Race and Class* 32 (1) July-September: 66-76.

Uri, P. (ed) (1968) *From Commonwealth to Common Market* Harmondsworth: Penguin.
Utley, T.E. (1968) *Enoch Powell: The Man and his Thinking* London: William Kimber.
Voloshinov, V.N. (1973) *Marxism and the Philosophy of Language* New York: Seminar Press.
Walden, B. (1969) 'The picture of prejudice' *Guardian* 10 July.
Walker, M. (1977) *The National Front* London: Fontana.
Waterhouse, K. (1973) 'The Brent goose' *Daily Mirror* 12 April.
Watkins, A. (1968) 'Enoch and After' *New Statesman* vol. 75: no. 1937.
Watkins, A. (1968) 'Brigadier Powell's Last Stand' *New Statesman* vol.76: no.1967.
Weber, C.G. (1986) *The Ideology of the British Right, 1918-1939* Kent: Croom Helm.
Wetherell, M., Potter, J. (1992) *Mapping the Language of Racism: Discourse and the Legitimation of Exploitation* Hemel Hempstead: Harvester.
Whale, J. (1970) 'Most angles are Right angles' Election '70: *Sunday Times* 7 June.
Wieviorka, M. (1994) 'Racism in Europe: Unity and Diversity' in: Rattansi A., Westwood S. (eds) *Racism, Modernity and Identity* Cambridge: Polity: 173-88.
Wieviorka, M. (1995) *The Arena of Racism* London: Sage.
Williams, R. (1961) *The Long Revolution* Harmondsworth: Penguin.
Williams, R. (1983) 'The Culture of Nations' in: *Towards 2000* London: Chatto and Windus: 177-199.
Wilson, H.J. (1964) 'Queen's Speech: debate on the address' *Hansard*: c.10-14: 3 November.
Wilson, H.J. (1971) *The Labour Government, 1964-1970: A Personal Record* Harmondsworth: Penguin.
Wilson, M. (1977) 'Grass roots Conservatism: motions to the Party Conference' in: Nugent, N., King, R. (eds) *The British Right* Farnborough: Saxon House: 64-98.
Winant, H. (1991) 'Racial Formation Theory: The Contemporary Agenda' in: Zegeye, A. Harris, L., Maxted, J. (eds) *Exploitation and Exclusion: Race and Class in Contemporary US Society* London: Hans Zell: 130-41.
Winant, J. (1994) 'Racial Formation and Hegemony: Global and Local Developments' in: Rattansi, A., Westwood, S. (eds) *Racism, Modernity and Identity: On the Western Front* Cambridge: Polity.
Wood, J. (ed) (1970) *Powell and the 1970 Election* Kingswood, Surrey: Elliot Right Way Books.
Woods, R. (1977) 'Discourse Analysis: the work of Michel Pecheux' *Ideology and Consciousness* 2 Autumn: 57-79.
Woolf, R.P., Moore, B., Marcuse, H. (1965) *A Critique of Pure Tolerance* London: Jonathan Cape.

Woolgar, S. (1988) *Science: the very idea* London: Ellis Horwood/ Tavistock.
Workers Against Racism (1985) *The Roots of Racism* London: Junius.
Worsthorne, P. (1985) 'End This Silence Over Race' *Sunday Telegraph* 29 September.
Wright, P. (1985) *On Living in an Old Country* London: Verso.
Young, H. (1971) 'The Treatment of Race in the British Press' in: Runneymede Trust *Race and the Press* London: Runneymede Trust: 29-41.
Young, R. (1990) *White Mythologies: Writing History and the West* London: Routledge.
Young, R. (1994) 'Egypt In America: Black Athena, Racism and Colonial Discourse in: Rattansi, A., Westwood, S. (eds) *Racism, Modernity and Identity* Cambridge: Polity Press: 150-69.
Yates, I. (1968a) 'Powell stokes up new Tory storm on immigration' *Observer* 21 April.
Yates, I. (1968b) 'Tories and Race' *Observer* 21 April.
Yates, I. (1968c) 'In Search Of Enoch Powell' *Observer* 28 April.
Zizek, S. (1989) *The Sublime Object of Ideology* London: Verso.
Zizek, S. (1990) 'Eastern Europe's Republics of Gilead' *New Left Review* 183 Sept/Oct: 50-62.
Zubaida, S. (ed) (1970) *Race and Racialism* London: Tavistock.
Zubaida, S. (1978) 'Theories of Nationalism' in: Little-John, G. Smart, B, Wakeford, J., Yuval-Davis, N. (eds) *Power and the State* London: Croom Helm: 52-71.
Zubaida, S. (1989) 'Nations: old and new. Comments on Anthony D. Smith's 'The myth of the "Modern Nation" and the myths of nations' *Ethnic and Racial Studies* 12 (3): 329-39.

Subject Index

BSA
-1969 Conference 44-5

-Commonwealth Immigrant Bill 1961 (Nov) 82-96
-assenting themes 83
-dissenting themes 84
-treatment 85-90
-ideological framework of 92-7

Commonsense
-Gramsci x
-commons'sense x
-new racist 39
-racism 63-8
-racist commonsense 68-70

Discourse
-anecdotal 202,
-archaeology xxvii
-enunciative field xxvii
-discursive repression xxviii
-of the state 11
-and text 16
-discursive formation 31
-and ideology 32-3
-discursive racialization 33-4
-eugenicist 288n

Deracialisation 21-3
-of Irish 13
-defined (Reeves) 21
-ideological 21-2

-deracialized discourse 22
-sanitary coding 23
-defined (Banton) 47

Forgotten Englishman xxii-xxiv
-indigenous English 123-5
-ordinary English 202-4
-englishman 93

Ideology
-autonomy of 14
-language 14
-ideological system 15
-epistemologically defied 29-30
-problem of 30-2
-of Conservatism 284n

Nation 57-9

Nationalism 28
-and racism 59-60

Nationality Debate (1981) 132-8

New Racism, The
- problem of ix-xiii
- modification of thesis xiii-xv
- and race politics 40-2
-thesis 47-9
- human nature 50, 55
-racist ideologies 51
- Barker's account 52-63
- pseudo-biological 55
- and Powellism 70-72
- as ethnocentrism 46
- slide to old 296-7
-debate 270n
-definition 273n
-problem of 279n

337

-as doctrine 279-80n
-and Hume 284n

New Right
-and anti-racism 295n
Parliamentary Debates
-structure and content 78-80
-method of study 80-3
-Immigration Control
(Dec.1958) 99-100
-Immigration Policy (April 1958) 97-9, 102-4
-Immigration 1976(5th July) 125-7
-Expiring Laws Bill Committee (1965) 163-5, 169-75, 178-181

Parliamentary leper 159-61

Political instinctivism 60-3

Political Language xvii
-of race xviii

Political Racism 148-50, 152, 155-6
-PR1 152
-PR2 153-4
-discursive formation of xxv
-discursive ensemble 153-5

Populism 193, 210-11
-authoritarian 42

Powellism
-researching xxvi
-epistemological break 107
-as empire blues 194-5
-as intellectual biography 195-6
-political impact 196-8
-and Thatcherism 201
-before Powell 202-7
-relations of signification 207-14

-and nationalism 214-17
-conceptual content 217
-as old racism 217-21
-as numbers game 221-31
-anecdotal discourse 202-7
-human nature 234
-patriotic nation 245-6
-repatriation 245-6
-patriotism 243-6
-imperialism 246
-Conservative institutionalism 251-4
-and commonwealth 254-5
-and 1981 Nationality Debate 255-8
-as political populism 258-61
-human nature theory 234-9
-political requirement 239-42
-empire myths and neo-nationalism 246-51
-Commonwealth and Queen row 254-5
-biography as explanation 288n
-idea of empire 302n

Race
-erasure of xix-xxi
-local politics of xxv-xxvi
-suppressed xviii
-de-centring xix-xx
-idea of 29
-science 29
-promotion 35
-thinking and feeling 36
-as ideology 278n
-public discourse of 287n

Race Politics 150-1
-mode of thematisation 2

Race Relations Debates
-1976 Debate (4th march) 112-16
-role of Powell 117-22
-role of Labour 130-2

-and discrimination (Bell) 121
-and PEP studies 293n

Racial language
-politics of 175-8

Racialisation
-approach 9-13
-postwar immigration control debates ch1, *passim*
-of black migration 1-2
- theory 3-6
-defined 19-21
-ideology 26
-defined (Banton) 47

Racism
-racist fictions xv-xvi
-as ideology xvi
-problematic 6-9
-functional to capitalism 17
-strong 24
-weak 24
-ideological signification 26-7
-definition (Miles) 26-7, 28
-functional equivalent 45
-as ethnocentrism 46
-differentialist 74
-inegalitarian 74
-as text xv
-biological fiction xv
-historical fiction xvi
-ideological field xxiv
-significatory properties xxvi
-ideological articulation 25-9
-parliamentary discourse 75-77
-English 289n

-old Racism xix, 213, 217

Racist Discourse
-point of transition xi
-nodal point xi
-conceptual transformation xiii
-discursive formation xiv, xxii-iii
-conceptual articulation xvi
-truth xvi
-untruth xvi
-disease and contamination xxii, 162-9,
-British 20-3
-anecdotal xiv-xv, 202-7

Signification
-empty signifiers xx
-racist signifiers xx
-social signifieds xxi
-signification of race xxi
-racist signifier 276n
-metonymic substitution 306n
-post-Saussurian semiotics 307n

Smethwick 141-7
-as national political phenomenon 147-8
-political treatment of 148
-impact as discourse 152-6
-and rise of race 156-9

Thatcherism 201

UNESCO xix

Urban blight 299

Name Index

Anderson, D. 215-6, 245
Axford, B. 2
Back, L. 31, 38, 220, 281n
Balibar, E. 274n
Banton, M. 44-7, 265, 273n
Barker, M. xi, xxii, 42, 48, 50, 52-68, 107, 110, 127, 235, 237, 271n, 272n, 283-4n, 301n
Barnett, A. 249, 255
Barthes, R. 148, 230, 247
Bauman, Z. 280n
Bell, R. 121-22, 293n
Benedict, R. 273n
Binns, J.MP 179-80
Ben-Tovim, G. 159
Benn, T. 200
Boyle, Sir E. 174-5
Brier, A. 2
Budgen, N. 122-3, 136, 257-8
Bulpitt, J. 150, 152, 300n
Butler, Lord 84-7, 93-4, 102-3
CCCS, xi, 4, 7, 70-2, 267
Callaghan, J. 108, 176
Carter, B. 11-13, 18-19, 286n, 303n
Casey, J. 244
Churchill, W. MP 112, 137-8
Cohen, P. 228
Coleman, T. 205, 255
Collits, T. 276n
Crossman, R. xxviii, 181-8
Deakin, N. 149, 222
Derrida, J. xix, 2, 220, 273n
Drewry, G. 76, 77
Drieberg, T. 163
Duffield, M. 50
Dummett, A. 156, 158, 162

Dummett, M. 162
Edelman, M. 2
Elton, Lord 226-7
Engels, F.W. 289n
Evans-Gordon, Major 226
Fanon, F. 245
Finney, D 144-5
Fisher, N.MP 171-3, 277n
Foot, D.MP 277n
Foot, P. xxiv, xxv-i, 141-7, 177, 194, 288n, 304n, 305-6n
Foucault, M. xviii, xxvii, 30
Fowler, R. 14
Fraser, J. 162
Freeman, G. 208
Freeson, R. 133
Fryer, P. 305n
Fuss, D. xv
Gabriel, J. 159
Gaitskell, H. 82, 91, 94-5, 277n
Gardener, E., MP 134-5
Gilroy, P. xi, xxii, 51, 107, 207, 271n, 289n, 292n, 296-7n, 303n
Goldberg, D. xx
Gordon-Walker, P. 82, 94
Gramsci, A. x
Gregory, F., MP 177
Griffiths, P. 141-7, 160, 180-1
Guillaumin, C. xxiv, 274n
Gunter, R. J., MP 173
Gurden H. 89-91, 205-6, 290-1n
Habermas, J. 4, 77
Hall, S. x, xii, 1, 4, 7, 8, 41-2, 153, 210, 220, 224, 266, 275n, 306n

Name Index 341

Harris, C. xxiii, 11-13, 18-19, 266, 276n, 286, 303n
Harvey Procter, K., MP 136-7, 258
Hattersley, R. 133-4, 141
Hiro, D.157
Hodge, R. 14-16, 275n
Hoogvelt, A. 46
Hornsby-Smith, P. 102, 103
Husband, C. 50
Husbands, C.T. 148
Hyne, H., MP 96, 101-3, 166, 291n
James, C.L.R. 168
Jenkins, P. 259
Jenkins, R. 130
Joshi, S. 11-13, 286n, 303n
Katznelson, I. xviii, 150, 300n
Kaufman, G. 154
Kress, G. 14-16, 275n
Laclau, E. xx, 220, 275n
Lawrence, D. xii
Lawrence, E. 51, 68-70, 226, 272n, 285n
Layton-Henry, Z. xxi, 107 147, 158, 159, 266, 272n
Lee, J. 176-7
Lennin, V.I. 76
Lindsay, M., MP 92, 96-7
Lloyd, G., MP 178
Lloyd, S., MP 169
Lucas-Tooth, Sir H. 202
Lyons, A., MP 131-2
Lyotard, J-F 30
Marshall, J. 134
Mazumadar, P. 288n, 290n
Mercer, K. xi, 38-40, 247, 271n, 279n, 281n, 306n, 307n
Miles, R. x, xv-i, 1, 2, 3-4, 9, 10, 17, 20, 25-9, 74, 152, 196-7, 198, 276n, 278n, 282n
Moore, R. 227
Morley, D. 305n
Nairn, T. 175, 208, 214, 216, 245, 246, 247, 282n, 307n
Norton, P. 76
Omi, M. xix-xx, 220

Osborne, C. xxiii, 87-9, 92, 98-101, 165-6
Patterson, S. 154
Phillips, K. 195, 260
Phizacklea, A. 152, 196-7, 198
Powell, J. (see Powellism)
Reeves, F. ix, 4, 20-5, 74, 78, 265, 277n
Reiper, D. 143
Rex, J. xxv, 45, 239, 282-3n
Richards, I., MP 169-71
Rogers, G., MP 127-8
Rose, E.J.B. 156, 175
Satzewich, V. 10
Schoen, D. 192, 207, 261
Seabrook, J. 204-5
Seidel, G. xvi-iii, 50, 281n
Seymour-Ure, C. 262
Sinclair, G., MP 120
Sivanandan, A. 132
Smith, A-M xi, xx, 270n, 271-2n, 279n
Smith, A.D. 59-60
Smith, D., MP 120
Solomos, J. xxv, 1, 10, 14, 31, 38, 198, 200, 220, 250, 274n, 281n, 295n
Sorensen, R., MP 164-5
Spearman, D. 46, 177, 301n
Steadman-Jones, G. 210, 211
Stokes, J. 123-5, 138, 203-4
Studlar, D. 265, 300n
Sykes, M. 34
Taylor, R., MP 128-9
Thorne, S., MP 133
Torney, T., MP 120
van Dijk, T. 287n
Volshinov, V. xvii, 16
Walker, M. 240
Watkins, A. 176
Whitelaw, W. 112-16, 125
Wieviorka, M. 74, 280n
Wilson, H.J. xxvii, 157, 168-9, 299n
Winant, H. xvi,xix-xx, 220
Wise, A., MP 165
Worsethorne, P. 201